Past Praise

I came away from this book with a heightened sense of the urgency of the problem of mind controlling cults, and a heightened admiration for Steven Hassan's work in understanding them and liberating people from them. It is a clear and valuable work.

Rabbi Harold S. Kushner
Author of *When Bad Things Happen to Good People*, *A Heart of Wisdom*, and many other books

I want to go on record as strongly endorsing Steven Hassan's approach to understanding the sources of cult power in controlling the minds and behavior of members. His now classic text on cultic mind control, *Combating Cult Mind Control*, integrates his personal experiences in a cult with his cogent analysis of the underlying dynamic processes, and then adds in to the mix current research and theory.

...Steven Hassan's approach is one that I value more than that of any other researcher or clinical practitioner...Hassan is a model of clear exposition, his original ideas are brilliantly presented in a captivating style.

Philip G. Zimbardo, Ph.D.
Former president of the American Psychological Association
Professor Emeritus of Psychology, Stanford University
Author of *The Lucifer Effect* and *Influencing Attitudes and Changing Behavior*
President and Founder of the Heroic Imagination Project

Steven Hassan is one of our most eloquent defenders of freedom of the mind. For decades he has labored mightily on behalf of the majesty of the human spirit. His good work has brought psychological and spiritual relief to countless victims and families who have unknowingly stumbled into the clutches of mind control perpetrators. As a spokesperson for the ordinary individual's right to be the master of his or her own thoughts and choices, Hassan has resisted the dangers and threats manufactured by manipulators who have sought to silence his courage.

Alan W. Scheflin
Professor Emeritus of Law, Santa Clara University
Coauthor of *The Mind Manipulators* and *Memory, Trauma Treatment and the Law*

We at My Life My Choice have been grateful for the opportunity to learn from Steven Hassan about mind control and its relevance to the trafficking field. As we learn new techniques to combat the debilitating effects of pimp control, Steven's wisdom as both a cult survivor and an expert in his field are invaluable.

Lisa Goldblatt Grace, LICSW, MPH
Co-Founder and Director, My Life My Choice

As a Baptist pastor for 35 years, I take no pleasure in testifying that religious abuse is one of the most pressing social problems in the world today. True religion always serves to liberate—never to enslave. Steven Hassan's work is instrumental for anyone seeking understanding of religious mind and thought control, and how to free themselves or loved ones from it. He not only brings exhaustive authority, research, and expertise to this critical field, but also compassion, respect, and sensitivity. Every pastor, minister, social worker, therapist, and counselor needs to read his books!

The Rev. Charles Foster Johnson
Pastor, Bread Fellowship, Fort Worth

Mind control is alive and well and in many varied forms across America. Steven Hassan understands like no one else the human need to belong, how it is exploited, and how to retrieve those who have fallen prey to the false allure of a perfect parent.

Douglas Rushkoff, Ph.D.
Professor of Media Studies, Queens College
Author of *Coercion*

Steven Hassan was the first to take on the Moonies, and understands cults better than almost anyone else. Happily, he's still sharing his knowledge, this time with a 25th anniversary updated and revised edition of his classic book, *Combating Cult Mind Control*. Fascinating and important reading.

Paulette Cooper
Author of *Scandal of Scientology*
Subject of Tony Ortega's book,
The Unbreakable Miss Lovely: How the Church of Scientology tried to destroy Paulette Cooper

This newly revised version of *Combating Cult Mind Control* is an eye-opening, must-read for victims and their families who are or were at one time trapped in a high-control pseudo-religious group or an abusive personal relationship. Steven Hassan skillfully describes the persuasion methods used by cult-like groups to overcome the free will and judgment of people who choose to listen and join. He also makes it easy to understand how and why intelligent people allow themselves to be unduly influenced and willingly sacrifice their best personal interests. In so doing, he makes a very compelling case for all readers about the clear and present danger of undue (unethical) influence in today's world. In fact, I predict that most people will read this book more than once and share it with friends; the book is that relevant and it is that good.

Richard E. Kelly
Board of Directors of the Open Minds Foundation
Author of *Growing Up in Mama's Club, Ghosts From Mama's Club*

We've known Steve Hassan personally, and his work, for over 25 years. Many times we have talked and shared information about particular gurus and cults as we are aligned in believing that healthy spirituality requires personal integrity and social responsibility. In 1989 we asked for his feedback on our booklet on gurus. He was so impressed that he said we should expand it into a book. The resulting book, *The Guru Papers: Masks of Authoritarian Power* (1993) has become a classic in helping free people from authoritarian teachers and groups. Steve Hassan has been at the forefront of investigating cults, cult behavior, and successfully helping many of those ensnared. He has shown the very real dangers that cults bring to individuals and society. His dedication to freeing people from insidious mind control has been his focus since 1976. Since cult dynamics are linked with terrorism and human trafficking, the new edition of his landmark book *Combating Cult Mind Control* is an important contribution to a deeper understanding of these global dangers and creating a better, safer world.

Joel Kramer and Diana Alstad
Authors of *The Guru Papers* and *Passionate Mind Revisited*

Steven Hassan has established himself as one of the foremost "how-to" authorities on fighting the effects of destructive mind control organizations like religious cults. His books and his website have long been a first-line defense in protecting those we love from the destructive temptations of these seductive groups. His advice and encouragement have helped thousands to escape.

Richard Packham, J.D.
Founder and first president of the Exmormon Foundation

Hassan explains in clear and cogent terms how coercive and manipulative leaders/groups create psychological and spiritual hostages out of vulnerable or well-intended human beings—people who are either going through painful life transitions or who are searching for higher truth. Early in my career this book was an invaluable resource to help me understand the nature of this unique type of victimization. Hassan's work inspired me, helping me create more effective pathways for healing for individuals emerging out of criminal and underground cults and trafficking situations….Hassan leads the reader on a journey unveiling the universal emotional and psychological vulnerabilities that leave all of us human beings susceptible to undue influence and group takeovers of our minds, hearts, and spirits. In very accessible and clear language this book offers excellent analysis and guidance, hope for cult survivors and their families, as well as clinicians and clergy who may be part of the individual's healing and integration process.

Harvey Schwartz, Ph.D.
Author of *Dialogues With Forgotten Voices* and *The Alchemy of Wolves and Sheep*

Steven Hassan has nearly 40 years of experience and knowledge that will advance our efforts to develop methods for breaking bonds held by human traffickers. Steven is a leader in the field of social psychology, and his one-on-one work to replace destructive bonds with healthy long-term relationships has the potential to improve responses to human trafficking rapidly and effectively. Steven's work goes far beyond physical removal of a victim from a perpetrator, empowering survivors to develop healthy memories and experiences in place of harmful and destructive thoughts and behaviors.

Carissa Phelps, J.D., MBA
CEO of Runaway Girl, Inc.
Author of *Runaway Girl*

Steve Hassan is a compelling spokesman on the topic of cult mind control, which encompasses issues of human identity and our innate psychological vulnerability to dissociate. In addition, he educates and challenges us to think about the groups using mind control techniques in our culture, and how to help those affected reclaim their lives. His commitment to this neglected area of human experience is exemplary. At my invitation, Steve has taught psychiatry residents at Brigham and Women's Hospital about these issues for the last 14 years. Knowledge of these issues is crucial for all mental health professionals.

Mary K. McCarthy, M.D.
Assistant Professor of Psychiatry
Harvard Medical School

Steve Hassan has successfully combined in one volume his personal story of involvement with a destructive cult, case histories of other cultists, and a sophisticated explanation of mind control from a psychological perspective. He has done a great job of pulling together a wealth of material. I especially liked the use of relevant literature in social psychology and psychiatry. I recommend it to parents, ex-cultists, and mental health specialists.

Arthur A. Dole
Professor Emeritus of Psychology, University of Pennsylvania

...a no-nonsense book which cuts directly to the core issues of destructive mind control. From firsthand experience he describes the power tactics used by cults to produce long-term psychological disorientation in unsuspecting "recruits"... Without question, this book will open your eyes to this serious continuing threat to our individual freedoms.

R. Reid Wilson, Ph.D.
Author of *Don't Panic: Taking Control of Anxiety Attacks*

Always informative, often riveting, written by one of the country's experts on mind control, *Combating Cult Mind Control* should be required reading for mental health professionals, clergy, and the many unfortunate families who are victimized by this ever-growing, insidious problem. Cult involvement is an often unseen and typically ignored problem worldwide. Pitifully few people realize the depth and breadth of the problem. Hassan is an ethical, informed, and dedicated crusader who has something to say to all of us.

Stephen R. Lankton, MSW, DAHB, LCSW
Editor: American Journal of Clinical Hypnosis
Author of *The Answer Within*

Combating Cult Mind Control combines superb research with authentic personal experience. The result is a remarkable achievement.

Rabbi A. James Rudin
Former Director, National Interreligious Affairs, The American Jewish Committee
Co-author of *Prison or Paradise: The New Religious Cults*

Steve Hassan has demonstrated his openness and ability to bring a broad range of knowledge and scholarship to bear on vexing questions of cult methods and alternatives for intervention. The result is a significant contribution to public understanding of the modern reality of mind control and the widening dimensions of the cult experience.

Flo Conway and Jim Siegelman
Authors of *Snapping* and *Holy Terror*

Combating Cult Mind Control is the best book available on the entire cult scene.... [Hassan's] explanation of mind control makes this frightening and sophisticated topic understandable to lay readers, and his own personal story is gripping....an indispensable tool for helping to educate young people about cults.

Marcia R. Rudin
Former Director, International Cult Education Program

I can think of no one more qualified than Steve Hassan for writing a book that explains in understandable and compelling terms what a truly serious and growing threat destructive cults pose for all of us. I only wish my family had known about the problem before it was too late. Steve's book should be required reading for every family in America.

Patricia Ryan
Lobbyist
Daughter of Congressman Leo J. Ryan (killed at Jonestown)The author probes beyond doctrine to uncover the thought control techniques common to many cults. Without this insight into the mental processes involved, a Christian worker can expend great effort trying to reach trapped individuals with no positive results.

David A. Reed
Christian Research Journal

Ultimately, this book is about empowerment—how individuals and societies can defend themselves against unethical applications of behavioral sciences. The reader is provided with resource lists, usable definitions, and simple communication and investigative strategies for when a loved one falls under cultic influences...

Frederick Clarkson
Senior Fellow, Political Research Associates

The book's practical value is enhanced by the author's extensive experience as a counselor to concerned families following his own involvement in a well-known cult. It is both readable and informed by scholarship.

Ronald M. Enroth, Ph.D.
Author of *The Jesus People, Why Cults Succeed Where the Church Fails,* and *A Guide to Cults and New Religions*

A valuable, well-written book on a topic of genuine importance. Steve Hassan explains precisely how cults operate to control minds and, in the process, he provides sharp insights into how the influence process works in everyday situations as well.

Robert B. Cialdini, Ph.D.
Author of *Influence and The Small Big: Small Changes That Spark Big Influence*

It is my hope that *Combating Cult Mind Control* will reach many readers, including parents of children in cults, ex-members, and the public at large. A result of Hassan's experience and laborious research, this work is a most crucial contribution to the understanding of cults and the prevention of their further destructive influence on our society.

Dr. Phillip Abramowitz
Former Director, Interfaith Coalition of Concern About Cults

Hassan is a master in the difficult task of opening closed minds. Anything he writes is on my booklist concerning destructive religious practices.

Robert Watts Thornburg
Former Dean of Marsh Chapel
Chaplain to Boston University

His book is well worth reading by professionals in mental health, particularly those involved with students, because early recognition and appropriate intervention depend on greater awareness of this menace.

Peter Tyrer, M.D.
Review of Books, *The Lancet* (British medical journal)

No one understands the cult experience better than Steve Hassan, and no one is better qualified to help people break free of their devastating effects. I wish there had been a Steve Hassan in my life when I needed one.

Mitchell Kapor
Technology entrepreneur and investor
Founder Lotus Development Corporation

Steven Hassan has developed a deep understanding of how individuals can be transformed from the identity they were raised in to become almost, or even completely, unrecognizable. The ease by which this happens is important for both scientific understanding and real world problems ranging from friends and family in cults to extremist movements. Consistent with complex systems science, his work dramatically expands our understanding of the role of context in psychology, following in the tradition of Philip Zimbardo's Stanford Prison Experiment. I look forward to his insights becoming more widely incorporated into scientific thought. His presentations at the International Conference on Complex Systems have been widely acclaimed.

Professor Yaneer Bar-Yam
Founding President ofthe New England Complex Systems Institute
Author of *Dynamics of Complex Systems* and *Making Things Work*

In my judgment this is a singularly important and valuable book. I was especially impressed by the author's candor in addressing his experiences both within the Unification Church and subsequent to his departure from it. Beyond the value of this illuminating personal account of a practitioner of "exit counseling" lies a remarkably useful collection of information about cult-related issues in contemporary American life. I heartily recommend this book to lay readers who for one reason or another wish to become better informed on this topic. It will also be valuable to professionals in health-related fields, clergy, attorneys, and others whose responsibilities bring them into contact with cults, their members, and the families whose lives are affected.

Louis Jolyon West, M.D. (1924-1999)
Former chairman of the Department of Psychiatry, UCLA
School of Medicine

A major contribution....For the first time, a skilled and ethical exit counselor has spelled out the details of the complicated yet understandable process of helping free a human being from the bondage of mental manipulation....Steve Hassan has written a "how to do something about it" book.

Margaret Singer, Ph.D. (1921-2003)
Department of Psychology, University of California, Berkeley

I strongly recommend *Combating Cult Mind Control*. Cults are a major problem that affects more than a few people....Steve Hassan is a bright and superior person who has authored an important book. Go to a bookstore to buy it....really try to get it!

Steve Allen (1921-2000)
Entertainer, comedian, and songwriter
Creator of the original *Tonight Show*
Parent of an ex-cult member
Author of *Beloved Son: A Story of the Jesus Cults*

...the serious clinician will find Hassan's book a challenge to the ignorance and prejudice that tragically surround the cult phenomenon.

Paul Martin, Ph.D. (1946-2009)
Founder of Wellspring Retreat and Resource Center, a rehabilitation facility for ex-cult members

COMBATING CULT MIND CONTROL

The #1 Best-Selling Guide
to Protection, Rescue, and Recovery
from Destructive Cults

Steven Hassan
America's Leading Cult Expert

30th Anniversary Edition
Revised and updated for today's new realities

Freedom of Mind Press
Newton, MA

COMBATING CULT MIND CONTROL

The #1 Best-Selling Guide to Protection, Rescue, and Recovery from Destructive Cults

Fourth edition, newly revised and updated

A Freedom of Mind Press Book

ISBN 978-0-9670688-2-4

Library of Congress Control Number: 2015935807

Cults-Psychology, Deprogramming, Brainwashing, Mind Control, Thought Reform, Persuasion, Religion-Cults, Human Trafficking, Terrorism, Social Influence, Self-Help, Recovery, Ex-cultists-Rehabilitation, Ex-cultists-Mental Health

Includes bibliographic references and index

For permission to reprint, media inquiries, and information on talks, presentations, and trainings by Steven Hassan, contact the publisher:

Freedom of Mind Resource Center
716 Beacon Street, #590443
Newton, MA 02459
Phone: (617) 396-4638
Fax: (617) 628-8153
center@freedomofmind.com
freedomofmind.com

Earlier editions of this book (1988, 1990) were published by Park Street Press, an imprint of Inner Traditions International under the title, *Combatting Cult Mind Control.*

Other works by Steven Hassan

Releasing the Bonds: Empowering People to Think for Themselves (2000)

Freedom of Mind: Helping Loved Ones Leave Controlling People, Cults and Beliefs (2012, 2013)

Co-developer of **Ending The Game,**© a **first-of-its-kind "coercion resiliency" curriculum** that reduces feelings of attachment to traffickers and/or a lifestyle characterized by commercial sexual exploitation, thereby reducing the rate of recidivism among sex trafficking survivors.
Endingthegame.com

I dedicate this book to people all over the world who have ever experienced the loss of their personal freedom, in the hope that it might help to ease their suffering and provide healing for themselves and their loved ones.

Contents

Introduction to the 2018 Edition

Fake News!

–Donald Trump, 45th President of the United States of America

In a time of universal deceit - telling the truth is a revolutionary act.

–George Orwell, (actual name, Eric Blair) in his dystopian novel *1984*, published in 1949

Spring, 2018. I am waiting to fly home to Boston, exhausted, but with a deep feeling of fulfillment. Last night I concluded a three-day intervention with a wonderful group of family and friends who had hired me to help a loved one wake up from a deep involvement with a Hindu guru group. Her marriage and their family business were threatened. The new guru had instructed believers to move to India and not speak with ex-members. Her husband and now two adult children had hired me, along with her sisters, to do my best to develop, guide and implement a Strategic Interactive Approach that culminated in this three-day voluntary intervention. Last night and again this morning tears came to my eyes as I read texts from everyone filled with gratitude. Her true believer trance was gone. She was now thinking for herself. Before we began, many had doubted we could be successful because she seemed so programmed. Thankfully, they were mistaken.

She agreed to listen because her sisters, children, husband and her close friends begged her to stay and learn. They asked her to have an open mind and learn about cults and mind control from me. With the help of long-term former members who had been her friends while in the group, she was overwhelmed with compelling and believable stories. She learned about horrible abuses of power that her daughter experienced and discovered had happened to others. She sat with and listened to her old friends she had previously dismissed and avoided. Love, patience, and respect guided the process. It worked beautifully!

As I am waiting at the airport, I get into a conversation with some fellow travelers who have recognized me from my appearance on the Leah Remini show exposing Scientology abuses. They have many questions. They ask me to tell them more about how I got interested in helping people out of cults.

I ask them if they have ever heard of the Moon cult? No, they haven't.

But they have heard of the newspaper owned by them, the Washington Times. As I'm describing how high-demand groups have proliferated over the past few years, reaching what I consider epidemic proportions, they stop me. They can't believe it's true. They are amazed to hear that cults are successfully recruiting people.

I go back through decades of big stories: "Charles Manson?" The woman had read that he was supposed to get married. "Patty Hearst and the SLA?" They've never heard of her. "Do you know about Jonestown and Jim Jones?" Astonishingly, no, they don't.

This edition is being published on the 40th anniversary of the Jonestown tragedy, which took place November 18th, 1978. The hardcover edition of *Combating Cult Mind Control* came out on the 10th anniversary of the Jonestown tragedy. While today most Americans know the expression "drink the Kool-Aid," many people have never heard of Jim Jones and his cult, the Peoples Temple. Even fewer know the grim story of how cyanide was mixed with Flavor Aid and forced down the throats of over 300 children and hundreds of adults. Jones told them it was an act of "revolutionary suicide." They believed he was God on earth. In total, he killed 912 people.

What about Waco, David Koresh, and Branch Davidians? Heaven's Gate? The Japanese cult Aum Shinrikyo and their sarin gas attack in the subways of Tokyo?" No, no. Sadly, no. They are not alone in not knowing. The world has changed. While the names of the big cults of the 1970s and 1980s have disappeared from the headlines, even more, insidious names—Al Qaeda, ISIS, Boko Haram, the Lord's Resistance Army, led by Joseph Kony—have taken their place. In fact, my traveling companions ask me about ISIS, also known as Islamic State or Daesh—it seems to them that it might be a cult. Yes! I tell them that, in my opinion, it is a political cult that uses religion to lure and influence people. It exhibits many of the classic signs—recruiting people through deception, whisking them away to isolated locations, giving them new names, clothes, controlling their access to food and information, implanting phobias, and making false promises.

We talk about North Korea, its nuclear arms development, and assassinations of enemies, cyber attacks against Sony Pictures, whose movie, *The Interview*, casts the North Korean leader, Kim Jong-un, in a decidedly unflattering light. I tell them that North Korea is a classic example of a mind control regime. They are entirely dependent and obedient to their "great leader," and his picture is everywhere. North Korean dictator Kim and President Trump, ignoring criminal human rights abuses, decided to meet in person. This event fascinates me as the United States' unorthodox move follows some of my significant principles of the Strategic Interactive Approach (SIA) including communicating directly in person rather than through others, or phone or email, rapport and trust building by giving respect. I also liked the 4 minute video shown to Kim of a future of economic promise.

We then discuss human trafficking—one of the most common felonies committed in the United States, second only to identity theft. Sex and labor trafficking are now multibillion-dollar industries. It is finally getting significant media attention. However, it seems everyone is missing the core issue. The human trafficking racket is accurately understood as a "commercial cult" phenomenon. Pimps are business people who operate like cult leaders. They use psychological techniques to recruit, indoctrinate, and control their members. I tell my companions about a book sold on Amazon, written by a pimp, showing men how to use mind control on women to get them to be sex slaves. I tell them that human trafficking has become a focus of my energies over the past few years.

In the summer of 2013, I was invited by Carissa Phelps and her Runaway Girl organization to speak at a training session for six hundred law enforcement personnel on the subject of trafficking. My role was to talk about the mind control tactics used by pimps and human traffickers, the effect on women, and how law enforcement can be most effective in responding. Later, Rachel Thomas, Carissa Phelps, D'lita Miller and I developed the first program for sex trafficking survivors to understand pimp mind control. It is called Ending the Game.

Had I taken the conversation further with them—had I scratched the surface of their personal lives a little deeper—chances are they would have mentioned someone they know, a friend or a relative, who has undergone a "radical personality change." It happens all the time. Someone has been acting strangely, possibly avoiding contact with parents, friends, or community. Maybe they've married a controlling spouse or become involved with a charismatic person on campus or a small group of people.

One of the most significant changes I have seen over the past decades is the rise of "mini-cults," which consist of anywhere from two to twelve people. The leader could be a husband or a wife, a teacher, a therapist, or even a client. One of my most memorable cases involved a therapist who had fallen victim to the undue influence of her client.

Today, the issue of unethical and psychological social influence permeates the fabric of our society, and societies all over the world. Destructive cults are just one manifestation of the application of what is now routinely studied academically, the science of social influence. The need for this book has not diminished. On the contrary, it is, if anything, even more pressing.

Cult Efforts To Stop Exposure

Since my deprogramming in May of 1976, I have written three books, given countless talks, workshops, and seminars all over the world, and done an incredible number of media interviews. I have been invited several times to speak in Professor Rebecca Lemov's History of Brainwashing course at Harvard University. When I ask the students if they are curious how I became interested in the science of brainwashing and mind control, and my involvement in the Moon cult, almost no one in the room knows what I am talking about. Most people have forgotten about the Korean cult leader Sun Myung Moon, who founded the Unification Church in 1954, declared himself the Messiah and arranged mass weddings between members—earning the group notoriety during the 1970s and 1980s.

Some Americans do remember the Moon cult, but they think the organization disappeared years ago. That is hardly the case. It is still very much alive, even though Moon himself died in 2012. The organization continues to be very active in world affairs. It owns, among many entities, The Washington Times and United Press International (UPI) in Washington, DC. For the past three decades, the media have provided little coverage on this group's destructive activities. This year, Hyung Jin Moon, made headlines with his Rod of Iron Ministry which advocates assault rifles are necessary for God's people. His brother Justin Moon owns Kahr arms, a gun manufacturing company that makes pistols, assault rifles, and submachine guns.

Back in the 1970s and 1980s, Scientology was also very well known. Since the early 1990s, however, it has received much less media attention. Not because of a lack of public interest, but because of Scientology's bottomless pockets and litigious nature. In fact, Scientology now holds the title of one of the most litigious organizations in the history of the world.

Scientology sued TIME Magazine over their 1990 cover story, "Scientology: The Thriving Cult of Greed and Power," and forced TIME to defend the article all the way to the U.S. Supreme Court. The lawsuit was eventually dismissed, but its writer, Richard Behar, was viciously and continuously harassed. Personal and legal harassment sent a strong message to other writers and news producers: Do a story on Scientology, and you will spend a fortune defending yourself while living in fear that you and your family will be harassed.

For decades after the TIME lawsuit, I was invited to appear on TV or radio programs, but would be warned by the producers to avoid mentioning Scientology. Because of similar fears about Moon's organization, which was also wealthy and litigious, I was told that I couldn't mention the Moonies, or say I'd been a member of Moon's Unification Church. When I mentioned it anyway, my comments would routinely be edited out, unless it was a live interview.

Scientology took over the most important counter-cult organization, the Cult Awareness Network (CAN)—an organization which was established to provide useful, accurate information on mind control groups. Contrary to cult propaganda it was not founded by deprogrammer Ted Patrick. CAN was made up of volunteers across the United States: parents, ex-cult members, mental health professionals, educators, lawyers, and other concerned citizens. When I first wrote this book, CAN was the essential information resource on cults. However, Scientology sued CAN into bankruptcy in 1996, and then bought their name, logo, and telephone number. They later obtained all of CAN's files and records. Scientology ran CAN as a deceptive front group for years. It now appears to be offline.

Scientology has also used legal warrants to raid databases around the world, including the counter-cult site factnet.org. Fortunately, this aspect of their legal maneuvering backfired, leading to greater public interest in the group, and sending Jon Atack's masterful exposé, *Let's Sell These People a Piece of Blue Sky*, into the Amazon top 100.

The media has done many stories on Tom Cruise, Katie Holmes, John Travolta and other celebrities associated with Scientology. Former top executives of the group have left and gone public, revealing how they managed, after 25 years of fighting and dirty tricks, to force the IRS to give them tax exempt status as a "religion" which it is not in my opinion.

In the years since the first edition of *Combating Cult Mind Control* was published, some of the larger mind control groups spent millions of dollars to retain top law firms, public relations agencies, and private investigators. Some of these professionals are paid handsomely to threaten former group members; to underwrite significant disinformation campaigns; to undermine the fundamental human rights of current members; and to defend the mind control organizations against prosecution for blatantly criminal acts.

Destructive cults have tried repeatedly, but unsuccessfully, to discredit other activists and me. Most of this has taken the form of disinformation campaigns, but some of it has been much shadier. For example, cult members would call my office, pretending to be ex-members or distraught parents, and ask for help. Their goal was to deceive or manipulate me into saying or doing something that could hurt my reputation. Cult agents have been sent out to sow seeds of distrust among cult activists by telling untruths about fellow activists. By undermining these collaborations and friendships, cult agents have occasionally disrupted or neutralized efforts to help victims of destructive cults.

Courageous former members who dare to speak out often suffer significant harm to their reputations, finances, or both. Careers and often marriages destroyed, people followed, tires punctured, dwellings broken into, and frivolous lawsuits filed. A book could be written just telling the stories of the heroes of the mind control awareness movement. Part of the reason I am republishing and updating this book is to share some of those critical and inspiring accounts.

Changes Since The 1988 Edition

This edition marks the 30th anniversary of this book. So many things have changed since it was first published. I still hear from people all over the world who tell me it was transformative and even saved their lives.

Over the years, I have heard from hundreds of people that the stories in *Combating Cult Mind Control* provided many parallels to their own experiences, and helped transform their lives. I am delighted to republish it fundamentally intact, but with many important updates and additions. Let me describe some of the changes and factors to consider as you read this new edition.

When I was deprogrammed from the Moonies in 1976, there was no Internet. Since then, life on planet Earth, especially our relationship to information and people around the world, has changed radically. I used to carry with me pounds of books and photocopies of information when doing my work. There was no Wikipedia. No Google. No Facebook. There were no cell phones, no text messaging, and no tracking GPS chips.

Before the Internet, no one knew where to go for help. Perhaps they would talk with friends, relatives, doctors, or clergy. Or they would use the card catalog at their local library to look for a book. People felt helpless, afraid, alone, and confused as they watched a loved one undergo a radical personality change.

Similarly, people recruited into a cult had few resources to reality-test what they were told while in the group. When people leave cults they are confused, ashamed, lonely, depressed, and often suicidal, but there were few places to turn to for helpful information or guidance.

The advent of the World Wide Web created a new era, as it was a fast and effective way to network and share information. In 1992, computer genius, Bob Penny, built factnet.org, the first dedicated counter-cult website, which was then launched by his fellow ex-Scientologists Lawrence Wollersheim, Gerry Armstrong, and Jon Atack. I had my website in 1995.

The Internet provided light on the dark deeds of megalomaniac cult leaders and their unethical, often criminal behavior. In those early days of the Internet, the information control of destructive groups was temporarily broken, and cults scrambled to cope with that fact.

Unfortunately, just as diseases evolve to resist or avoid new medical treatments, many organizations now use the Internet to mislead and misinform the world. Some examples:

• Unfortunately, Wikipedia is constantly patrolled by agents of destructive groups. Critical information is removed or confusing information is added. These wealthy groups with free labor have the advantage when it comes to information control and currently, Wikipedia has not found a way to protect the public and mitigate their power. Perhaps they are substantial donors? Members continuously try to remove accurate information about their organizations and replace it with falsehoods. Some of the larger organizations have staff whose sole job is to erase truth from the web and upload propaganda. Valuable sites, such as factnet.org, are hacked and driven out of operation. Thankfully, there is the Wayback Machine Internet archive. If you know the critical site URL, there is a chance the useful information has been saved and archived.

• Mind-control organizations routinely sponsor websites that purport to provide help, empathy, and guidance to former members, as well as to current members who are thinking of leaving. Some of these sites include links to ostensibly supportive professionals. Unfortunately, some of these websites are shams. They are run by the mind control organizations themselves and are used to lure ex-members back in and to identify and isolate people who are thinking of leaving. There are also some disturbed people, including hucksters pretending to be deprogrammers and cult experts trolling for business. They have questionable personal histories, lack credentials and will attack me or colleagues in an attempt to harm our reputations. Do not believe information that does not make sense. Ask for verifiable proof. Or ask me what is going on. Legitimate experts have legitimate other experts to verify they are responsible and trustworthy.

• Because vast amounts of personal information are now available for purchase online, cult recruiters (as well as ordinary scam artists) can now go online and develop extensive profiles about future targets. They then pretend to read people's minds, or intuit their deepest hopes and fears, or channel spirits, or act as agents of divine inspiration. This technique of mystical manipulation often plays a significant role in a person's recruitment. The Internet has provided an entirely new way to influence people and control them. Totalitarian countries block access to sites they consider to be "dangerous" for their continued control. AI, sophisticated deep data mining algorithms, and social media represent a far greater danger for mass mind control.

In the past several years, a number of fiction movies and television series have been developed around the idea of destructive cults with charismatic leaders. Unfortunately, they all far short in giving useful information that will enable people to truly understand cult mind control and protect themselves and loved ones.

What Else Has Changed

In this edition of *Combating Cult Mind Control*, I will often use the terms mind control and undue influence. In previous versions, I regularly used mind control but rarely used undue influence. Both refer to the process of controlling people by mentally hijacking their rational thought processes. Undue influence has been primarily used in a legal context, but one of my hopes is that undue influence will be understood and used by the general public soon. In many ways, undue influence is a better term than mind control, as exploitation is part of the definition of undue influence. In truth, undue influence can infect people to such an extent that they form a programmed cult identity. It is a kind of "virus of undue influence" which invades and alters its host. I have become a member of the Program in Psychiatry and the Law at Harvard, a forensic think tank, where I discuss these concepts with esteemed colleagues. I have taught Psychiatry Grand Rounds at Harvard Medical School and have begun teaching there. And, I have entered a doctoral program at Fielding Graduate University to do scholarly research on my BITE model. Hopefully it might be shown to be a useful instrument for helping to define undue influence.

I would like to talk about and define three other terms: intervention, deprogramming, and exit-counseling. Over the years, my work has evolved dramatically to deal with the many new realities in mind control or undue influence. As a result, none of these terms accurately describes what I usually teach and do.

An intervention is a sit-down, ideally three-day process in which I, along with former cult members, experts and key family members and friends surprise someone who is in the grips of mind control. We then use friendly persuasion to secure their voluntary agreement to sit with us, listen, and learn.

Before the first edition of this book was published, it was relatively simple to do an intervention, and many of them were successful. But after this book's initial success, many leaders of mind control organizations adapted their strategies in response. So—especially with the major groups I've written about—members were told never to go home alone, especially for more than a day or two.

Also, since the advent of the smartphone, people under undue influence are regularly monitored and controlled via voice mail messages, texts, phone calls, and emails. As a result, the old intervention techniques are no longer as effective. These days, I agree to do interventions only when I'm sure there is no better way to help, and I am reasonably sure that the person will not get up and walk out (or call the cult).

I also stopped using the term exit-counseling many years ago. For one thing, the term proved counterproductive. When a cult member was told that Steve Hassan, an exit-counselor, had arrived to talk with them, they would refuse to speak with me unless they were already interested in leaving. Furthermore, in parts of Europe, the term exit-counseling is used to describe counseling someone who is dying.

Although I did some deprogramming very early in my career, I have avoided the practice for over three decades. As you will see, I differentiate deprogramming—which is conducted by force, and which sometimes included actual abduction—from voluntary, respectful, and legal methods of helping.

Over the years, my colleagues and I have endeavored to find a more descriptive term than deprogramming. For a vast number of people in the media, as well as the general public, the word has positive connotations. For a time I would say that I was a cult exit-counselor, and everyone would ask, "What is that?" When I added, "voluntary, legal deprogramming," they would understand that I was involved in helping group members think for themselves and make their own decisions. But the word deprogramming continues to be problematic for me to feel comfortable using as a term. People don't erase people's mental hard drives. Instead, I give people a toolkit for helping them make their own decisions and taking back their lives. I help people detect and remove the virus of mind control on their own. Reclaiming one's power is something they ultimately need to do themselves, for themselves, not something I do to them.

However, when people are operating in full cult-identity mode, they often need help to encourage them to step back and reality-test their commitments, including their beliefs and behaviors. Helping people reclaim their integrity and free will is a complicated process.

In any case, all of these terms are just sound-bites. The full name for what I teach and do is the Strategic Interactive Approach. A mouthful. What does it mean? It's a customized, sophisticated, complex systems-theory approach, whereby I create a unique and ethical influence campaign to help individuals acquire a set of experiences and realizations that help them remove many of the invisible chains of mind control.

The goals of every SIA effort are to empower the individual to be their own person: to think critically, to evaluate, and to reality-test and to exercise their own free will. The person learns to listen to their inner voice, rather than the instructions of an authority figure. In this process, I engage family and friends and employ a wide variety of helpful strategies and resources.

In this edition, I have re-titled chapter 6 Courageous Survivor Stories and added new stories of people who were members of mind control groups, which includes terrorism and sex trafficking. I also have highlighted several people's courageous activities to help others, and de-stigmatize their own earlier involvement in these groups.

These stories shed light on the full range of such organizations. Some are relatively unknown, such as the apocalyptic cult Eternal Values, or the Zen Buddhist organization Shasta Abbey or the Iranian terrorist group

MeK. Others, such as Scientology and Transcendental Meditation (TM), are more recognizable to the average reader.

Still others, such as Jehovah's Witnesses and the Mormons, have been highly visible for many decades. In the early editions of *Combating Cult Mind Control*, I did not include stories about those aberrant Christian groups. However, over the years I have been contacted by many people who were born into those organizations, telling me how the book helped them. Paradoxically, because the earlier editions didn't mention either group, the book wasn't banned by church leaders, and so it was widely read by church members as a result.

An Invitation To Safety

The techniques of undue influence have evolved dramatically, and continue to do so. Today, a vast array of methods exists to deceive, manipulate and indoctrinate people into closed systems of obedience and dependency.

Sadly, the essential information in this book is still not widely known or understood. People around the world remain largely unprepared for the new realities of mind control.

But we are far from helpless. There is a great deal you can do to stay safe, sane, and whole—and to help the people you care about to do the same. And if someone you love is already part of a mind control group, there is much you can do to help them break free and rebuild their lives. This book will give you the tools you will need.

As you read this book, you will learn to develop, use, and trust your critical thinking skills, your intuition, your bodily and emotional awareness, your ability to ask the right questions, and your skills at doing rapid and useful research. You will also learn to cultivate a healthy balance of openness and skepticism. As you will see, the entire process begins and ends with you.

Welcome!

Foreword to the 1988 Edition

The phone was frighteningly loud. The clock read 4:30 a.m. It was difficult to take in what a reporter from *The Berkeley Gazette* was saying on the phone: "Margaret, I hate to bother you this early, but we have just learned that Jim Jones has decided to pull the trigger down in Guyana. I've been here all night at a house in Berkeley talking with ex-members of Peoples Temple and with relatives of persons down in Jonestown. There's a mother here whose husband and 12-year-old son are down there and she is desperate. It is not known if everyone's dead, or if there are survivors. I know I've told you not to work with ex-members of Peoples Temple because of the dangerous harassment that Jones' so-called 'Angels' direct against former members. But these people need to talk with you and get some help with what has happened."

As daylight was breaking, I passed up the steps guarded by somber Berkeley police, as it was feared that Jones had left "hit orders" for members still in the area to wipe out defectors when he ordered the final "White Night," his term for the often-rehearsed moment when he would have all his followers drink poison.

The reporter, my son (also a reporter), and a few police officers had warned me not to give my usual gratis consultation services to ex-Peoples Temple members, even though I had long given these services to former cultists. Jones allegedly used his "angels" to wreak vengeance against members who left, and against their supporters as well.

The woman whose husband and young son were eventually identified as dead in Jonestown was only one of many. I spent hours and days meeting and talking with various survivors as they returned from Guyana to the Bay Area and attempted to get their lives going again after the Guyanese holocaust. There were attorney Tim Stoen and his wife, Grace, whose young son had been held captive by Jones and died in Jonestown. There were the members of the basketball team who missed the mass suicide-murder. There was a nine-year-old girl who had survived having had her throat slit by a woman who then killed herself in Georgetown, Guyana, as part of Jones' mass death orders. There was Larry Layton, who faced courts in two countries for allegedly carrying out Jones' orders at the airport in Guyana where Rep. Leo J. Ryan and others died.

I began to work with ex-cultists about six years before Jonestown and continue to do so to this day.

I have provided psychological counseling to more than 3000 persons who have been in cults. I have written about some of this work and have talked with lay and professional groups in many countries about thought reform programs, intense indoctrination programs, cults, and related topics.

My interest in the effects of thought reform programs began when I worked at the Walter Reed Army Institute of Research after the Korean War. At that point I met and worked with Edgar H. Schein, Ph.D., Robert Jay Lifton, M.D., and Louis J. West, M.D., pioneers in the study of the effects of intense indoctrination programs. I was involved in the follow-up studies of former prisoners of war, interviewed long-term prisoners of the Chinese, and participated over the years in much of the work on conceptualizing thought reform programs. As Steve Hassan does in this volume, I have repeatedly described the specific needs of persons who have been subjected to such and have emphasized the lack of knowledge that most citizens as well as mental health professionals have about the processes, effects, and aftermath of being subjected to thought reform programs.

Steve Hassan has clearly and convincingly described how mind control is induced. He integrates his personal experience in a cult, and his practical skills developed in years of exit-counseling of persons who have been in mind control situations, with theories and concepts in the scientific literature. The book comes alive with real-life examples.

For the first time, an experienced exit-counselor outlines step by step the actual methods, sequence, and framework of what he does and how he works with families and the persons under mind control. He draws on the various scholarly works in the fields of thought reform, persuasion, social psychology, and hypnosis to offer theoretical frameworks for how mind control is achieved.

Exit-counseling is a new profession, and Steve Hassan has spelled out here a type of ethical, educational counseling which he and others have developed. He has devoted the time and has the literary skill and educational background to make this volume a major contribution. The reader is taken from Steve's first telephone contacts with desperate families to the final outcome of his interventions. These counseling techniques and tactics are socially and psychologically well worked out. They are ethical and growth enhancing. While the need is great, there are few really adequately prepared and experienced exit-counselors. They do not offer what psychologists and psychiatrists offer, nor can they be replaced by these or other mental health professionals. Exit-counseling is a special field, one that demands specific knowledge, special techniques and methods, and a high level of skill.

This book should have a wide appeal. Anyone with a relative or friend who has become involved with a group using mind control procedures will find it useful. Any citizen can profit from seeing how vulnerable to influence we all are and learning that mind control exists—that it is not a myth.

We must heed the potentially destructive and frightening impact that the use of mind control by selfishly motivated groups can have on the very fabric of a society. This book fills a need and deserves a wide audience.

Margaret T. Singer, Ph.D.
Adjunct Professor, Department of Psychology
University of California, Berkeley
Recipient of the Leo J. Ryan Memorial Award

This foreword was written for the first edition of *Combatting Cult Mind Control*, published in 1988. Unfortunately, Dr. Singer died in 2003. She authored two books with Janja Lalich, *Cults in Our Midst* (Jossey–Bass, 1995) and *Crazy Therapies* (Jossey- Bass, 1996).

Preface to the First Paperback Edition

Since the first publication of *Combating Cult Mind Control* in the fall of 1988, I have heard from hundreds of people who have told me about the positive impact this book has had on their lives. Lawyers, educators, mental health professionals, and clergy have let me know how valuable it has been in their work. Families have told me incredible stories of how reading it led to a series of phone calls, meetings, and, ultimately, successful interventions with loved ones. Yet nothing gratifies me more than to hear from individuals who were involved with a destructive cult for many years, and who felt that reading this book helped them open a door to freedom.

For each of you who might be a current or former member of an organization that is controversial, and to those who are friends or relatives of someone involved with such a group, I have some special words of advice:

- **If you are currently a member (or former member) of a group or organization that has been alleged to be a cult:**

You may find that it takes a great deal of strength, courage, and integrity to make the effort to learn about this phenomenon. But as difficult as it is, keep in mind how much you stand to gain by reading this book in its entirety. Knowledge is power. You may even discover that, although the public views your group as a cult, there in fact is no mind control being used. I have been thanked countless times by members of unorthodox organizations who were able to, once and for all, discuss with their families and friends the criteria I outline in this book. By reading and discussing the material, they can demonstrate that they *are* exercising their own free will, and continue their involvement with a clear conscience.

If you are questioning the ethics, policies, or practices of your group, approach this book with an open mind. However, please be careful about letting other group members know you are reading it, as this might invoke unwanted attention and disciplinary measures from the group's leadership. If it is at all possible to take some time off and get some distance from other members, I urge you to do so. Find a place where you have minimal pressure and few distractions.

I also strongly suggest reading the book at least two times. When reading it for the first time, do so with the perspective that it is describing *other* groups (preferably ones that you do believe are destructive), and really allow yourself the opportunity to understand the process of mind control and the characteristics of destructive cults. Be sure to make notes as you read, writing down everything you agree with or disagree with, as well as things you want to research further. Then do all the follow-up research necessary to fully answer your questions.

Once you have finished the book, give yourself at least a few days before reading it again. When you pick it up a second time, read it objectively, as though it may or may not apply to your own personal situation. Make a new set of notes on what you agree with, what you disagree with, and what you need to research further. On completing this second reading, go find the answers to the issues that are raised pertaining to your own group. Take some time off (if possible, a minimum of a few weeks) and go to a restful place, away from other group members, and gather more information from other sources. *Remember, if the group is a legitimate, valid organization, it will stand up to any scrutiny.* It is far better to find out the truth now than to invest more time, money, and energy, only to discover years later that the group is very different from its idealized image.

Truth is stronger than lies, and love is stronger than fear. If you are involved with a religious organization, keep in mind that God created us with free will, and that no truly spiritual organization would *ever* use deception or mind control, or take away your freedom.

- **If you are a family member, friend, or loved one of someone who is involved in what you suspect is a destructive cult:**

It is best to approach the problem in a systematic and methodical manner. Avoid overreacting and getting hysterical. Don't jump the gun and tell the person that you have bought this book or are reading it. Wait until you and other relevant people have had a chance to read and get prepared before planning a team Strategic Interactive Approach (SIA). Be sure to also read my book *Freedom of Mind: Helping Loved Ones Leave Controlling People, Cults and Beliefs*, which will offer a great deal of further information and guidance. Unfortunately, there have been cases in which people have bought *Combating Cult Mind Control* and impulsively given it to cult members. This can backfire badly if anyone from the cult finds out.

Most cult groups fear anything and anyone that might cause them to lose members, and giving a member this book will tip them off that you are educating yourself. Be careful! Instead of sounding the alarm, adopt a *curious yet concerned* posture. Try to avoid confrontations and ultimatums.

Read this book as many times as you need to in order to clearly explain to others the characteristics of mind control, the criteria of a destructive cult, and the basics of cult psychology. The BITE model in Chapter 4 will be a particularly valuable tool.

Get as many concerned friends and relatives involved as you can. A strong first step will be for them to read this book, too. If everyone is prepared, they will not be caught off guard.

Although this book is meant as a resource, there is no substitute for professional advice geared to your own unique situation. Do not hesitate to seek such help from people who are qualified and informed. I am now developing programs to train mental health professionals, former cult members, and activists on mind control, undue influence, and cult psychology. Also please consult the wealth of free interviews, talks, workshops, and other resources on the freedomofmind.com website.

Chapter 1

My Work as a Cult Expert

Finally, a chance to relax, forget about work, and enjoy some social time with my friends. Maybe meet some new people at this party.

"Hi. My name is Steve Hassan. Nice to meet you." (I just hope no one asks me to talk about work.)

The question: "So, what do you do?" (Oh no, not again!)

The dodge: "I'm self-employed."

"Doing what?" (No escape.)

"I'm a cult expert." (Here come the 50 questions.)

"Oh, really? That's interesting. How did you get into that? Can you tell me why...?"

Since February 1974, I have been involved with the problems caused by destructive cults. That was when I was recruited into the "One World Crusade,"[1] one of hundreds of front groups of the Unification Church, also known as the Moonies. After two and a half years as a member of that cult, I was deprogrammed after I fell asleep while driving a fundraising van, and smashed into a tractor trailer truck at 80 miles an hour.

Ever since then, I have been actively involved in fighting destructive cults. I have become a professionally trained therapist and fly anywhere my help is genuinely needed. My phone rings at all hours of the day. My clients are people who, for one reason or another, have been damaged emotionally, socially, and sometimes even physically, by their involvement with destructive cults. I help these people recover and start their lives over. My approach enables them to make this transition in a way that avoids the trauma associated with the often-illegal abduction method Ted Patrick called *deprogramming*.

My work is intensive, totally involving me with a person and their family, sometimes for days at a time. My approach is legal and respectful. Usually, I am able to assist a person in making a dramatic recovery, accessing and reclaiming their authentic identity, or, at least, understanding that they have a better life ahead of them if they decide to leave the group. Only a handful of people in the world work with members of destructive cults. This book reveals most of the significant aspects of my approach to this unusual profession.

This is work and a way of life that I never imagined. I undertook it because I thought I could help people. Having seen how destructive cults deliberately undermine basic human rights, I also became an activist. I am especially concerned with everyone's right to know about how destructive cults recruit, keep control of and exploit highly talented, productive people.

My life as a cult expert often makes me feel as though I'm in the middle of a war zone. All kinds of incredible cases and media situations come my way and I do the best I can to help. Even though I try to manage the number of active cases and see only a reasonable number of clients each week, unexpected emergencies sometimes command my attention. Here is one such story:

I came home late one Friday evening after a night out with friends and checked my phone messages. There were four calls, all from the same family in Minnesota. "Call us any time—day or night—please," said a woman's voice. "Our son Bruce has gotten involved with the Moonies. He's going on a three-week workshop with them in Pennsylvania on Monday. He's a doctoral student in physics at MIT. Please call us back."

I called right away and talked with the mother and father for about an hour. They had heard that their son had become a member of an organization called the Collegiate Association for the Research of Principles (C.A.R.P.) They had done some investigation and discovered that C.A.R.P. was the international student-recruiting arm of the Unification Church.[2] I had started a branch of C.A.R.P. on the Queens College campus, so I knew all about it. We agreed there was no time to lose.

After some discussion, we decided on a course of action. They would take a 6:45 a.m. flight to Boston, the next day. They would go to their son's apartment, take him out to a restaurant, and assess his situation. Their success or failure would depend on Bruce's close relationship to them, and on how far the Moonies had already indoctrinated him. Had they gotten to the point where they could make him reject his family as "satanic?" His mother and father assured me they would be able to talk to their son. I wasn't so sure, but agreed it would be well worth the attempt. From my experience with the Moonies, I felt that if Bruce went to the three-week indoctrination, he would most very likely drop out of school and become a full-time member.

The next step would be for the parents to persuade Bruce to talk to me. I was worried about whether they could. The Moonies do a very thorough job of convincing people that former members are satanic and that even being in their presence could be dangerous.[3] I mentally reviewed the possibilities. There were a number of ways things could go badly: Bruce could refuse to meet with me, or meet with me and walk away before we had enough time. He could later tell the Moonies his parents asked him to meet with me, in which case he might be whisked away and given deep phobias about Satan working through his family. He would have come to believe what I believed while I was a Moonie. I was programmed to fear my family and cut off personal contact for over a year. For the moment, then, all I could do was wait.

The next morning I was interviewed for a television show on cults, something I do frequently all over the country. After the taping, I canceled all my appointments for the day. Bruce's parents called from the Boston airport. They were about to leave for their son's house. We reviewed our strategy one more time. I crossed my fingers.

Two hours later the phone rang. They had managed to bring Bruce to a Chinese restaurant not far from my house. Bruce had agreed to meet me. I grabbed whatever I thought I might need to show him—file folders, photocopies of articles, and books—and threw them into the car and drove to the restaurant.

When I arrived and met the family, the parents' faces were full of worry and concern. Bruce tried to smile at first and shook my hand. But it was clear to me that he was thinking, "Can I trust this guy? Who *is* he?"

I sat down in the booth with them. I asked Bruce about himself and why he thought his parents were so concerned that they flew from Minneapolis. Within an hour, after asking him enough questions to get a good handle on his state of mind, I decided to "go for it."

"Did they tell you about pledge service yet?" I asked.

He shook his head and looked surprised. "What's that?"

"Oh, that's a very important ceremony members do every Sunday morning, on the first day of every month, and on four holy days the group observes," I started. "Members bow three times with their face touching the floor before an altar with Sun Myung Moon's picture on it and recite a six-point pledge to be faithful to God, to Moon, and to the fatherland—Korea."

"You're kidding!"

At that moment I knew Bruce would be all right. I could see that he was not yet fully under the group's mind control. I thought he would respond well to hearing more information about the group's leader, multimillionaire Korean industrialist Sun Myung Moon. I began telling him facts about the Moonies unrelated to mind control—Moon's felony tax fraud conviction; the Congressional report on the Moonies' connections to the Korean CIA; and their suspected illegal activities.

"You know, I've been looking for someone like you for a few months," Bruce said after hearing me out. "I went to the priest at MIT to ask him for information. He didn't know anything."

Bruce was still thinking for himself, but in my opinion, he had been on the verge of being inducted into the cult. The three-day and seven-day workshops he'd been through had set him up for the 21-day program. When I was a member, it was common practice after this latter program to ask recruits to donate their bank accounts, move into the Moonie house, and become full time members.[4]

Bruce and I spent the next couple of days going over more information, watching videotapes, and talking about mind control and destructive cults. Much to his parents' relief, he finally announced he wasn't going to the workshop. He spent a lot of time photocopying stacks of documents and wanted to try to talk to the other students being recruited at MIT. He went back to the priest and told him about his close call. A week later the priest called to see if I would conduct a briefing session for college administrators.

That case was an easy one with a happy ending. The family had been quick to spot their son's personality changes, discover that C.A.R.P. was a front for the Moonies, and locate me. Their fast action enabled them to help their son easily and quickly.

The phone calls I receive are usually variations of the same plea for help. A son or daughter, sister or brother, husband or wife, mother or father, boyfriend or girlfriend is in trouble. Sometimes he or she is just being recruited; other times the call is about someone who has been in a cult for many years.

It is relatively easy to deal with someone not yet fully indoctrinated, like Bruce. Most people who call me, though, have had a longer-term problem. Some cases can be resolved quickly; others require a slower, more methodical approach. Emergencies like Bruce's are tricky because there is little or no time to prepare. Nonetheless, I have learned that fast action is often necessary. If someone is being worked on in a mind control environment, sometimes even a few hours can be crucial.

For some unknown reason, the calls for help seem to come in waves; only a few a day for a while, then suddenly ten or fifteen calls. Although I have traveled overseas to help people in cults, I spend most of my time traveling all over the United States and Canada. More than once in my travels, I have found myself on a train or plane sitting next to a dissatisfied member of a destructive cult. During the encounter, I have discovered that the person wanted more information about how to change his or her life. I freely offer this information. These "mini-interventions" can help plant a seed or actually turn on a "light bulb" of awareness—enabling the person to reclaim his or her personal autonomy.

My work entails two parts: counseling individuals and alerting the public to the cult phenomenon. I believe that sensitizing the public to the problem of mind control—or undue influence—is the best way to counter the growth of these groups. It is fairly easy to advise people about what to watch out for. It is much harder and far more complicated to help someone leave a cult. That's why the best way to deal with this problem and damage done to people in destructive cults is to "inoculate" people through education about cult mind control—particularly helping people learn how undue influence works. People's resistance is higher when they are aware of the danger. To this end, I give lectures and seminars and appear on television and radio shows wherever possible. And I write books such as this one.

Cults: A Nightmare Reality

Had someone told me when I was in high school that I would one day become a cult expert, I would have thought the idea bizarre. I wanted to be a poet and writer. I thought I might like to teach creative writing and possibly become an English professor. If that person had added that my clients would be people who had been systematically lied to, physically abused, separated from their families and friends, and forced into servitude, I would have accused them of borrowing images from George Orwell's novel, *Nineteen Eighty-Four.*

Orwell depicted a world where "thought police" maintain complete control over people's mental and emotional lives, and where it is a crime to act or think independently, or even to fall in love. Unfortunately, such places do exist right now, all over the world. They are mind control cults.

In these groups, basic respect for the individual is secondary to the leader's whims and ideology. People are manipulated and coerced to think, feel, and behave in a single "right way." Individuals become totally dependent on the group and lose the ability to act or think on their own. They are typically exploited for the sake of the group's economic or political ends.

I realize that this entire field is fraught with controversy, and I invite readers to consider that some people object to the word "cult" and some deny the reality of mind control. They are entitled to their opinions. But whatever we may call these things, they are real and often play decisive and, too often, destructive roles in people's lives. I have lived it and I see it all the time. Throughout this book, we will delve more deeply into these issues and determine what is or is not a cult. But for our immediate purposes: I define any group that uses unethical mind control to pursue its ends—whether religious, political, or commercial—as a destructive cult.

The popular view of cults is that they prey on the disaffected and the vulnerable—losers, loners, outcasts, and people who simply don't fit in. But the truth is very different. In fact, most cult recruits are normal people with ordinary backgrounds—and many are highly intelligent.

The world of *Nineteen Eighty-Four* was a far cry from the typically middle class American world of my childhood. I grew up in a conservative Jewish family in Flushing, Queens, New York, the youngest of three children and the only son. I vividly remember helping my father in his hardware store in Ozone Park. My mother, a junior high school art teacher, raised me in a warm, loving, unconditionally supportive way. Compared to many families, mine was boringly normal. My parents didn't smoke, drink, gamble or have affairs. We lived in a humble attached row house near Union Turnpike, across the street from St. John's University, for my entire childhood. My folks remained married for over sixty-five years.

I look back on my childhood and remember myself as an introvert, not a joiner. While I always had a few close friends, I preferred reading books to going to parties. The only groups I really belonged to were my synagogue's basketball team and a sixth grade chorus. I was an extra-honors student and was able to skip eighth grade. I graduated high school when I turned seventeen and turned my father down when he asked me if I wanted to take over his hardware business.

I decided to pursue a liberal arts education at Queens College, which is where I first encountered the cult recruiters who conned me out of my dreams—and out of my Jewish faith—and turned me into a disciple of Sun Myung Moon, one of the most notorious cult leaders of our time. Collectively, we were known as "the Moonies." We were as proud to call ourselves Moonies as the cult leader was that his followers had adopted the societal nickname.

Before we get any farther into our story, let me say since I was a member, the Moon organization waged a successful public relations campaign, culminating in 1989 claiming that the term "Moonie" is one of religious and racial bigotry. It has since fallen into general disuse. So much so, that when I speak to college classes, few have even heard of the Moonies. But I remember when we wore tee shirts in the style of "I Love New York"—but emblazoned with the slogan: "I'm a Moonie and I Love It!"[5]

Even though others no longer use the term, I still do and I want to explain why. I recognize that hateful people can turn any term into an epithet. This is especially so for members of religious, racial and other minorities—as those of us who identify as Muslim or Jewish can attest. I experienced such abuse when I was a Moonie, and there is no excuse for anyone to be treated in this way. But when I was a Moonie, Sun Myung Moon and his empire embraced the term—but only much later decided that it was inconvenient—and used the PR campaign as a bludgeon against critics, particularly reporters. To me, the Moon organization will always be The Moonies, although I understand that other people may choose other terms, and undoubtedly for the best of motives. I hope they will extend the same courtesy to me. Either way, I will not be silenced.

Who Are The Moonies?

The Unification Church (whose formal name is The Holy Spirit Association for the Unification of World Christianity) was once one of the wealthiest, most influential, most visible, and most destructive cults operating in the United States. The organization was completely dominated by its absolute leader, Sun Myung Moon,[6] a Korean-born businessman. In 1982, Moon was convicted of felony tax fraud and served 13 months in the federal penitentiary in Danbury, Connecticut.[7]

During the 1970s, the Moonies were a well-known feature of most American cities, especially college towns. They stood on street corners selling flowers, candy, puppets, and other small items. They also actively recruited young people from colleges and universities. Generally clean-cut, courteous, and persistent, they proliferated for years, gaining unfavorable media attention almost everywhere.

As far as the media were concerned, the Unification Church and its followers faded away in the 1980s. The truth is that the Moon organization became *more* sophisticated, expanding its many religious, political, cultural, and business front groups. Because the Unification Church keeps its vital statistics secret, there have never been any reliable figures of church membership in the United States. Church officials have claimed to have 30,000 members here (and some 3,000,000 in the world), but the numbers are undoubtedly much lower. There are probably some 4,000 Americans and another 4,000 foreigners (many married to American members) working for the cult in the United States today.[8]

Another aspect of the Unification Church, still insufficiently recognized, is that members justify the use of deception to recruit people.[9] When I was a Moonie recruiter, we also used psychological pressure to convince members to turn over all their personal wealth and possessions to the church.[10]

Members are subjected to workshops that thoroughly indoctrinate them in church beliefs,[11] and typically undergo a conversion experience in which they surrender to the group. As a result, they become totally dependent upon the group for financial and emotional support, and lose the ability to act independently of it. Under these conditions, members are required to work long hours; exist on little sleep; eat boring junk food, sometimes for weeks on end; and endure numerous hardships for the sake of their "spiritual growth." They are discouraged from forming close relationships with members of the opposite sex[12] and may be married only under arrangements made by Sun Myung Moon himself or his proxy.[13] They are sometimes asked to participate in political demonstrations and other activities which aid causes, candidates, and public office holders supported by the Moon organization.[14] If they snap from the pressure and begin to challenge their leaders' authority or otherwise fall out of line, they are accused of being influenced by Satan and are subjected to even greater pressure in the form of re-indoctrination.

I know these things are true. I was a leader in the Moon cult.

What Is Mind Control?

There are many different forms of mind control. Most people think of brainwashing almost as soon as they hear the term. But that is only one specific form. Mind control is any *system* of influence that disrupts an individual's authentic identity and replaces it with a false, new one.

In most cases, that new identity is one the person would strongly reject, if they had been asked for their informed consent. That's why I also use the term *undue influence*—"undue" because these practices violate personal boundaries and human integrity, as well as ethics and, often, the law.

That said, not all of the techniques used in mind control are inherently bad or unethical. The intent, the methods used, and the end result need to be part of the evaluation. They span a continuum from entirely ethical to grossly unethical. It is fine to use hypnosis to stop smoking, for example—but it must be used ethically, to empower the person, not for manipulative, exploitive ends. The locus of control of one's mind and body should always remain within the adult individual, *never* with an external authority.

Today, many mind control techniques exist that are far more sophisticated than the brainwashing techniques used in the Chinese thought reform camps and the Korean War. Some involve subtle forms of hypnosis or suggestion; others are overt, and are implemented in highly rigid and controlled social environments.

In this book, I discuss many groups I characterize as destructive cults that use mind control techniques. When I identify an organization in this way it is only after thorough research and close examination. I would never slap unfair labels on unpopular or controversial groups. Any designation I may give them is well earned. For example, I have no qualms about referring to the Unification Church as a *destructive cult*.[15] The group's record speaks for itself.[16] Of course, members of this and many other groups would likely be offended and deny that destructive mind control is happening. It is also true, however, that although many people sincerely believe that they had a fair choice in joining—and always have a fair choice about leaving—that is, sadly, too often a delusion created by the cult itself.

The Many Faces Of The Unification Church

How did this group start out?

One of the best summaries is in the Fraser Report, published on October 31, 1978 by the U.S. House of Representatives' Subcommittee on International Organizations of the Committee on International Relations. Chaired by Rep. Donald Fraser, a Democrat from Minnesota, the committee unearthed many astounding and previously unreported facts about what they called the "Moon organization," out of a recognition that it was not just one, but many moving parts working towards common ends, under the direction of Sun Myung Moon. Among the investigation's findings was the Unification Church's intimate involvement with the Korean Central Intelligence Agency (KCIA). The investigation revealed that the Unification Church was not merely a body of believers but also a political organization with an active political agenda. Here is what the Fraser Report documented:

In the late 1950s, Moon's message was favorably received by four young, English-speaking Korean Army officers, all of whom were later to provide important contacts with the post-1961 Korean government. One was Bo Hi Pak, who had joined the ROK (Republic of Korea) army in 1950. Han Sang Keuk...became a personal assistant to Kim Jong Pil, the architect of the 1961 coup and founder of the KCIA. Kim Sang In retired from the ROK army in May, 1961, joined the KCIA and became an interpreter for Kim Jong Pil until 1966. At that time, [Kim Sang In] returned to his position as KCIA officer, later to become the KCIA's chief of station in Mexico City. He was a close friend of Bo Hi Pak and a supporter of the Unification Church. The fourth, Han Sang Kil, was a military attaché at the ROK embassy in Washington in the late 1960s. Executive branch reports also link him to the KCIA. On leaving the service of the ROK government, Han became Moon's personal secretary and tutor to his children.

Immediately after the coup, Kim Jong Pil founded the KCIA and supervised the building of a political base for the new regime. A February 1963 unevaluated CIA report stated that Kim Jong Pil had "organized" the Unification Church while he was KCIA director and has been using the Unification Church as a "political tool."[17]

Journalist Frederick Clarkson, who has written widely about the politics of the Moon organization, adds these insights:

Though the Fraser Report noted that "organized" is not to be confused with "founded," since the Unification Church was "founded" in 1954, the Fraser Report goes on to state that "...there was a great deal of independent corroboration for the suggestion in this and later intelligence reports that Kim Jong Pil and the Moon organization had a mutually supportive relationship, as well as for the statement that Kim used the Unification Church for political purposes."[18]

It is remarkable that in the 1970s, and thereafter, so many people were deeply involved with the Moon organization, blindly believing the stories they were told by leaders, knowing almost nothing about its real history. Certainly, if I had learned that the Moon organization, as Congressional investigators called it, was connected with the KCIA, or that in 1967 Moon had forged an organizational link with Yoshi Kodama, a leader of the *Yakuza*, the Japanese organized crime network,[19] I would have never become involved. [20]

While the story of the Unification Church's theology is too involved to detail here, the most important feature of it is the Church's position that Sun Myung Moon was the new Messiah and that his mission was to establish a new "kingdom" on Earth (he actually died in 2012). Yet, many ex-members, like me, have observed that Moon's vision of *that* kingdom was distinctly Korean. During my two-and-a-half-year period in the church, I understood that the highest positions of membership (closest to Moon) were available only to Koreans, with the Japanese coming in second. American members, myself included, were on the third rung of the ladder. Members of the Unification Church believe, as I did, that their donations of time, money, and effort are "saving the world." What they do not realize is that they are the victims of mind control.[21]

It is impossible to gain a full picture of Moon and his influence in the United States by only looking at the Unification Church, although there is plenty there to see. Moon and his colleagues developed a complex organization that—even today—embraces both business and non-profit organizations in his native Korea, in the United States, and in many other countries, on every continent. The Moon organization comprises enterprises ranging from ginseng exportation to the manufacture of M-16 rifles.[22] In the United States, perhaps the most visible Moon controlled entity is *The Washington Times*—a newspaper which has enjoyed considerable influence both in Washington and internationally.[23] Former President Ronald Reagan said it was his favorite newspaper and that he read it every day.[24] When the *Times* celebrated its 25th anniversary in 2007—former President George H.W. Bush was the headliner.[25] Han Sang Keuk and Bo Hi Pak have both been top executives of the *Times*. It is reported that the Moon group spent some $2 billion on a newspaper that has never returned a profit.

Until recent years, a thread running through all of Moon's myriad organizations was anti-Communism. To put it simply, the Moonies believed that Christians and the citizens of the non-Communist world were locked in a mortal struggle with the satanic forces of materialistic Communism. To the extent that America and other countries did not fight Communism, they would grow weak and fall. The world's only salvation lay in Moon and in the establishment of a divine theocracy, so God could rule the world through him and his minions.

This may seem a bit absurd to Americans today, now that Communism is limited to North Korea and Cuba (though it understandably seems less absurd to South Koreans). It is also true that Moon's organizations have moved significantly away from their anti-communist stance over the past two decades. The fall of the U.S.S.R. and the adoption of capitalism by China were major factors behind this—although, interestingly, Moon claimed to his followers that *he* was the reason Communism fell apart. The Moon empire went on to invest millions in enterprises in China and North Korea, two countries he had previously deemed deeply satanic.

Had it not been for the Congressional Subcommittee Investigation and the work of Rep. Donald Fraser, Moon would very likely have increased his power. I was glad to give Fraser's investigators my collection of *Master Speaks*, a set of internal, unedited Moon speeches. These documents were available only to Unification Church leaders and were submitted as evidence in the investigation. The report of the Fraser investigation quoted from a 1973 speech, in which Moon declared, "When it comes to our age, we must have an automatic theocracy to rule the world. So we cannot separate the political field from the religious...Separation between religion and politics is what Satan likes most."[26]

True believers still believe that the world's only salvation lay in devotedly following Moon's wife, Hak Ja Han and her sons, and in the establishment of a divine theocracy. They actually believe what they have been told: that Sun Myung Moon is working in the "spirit world" with his wife and heirs so that God can rule the world through him and his minions.

Moon's belief in the necessary fusion of religion and politics underscores his organization's involvement in a wide variety of extreme right-wing groups. While there have been many such involvements over the years, his political arm in the 1980s was an organization known as CAUSA,[27] which was founded in 1980 after a tour of Latin America by Moon's right-hand man, Bo Hi Pak. The organization spread to every continent in the ensuing years and was very active in the United States, providing seminars for people in leadership positions. "The general thrust of CAUSA," Frederick Clarkson wrote at the time, "is anti-communist education from a historical perspective. The CAUSA antidote to communism is 'Godism,' which is simply the Unification Church philosophy without Moonist mythology."

Through the late 1980s, the Moon empire continued to expand its power and influence. Moon attempted to buy legitimacy, lending and giving millions of dollars to conservative causes in the U.S.[28]

But it's hard to gain legitimacy when you're making big profits from selling schlock while doing "spiritual sales." A major newspaper investigation in 1987 reported that "door-to-door Moonie salesmen (in Japan) using illegal high-pressure sales tactics bilked buyers of their cheaply-made religious artifacts, charms and talismans out of at least $1 billion by defrauding over 33,000 victims."[29]

The victims were predominantly "women who have had an accidental death or fatal illness in the family, are widowed or divorced, or have had a miscarriage." They allegedly at times paid more than $100,000 for urns, pagodas, and other charms that would, Moonie salesmen persuaded them, "ward off the evil spirits affecting them."

It seems probable that much of this money was funneled to the United States to underwrite the famously unprofitable *Washington Times*. The paper sought to be a conservative flagship newspaper. And while it is debatable if it achieves this end, the *Washington Times* has never been just a newspaper. It has enabled Moon's organizations unusual access to the power brokers of American politics, and influenced people and even governments around the world.[30]

In addition to the Church and the *Washington Times*, Moon started a number of think tanks and organizations over the years, to engage the culture in every possible sphere, staging scientific, academic, religious, media and legal conferences and cultural interchange programs—which have served to build its network for power.

The empire that Moon built is gridlocked by lawsuits, among members of Moon's large, extended family and between the family and outsiders. It will take years to sort through the legal claims and power struggles. But the myriad entities of the Moon empire live on. Currently the empire's primary organization is the Universal Peace Federation (UPF). Here are a few of the Moon empire's current projects and institutions that are just the tip of the iceberg of its involvement in American public life: The UPF owns the University of Bridgeport, a private university in Bridgeport, Connecticut, and has used it to facilitate recruiting some people into the group by offering them a scholarship to come to study in the U.S. The Moon empire has substantial holdings in the fishing industry on the east and west coasts, as well as the Gulf of Mexico, especially the fish used in sushi, such as shrimp. Kahr Arms, a handgun manufacturer, is also part of the Moon network. Kahr's corporate headquarters is located in Blauvelt, New York, while production and assembly operations are located in Worcester, Massachusetts. For up-to-date information on the Unification Church and many other Moon family organizations, see my website, freedomofmind.com.

• • •

The Unification Church is a destructive cult *par excellence*. However, many other groups in this country also espouse strange doctrines and have members who engage in practices which, to many people, might seem downright bizarre. Are all these groups "destructive cults?"

Not by any means. The United States of America has always been a land where freedom of thought and tolerance of differing beliefs have flourished under the protection of the First Amendment of the Constitution.

As difficult as it may be to believe, in recent decades we have seen the rise of organizations in our society that systematically violate the rights of their members, subject them to many kinds of abuse, and actively diminish their capacity to think and act as responsible adults. People who stay in these organizations suffer not only damage to their self-esteem, but to their whole sense of identity and their connection with the outside world. In some cases they completely lose contact with family and friends for long periods of time. If they leave, those born into destructive groups are often shunned as evil and as "unbelievers" or "apostates". Often, they are vilified and lies are told about them to members to keep them "faithful" and afraid to speak with defectors to hear their side of the story. Family members and friends are typically ordered to reject them and often have no contact with them.

The damage from living in a cult may not be readily apparent to family members or friends or even—in the early stages—to someone casually meeting such a person for the first time. But many forms of violence, from the gross to the very subtle, are the inevitable result. Some members of destructive cults suffer physical abuse during their involvement, in the form of beatings or rape, while others simply suffer the abuse of long hours of grueling, monotonous work—15 to 18 hours a day, year in and year out. In essence, they become slaves with few or no resources, personal or financial. They become trapped in the group, which does everything it can to keep them, as long as they are productive. When they fall sick or are no longer an asset, they are often kicked out. Nowhere is this more evident today than human trafficking.

Many mind control groups appear, on the surface, to be respectable associations. Their members talk convincingly about how they exerted their own free will in deciding to become involved. Many are very intelligent and seem to be happy. This may seem like a contradiction.

It is also important to recognize that there are different kinds of cults and they often operate quite differently. Different cults appeal to the many different human impulses: such as desire to belong; to improve oneself and others; to understand the meaning and purpose of life. Religious cults are the most well known. They often have a charismatic leader and operate with religious dogma. Political cults, often in the news, are organized around a simplistic political theory, sometimes with a religious cloak. Psychotherapy/educational cults, which have enjoyed great popularity, purport to give the participant "insight" and "enlightenment." Commercial cults play on people's desires to make money. They typically promise riches but actually enslave people, and compel them to turn money over to the group. None of these destructive cults deliver what they promise and glittering dreams eventually turn out to be paths to psychological enslavement.

Destructive cults do many kinds of damage to their members. I will illustrate this with several case histories, including my own. It is not easy to recover from the damage done by membership in a destructive cult, but it is possible. With the right help, almost everyone can recover. My experience proves that some definite steps can be taken to learn how to help anyone return to a normal productive life after taking the exit to freedom.

I believe that people want to be free. They want to read what they want to read, and they want to form their own opinions. They want honesty and do not like being lied to or exploited. They want trustworthy leaders who are responsible and accountable. They want people they can look up to, and who provide good role models. They want love and respect.

In my experience, many people eventually walk away from cults, even those who have spent their entire lives inside one. They crave the freedom to be themselves.

Chapter 2

My Life in the Unification Church

As a child, I had always been very independent. I wanted to be a writer and poet, but during my college years I struggled to find a career path in which I could make enough money to pursue my dreams. When my girlfriend dumped me in January 1974, I wondered if I would ever find true love.

I had always been an avid reader; during that time I began to read a great deal of psychology and philosophy. My neighbor next door, a mathematician, introduced me to the writings of G. I. Gurdjieff and P. D. Ouspensky. I became interested in what was presented as ancient, esoteric knowledge. Much of what I read described humanity's natural condition as being "asleep" to the truth and in need of someone more spiritually advanced to teach us about higher levels of consciousness. The suggestion that one should join a spiritual school was embedded in those books.

At age 19, I knew I was never going to be happy as a businessman, like my father, living my life to pursue money. I wanted to be a creative writer. I wanted answers to the deeper questions. Is there a God? If so, why is there so much suffering? What role was I to play in the world? Could I do anything to make a difference? I felt extreme internal pressure to make a big contribution to humankind. I had been told all my life how intelligent I was and how much I would accomplish when I grew up. But I was going to graduate in another year and I felt like time was running out.

I had already become a "foster parent" of a little girl in Chile to whom I sent money each month. I had decided that writing was probably my most important pursuit, and so I wrote. Still I felt it wasn't enough. I looked out at the world and saw so much in the way of social injustice, political corruption, and ecological destruction that it seemed I could do very little. I knew that I wanted to help change things, but I didn't know how to go about doing it.

One day, as I was reading a book in the student union cafeteria, three attractive Japanese women and an Italian-American man approached me. They were dressed like students and carried college textbooks. They asked if they could share the table. I nodded, and within minutes, they engaged me in a friendly conversation. I thought the women were pretty cute. Since I had a three-hour break between classes, I stayed and talked. They told me they were students too, involved in a small community of "young people from all over the world." They invited me to visit them.

The semester had just started and I thought I might be able to get lucky with one of the women, so I drove to their house that night after class. When I arrived I found a lively group of about 30 people from half a dozen countries. I asked if they were a religious group. "Oh, no, not at all," they said, and laughed. They told me they were part of something called the One World Crusade, dedicated to overcoming cultural differences among people and to combating major social problems, such as the ones I was concerned about.

"One world where people treat each other with love and respect," I thought to myself. "What idealists these people are!"

I enjoyed the stimulating conversations and energetic atmosphere at the meeting. These people related to each other like brothers and sisters and clearly felt they were part of one global family. They seemed very happy with their lives. After a month of feeling depressed, I was invigorated by all that positive energy. I went home that night feeling lucky to have met such nice people.

The next day I ran into Tony, the man who had approached me in the cafeteria. "Did you enjoy the evening?" he asked. I answered that I had. "Well, listen," Tony said. "This afternoon Adri, who's from Holland, is going to give a short lecture on some interesting principles of life. Why don't you come over?"

I listened to Adri's lecture a few hours later. It seemed vague and a bit simplistic, but optimistic, and I could agree with nearly everything he said. However, the content of his speech didn't explain why everyone in this group seemed so happy all the time. I felt there must be something wrong with me or something exceptional about them. My curiosity was engaged.

I wound up going back the next day. This time another person gave a talk about the origin of all the problems that humankind has had to face. This lecture had a decidedly religious tone; it dealt with Adam and Eve and how they were corrupted by a misuse of love in the Garden of Eden. At that point I didn't notice that my questions were never answered, and didn't suspect I was being deliberately strung along. However, I did feel a bit confused and said I didn't think I'd be coming back.

When I said this, a silent alarm seemed to go off among the people in the house. As I walked out and got into my car, a dozen people came running out into the icy February air in their stockinged feet (it was the custom to remove shoes in the house) and surrounded my car. They said they wouldn't let me leave until I *promised* to come back the following night. "These people are crazy," I thought, "standing outside in the freezing cold without shoes, without jackets, holding me hostage because they like me so much." After a few minutes I relented, mostly because I didn't want to feel guilty if one of them caught a cold. Once I had given my word, I wouldn't think of not following through, even though I didn't really want to go back.

When I returned on Thursday night, I was barraged with flattery from all sides, all evening. This practice, I would later learn, was called "love bombing." I was told over and over what a nice person I was, what a good person I was, how smart I was, how dynamic I was, and so forth. No fewer than thirty times they invited me to go with them for a "weekend away from the city for a retreat in a beautiful place upstate."

Over and over I told them that I had to work as a waiter on weekends and could not go. Before I left, I was pressured to promise that if I were ever free on a weekend, I would go. I had not had a free weekend for a year and a half, so I was certain I would not have to keep my promise.

The next day I phoned my boss at the Holiday Inn banquet office to get my schedule for the weekend. He said, "Steve, you're not going to believe this, but the wedding was called off this afternoon. Take the weekend off!" I was flabbergasted. Was this a sign that I was *supposed* to go to this weekend outing? I asked myself what Gurdjieff or Ouspensky would have done in my situation. They had spent years searching for greater knowledge.

I called the people at the house, and off I went that Friday night.

My Indoctrination: How I Became A Moonie

As we drove through the tall, black, wrought iron gates of a multimillion-dollar estate in Tarrytown, New York, someone leaned over and told me, "This weekend we'll be having a joint workshop with the Unification

Church." My immediate reaction was a series of questions. "Workshop? Church? What is going on here? Why didn't anyone tell me this before?" I protested. "How can I get back to Queens?" Instead of responding to my questions, they immediately turned it around on me and made it my issue. "What's the matter, Steve? Have a problem being with Christians?" one man asked me with an attitude. "No," I said. "Afraid we are going to brainwash you or something?" another person asked. "Not at all," I said, indignant at the insinuation that I was weak-minded.

We were herded from the van into a small wooden structure nestled in some large trees. I had a feeling of dread. I gave myself a little pep talk. I reminded myself that I had bicycled across the U.S. when I was 16, worked on an archaeological dig in the Negev desert in Israel when I was 17, and driven across Canada to Alaska when I was 18.

I got my courage up. "Listen, I really think I would like to go back to Queens," I told one of the members, a pleasant young man with blond hair and a smile pasted to his face. "Oh, come on, you'll have a good time!" he said, patting me on the back. Anyway, there's no one driving back to the city tonight." I decided to make the most of the situation and avoid creating a scene. We climbed the stairs and entered a room that I later learned had once been an artist's studio. A large blackboard was at the other end of the room. Metal folding chairs were stacked neatly in a corner.

Within a few minutes we were divided up into small groups. The leaders handed us sheets of paper and crayons and asked us to draw a picture with a house, a tree, a mountain, a river, the sun, and a snake. Nobody asked why; everyone just obeyed. (Much later I was told that it was a form of projective personality test used to learn about people's psyches.)

We all took turns introducing ourselves while seated cross-legged on the floor of the handsome wooden structure, all part of a large estate with an enormous mansion, which I later learned had been purchased from the Seagram family for millions. We were led in singing folk songs. I was embarrassed by the childishness of it all, but no one else seemed to mind. I loved to sing and grew up listening to Peter, Paul and Mary and many others. The atmosphere of the event, with lots of enthusiastic young people all together, brought back warm memories of summer camp. That night we were escorted to bunk beds above a converted garage, and the men and women were put in separate rooms. As it turned out, getting a good night's sleep was nearly impossible. Not only was it crowded, but also there were two loud snorers! The other newcomers and I slept very little.

When morning came, an intense young man from the group house in Queens sat down and talked with me. I asked again when the van was going back to Queens. He told me, "We're so sorry, but the brother left already much earlier this morning." He told me that he too had been put off at first by some of the strange things he had heard and seen at his first workshop. He begged me not to have a closed mind but to give "them" a chance to present what he called the Divine Principle. "Please don't judge them until you've had a chance to hear the whole thing," he pleaded. He told me that if I left now, I would regret it for the rest of my life.

His voice was so full of mystery and intrigue that it offset my suspicions and piqued my curiosity. "Now," I said to myself, "I'll finally get all my questions answered." Or so I thought.

In the morning we were led in calisthenics before breakfast. Afterward, we sang more songs. As we sat on the floor, a charismatic man with ice-blue eyes and a penetrating voice introduced himself and the ground rules for the weekend. He was the workshop director. We were told we had to spend all of our time together in the small groups to which we were assigned. There was to be no walking around the estate alone. Questions were to be asked only after a lecture was over, when we were back in our small group. He then introduced the lecturer, Wayne Miller.

An American in his late twenties, dressed in a blue suit, white shirt, and red tie, Mr. Miller exuded the charm and confidence of a family doctor. He began to talk, and talk, and talk. As he lectured for hour after hour, I became very uncomfortable. The workshop was just too weird. I liked almost everyone there: they were bright, goodhearted college students like myself. But I disliked the overly structured environment, the childishly religious atmosphere, and having been misled about the nature of this weekend retreat. Whenever I started to object, which I did several times, I was told to save my questions until after the lecture. In the small group, I was always told, "That is a very good question. Hold onto it because it will be answered in the next lecture." Again and again, I was told not to judge what I was hearing until I had heard it all. Meanwhile, I was listening to an enormous amount of material about humankind, history, the purpose of creation, the spiritual world versus the physical world, and so forth, much of which presumed an acceptance of what had been said earlier.

The entire weekend was structured from morning until night. There was no free time. There was no possibility of being alone. Members outnumbered newcomers three to one and kept us surrounded. We newcomers were never permitted to talk among ourselves unchaperoned. Day one came and went, leaving my sense of reality more or less intact. Before we went to bed we were asked to fill out "reflection" sheets to reveal all we were thinking and feeling. Naively, I filled them out. I had another restless night but was so exhausted emotionally and physically that I did manage to get a few hours' sleep.

Day two, Sunday, began in exactly the same way. But now we had all been in this crazy, intense environment for 36 hours, which felt more like a week. I started asking myself, "Is something wrong with me? Why do I seem to be the only person questioning this stuff? Is it more profound than I'm able to grasp? Am I not spiritual enough to understand what they're teaching?" I started listening to Mr. Miller more seriously and began to take notes.

By Sunday evening I was more than ready for the ride back home. But it grew later and later, and nobody made any move to depart. Finally I spoke up and said I had to leave now. "Oh, *please* don't go!" several people pleaded. "Tomorrow is the most important day!"

"Tomorrow? It's Monday and I have classes!" I explained that it was impossible for me to stay another day.

The workshop director took me aside and told me that everybody else had decided to stay for the third day. "No one told you this was a three-day workshop?" he asked.

"No," I responded. "I never would have come if I'd known it would make me miss a day of school."

"Well, since you've heard the first two-thirds, don't you want to know the conclusion?" he asked, intriguingly. Tomorrow, he promised, everything would become clear.

Part of me *was* really curious to hear the whole thing. But also, I was dependent on these people for transportation. I didn't want to bother my friends or family with an emergency call to drive all that way to get me—or, worse, start hitchhiking in upstate New York at night in the middle of winter.

I agreed to stay for one more day.

On the third day, we were given an unprecedented emotional high. The most powerful of Mr. Miller's lectures that day was called "The History of

Restoration." It claimed to be a precise and accurate map of God's method for directing humankind back to His original intention. "It is scientifically proven that there is a pattern of recurring cycles in history," Mr. Miller declared. Throughout his hours of lecturing, he explained that these cycles all pointed to an incredible conclusion: God had sent His second Messiah to the earth between 1917 and 1930. But who was this new Messiah? No one at the workshop would say.

By the time we were ready to drive back to the city, I was not only exhausted, but also very confused. I was elated to consider the bare possibility that God had been working all of my life to prepare me for this historic moment. At other moments, I thought the whole thing was preposterous—a bad joke. Yet, no one was laughing. An atmosphere of earnest seriousness filled the crowded studio.

I can still remember the final moments of Mr. Miller's lecture:

"What if?...what if?...what if... it is true? Could you betray the Son of God?" Mr. Miller had questioned with passion in his voice, his eyes moving slowly upward as he concluded. Finally, the workshop director had stepped up and prayed a very emotional prayer about how we were God's lost children and needed to be open-minded to follow what God wanted in our lives. On and on he went, praying that all of mankind would stop living such selfish materialistic lives and return to Him. He apologized over and over for all the times in history that God called people to do His will and was forsaken. He pledged himself to a higher level of commitment and dedication. His sincerity was overpowering. One couldn't help but be moved.

When the van finally returned late that night to the Queens center, I was completely exhausted and wanted only to go home and sleep. But I was still not permitted to leave. Jaap Van Rossum, the house director, insisted that I stay and talk with him for a while. I wanted desperately to go. He was emphatic. He sat me down in front of a crackling fire and read me the biography of a humble Korean man I had never heard of before, Sun Myung Moon. The story was that Moon had suffered through tremendous hardships and tribulations to proclaim the truth of God and to fight Satan and communism. When he had finished, Jaap begged me to pray about what I had just heard. He told me that I was now responsible for the great truth I had been taught. If I turned my back on it, I would never forgive myself and God would be heartbroken. He then tried to persuade me to stay in the house overnight.

My insides were screaming at me, "Get out! Get out! Get the hell away from these people! You need time to think." In order to escape I had to get angry and yelled, "No! Get off my case!" and charged out into the night. Nevertheless, I felt guilty for being rude to those sincere and wonderful people. I drove home, almost in tears.

When I arrived home, my parents (they told me later) thought I had been drugged. They said I looked awful: my eyes were glassy, and I was obviously very confused. I tried to explain to them what had just happened. I was exhausted and semi-coherent. When I told them the workshop was affiliated with the Unification Church, my parents became upset and thought I was turning my back on our Jewish heritage and wanted to become a Christian. My mom said, "Let's go talk with the rabbi tomorrow." I was happy to agree.

Unfortunately my rabbi had never heard of the Unification Church, nor had he ever dealt with anyone involved with a cult. He thought I was interested in becoming a Christian. He didn't know what to say or do. I came away telling myself, "The only way I can get to the bottom of this thing is investigate it myself." Still, I was afraid. I wished I could speak with someone who knew about this group but wasn't a devoted member. In February 1974, no one I knew had ever heard of the Moonies.

Ceaseless questions ran through my mind. Had God been preparing me throughout my life for the mission of setting up the Kingdom of Heaven on earth? Was Sun Myung Moon the Messiah? I prayed earnestly to God for Him to show me a sign. Was the Divine Principle the new truth? What should I do? It didn't dawn on me in my agitated state of confusion that I had been subjected to mind control[31]—that whereas one week earlier, I had had no belief in Satan, now I was afraid that he was influencing my thoughts.

My parents told me to stay away from the group. They didn't want me to abandon Judaism. My grandparents were Orthodox Jews and I went to Temple, my mom kept kosher and I had a Bar Mitzvah when I turned thirteen. I was very educated about the Nazis and the Holocaust. I didn't want to change my religion; I just wanted to do the right thing. If Moon was the *Moshiach* (Hebrew for Anointed One), I reasoned, then I will be fulfilling my Jewish heritage by following him. Even though my parents opposed the group, I believed that as an independent 19-year-old person,

I was capable of making my own decision in this matter. I wanted to do what was right. In doing so, I had been told by members of the group, I could later intervene on my parents' behalf and save them spiritually.

After several earnest days of prayer, I received what I thought was the "sign." Unable to concentrate on my schoolwork, I was sitting on the edge of my bed. I reached down, picked up an Ouspensky book, and opened it to a paragraph at random, which said that history goes through certain cycles to help human beings evolve to a higher plane. At that moment I believed I had had a spiritual experience. How could I have chanced to open the book to that paragraph? I thought that God was surely signaling me to heed Mr. Miller's lectures. I felt I had to go back and learn more about this movement.

Tying The Knot: Becoming An Insider

As soon as I called the center, I was whisked off to another three-day workshop. When I asked a member why I hadn't been told the truth about the group being religious, he asked, "If you knew in advance, would you have come?" I admitted that I probably wouldn't have.

He explained that Satan controlled the world after he had deceived Adam and Eve into disobeying God. Now God's children had to deceive Satan's children into following God's will. He said, "Stop thinking from fallen man's viewpoint. Think about God's viewpoint. He wants to see His creation restored to His original ideal—the Garden of Eden. That's all that matters." (Later, it became evident that this "heavenly deception" was used in all aspects of the organization, including recruiting, fundraising, and public relations. Since members are so focused on meeting their assigned goals, there is no room for the "old morality." The group even uses the Bible to "show" that God condoned deception several times in history in order to see His plan accomplished.[32]) By accepting the way in which I was deceived, I set myself up to begin deceiving others.

Although the workshop was almost identical in content to the one I had taken the previous week, I felt that this time I needed to listen with an open mind and take notes. "Last weekend I was too cynical," I said to myself.

This time Miller added a lecture on Communism. He explained that Communism was Satan's version of God's ideal plan, yet it denied the existence of God. It was therefore Satan's own religion on Earth and must be vehemently opposed. He said the final World War would be fought within the next three years between communism and democracy (at that time, by 1977), and that if members of the movement didn't work hard enough, incredible suffering would result.

By the end of those three days, the Steve Hassan who had walked into the first workshop was gone, replaced by a new "Steve Hassan." I was elated at the thought that I had been "chosen" by God, and that I knew what I needed to do with my life. I experienced a wide range of other feelings, too: I was shocked and honored that I had been singled out for leadership, scared at how much responsibility rested on my shoulders, and emotionally high on the thought that God was actively working to bring about the Garden of Eden. No more war, no more poverty, no more ecological destruction. There was hope! Also love, truth, beauty, and goodness.

At that point, I was still aware of a muffled voice deep within me that was warning me to watch out, to keep questioning everything.

After that workshop, I returned to Queens. I was advised to move into the local Moonie house for a few months to get a feel for the lifestyle and to study the Divine Principle before I made a lifetime commitment. Within the first few weeks of my residence there, I met a powerful leader, Takeru Kamiyama, a Japanese man in charge of the Unification Church throughout New York City. [33]I was instantly drawn to him. He struck me as having a very spiritual, humble character. I wanted to learn everything I could from him.

In retrospect, I realize that Mr. Kamiyama appealed to me because he was very different from my father. He was a visionary. He had a great deal of power and status. My father, a simple businessman, had repeatedly told me that no one person could ever change the world. Kamiyama very much believed that one person could make a huge difference. He was very religious and emotionally expressive. My father, a sincere, intense man in his own quiet way, was not. In looking back and analyzing the relationship, I see that Kamiyama became a surrogate father figure. The verbal approval and physical affection I wanted from my father was given to me by this man, who used this emotional leverage to motivate and control me.

As it turned out, I was the first new person to join the center in Queens.

Just a month earlier, the big center in Manhattan had been divided into eight satellite centers spread out in different boroughs. Since I was the first, Mr. Kamiyama said it was a sign that I was meant to become a great leader. He made me one of his 12 American disciples and oversaw everything I did. I never attended a 7-, 21- or 40-day workshop—the normal sequence. I was groomed very carefully by Kamiyama and Moon.

Although I had never liked being in groups before, my elite status in this group made me feel special. Because of my relationship with Kamiyama, I would even have access to the Messiah himself—Sun Myung Moon—who was a projection of the ultimate father figure.

Life With "Father": Get Closer To Moon

Sun Myung Moon was a short, stocky man who had more than the average share of charisma. He was born in 1920 in what is now North Korea. He carried himself like a small sumo wrestler in a extremely expensive business suit. He was a shrewd manipulator and communicator, particularly with those who were indoctrinated to believe he was the greatest man ever to walk the face of the Earth. Moon usually spoke either Korean or Japanese and used a translator. I was told he did so for "spiritual" reasons. During my membership, I was present at more than 100 of his lectures and participated in about 25 leadership meetings with him.

Mr. Moon and Mr. Kamiyama knew how to cultivate their disciples to be loyal and well disciplined. Members of the core leadership were trained to follow orders without question or hesitation. Once I had become totally indoctrinated, all I wanted to do was to follow my *central figure's* instructions. I was so committed that my new identity completely suppressed the real me. Whenever I look back now, I am amazed at how I was manipulated and how I learned to manipulate others "in the name of God." I can also see very clearly that the higher I rose in the hierarchy, the more corrupted I became: Moon was making us over in his image. Once he actually told the leaders that if we remained faithful and carried out our missions well, we would each be President of our own country one day. We too would have Mercedes Benz automobiles, personal secretaries, and bodyguards. By this point, I was encouraged to decide what country I might like to run when Unificationism took over the world.

I learned how to present the introductory lectures of the Divine Principle within the first three months of my membership. By that time, I had recruited two more people, who became my "spiritual children," and was instructed to drop out of school, quit my job, and move into the center. My hair was cut short and I started to wear a suit and tie. At the suggestion of a senior member, I had done a 40-day "indemnity condition"—giving up my friends and family for forty days, not seeing them or communicating with them in any way. This is a practice used by several cults and in particular about the two years Mormon 'missionaries' are kept from their families.

I donated my bank account to the center and would have given my car, except that my parents had the title. I had to abandon my Chilean foster child because I had no way to earn money to send to her. I was asked to sacrifice my "Isaac." The Moonies reminded me of the Biblical story of Abraham and how God asked him to sacrifice his beloved son. I was told my creative writing, especially my poetry, was my "Isaac." I dutifully threw out everything I had written—some four hundred pieces. Of course, Isaac never actually had to be sacrificed, but the Moonies manipulated me. They got my cult self to throw out a large stack of papers that my authentic self spent countless hours on, over many years. Work that I had nurtured as if it were nurturing like a child. I put my poems into the garbage can while my superiors watched. The psychological effect was powerful.

Once I had officially dropped out of college, I was sent back to the campus to recruit new members. The leaders told me I could go back to finish my degree the following year. A lie. When I later told them about my desire to teach, they informed me that the Family—as members refer to the movement—was planning to start its own university in a few years, and I could be a professor there.

I was also ordered to set up an official student club at Queens College, even though I was no longer a student. The club was to be called Collegiate Association for the Research of Principles, or C.A.R.P. Within a couple of weeks I had done so, and I was made C.A.R.P.'s director. Although I told students that C.A.R.P. had no affiliation with any other group, I received all of my instructions and funding from the director of the Unification Church in Queens. We sponsored free lectures, poetry readings, anti-Communist political rallies, and free movies, all while seeking to meet potential converts. I recruited several people, and they were instructed to drop out of college, too. At that point, we were the most successful C.A.R.P. chapter in the country.

I was in a high-speed daze of exhaustion, zeal, and emotional overload. I generally slept between three and four hours a night. Almost all my time that first year was spent recruiting and lecturing. Occasionally I went out with others "fundraising"—selling flowers or other items on the street—to support the house and the operations of the New York church. I was also ordered to fast for three days, drinking only water. Later, I would do three separate seven-day fasts, having been told that fasting was an "indemnity condition" (a supposed restitution to God for some past transgression).

During my time in the group, I was directly involved in many political demonstrations, though they were usually organized under the names of front groups. (Over the years, the Moon organization has created and used hundreds of such groups.)[34] For example, in July 1974, I was sent to the Capitol steps with several hundred Moonies, under the name National Prayer and Fast for the Watergate Crisis, to fast for three days and demonstrate in support of then-President Richard Nixon.

Before joining the Moonies I had had several arguments with my father at the dinner table about Nixon. My father, a businessman, was at that time a die-hard Nixon supporter. I voted for McGovern and had always felt strongly that Nixon was not to be trusted. In fact I had often referred to him as a crook. Now, in the heat of my Moon-inspired prayer vigil *for* Nixon, I called my parents from Washington to tell them about the fast. Because my father had always been so staunchly behind Nixon, I thought he would be pleased.

When I told him the news, my father said to me, "Steven, you were right. Nixon's a crook!"

"But Dad, you don't *understand*; God wants Nixon to be President!"

"Now I *know* you are brainwashed," my father said. "The guy's a crook."

It was only after I left the group that I laughed at the irony of that moment.

Later in 1974, I was part of a seven-day fast in front of the United Nations.[35] There was a pending vote on whether the UN would withdraw its troops from South Korea because of human rights violations. We were personally instructed by Sun Myung Moon not to tell anyone that we were members of the Unification Church or had any political motivation. That time we had a front group called The American Committee for Human Rights for Japanese Wives of North Korean Repatriates. We successfully shifted the delegates' focus from human rights abuses in South Korea to those perpetrated by North Korea. The vote to withdraw was defeated. The Moonies claimed a victory and we were told the South Korean government was pleased.[36]

Being so close to "the Messiah" was exhilarating. I felt incredibly fortunate to be part of this movement. I took things very seriously because of the potential spiritual repercussions of everything I did. I thought my every action had monumental and historical implications. I strived to be the perfect son of the "True Parents"[37]—obedient and loyal. (These two virtues were valued above all else.) I always did what I was told, and then some. I wanted to prove my loyalty, and I was tested many times by Kamiyama and other leaders.

As a leader myself, I was able to see and hear things that rank-and-file members never could. Once, in late 1974, Moon took a few of us to inspect some new real estate he had acquired in Tarrytown. As usual, he gave an impromptu talk. "When we take power in America," he said, "we will have to amend the Constitution and make it a capital offense for anyone to have sexual relations with anyone other than the person assigned to them." He explained that any sex that was not God-centered was the greatest sin a person could commit. If a person could not overcome temptation, it would be better to take away their physical body. We would be doing them a favor, and make it easier to restore them to righteousness in the spirit world. I thought of all the married people not in the movement who were destroying their spiritual bodies by having sex. At the time, I didn't stop to think of the mass genocide that might result if we took over America and the world.

Leadership had other benefits, too. On one occasion, Moon gave me an Italian hand-blown glass figurine and $300 in cash as presents. I even played softball with his son and heir apparent, Hyo Jin Moon. Twice I ate with Moon at his lavish dinner table. I came to love the feeling of getting up in front of hundreds of people and giving a Sunday service or a Divine Principle lecture; of having members look up to me as a wonderful, spiritual person.

There were even "miracles" in my life. At one point I learned that all American members had been ordered by Moon to undergo 120-day leadership training. Much to my surprise, Kamiyama interceded with Moon to keep me from being sent to that training session. I was brought before Moon—referred to by members as "Father"—and before I knew what had happened, he put his hand over my head and announced that I had just graduated from the 120-day program! When I asked Kamiyama why he had requested my exemption from the training, he told me that I was too important where I was in New York and that he didn't want to lose me. I had received the approval of a man who, I thought, was God's representative on Earth.

Moon had an interesting, fairly typical narcissistic way of behaving—nice then nasty, double bind of motivating leaders. He would be nice to us at first, buying us gifts and taking us out for dinner or a movie. Then he would bring us back to his estate and yell and scream about how poorly we were performing.

Moon also liked to stimulate the highest degree of competition between leaders in order to maximize productivity. He would single out someone who was very successful at recruiting or fundraising (he did this with me), and present that person as a model of excellence, shaming the others into being more successful. It is ironic that whereas Moon's stated goal was to unify the world, many of his strategies fostered jealousy and spite among leaders, virtually ensuring a lack of unity.

When I knew him, Moon was a movie junkie. One of his favorite movies was *Rocky*, which he watched repeatedly, he told us. On one memorable occasion he told us that we had to have the same determination as Rocky Balboa to defeat our enemy. Later he spent $48 million to make a film of his own, *Inchon*, about General Douglas MacArthur's landing in Korea to stop the Communist invasion. Even though Moon bought top talent in Laurence Olivier and Jacqueline Bisset, *Inchon* was an abysmal failure. It was the most expensive movie ever made up to that time, and received resoundingly bad reviews from critics.[38]

Looking back on it all now, I believe one of Moon's major problems was his incredible narcissism and unwillingness to admit he didn't know everything. He had grandiose plans, but he was often shortsighted, as he thought he was above the law. He always seemed more concerned with immediate results than with possible negative consequences in the future. His disregard for legal and accounting advice eventually landed him in jail.[39] His use of deception in order to buy real estate and businesses caused great enmity in many communities. His use of political shortcuts, like supporting Nixon, brought him into the national spotlight, but also alerted people to his background and his unethical practices. This lack of foresight eventually caused his organizations tremendous problems.

I became the main lecturer at the national Unification Church office opposite the main public library in Manhattan. That month the headquarters had been moved from Washington, D.C., to bring its American leadership under stricter control. I was made assistant director of the Unification Church at national headquarters and was told to set an example to Neil Salonen, then president of the Unification Church of America. Mr. Kamiyama told me that Neil needed to learn how to submit totally to the Korean and Japanese leadership in the church, as I had. I had been placed in the headquarters to teach him the "Japanese standard."

In my new position, it was my job to recruit newcomers to workshops. There had been a good deal of negative media reports, and we felt we were being "persecuted." We were told to identify with Jesus and the early Christians: the more people opposed us, the more committed we felt to "go the way of the cross." At that time the media carried some sensationalistic articles and television shows about the Moon cult, which reinforced our fears that Communists were now taking control of America. Re-motivated by our increased level of fear, we continued our recruiting activities at a blinding pace. We all felt a great deal of pressure to recruit a minimum of at least one new person per member per month, and all members had to report their activities each night to their *central figure*. It was as if we were God's army in the middle of a spiritual war—the only ones who could go to the front lines and fight Satan each day.

When Moon decided to give a lecture at Yankee Stadium in 1976, he needed to raise several million dollars for the publicity campaign. At this point, I was sent out with other American leaders as part of a model fundraising team in Manhattan. We fundraised 21 hours a day. We were constantly out on the streets, in the worst places imaginable. Once I was almost mugged in Harlem by someone with a garrote who saw me selling candles at night. Another time a man demanded my money and threatened me with a knife near my stomach. As a loyal, dedicated Moonie, I would never let anyone steal God's money and refused. Both times, I narrowly escaped.

Falling Asleep At The Wheel

One irony of my experience in the Moonies is that the higher I rose in the organization, the closer I got to the total burn-out and exhaustion that eventually led to my exit from the group. Because I was so successful at fundraising, I pressed myself to the limit again and again. I had been trained to have little concern for my overall well-being during those days. The most important thing was to work as hard as I could for "Father." Fortunately for me, though, my family had not forgotten about me. They were deeply concerned and desired to see me back to my creative, independent self.

Members were repeatedly told horror stories about deprogramming. I had come to believe that group members were brutally kidnapped, beaten, and tortured by deprogrammers—Satan's elite soldiers committed to breaking people down and destroying their faith in God.[40] A couple of members were sent around to different centers to tell us about their deprogramming experiences. Fear of the outside world, particularly of our parents, was drilled into our minds. Although I didn't realize it then, each successive deprogramming story was more terrifying—and more exaggerated—than the one before.

After my time on the model fundraising team in Manhattan, I was told that my family was trying to kidnap and deprogram me. I was sent "underground" to Pennsylvania. I was instructed not to tell my family my whereabouts and to have all my mail forwarded through another city. Years later, after I left the group, I suspected I had been sent out of town as a distraction. The Moonies wanted to keep me from pursuing some disturbing questions about the validity of the "time parallels" used in the *History of Restoration* lecture. I had discovered some glaring inconsistencies. It was dangerous for someone in my position in the organization to ask questions that couldn't be answered. The other group leaders filled me with so much fear about deprogrammers that my questions were shelved. I believed my spiritual survival was at stake.

After a couple of months of fundraising on a model team in Pennsylvania, I was put in charge of all fundraising in Baltimore. My regional commander ordered me to have each member bring in a minimum of $100 a day, even if it meant staying up all night to reach that goal. I had a team of eight inexperienced fundraisers. As a good leader, I had to set an example and stay up with them.

I drove my team hard, and together they averaged over $1,000 a day in total profit—tax-exempt cash. It was also my responsibility to feed, clothe, and shelter my team, as well as to order, buy, and pick up product—the items we pushed on people—and to collect the cash nightly and wire it to New York twice a week. We sold chocolate mints, peanut brittle, chocolate bars, roses, carnations, and candles. The markups were enormous. A box of mints that cost us 30 cents was sold for two dollars. A ten-cent flower was sold for a minimum of a dollar, and usually two dollars.

People would buy these items from us because they thought they were donating to a charitable cause. Our consciences had been reprogrammed by Moon's value system. We told people we were sponsoring Christian youth programs: a lie. We told them we operated drug rehabilitation houses: another lie. We told them that we were helping orphaned kids: another lie. On the spur of the moment we told them anything that we thought would work.[41] Since we thought saving the world from evil and establishing God's kingdom on Earth was the most important effort on the planet, we didn't see it as "real" lying.

After all, every person but us was being controlled by Satan, and it was up to us "Heavenly Children" to claim money back from Satan for God's Messiah, Sun Myung Moon. We believed we were saving the world from Satan and Communism by selling those products, and that we were giving people the opportunity to help the Messiah create the Garden of Eden on Earth.

At about 5:30 a.m. on April 23, 1976, I was driving the van to pick up the last member of my group, who had been out all night fundraising in front of a 24-hour convenience store. I hadn't slept at all in the previous two days and was driving alone. Usually I had someone ride "shotgun" position to protect me from being attacked by evil forces, including "sleep spirits." As ridiculous as it seems now, I actually believed that spiritual entities were all around me, waiting to invade me and possess me. This was all part of the mind control indoctrination. Staying focused on the True Parents was the only way to ward off the evil spirits. If my attention wavered, I could be taken over. Phobias such as this kept me and other members dependent and compliant.

This time I was overconfident. I fell asleep and awoke abruptly. All I could see was the red back end of the eighteen-wheeler I was driving into at high speed. I hit the brakes, but it was too late. The impact was terrifying. The van was crushed and I was pinned. The pain was excruciating, but I could do nothing—I was trapped. The door had to be sawn off. It took an emergency team about thirty minutes to set up a winch and pull the steering column forward to make enough room to free me. The whole time they worried that the van might catch fire and blow up. My rescuers told me it was a "miracle" that I survived.

All I could think was "Father, forgive me" and "Crush Satan." Over and over I chanted those lines to try to focus my mind on God and beg His forgiveness. I thought what had happened was "spiritual"—that I had been tested by Satan in the spirit world and had been defeated, and that this was what caused the accident, not the fact that I hadn't slept in days. Like any dedicated cult member I blamed myself for not being "pure" enough. It didn't dawn on me that I was programmed to be chronically sleep deprived.

I felt that I had been chosen by God, tested by this holy mission, but had failed.

Deprogramming: How I Found My Way Back To Myself

After two weeks in the hospital and an operation for my broken leg, I got permission from my Moonie superior to visit my sister Thea. I was able to do this for several reasons. Thea had never openly criticized my involvement in the Moonies. When I talked with her, she appealed to my love and told me that she wanted her newborn son to know his Uncle Steve. I made a deal with her: don't tell my parents or Stef, my oldest sister, that I was coming to visit, since I feared they might try to deprogram me. Also I was a trusted leader—someone whose faith in God and in the group was believed to be absolute. I convinced Kamiyama that it would be a "good condition" for Satan (my sister) to take care of one of God's soldiers (me), not diverting members from their work by tending to me.

The accident, however, began breaking the Moonies' hold over me in several ways. First, I could sleep, eat, and rest. Second, I could finally see my beloved sister. Third, I could slow down and think, being away from the group's constant reinforcement. Fourth, Thea decided to tell my parents, so a plan to rescue me was put into place. Fifth, I had a cast on my right leg from my toes to my pelvis, so I couldn't move without crutches. I could neither fight nor run away.

I was sitting on the living room couch at my sister's home, when my father appeared unexpectedly. He sat down next to me and asked, " How are you doing?" When I said "fine," he stood up. He said, "That's great!" He took my crutches to the other side of the room. Suddenly, on cue seven more people appeared and announced that they had come to "talk to me about my affiliation with the Unification Church." I was shocked, and realized I was trapped. I told them to call my office and make an appointment to speak with me.

Since I was thoroughly programmed, I immediately "knew" that the deprogramming team had been sent directly by Satan. In my terror, their faces looked like images of demons. It was very surprising to me, then, when they turned out to be warm and friendly. They spent several hours talking at me about what they knew to be wrong with the Moonies. As a committed member, I did thought-stopping, sang "holy songs," chanted and prayed silently to keep from hearing them. After all, I had been told all about deprogramming by leaders of the group. I wasn't going to allow my "faith in God" to be broken by Satan. I kept telling them that they needed to make an appointment and that I did not want to speak with them.

The next morning my father said that we were going to go for a drive to see my mother. What had actually happened, I learned later, was that the Moonies had called to see why I hadn't reported in and were on their way to rescue me. Believing that my mother would be sympathetic and put an end to the deprogramming, I eagerly hobbled on my crutches and got into the back seat of the car, with my broken leg outstretched. My father was driving, and two of the deprogrammers sat next to him. I became angry, though, as my father passed the exit from the Long Island Expressway to my parents' home. While it might seem hard to believe, my first impulse was to kill my father by reaching over and snapping his neck. I actually believed it was better to do that than betray the Messiah! As a member, I had been told many times that it was better to die or kill than to leave the church.[42]

At that point, however, I was still confident that they could never break me. I knew I would have other chances to escape, so I decided not to kill my father, myself and the others in the car. When we arrived at the apartment in which the deprogramming was scheduled to continue, I refused to get out of the car without a fight. I threatened my father with extreme violence. I told him that I would fight to my death and if I bled to death, it would be on his conscience.

My father turned around from the driver's seat and started to cry. I had seen my father cry only once before: a couple of tears when I was fifteen when my grandmother died. Then, as now, I felt a big lump in my throat and an ache in my heart. "This is crazy," he pleaded. "Tell me, what would you do? How would you feel if your son—your only son—went away for a weekend workshop and all of a sudden disappeared, dropped out of college, quit work, and got involved with such a controversial organization?"

That was the first time since I had joined that I allowed myself to think—for even a moment—from his perspective. I felt his pain, his anguish and worry, as well as his parental love. But I still believed he had been brainwashed by the Communist media.

I answered, "Probably the same thing that you're doing now." I meant it. "What do you want me to do?" I asked.

"Just talk to these people," he replied. ''Listen to what they have to say. Then your mother and I will be able to sleep at night, knowing that you have heard the other side and that we have done the responsible thing."

"For how long?" I asked.

"For five days." he said.

"Then what—can I go back if I want to?"

"Yes, I will drive you back myself. If you want to come out, that will be your choice."

I thought about the proposition. I *knew* that what I had been doing was right. I *knew* that God wanted me to remain in the group. I *knew* the Messiah personally, in the flesh. I *knew* the Divine Principle by heart. What did I have to fear? Besides, I believed that I could prove to my parents once and for all that I wasn't brainwashed. Also, I knew that if I remained with my parents involuntarily and then escaped, I could be ordered to press kidnapping charges against them. I didn't want to do that.

I agreed to stay and listen, voluntarily. I would not contact the Moonies for five more days. Also, I would make no effort to escape. I would talk to the ex-members and listen to what they wanted to tell me, taking breaks as often as I wished.

The former members were not at all what I expected. I assumed, because of my training, that they would be cold, calculating, unspiritual, money hungry, and abusive. They were warm, caring, idealistic, and spiritually minded, and they treated me with respect. As former members, they should have been miserable and guilt-ridden. They weren't. They were very happy that they were out and free to lead their lives as they were doing. All of this was very perplexing.

I was a very difficult person to deprogram. I fought the process with prayer and chanting and threw up expert barricades of denial, rationalizations, justifications, and wishful thinking. The former members brought out psychiatrist Robert Jay Lifton's book *Thought Reform and the Psychology of Totalism* and discussed the techniques and processes used by the Communist Chinese (the enemy!) to brainwash people during the 1950s. It became obvious to me that the processes we used in the Moonies were almost identical. A big question for me began to emerge, "Does God have to use the same tactics as Satan in order to make an ideal world?" Thinking and reasoning for me at that time felt like wading through waist-high mud.

On the fourth day they discussed Hitler and the Nazi movement, comparing Moon and his philosophy of world theocracy to Hitler's global goals for German National Socialism. At one point, I remember getting angry and saying, "I don't care if Moon is like Hitler! I've chosen to follow him and I will follow him till the very end!" When I heard myself say that, an eerie chill went down my spine. I quickly suppressed it.

On the morning of the last day of deprogramming, I had the indescribable experience of my mind suddenly opening up, as if a light switch had been thrown. The former members had asked me to read one of Moon's speeches to members of Congress.[43] He was talking about how he said that Americans were too smart to allow themselves to be brainwashed by a Korean, and how that he respected Americans very much. I had listened to him say, on at least a dozen occasions, how stupid, lazy, and corrupt Americans were, particularly politicians. Also, three Americans, former members, were sitting in front of me, and they each took turns telling me that they had been brainwashed by Moon.

I had the first negative thought about Moon in over two years: "What a snake!"

That was it. Over two years of programming started collapsing like an elaborate house of cards. It had all been built upon one belief, that Moon was God's greatest chosen man in all history—the Messiah. But if he was a liar, that meant he wasn't trustworthy and wasn't of God.

I believed in a God of Truth.

I started to cry inconsolably.

I asked everybody to leave the room.

I cried for a very long time. Someone returned and gave me a cold compress for my forehead. My head pounded, and I felt like a large throbbing open wound. That night was the most painful time of my whole life.

Recovery: Returning To Me

After rediscovering myself, I had a whole new string of questions in my mind. How could I have ever believed that a multimillionaire industrialist from Korea was the Messiah? How could I have turned my back on almost every moral and ethical principle I'd ever had? How could I have done so many cruel things to so many people? The fantasy I had used to inspire myself day after day and month after month was gone. What was left was a frightened, confused, indignant person. I felt as though I had awakened from a surreal dream and wasn't sure what was reality—or as if I had stepped off a skyscraper and was headed toward the Earth, but I kept falling and never hit the ground.

I was overwhelmed by many emotions. I was sad and missed my friends in the group, particularly my "spiritual children," the people I recruited. I missed the excitement of feeling that what I was doing was cosmically important. I missed the feeling of power that single-mindedness brought. Now, all I knew was that my leg was broken. I was broken. I felt tremendous embarrassment about having fallen for a cult. My parents had told me it was a cult. So had my friends. Why hadn't I listened to them? Why hadn't I trusted them? It took me many weeks before I could thank my family for helping me. It was months before I could even refer to the Moonies as a cult, publicly.

I read for months. For me, the burning issue was how the Moonies had ever managed to convert me and indoctrinate me so thoroughly that I could no longer think for myself. I read everything I could get my hands on about brainwashing, attitude change, persuasion, thought reform, mind control, undue influence, and cults. At first, the act of reading itself was extremely difficult. I had read only Moon literature for more than two years. I had trouble concentrating and was sometimes spaced out for long periods, not comprehending what I was reading. I was told that the mind is like a "muscle" and would regain its power through exercise. I forced myself to look up words in the dictionary. I forced myself to read line by line until I worked my way back to being able to concentrate and read pages at a time and be able to explain what I had read.

Living at home was difficult. I was pretty depressed. My leg needed a second operation. Since I still had a full cast on my leg, I needed crutches to move about, to eat, even to go to the bathroom. I was unaccustomed to being so dependent. I had been running a house and controlling the lives of many members. Now I was a captain with no one to lead. I felt terrible for what I had put my family through. They were wonderful to me, but I felt a tremendous sense of guilt.

I felt even more guilt for what I had done as a Moonie. I had lied to people, manipulated them, tricked them, and induced them to abandon their families, education, and relationships to follow a would-be dictator.[44] The guilt turned to anger the more I studied mind control.

I tracked down Dr. Robert Jay Lifton and arranged a meeting at his apartment in Manhattan. He was curious to know why I was so interested in a book about Chinese brainwashing he had written 15 years earlier, in 1961. He was amazed when I described to him, in detail, what the Moonies do to recruit members and how they run their 3 day workshops, their 7 day workshops, and their 21 day, 40 day, and 120 day workshops. He said, "What you are telling me is so much more sophisticated than what the Chinese did in the '50s. It's like a hybrid mutation of a virulent virus strain!"

Lifton shifted my entire perspective on myself when he said, "Steve, you know more about this than I do, because you've lived it. You know it instrumentally. I only know it theoretically and second-hand. You must study psychology and take what you know through your experience and tell others about it." He later asked me to co-author a book with him on mind control (something that was never to be). I was flattered by his offer and intended to take him up on it, but the timing wasn't right for me.

I Decide To Go Public

Meeting Lifton transformed my life. Instead of looking at myself and seeing a college dropout, a poet with no poetry (I sorely regretted throwing those four hundred poems away), and a former cult member, I saw that perhaps there was a higher purpose for me. At that time, although I was no longer a Moonie, I was still thinking somewhat in black and white terms: good versus evil, us versus them. The world's most renowned expert on brainwashing thought that I had an important contribution to make, that what I had experienced could be useful in helping people. By this time I had started attending cult awareness meetings of people affected by the problem and was approached by many parents of people in the Moonies. They asked me if I would talk to their children still trapped in the Moonies. I agreed.

It was then, in 1976, that I seriously began taking steps to become a professional counselor. At first I had my work cut out for me; there were then no alternatives to forcible deprogramming. I had undergone a little training as a peer counselor at college before joining the Moonies. I myself had been deprogrammed. Most helpful of all in talking to members was that I had been a Moonie at a high level, and I knew the group doctrine and policies inside and out. I reread Moon's *Divine Principle*. I studied the Bible and sorted out which things Moon said about it were true, which ones weren't, and what was taken out of context. I established my own belief system. I was involved with deprogramming for about a year. A couple of the cases may have involved abduction by parents or people they hired; most were cases in which members came home to visit and weren't allowed to leave. Some of these were legal conservatorship cases, in which the family received legal custody of an adult child. (Such conservatorship laws are now gone. This change is partly the result of legal and lobbying efforts by cult lawyers, as well as by more well-intentioned people who did not understand the gross human rights violations of mind control cults.)

Fortunately, I was never sued. All of my cases were successful, except two, when the Moonies went back to the group. The exhilaration of helping someone reclaim their life and be restored to their loved ones is beyond words. The closest thing I can use to describe the feeling is how I felt when a friend of mine had a leg cramp in the ocean and was going under and I ran out to the waves, dived in, swam as hard and fast as I could and managed to pull him safely to shore. However, I disliked the stress of forcible deprogramming and wanted to find some other way to help members of destructive cults.

After a year of going public, giving lectures, and doing television and radio interviews, I decided that I needed to figure out who I was again. I went back to college for a semester at Yale and temporarily dropped out of my life as a full-time cult fighter. I wrote poetry, played basketball, went out on dates, and tried to be normal. I did not like Yale, switched to Boston University, volunteered to be a counselor in two student counseling agencies and got in touch with myself again.

During this time, though, Moon was making new and bigger waves. In Congress, the House Subcommittee on International Relations held a lengthy investigation into Korean CIA activities in the United States and other efforts by Korean agents to influence United States' government decisions. I agreed to help the investigation as much as the committee wanted, provided they not ask me to testify publicly. The truth was, as the highest-ranking recent defector who knew a lot of the inner workings, I was afraid of being harassed and possibly murdered. I didn't really follow the "Koreagate" investigation, except when I read an occasional article. I was absolutely confident that the government would expose the Moon group and it would be destroyed.

The final report of the investigation had an 80-page section on the Moonies.[45] The report found that the Moon organization "systematically violated U.S. tax, immigration, banking, currency, and Foreign Agents Registration Act laws, as well as state and local laws relating to charity fraud." It called for an interagency task force to continue to gather evidence, and to prosecute Moon and other Unification Church leaders for their criminal violations. The subcommittee's Republican minority included its own statement, which said, in part, "It is difficult to understand why the appropriate agencies of the Executive Branch have not long since taken action against those activities of the Moon organization that are illegal."

The report was released October 31, 1978. Three weeks later, California Congressman Leo J. Ryan, a member of the Koreagate investigation, was gunned down at an airstrip near Jonestown, Guyana, while trying to help members of another cult, the People's Temple, escape the horrors of Jim Jones' camp. Others with Ryan were shot or killed. I watched the news bulletins about the nine hundred people who were dead because a cult leader had ordered mass murder. Chills went down my spine. I had never heard of the People's Temple before, but I completely identified with the mindset of its members. I remembered listening to Moon harangue us and ask if we were willing to follow him to our deaths. I remembered hearing Moon say that if North Korea invaded South Korea, he would send American Unification members to die on the front lines, so that Americans would be inspired to fight another land war in Asia.

I spent days thinking about the cult problem. More than anything else, the Jonestown massacre motivated me to become a public activist again. I accepted several invitations to appear on television. I was asked to speak at Senator Robert Dole's public hearing on cults, on Capitol Hill, in 1979. But at the last moment, all the ex-cult members invited to speak were taken off the program due to political pressure from cults. The hearing was a disaster and the effort to educate the Government officials and the public about the dangers of destructive cults was undermined.

After that, Moon's political influence began to grow. When Ronald Reagan became president, Moon-controlled groups began funding the New Right political movement in Washington. When it was clear the federal government would do nothing about the Moonies, I decided to organize. I started a group called Ex-Members Against Moon, later Ex-Moon, Inc. I sponsored press conferences, edited a monthly newsletter, and gave numerous interviews. I had considered starting a group of former members from many different cult groups, but I decided that with the release of the Congressional investigation, it would be more effective for me to focus on the Moonies.

I filed a Freedom of Information Act request with the Department of Defense, asking why a Moon company, Tong Il Industries, was permitted to make American M-16 rifles in Korea when only the South Korean government had legal permission to do so. Was the Moon organization part of the Korean government? Was the Department of Defense giving it favored treatment? The request was turned down on the grounds that revealing the information I asked for would compromise the security of the United States. To this day I cannot confirm what I believe to be the truth—that the Moon group was a creature of the Intelligence agencies.

Meanwhile, I knew that I would not do any more forceful deprogramming. I had to find a way to help people out of cults that would be less traumatic and less expensive, and that would not violate the law. I had read many dozens of books and thousands of pages—everything I could get my hands on—about thought reform, brainwashing, attitude change, persuasion, and CIA recruitment and indoctrination. The next and most important area to research was the field of hypnosis.

In 1980, I attended a seminar by Richard Bandler on hypnosis that was based on the work of the psychiatrist Milton Erickson. Bandler and John Grinder had also developed a model based on the work of therapist Virginia Satir and Gregory Bateson. They called it Neuro-Linguistic Programming, or NLP. The seminar gave me a greater understanding of techniques of hypnotic mind control and how to combat them. I spent nearly two years studying NLP with everyone involved in its formulation and presentation, even moving to Santa Cruz, California to do an apprenticeship with John Grinder. By this time, I had fallen in love and married. Eventually I moved back to Massachusetts when my wife, Aureet Bar-Yam, was given a scholarship to work toward her master's degree in psychology at Harvard.[46]

Over time, however, I became more and more concerned about the ethics of NLP. It seemed to me that its leaders had launched a mass-market campaign to promote NLP as a tool for power enhancement. Bandler and Grinder shifted their focus from training away from therapists and teachers. They started training anyone, especially salespeople and business executives. One of my big problems was their dictum, "Do what works." Eventually I realized that NLP was amoral. It depended entirely on the conscience and good will of the practitioner. This was not too much of an issue with a licensed therapist who had strict ethical guidelines. But it was another matter entirely when practitioners were salespeople or corporate executives who were interested in power, money, or sex. I left my association with NLP forever.

I earned my master's degree in counseling psychology from Cambridge College in 1985, allowing me to begin to receive training from experts in the field of clinical hypnosis. I studied the work of Dr. Milton Erickson from his books and tapes, and from people trained by him. I learned a great deal about how the mind functions, as well as how to communicate with people more effectively. These studies gave me a better way to apply what I had learned to help people trapped in cults. It was possible, I discovered, to create a model of the entire process of change that occurs when a person gets drawn into a cult group and then successfully leaves it.

I asked myself a range of essential questions. What specific factors make a person able to move out of a mind controlled psyche? Why are certain interventions successful and others not? What goes on in the thought processes of people who simply walk out of cults? Patterns began to appear. I found that people who were able to walk away without intervention were those who had maintained contact with people outside the destructive cult. When people could maintain communication with outsiders, valuable information that could change their life could penetrate cult-constructed mental walls.

I knew how important my father's tears had been for me. More importantly, I realized that he had been able to *invite me to look at myself from his perspective*, and re-examine my own information from his viewpoint. In analyzing my own experience, I recognized that what helped me most was my own internal voice and my own first-hand experiences, buried beneath all the emotional suppression and the thought-stopping rituals of chanting and praying. Underneath, the real me wasn't dead. Maybe it had been bound and gagged, but I was still very much alive. The accident and the deprogramming had helped move me physically and psychologically to a place where I was able to get in touch with myself. Indeed, it was my ideals and my own fantasy of an ideal world that had lured me into the Moonies. Those ideals ultimately enabled me to walk out and publicly condemn cult mind control.

No matter how deeply the Unification Church virus had invaded the "child parts" of my identity—the real Steve Hassan had not been destroyed. After decades of membership, I have learned that all of my "spiritual children"—the people I recruited—have exited the cult. A very great relief.

After receiving my master's degree, I began a new phase of my life. While practicing psychotherapy and conducting my public education activities, I also worked as the national coordinator for FOCUS, a support group of former cult members who want to help each other. For the past years, I have worked to increase public awareness of destructive cults, undue influence, and mind control. These cults did not go away as the idealistic youth of the 1970s became the young professionals of the 1980s, the leaders of the 1990s and 2000s, and the new retirees of the 2010s. Sadly, destructive cults continue to grow, thrive, and recruit people of all ages and from all walks of life.

Yet, while destructive cults continue to grow, so too does our understanding of the process of mind control and undue influence. The availability of help for mind control victims continues to increase. We know far more about the neurological processes of the brain than we did even a decade ago. As more and more people—especially mental health professionals, social workers, doctors, and lawyers—lose loved ones to mind control cults, a sense of urgency is building. There *are* some basic ways to identify destructive cults, protect yourself from mind control, and help others shake free of its influence. Giving the keys to that knowledge is what this book is all about.

Chapter 3

The Threat: Mind Control Today

Imagine, if you will, the following scenes.

Saffron-robed men on street corners, dancing and chanting with cymbals and drums. Bedraggled young people running from car to car, selling flowers in the pouring rain. Glassy-eyed men and women confronting people behind folding tables near busy intersections, asking for money to quarantine AIDS victims and build particle-beam weapons. Over nine hundred people—men, women, and children—lying dead, face down in the mud.

Mention cults to someone and these might be some of the images you'll evoke. Yet these images do not accurately represent cults, mind control, and undue influence as they exist today. They represent only a small fraction of these phenomena.

Imagine, then, a different set of images.

Business executives in three-piece suits sitting in hotel ballrooms for company-sponsored "awareness" training, not permitted to stand up or leave, even to go to the bathroom. Housewives attending "psych-up rallies" so they can recruit friends and neighbors into a multi-level marketing organization. Hundreds of students gathering at an accredited university, being told they can levitate and fly through the air if only they meditate hard enough. High-school students practicing satanic rituals involving blood and urine, being directed by an older leader who claims he will help them develop their personal power. "Troubled" teens being sent off to boot camps by their deceived parents, unregulated by the government, some run by religious groups who seek to convert them.[47]

Hundreds of women and men of every description paying huge sums to learn cosmic truths from some channeled spirit. Tens of thousands of women dressed in long dresses, living in harem-type households run by men with long beards. Young girls and women (and men and boys, too) being sold for sex, making their traffickers rich. Young Muslims being trained to kill, rape and even blow themselves up in the name of Allah.

These are some of the forms that mind control takes today.

The Pervasiveness Of Cults

Do you know anyone who has undergone or witnessed a radical personality change because of such a group? The odds are that you do. Someone you know—someone in your family, at work, or in your circle of friends—has likely been directly and profoundly affected by undue influence.

In the past decades, the destructive cult phenomenon has mushroomed into a problem of tremendous social and political importance. It is estimated that there are now over three thousand destructive cults in the United States, directly affecting more than three million people.[48] These organizations come in many different types and sizes. Some have hundreds of millions of dollars; others are relatively poor. Some, however, are clearly more dangerous than others. The largest and most destructive are not content to simply exercise their control over the lives of their members. They have an agenda to gain political power and use it to reshape American society—or even the world.

Considering how well these cults have been largely able to shield themselves from public scrutiny, it might seem alarmist to regard them as a threat to individual liberty and society as a whole. Yet, some are influencing the political landscape through extensive lobbying efforts and electioneering for candidates.[49] Some are attempting to influence United States foreign policy by lobbying covertly for foreign powers.[50] The Moonies, for example, were a major supplier of money and guns to the Contra forces in Nicaragua.[51] They also invested between $70 and $100 million in Uruguay,[52] in a failed attempt to turn that country into the cult's first theocratic state—a springboard from which to pursue its declared goal: "to conquer and subjugate the world."[53]

In the United States, cults exert tremendous economic clout by buying up huge blocks of real estate and taking over hundreds of businesses. Some enter corporations under the pretense of offering executive leadership training, while harboring a covert agenda of taking over the company. Some seek to influence the judicial system by spending millions of dollars annually on top attorneys to bend the law to their will.

Since all destructive cults believe that their ends justify any means, no matter how harmful, they typically believe themselves to be above the law. As long as they believe that what they are doing is right and just, many of them feel justified to lie, steal, cheat, or to use any and all forms of undue influence to accomplish their ends. They routinely violate, in the most profound and fundamental way, the civil and religious liberties of the people they recruit. They turn unsuspecting people into slaves.

When I call a cult "destructive," I do so because it meets the specific criteria described in detail in the next chapter of this book. Briefly, a destructive cult is a group that violates its members' rights and damages them through the abusive techniques of unethical mind control. It distinguishes itself from a normal, healthy social or religious group by subjecting its members to systematic control of behavior, information, thoughts and emotions (BITE) to keep them dependent and obedient.

When domestic abuse survivors hear this definition, they often describe their relationship with their abuser as a cult with one follower and one leader. A pimp with four women (or men) under his control forms a cult of five. A sweatshop of foreign workers who have been economically lured there, and who now cannot leave, is a labor trafficking cult. A multi-level marketing business that makes its money not from selling products to buyers, but by misleading and recruiting ever more sales associates, is a marketing cult. A corporation that demands obedience and unpaid overtime from its workers, and forces them into "motivational training" sessions that are in fact mind control, is a business cult. Methods of operation are what makes a cult destructive.

If I had not personally suffered from mind control for two and a half years, I would probably be a staunch defender of the rights of such groups to practice freely, unhindered by public scrutiny. I am extremely concerned about protecting personal liberty and defending the Constitution's guarantees of religious freedom. I fully support people's rights to believe as they choose, no matter how unorthodox their beliefs. If people want to believe that Sun Myung Moon—or Charles Manson, or their dog—is the Messiah, that is their right. However—and this is a crucial point—people need to be protected from processes that *make* them believe Manson or Moon is the Messiah.

This chapter looks at the different areas of society in which cults arise, and the different techniques used to recruit members. How a group recruits and what happens during membership determine whether or not it respects people's rights to choose *for themselves* what they do and believe. If deception, hypnosis, or other mind control techniques are used to recruit and control followers, then people's rights are being infringed upon.

Cults 101

Cults are not new. Throughout history, groups of enthusiasts have sprung up around charismatic leaders of every possible description. But in recent decades, something has been added: the systematic use of modern psychological techniques to reduce a person's will and gain control over their thoughts, feelings, and behavior.

While most people usually think of cults as religious—the first definition of *cult* in *Webster's Third New International Dictionary* is "religious practice: worship"—they are often completely secular. *Webster's* also defines *cult* as "a usually small or narrow circle of persons united by devotion or allegiance to some artistic or intellectual program, tendency, or figure (as one of limited popular appeal)." That second definition comes closer to the meaning of a modern cult, but still falls a bit short. Modern cults have *virtually unlimited* popular appeal. For the sake of brevity, from here on I will refer to any group in which mind control is used in destructive ways as simply a cult.

In times past, cult or sect leaders could be very compelling, often abusively so. Charges of mind control against them have a long history. But, until recently, leaders gained their dominance over followers in a relatively hit-or-miss way, learning as they went along. Cult leadership was an art successfully practiced by relatively few. In some cases, groups that were considered cults in their earliest days are now considered to be mainline religions. Of course, even mainline religious organizations can have destructive aspects, use undue influence, or become destructive cults. Cults can arise within major religions, too.

Over the past half century, undue influence has become more of a science. Since World War II, intelligence agencies around the world have been aggressively engaged in mind control research and development. The CIA admits to having performed drug, electroshock, and hypnosis experiments since the early 1950s under the code name MK-ULTRA.[54] Research has expanded into other areas since then.

Two generations ago, the human potential movement in psychology began to experiment with techniques to direct individual and group dynamics. These techniques were developed with the best of motives: to force people out of debilitating mental ruts and show them how truly different they could become. During the late 1960s, a form of group therapy known as *sensitivity training* became popular. In such a group, people were encouraged to speak about their most intimate personal matters in front of other members. One technique widely popular at that time was the "hot seat" which was first used by the drug rehab cult, Synanon. A member of the group sat in the center of the circle, while other members confronted them with what they considered to be the person's shortcomings or problems. Needless to say, without the supervision of an experienced therapist (and sometimes even with it), such a technique opens up considerable possibilities for abuse. Today the "hot seat" is used by some destructive cults to demean and control their members.

Another development that began to affect the general population was the popularization of hypnosis. People were introduced to certain techniques for inducing hypnotic trance—but often without adequate consideration of the ethical aspects of working with the subconscious mind. Originally these group process methods were used only on willing participants, and many people reported positive experiences. Soon, though, some of these techniques percolated out into the general culture, where they became available for anyone to abuse. Unscrupulous persons began using them to make money and gain power by manipulating a coterie of followers. (My earlier discussion of Neuro-Linguistic Programming provides one common example.) Unfortunately, with the Internet, it is easy to download such information and training and to use it to manipulate and program others into new beliefs, behaviors and even identities.

Because of increased media coverage, people in the United States began to become aware of the new cults in the middle to late 1970s. No one of my generation can forget the spectacle of Patty Hearst, the daughter of one of the country's most powerful newspaper publishers, William Randolph Hearst III, who transformed into Tania, a member of the Symbionese Liberation Army, a left-wing terrorist cult.[55]

As public awareness of the destructive potential of cult membership began to grow, we saw the birth of deprogramming. Professional deprogrammers, like Ted Patrick, hired by a cult member's family, would forcibly abduct the person and, often in a secluded motel room, try to reverse the cult's brainwashing.[56] Thousands of cult members, like myself, were indeed de-brainwashed successfully, and later gave dramatic public testimony of how cult mind control worked. But many deprogrammings failed, and members and cults sometimes brought lawsuits against families and deprogrammers. Worst of all, deprogramming could be harmful to the cult member.

Many families with members in destructive cults found abduction and forceful detention repugnant. They also found the financial burden great and the threat of lawsuits intimidating. If they didn't want to try a forcible deprogramming, they had no choice but to be patient and hope that something would happen. As a result their family members or friends remained in cults throughout the 1970s. Then something happened to change the way the whole nation perceived destructive cults: the massacre at Jonestown.

Above Jones's throne was affixed a sign which read, "Those who do not remember the past are condemned to repeat it." While no one can explain why Jones chose this saying from George Santayana as his motto, the truth in the message, ironically, is relevant to us today as we examine the history of cults and think about the implications.

The Four Main Types Of Cults

News of the Jonestown massacre shocked the world. In the 1970s, there was little general understanding of unethical mind control or of how widespread its use had already become in society at large. In the decades following that massacre, cult groups have continued to grow, unabated. New cults appear and older ones grow more sophisticated. Currently, there are groups using mind control in many different areas of society. These organizations include religious cults, political cults, psychotherapy/educational cults, and commercial cults.

Religious cults are the best known and most numerous. These groups focus on religious dogma. Some use the Bible or Koran; some are based on an Eastern religion; others draw on occult lore; and some are purely the inventions of their leaders. Although most claim to involve the spiritual realm, or to follow a strict code of religious principles, it is more common than not for these cult leaders to enjoy a luxurious lifestyle, with the groups owning millions of dollars of real estate, and/or running extensive business enterprises. Think of ISIS, Boko Haram, the Unification Church, Scientology,[57] Church Universal and Triumphant,[58] The Way International,[59] or the organization of Osho (Bhagwan Shree Rajneesh, rebranded Osho by his followers after his death in 1990).[60] Scientology is unusual, as it began as a psychotherapy cult and also functions as a commercial cult. It functions under the cloak of religion.

Political cults often make the news, usually with the word "fringe" or "extremist" attached. Rarely do people hear about the deceptive recruitment and mind control practices that distinguish these organizations from run-of-the-mill fanatical groups. These groups are organized around a particular political dogma. One such group's leader, Lyndon LaRouche, has run for president in the past eight elections, and claims to advise top government and business leaders.[61] Another group, known simply as Move, was bombed by police in Philadelphia after holing up with an arsenal of weapons.[62] Yet another, Aryan Nation, believes in white supremacy, for many years ran survivalist training camps, and has plans to take over the United States or die trying.[63] The now-defunct Democratic Workers' Party of California was for years an extreme left-wing cult.[64]

Psychotherapy/educational cults hold expensive workshops and seminars that provide participants with "insight" and "enlightenment," usually in a hotel conference room. These cults use many basic mind control techniques to provide participants with a peak experience—which is to say hypnotic euphoria, although I don't think that Maslow would describe such events as 'peak experiences'. That experience is all that happens to most customers, but others are manipulated to sign up for the more expensive advanced courses. Graduates of the advanced courses may then become enmeshed in the group. Once committed to the group, members are told to bring in friends, relatives, and co-workers, or else cut off relations with them. Recruiters are typically not allowed to disclose much about the program.

Many of these groups have caused nervous breakdowns, broken marriages, and business failures, as well as suicides and accidental deaths by reckless accidents. The people who run these groups sometimes have questionable personal backgrounds, and, often, few or no credentials.

Commercial cults believe in the dogma of greed. They deceive and manipulate people to work for little or no pay in the hope of getting rich. Many such pyramid-scheme or multi-level marketing organizations promise big money, but in fact fleece their victims. They also destroy their victims' self-esteem so they will not complain. Success depends not on selling products or services, but on recruiting new people, who in turn recruit others.

Some commercial cults browbeat people into hawking magazine subscriptions or other items door to door. These cults take out ads in local newspapers, promising exciting travel and lucrative careers. Cult recruiters set up interviews inside their hotel rooms, preying on high school and college students. When people are accepted into the program, they usually have to pay money to be trained, and then are sent far away in vans to sell merchandise. Salespeople are manipulated through fear and guilt, and are sometimes physically and sexually abused. These people sometimes become slaves to the company and turn over their money in order to pay for living expenses.

Pimps and human traffickers run their own versions of commercial cults. Since 2013, I have been working with survivors of trafficking, helping them to understand how they were controlled and indoctrinated into slavery.

Recruitment: How It's Done

As we will see, there are many different ways people can be ensnared into a relationship or group that uses mind control. Many cults deliberately seek out people who are intelligent, talented, and successful. As a result, its members are often powerfully persuasive and seductive to newcomers. Indeed, the sheer number of sincere, committed members whom a newcomer meets is probably far more convincing than any doctrine or structure. The large cults know how to train their "salespeople" well. They indoctrinate members to show only the best sides of the organization. Members are taught to suppress any negative feelings they have about the group, and to always show a continually smiling, happy face. Recruiters are taught to size up each newcomer, and package and sell the cult in whatever way is most likely to succeed.

In the Moonies, I was taught to use a four-part personality model to help recruit new members. People were categorized as *thinkers*, *feelers*, *doers*, or *believers*. Thinkers are people who approach life with their minds, as intellectuals. Feelers lead with their emotions. Doers are action-oriented and very physical. Believers are spiritually oriented.

If a person was categorized as a thinker, we would use an intellectual approach. We would show him pictures of Nobel Laureates at a Moonie-sponsored science conference, or philosophers discussing a variety of interesting topics. A deliberate misimpression was given that these giants of the scientific and academic communities were supporters of the movement. In fact, to my knowledge, not one of them actually supported the Moon cause. They were interested in meeting with professional colleagues and friends. Of course, their expense-paid trips and the thousands of dollars paid to them as honorariums were added incentives. Many academics and some celebrated politicians took advantage of these paid holidays with no concern for the allure that their names were adding to an invidious cause.

Feelers would always respond well to a loving, caring approach. With these people, my group would accentuate our emotional well-being, as well as the extended family aspect of the group. We would always talk about love with such people, and how there wasn't enough of the *real* kind of love in the world. Feelers automatically long to be accepted and loved, so we would go out of our way to provide the person with a warm and enticing feeling of unconditional approval.

Doers are action-oriented. They like challenges and strive to accomplish as much as they can. If they saw poverty and suffering in the world and longed to make it end, we would tell them how much we were doing along these lines. Perhaps they were concerned about war, or Communism. We would always make it sound as though we were the only organization with a workable plan of action (even if it was objectively untrue, we believed it was true). We would tell doers about the hundreds of programs we sponsored to heal a broken world.

We saw believers as people searching for God, or looking for spiritual meaning in their lives. They typically would tell us about their spiritual experiences—dreams, visions and revelations. For the most part, these people were "wide open," and often recruited themselves. It was always amazing to me to realize how many people told us they had just been praying to God to reveal to them what He wanted them to do with their lives. Many believed they were spiritually led to meet one of our members. With them it was simply a matter of sharing our testimonies and we would convince them they had been led to us by God.

Contrary to public perception, most of the people we recruited did *not* fall into the believer category. Most were either feelers or doers. Many of the so-called thinkers eventually became leaders within the organization.

With this one simple personality model to guide recruiters, and hundreds of front groups to operate behind, the Moon organization cast a broad recruitment net that drew in diverse range of people.[65] Indeed, members regard themselves as "fishers of men," a term taken from Jesus' metaphor for describing his disciples in the New Testament. Unfortunately, four decades later, the methods of mind control used by many cults are far more nuanced and sophisticated—and potentially far more damaging.

The recruiter's work is made considerably easier because most people have no idea how deep the pockets of major cults can be. Many of the larger ones have grown hugely wealthy through public fundraising techniques, as well as by tapping their own members' bank accounts and property. They reinvest a huge part of their capital into recruiting more members.[66]

Today, it is also quite common for some cult groups to spend huge sums of money on public relations firms and marketing specialists. They pay top dollar to experts to help present a positive image and design recruitment campaigns.[67]

The average person doesn't understand mind control; doesn't know how cults operate, doesn't know what questions to ask and what behaviors to watch out for, and doesn't believe they could ever be sucked in. That's why so many ordinary people are prime candidates for cult recruiters.

Why Do Cults Have So Much Success?

Why is there so much complacency about the threat of mind control cults?

First, accepting that mind control can be effectively used on almost anybody challenges the age-old notion that human beings are rational, and responsible for (and in control of) all their actions. Such a worldview does not allow for any concept of mind control.

Second, we all have *a belief in our own invulnerability*. It is too scary to think that someone could take control of our minds. We all want to have a belief in our own ability to completely control our lives.

Third, the processes of influence start from the moment we are born, so it's easy to take the position that everything is mind control. *Why worry about it?* We tell ourselves, "It's a normal part of life." But, just as sex is a normal part of life but seduction by a womanizer or femme fatale, or rape is not, influence is a natural part of life, but *undue* influence is not.

Let's dig into each of these preconceptions.

First there is the idea that a human being is inherently rational. If people operate from such a viewpoint, they believe that cult members have rationally chosen to live a deviant lifestyle. If the person is an adult, goes the argument, then they have a right to live any way they choose. That argument might be true if no deceptive, social influence techniques were used to unduly influence a person's choice. But, of course, these techniques are used.

Furthermore, we human beings aren't totally rational creatures. Complete rationality denies our emotional and physical nature. We can't function without our emotions. We all need love, friendship, attention, and approval. Most of us agree on the wonderfulness of falling in love. Most of us also understand that the condition of our bodies has a tremendous impact on the way we function psychologically. Have you ever gone for a few days with little or no sleep? If so, you probably weren't functioning rationally and likely weren't in total control of your every action. Have you ever gone without food for days? The mind begins to hallucinate when the body doesn't have enough sleep or food. In such circumstances, our physiology undermines our rationality.

Then there is the belief in our own invulnerability. We all need to feel that we are in control of our lives. We don't like feeling that events are out of control, so we put reality into an order that makes sense to us. When we hear that something bad has happened to someone (perhaps being mugged or raped), we usually try to find a reason to explain why that person was a victim. Was he or she walking at the wrong time in a bad neighborhood? People try to ascribe a direct cause-and-effect relationship to what happened: if something bad happened to her, then she must have done something wrong. This kind of behavior is called *blaming the victim*.

Although there is value in trying to assess possibly careless behavior (indeed, we must learn from life's tragedies), the reality is that the person just might have been in the wrong place at the wrong time. Blaming the victim plays an important psychological role in allowing us to distance ourselves from the person who was hurt. In this way, we say to ourselves, "Such a thing couldn't happen to me because I am different. I know better." Often people look at a cult victim and say mistakenly, "What a weak-minded person; he must have been looking for a way to escape responsibility and have someone control his life." In that way people deny the reality that the same thing could happen to them.

People believe that "it can never happen to them" because they want to believe they are stronger and better than the many millions who have fallen victim to mind control. Our need to believe that we are invulnerable, though, is actually a weakness that is easily played upon by cult recruiters. For example, a recruiter could say, "Now, Bill, you strike me as a very intelligent, worldly type of person. You would never allow anyone to force you to do something you wouldn't want to do. You like to make up your mind for yourself. So you won't let the biased media scare you with bizarre claims of mind control. You're too smart for that. So what time do you want to come over for that lecture?"

As for the philosophical position that everything is a form of mind control, it is certainly true that we are constantly being influenced by all kinds of people, ideas, and forces. Yet there is actually a continuum of influence. At one end are benign or even helpful influences, such as a friend suggesting that the two of you see a particular movie. At the other end are deeply destructive influences, such as indoctrinating people to kill themselves or harm others. Most of the groups I'm concerned with fall near the destructive end of the continuum.

Influence Continuum

From the **BITE** Model:
Behavior, **I**nformation, **T**hought, and **E**motional Control

Constructive / ***Healthy***		***Destructive*** / ***Unhealthy***
Authentic Self Unconditional Love Conscience Creativity and Humor Free Will / Critical Thinking	**For Individuals**	False (Cult) Identity Conditional "love" Doctrine Solemnity, Fear and Guilt Dependency / Obedience
Psychologically Healthy Knows Own Limits Empowers Individuals Trustworthy Accountable	**For Leaders**	Narcissistic / Psychopathic Elitist / Grandiose Power Hungry Secretive / Deceptive Claims Absolute Authority
Checks and Balances Informed Consent Individuality / Diversity Means Create End Encourages Growth Free to Leave	**For Organizations** **(and Relationships)**	Authoritarian Structure Deceptive / Manipulative Clones People Ends Justify Means Preserves Own Power No Legitimate Reasons to Leave

An organization that provides helpful or constructive influence has these essential traits:

- It routinely seeks the informed consent of its members.
- Checks and balances are built into its systems of governance, so that no one person or sub-group can seize control.
- It is transparent about its mission, its finances, its governance, and its decision-making processes.
- It encourages the growth, health and sanity of its members.

Leaders of these organizations are honest, trustworthy, accountable and transparent about what they do and decide, and why. Their approach to leadership respects all group members' individuality, choice, and free will. They provide members and others with free and open access to information about the group. Ideally, they are also sincerely loving, compassionate, wise (or at least reasonably intelligent) human beings.

If we look at a typical organization on the opposite end of the continuum, we find that it exhibits these traits:

- No informed consent. Information is manipulated and controlled.
- It has a top-down structure, with a single leader at the top and a small inner circle immediately below.
- It is authoritarian: orders are issued from the top, sometimes without explanation or rationale, and those below must follow them without question.
- It has no guiding ethical principles; all goals justify the use of any means.
- It focuses on controlling, preserving, and acquiring power and information, but shares little of these with rank and file members—and none with outsiders.

People at the top of these organizations do not lead through wisdom, consensus, compassion, or even brainpower. They lead by making their followers frightened and dependent. They demand obedience and subservience. They often require their followers to dress, act, and think exactly alike.

As we will see in Chapter 4, one highly effective way to determine where an organization falls on this continuum is to apply the BITE model. As I mentioned, this model looks at four aspects of potential control: behavior control, information control, thought control, and emotion control.

These four components are inherently neither good nor evil. If mind control techniques are used to empower an individual to have integrity and more choice, and the authority for his life remains within himself, the effects can be very beneficial. However, if mind control is used to change a person's belief system *without informed consent* and make him *dependent on outside authority figures,* the effects can be devastating.

The more a group seeks to control any or all of these aspects of its members lives, the closer to the extreme end of the influence continuum it falls—and the more likely it is to be a cult.

Authoritarian, Destructive Cult Structure

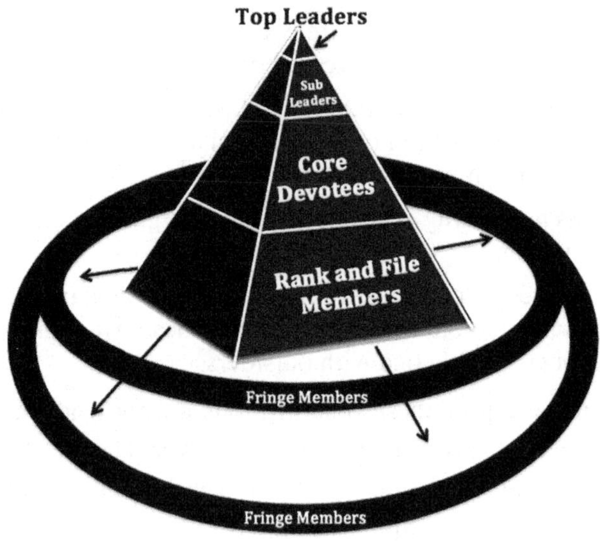

Another important model to help discern the core characteristics of a group is this diagram of a destructive cult. When I evaluate a group and its use of the BITE model, it is important to use information that is descriptive of the pyramid and not the circle outside the pyramid—I refer to these people as "fringe members." A person who is affiliated very loosely in a behavioral sense may still be indoctrinated into the belief system through sleep deprivation, trance states, intensive workshops, time on discussion boards, YouTube video indoctrination, not to mention telephone calls, texts, webinars and more. They are influenced and involved with the destructive cult, but not to the extent of someone who works on staff 80 hours a week and has no vacation time. That individual may be evaluated as less extremely mind controlled than the staffer, but is still in a destructive experience.

Sometimes I am asked to consult with a person who is just beginning to get involved with the group and has yet to experience the extremes of the BITE model. By showing them the "bigger picture" and helping them to see the "whole elephant" and not just the tail, it empowers them to reality-test. Stepping back to visualize the entire entity is important.

People are being incorrectly described as "self-radicalized" into becoming terrorists. These folks can be better understood as being on the fringes of a destructive cult—but in the "sphere of influence" of mind control. They are absolutely being recruited—by people in person and online. Cult recruiters are expert at targeting vulnerabilities and activating motivation. Political and religious cults that use terrorist tactics are aggressively recruiting and some people are being sucked into their vortex.

Before we move on to a more comprehensive description of mind control, there are a few more major points I wish to cover.

Phobias: The Force That Robs Cult Members' Freedom[68]

We all know someone who has had a phobia. Yourself, perhaps? The most common phobias include fears of flying in airplanes, public speaking, taking elevators, driving in tunnels or over bridges, and children commonly develop phobias about certain animals like snakes, spiders, and even dogs.

Basically, phobias are an intense fear reaction to someone or something. A phobic reaction can range from very mild to very severe. An intense phobic reaction can cause physical responses like racing heartbeat, dry mouth, sweating, and muscle tension. Phobias can immobilize people and keep them from doing the things they truly want to do. Indeed, phobias can rob people of free choice.

Often people develop phobias as a result of a traumatic life experience. For example, a friend dies in a plane crash. An elevator someone is traveling in gets stuck for hours without light. Someone is bitten by a snake. We learn to associate extremely negative feelings with the object. After such an experience, our fears can then take on a life of their own and, in minutes or over several years, can become full-blown phobias.

The structure of a phobia involves several internal components that interact to cause a vicious cycle. These components include worrisome thoughts, negative internal images, and feelings of dread and being out of control. Just thinking about the object can sometimes trigger the cycle into action. The person may say to himself, "Oh, I hope the teacher doesn't call on me to give my report." That thought is enough to cause them to start feeling tense and anxious. They see—usually unconsciously—a picture of themselves going to the front of the class and freezing up. In this vivid "motion picture," they see themselves sweating and fidgeting, and their minds turning blank. Everyone is laughing and the teacher starts yelling at them. This imagined ridicule causes them to feel even more upset and fearful that they will be called upon. Such a person could be well on their way toward having a fully developed phobia.

People who were sexually abused as children often have crippling phobias about themselves programmed into them by their perpetrators. Many children have no conscious memories of the phobia installation. However they suffer deep trauma issues about identity and sexuality. They are unable to visualize themselves being healthy and valued as a unique human being. Not surprisingly, a large number of sex trafficking victims were sexually abused as children, making them especially vulnerable to recruitment and continued abuse. This childhood mind control abuse set them up for being abused again and again.

What do phobias have to do with cult groups and mind control? In some cults, *members are systematically made to be phobic about ever leaving the group*. Today's cults know how to effectively implant vivid negative images deep within members' unconscious minds, making it impossible for them to even conceive of ever being happy and successful outside of the group. When the unconscious is programmed to accept such negative associations, it behaves as though they were true. The unconscious mind of the typical cult member contains a substantial image-bank of all of the bad things that will occur if they, or anyone, were to ever betray the group. Members are programmed, either overtly or subtly, to believe that if they ever leave, they will die of some horrible disease, be hit by a car, be killed in a plane crash, or perhaps cause the death of loved ones. Some cults program members to believe that if they leave the group, planetary nuclear holocaust will be the result. Yet cult-induced phobias are so cleverly created and implanted that people often don't even know they exist.

Of course, these thoughts are irrational and often nonsensical. However, keep in mind that *most* phobias are irrational. Most planes don't crash, most elevators don't get stuck, and most dogs aren't rabid.

Imagine what it would be like if you believed that mysterious people were determined to poison you. If this belief were implanted deep in your unconscious, do you think you would ever be able to go to a restaurant and enjoy your meal? How long would it be before you only ate food that you bought and prepared yourself? If, by chance, someone you were eating with in a restaurant suddenly became ill, how long would it be before you stopped eating out altogether?

Such a belief—whether conscious or unconscious—would substantially limit your choices. If the belief were not conscious, you might try to rationalize your behavior by telling your friends that you don't like eating out because you are on a diet, or because many restaurants are unsanitary. Either way, your choices no longer include simply going to a restaurant and enjoying a good meal.

In the same way, cult phobias take away people's choices. Members truly believe they will be destroyed if they leave the safety of the group. They think there is no way outside the group for them to grow—spiritually, intellectually, or emotionally.

However, once they become conscious of their desire to leave, it is usually only a matter of time before the authentic self develops a stronger and stronger voice. Why? Because mind control groups constantly change their doctrines and policies. Members are constantly exiting, and leaders need to keep lying and change policies to try to maintain control.

NOTE: Working with extremist cult members and victims of human trafficking, it is essential to professionally evaluate threats of harm. They might not be all phobias. Unfortunately, for these cult survivors, threats of harm to themselves or loved ones are often real. Special steps must be taken to make sure they are safe.

The Unconscious Mind: The Key To Creativity—And Vulnerability

What makes us all so vulnerable to these influence processes? The answer lies in the nature of the mind itself.

The human mind has been described as an extraordinarily sophisticated biocomputer that is oriented for learning patterns for survival—and much more. It is remarkable in its ability to creatively respond to a person's needs, as well as to their environment. Our mind filters out floods of information every second, so that we can cope with those things that we consider important.

Our minds are huge reservoirs of information, stored as images, sounds, feelings, tastes and smells. All this information is systematically connected in meaningful ways.

Our sense of self develops over years of life experience. As we grow and change, our beliefs about ourselves and the world change, too. Our beliefs serve as the major means of processing information—and of determining our behavior.

We have a certain degree of conscious control, but most matters are controlled unconsciously. The conscious mind has a narrow range of attention. The unconscious does all the rest, including regulating all body functions. Imagine having to tell your heart to beat 72 times every minute. You would never have time for anything else. The unconscious mind is the primary manager of information.

It is our creative unconscious that allows us to make mental pictures and to experience them as "real." Try this experiment. Take a moment and allow your mind to transport you to a beautiful tropical paradise. Feel the warmth of the sun, a cool breeze, and the smell of the ocean. Even if you have never been to such a place, it is still possible to perform this experiment. Did you go somewhere else for that moment? Our imagination can be channeled in other ways too. For example, professional basketball players visualize the ball leaving their fingers and going through the net before they shoot. These capacities to fantasize and visualize exist within everyone and are an essential component of being human. We all have dreamed about happier times in our lives—perhaps meeting the "perfect" person, perhaps winning the lottery. But hypnosis can also be used to create in our unconscious minds a fantasy world that can be used to enslave us.

As we grow, the mind does not erase previous memories: it layers new experiences over them in a very systematic way. It is amazing how easily we can shift back into past memories. For example, try to remember playing with your favorite toy when you were a child, or eating your favorite food. Our memories of childhood form a vast storehouse that can be tapped and exploited by hypnotic techniques. It is not accidental that many destructive cults tell their members to "become like little children," mimicking Christianity: "You must be as one of these to enter the Kingdom of Heaven." Adults can easily be age-regressed to a time when they had little or no critical faculties. As children, we were helpless and dependent on our parents as the ultimate authority figures.

The mind, despite all of its strength and ability, has weaknesses too. It is dependent on a stream of coherent information to function properly. Put a person in a sensory deprivation chamber, and within minutes he will start to hallucinate and become incredibly suggestible. Likewise, put a person into a situation where his senses are overloaded with non-coherent information, and the mind will go "numb" as a protective mechanism. It gets confused and overwhelmed, and critical faculties no longer work properly. It is in this weakened state that people become very open to suggestion.

The mind needs frames of reference in order to structure reality. Change the frame of reference, and the information coming in will be interpreted in a different way. Take, for example, the Jewish rite of circumcision. If you take away the cultural meaning and the medical advantages, it looks like an assault on a defenseless infant. Our belief system allows us to interpret information, make decisions, and act according to our beliefs. When people are subjected to a mind control process, most do not have any frame of reference for the experience, and consequently they often accept the frame of reference given to them by the group.

When we make decisions, we usually base them on information we believe to be true. We don't have the time to verify every piece of information that comes at us. When we shop, we tend to believe it when we are told that a particular item is cheaper here than at any other store. After all, why would the salesperson lie, particularly if you can come back and complain? If we distrusted everything, we would be paranoid. If, at the other extreme, we were to trust everything and everybody, we would be naive and taken advantage of for the rest of our lives. Therefore, we strive to live our lives in a balance between skepticism and trust. A person with an open mind seeks to live within that healthy balance. Mind control techniques seek to upset that balance.

Con artists are professional liars. Their greatest assets are their looks and their ability to 'charm'. Many victims of con artists remark that they trusted the person because they "didn't look like a criminal." The successful ones—Bernie Madoff, for example—never do. They convey a humanness that bypasses a person's defenses. They are usually great talkers but do not appear to be too slick. Slickness would give them away. Con artists size up their victim, make the con, get the money, and leave.

Cult recruiters use many of the same skills, but they don't leave. They want you to join them. Almost all of them were victims themselves at one point. They believe that what they are doing is truly beneficial for you. However, they want something more valuable than your money. They want your mind! Of course, they'll take your money too, along the way. But they don't run away like common criminals. They want you to move in with them. Not only that, they want you to go out and do the same to others.

Like it or not, everyone is vulnerable to mind control. Everyone wants to be happy. Everyone needs affection and attention. Everyone is looking for something better in life: more wisdom, more knowledge, more money, more status, more meaning, better relationships, or better health. These basic human qualities and needs are exactly what cult recruiters prey upon.

It is important to remember that, for the most part, people don't join cults. *Cults recruit people.*

Basic Recruitment Approaches

How can one become more aware of cult recruitment? The best way is to be able to instantly recognize the ways in which cults make their appeals for membership. People being recruited by cults are approached in four basic ways: 1) by a friend or relative who is already a member; 2) by a stranger (often a member of the opposite sex) who befriends them; 3) through a cult-sponsored event, such as a lecture, symposium, or movie; or 4) through social media such as Facebook, YouTube, Vimeo, Instagram, websites, blogs, and so forth. Even Wikipedia is now being actively manipulated by wealthy cult groups. Google, Bing and other search engines are routinely manipulated by some of the wealthier cults, which have small online armies that bury critical information or mount disinformation campaigns against critics.

Usually an individual does not suspect he or she is being recruited. The friend or relative wants to share some incredible insights and experiences. Or they say they "just need your opinion," in order to trick you into an indoctrination session. If the recruiter is a stranger, more often than not you think you've made a good friend. Surveys of present and former cult members indicate that the majority of people recruited into destructive cults were approached *at a vulnerable time of stress in their lives.*[69] The stress is often due to some kind of major transition: moving to a new town, starting a new job, breaking off a relationship, experiencing financial instability, or losing a loved one. People in such situations tend to have defense mechanisms that are overloaded or weakened. If they don't know how to spot and avoid destructive cults, they are easy prey.

It is important to recognize that recruitment doesn't just happen. It is a process imposed on people by other people. High-powered business executives pressured by competition and driven by a need to succeed are recruited by *colleagues*, who tell them about the incredible benefits to be obtained from taking the "course." College students pressured by academic work and a need for acceptance make friends with a *professional cult recruiter*, or go to a group's presentation on some current social issue. A housewife driven by the need to do something with her life follows the example of a *friend* and buys into a pyramid-style household supplies company. A high school student is dared by *peers* into dabbling in satanic rituals.

Other people are initially brought into contact with a cult through an impersonal medium. Some people begin by buying a cult book advertised on TV as a bestseller. Others receive in the mail an invitation to a seemingly harmless Bible-study session. Some people answer a want ad. Some are recruited when they take a job with a cult-owned business.

Whatever the approach, personal contact is eventually made. The recruiter starts to learn all about the potential recruit—their hopes, dreams, fears, relationships, job and interests. The more information the recruiter can elicit, the greater their opportunity to manipulate the person. The recruiter then strategically plans how to bring the person into the group, step by step. The plan might include effusive praise and flattery; introducing the person to another member with similar interests and background; deliberate deception about the group; or evasive maneuvering to avoid answering questions.

Virtually anyone can be seduced into a mind control relationship or recruited into a cult, especially if they don't understand what to watch out for. In the 1970s and early 1980s, the typical cult member was college-aged, but by the late 1980s it had become commonplace for people of all ages to fall victim. Elderly people are quite likely to be recruited.[70] The elderly tend to be solicited for heavy financial contributions or public-relations endorsements. Many middle-aged people are recruited for their professional expertise, to help set up or run cult-owned businesses. Still, young people, for the most part, represent the core workers. They can sleep less, eat less and work harder.

Although the white middle class is still the main target of recruitment, several groups are now actively seeking out blacks, Hispanics, and Asians. As they gather individuals from these communities, they use them to design programs that will bring in others. The big cults have already developed indoctrination programs in Spanish, for example. Another target population is made up of Europeans visiting, going to school or working in the United States. After a few years of training and indoctrination (usually with expired visas), they are sent home to recruit in their own countries. Cults also reach into foreign countries to provide workers. For decades, Scientology has recruited in Africa, eastern Europe and Asia to provide staff for its U.S., UK and Australian organizations. Recruits are offered a 'scholarship' which in reality is a 90-hour work week.

Interestingly, cults generally avoid recruiting people who will burden them, such as those with physical disabilities or severe emotional problems. They want people who will stand up to the grueling demands of cult life. If someone is recruited who uses illegal drugs, they are usually told to either stop using them or leave. To my knowledge, there are few people with disabilities recruited in cults, because it takes time, money, and effort to assist them. People born into cults who develop disabilities are often distanced and sent to government welfare programs.

Cult Life: Illusion And Abuse

Once a person joins a destructive cult, for the first few weeks or months they typically enjoy a "honeymoon phase." They are treated as though they were royalty. They are made to feel very special as they embark on a new life with the group. The new convert has yet to experience what life in the group is really going to be like.

Even though most cult members say publicly that they are happier than they've ever been in their lives, the reality is sadly different. Life in a destructive cult is, for the most part, a life of sacrifice, pain and fear. People involved full-time in a destructive cult know what it is like to live under totalitarianism, but can't objectively see what is happening to them. They live in a fantasy world created by the group.

Some destructive groups essentially make addicts out of their members. With alcoholism and substance abuse treatment so much in the national spotlight today, it is important that mental health professionals pay attention to this former cult member population. People indoctrinated to perform excessive (hours-long) meditation or chanting techniques every day can become psychologically and physiologically addicted to the mind control technique. Such mind-stilling generates strong releases of brain chemicals which cause not only a dissociated mental state but also a "high" similar to that created by drugs and other addictions. Some former members who have used these techniques for several years report a wide variety of deleterious side effects, including severe headaches, involuntary muscle spasms and diminution of cognitive faculties like memory, concentration, and decision-making ability. Of course, some pimps get their victims hooked on heroin or meth or other drugs to control their minds, make them dependent so there are serious health effects and long rehabilitation is needed.

Cult members tend to spend all their time either recruiting more people, fundraising, or working on public relations projects. When people are fully hooked, they donate large amounts of their own money and assets to the group—sometimes everything they own. In exchange, they are promised care and meaning for the rest of their lives. This transaction leaves the person dependent on the group for everything: food, clothing, shelter and health care.

In many groups, however, this care is less than adequate. Medical neglect is rampant. People are made to feel that any medical problem is the result of some personal or spiritual weakness. All they need to do is repent and work harder, and the problem will go away.

Few cults carry health insurance for their devotees, so when a person becomes critically ill, they are often sent as an indigent to a hospital or free clinic. People who worked devotedly for years, sometimes making hundreds of thousands of dollars for the group, are told that the group can't afford to pay their medical bills. Often they are asked to leave the group until they have healed. A person who requires expensive treatment will often be asked to go back to their family, so that the family will pay the bills. If the person doesn't have a family who will help, they may be driven to a hospital and abandoned.

Some cults, like the Followers of Christ,[71] advocate faith healing as the sole treatment for medical problems. The outcome can be great suffering, or even death. People are told that their illness has a spiritual cause, and are made to feel guilty for not totally devoting themselves to the group. Some cults tell members that going to a doctor would show their faithlessness. A few will even threaten to excommunicate members if they seek medical attention.

A related problem is child abuse. Many children have died or been scarred for life because of their parents' involvement in destructive cults.[72] Many people have forgotten that nearly 300 children were murdered during the Jonestown massacre. Those children had no choice but to drink the poisoned Kool-Aid. The public also doesn't know that many of these children were the wards of the state of California and had been adopted by Peoples Temple members to provide more income as well as serve as cheap labor.

Some groups advocate beating and even torturing children to enforce discipline. At Jonestown, at night, some children were put into dark pits that they were told were filled with snakes. Members would dangle ropes from above to scare them. Although Jonestown was an extreme example, several groups do use rods and sticks to beat children, at times for hours and sometimes all over their bodies. Some groups subject children to sexual abuse as a matter of doctrine. Because children are often kept out of school and away from other contact with society, the abuse goes unreported.

Children are often raised communally and allowed only infrequent visits with their parents. The children are taught to place their allegiance with the cult leader or the group as a whole, not with their parents. Playtime is limited or denied altogether. Children typically receive an inferior education, if any. Like their parents, they are taught that the world is a hostile, evil place, and they are forced to depend on cult doctrine to understand reality. Although they may be regarded as the future of the group, they are also usually seen as a hindrance to the immediate demands of the cult's "work."

Terrorist cults are known to abduct children and turn them into killers and rapists. I wish to make special mention of Harvey L. Schwartz's book about trauma inflicted on children recruited to become soldiers, *The Alchemy of Wolves and Sheep: A Relational Approach to Internalized Perpetration in Complex Trauma Survivors*.[73]

The casualties of mind control thus include millions of cult members, their children, and society as well. Our nation is being robbed of our greatest resource: bright, idealistic, ambitious people who are capable of making an enormous contribution to humankind. Many of the former cult members I know have become doctors, teachers, counselors, inventors and artists. Imagine what so many cult members could accomplish if they were all set free to develop their unique talents and abilities. What if they channeled their energies into problem solving, rather than trying to undermine the world's freedoms with some warped totalitarian vision?

In the meanwhile, destructive cult groups continue to grow more numerous and powerful, operating with virtual free license to enslave people. It is ironic that in the United States, a country that cherishes freedom and liberty, citizens are better protected from sales pressure at a used-car lot than they are from organizations whose intent is to hijack their minds and hearts. Until the law sets restrictions on such practices and recognizes the existence of modern mind control techniques, people are mostly left to protect themselves.

Perhaps the single most important thing to realize in dealing with destructive cults is that *we are all vulnerable*. The most we can do to protect ourselves is inform ourselves thoroughly about the ways in which destructive cults operate, and be "good consumers" when approaching any group we might be interested in joining. Friends or relatives of people seeking some kind of major group involvement or passing through times of unusual stress should remain alert to sudden personality changes in those people. If you do suspect that someone you know is coming under the influence of a mind control person or organization, act quickly to seek competent help. Most medical problems respond better to early detection and treatment, and the same principle holds true here.

Be a good consumer about any group that interests you, before you make any commitments. First and foremost, do careful research. One place to start is with my own free site, freedomofmind.com. Other helpful sites include icsahome.com, openmindsfoundation.org, and apologeticsindex.org. However, please don't assume that if a group isn't mentioned on any of these sites as potentially worrisome, it's automatically okay. Dig deeper. In Google or some other search engine, type the name of the organization (with the entire name inside quotation marks) and the word *cult*; also try the name of the group (again, inside quotation marks) and the word *scam* or *scandal*. Try variations with the name of the leader of the group, and words like *criminal*, *abuser* or *sex*. Look at more than the first page or two of results. Cults have learned how to bury negative articles and blogs by manipulating search engines.

In the 21st century, when it comes to *any* group, it's important to do at least as much background research as you would before buying a TV, computer or car.

Chapter 4

Understanding Mind Control

When I do trainings or lectures at colleges, I usually challenge my audience with this question: "How would you *know* if you were under mind control?"

After some reflection, most people realize that if they were under mind control, it would be impossible to determine it without some help from the outside. In addition, they would need to understand very clearly what mind control is. When I was under mind control, I didn't understand what it was all about. I assumed that mind control would involve being tortured in a dank basement somewhere, with a light bulb shining in my face. Of course, that never happened to me while I was in the Moonies. Whenever people yelled at me and called me a "brainwashed robot," I just took it as an expected persecution. It made me feel more committed to the group.

At that time, I didn't have a frame of reference for the phenomenon of mind control. It wasn't until my deprogramming that I was given a credible model of what it is and how it works. Since I was a member of the Moonies and we regarded Communism as the enemy, I was very interested in the techniques that the Chinese Communist Party used to convert people into Communism during the 1950s. I didn't resist, then, when my counselors asked to read me parts of Dr. Robert Jay Lifton's book *Thought Reform and the Psychology of Totalism*.[74] Since the book had been published in 1961, I could not accuse Lifton of being anti-Moon.

That book had a major impact on my understanding of what had happened to me in the Moonies. Lifton identified eight basic elements of the process of mind control as practiced by the Chinese Communists. My counselors pointed out that no matter how wonderful the cause, or how attractive the members, if any group employed all eight of Robert Jay Lifton's elements, then it was practicing mind control. I was eventually able to see that the Unification Church used all eight of those elements: milieu control, mystical manipulation or planned spontaneity, the demand for purity, the cult of confession, sacred science, loading of the language, doctrine over person, and dispensing of existence. (In the Appendix of this book, Lifton describes these eight elements in more detail. Two video interviews with Lifton can be found on my website, freedomofmind.com.)

Before I could leave the Moonies, though, I had to wrestle with several moral questions. Does the God I believe in need to use deception and mind control? Do the ends truly justify the means? Do the means determine the ends? How could the world become a paradise if people's free wills are subverted? What would the world truly look like if Moon assumed total power? Through asking myself these questions, I decided I could no longer participate in an organization that used mind control practices. I left behind the fantasy world I had lived in for years.

Over the years, I have come to realize that millions of people have actually been subjected to a mind control regimen but don't even know it. Hardly a week goes by that I don't talk with several people who are still experiencing negative side effects from their experience of mind control. Often, it is a great relief for them to hear that they are not alone and that their problems stem from their past involvement with such a group.

Perhaps the biggest problem faced by people who have left destructive cults is the disruption of their own authentic identity. There is a very good reason: they have lived for years inside an "artificial" identity given to them by the cult. While cult mind control can be talked about and defined in many different ways, I believe it is best understood as *a system that disrupts an individual's healthy identity development*. An identity is made up of elements such as beliefs, behavior, thought processes and emotions that constitute a definite pattern. Under the influence of mind control, a person's authentic identity given at birth, and as later formed by family, education, friendships, and most importantly that person's own free choices, becomes replaced with another identity, often one that they would not have chosen for themself without tremendous social pressure.[75]

Even if the person gets along through deliberate play-acting at first, the act eventually becomes real. They take on a totalistic ideology that, when internalized, supersedes their prior belief system. Ultimately, the person usually experiences—and shows—a radical personality change and a drastic interruption of their life course.

The process can be initiated quickly, but usually requires days or weeks to solidify. Those unfortunate enough to be born to members of a destructive cult are deprived of a healthy psychological environment in which to mature optimally. That said, children are remarkably resilient and I have met many who described never completely "buying in" to the crazy beliefs and practices. Most ran away or found a way to escape before they became adult. Yet, for others, it took decades to find the strength and the courage to be "true to themselves." Family ties can enforce silence on disbelieving second-generation members. It is easier to go along with the cult than to express their true opinions.

It's worth noting that a group can use mind control in positive ways. For example, many drug rehabilitation and juvenile rehabilitation programs use some of these same methods to re-integrate a person's old identity. But such programs, successful as they may be, are fraught with danger. After the person is broken and given a new identity, they must also have their autonomy and individuality restored. Whether that happens depends entirely on the altruism and responsible behavior of the group's directors. As mentioned earlier, one drug rehabilitation program, Synanon, drew repeated allegations that it abused the most basic rights of its members and was actually a full-fledged cult.[76]

Of course, we are all subjected to various social pressures every day, most noticeably in our families and our work. The pressure to conform to certain standards of behavior exists in nearly every institution. Many kinds of influence are at work on us all the time, some of them obvious and benign (such as "Fasten Your Seat Belt" billboards) and others subtle and destructive. I cannot emphasize too strongly, then, that when I use the term "mind control," I am specifically referring to the destructive end of the spectrum. Therefore, as I have stressed before, the term "mind control" in this book will not apply to certain technologies (biofeedback, for example) that are used to enhance personal control and promote choice. It will refer to only those systems that *seek to undermine an individual's integrity in making independent decisions*. The essence of mind control is that it encourages dependence and conformity, and discourages autonomy and individuality.

Mind Control Versus Brainwashing

While it is important to have a basic understanding of mind control, it is just as important to understand what mind control is not. Unfortunately, in popular discussions of the subject, the term *brainwashing* is often used as a synonym for *mind control* or *undue influence*. On the influence continuum, however, brainwashing belongs closer to the most negative, injurious and extreme end.

The term *brainwashing* was coined in 1951 by journalist and CIA agent Edward Hunter. He used it to describe how American servicemen captured in the Korean War suddenly reversed their values and allegiances, and believed they had committed fictional war crimes. Hunter translated the term from the Chinese *hsi nao*, which means "wash brain."

I think of brainwashing as overtly coercive. The person being brainwashed knows at the outset that they are in the hands of an enemy. The process begins with a clear demarcation of the respective roles—who is prisoner and who is jailer—and the prisoner experiences an absolute minimum of choice. Abusive mistreatment, even torture, and sometimes rape are involved.

Perhaps one of the most famous cases of brainwashing and cult mind control in the United States involved newspaper heiress Patty Hearst. She was kidnapped by the Symbionese Liberation Army (SLA), a small, political, terrorist cult, in 1974, the same month I was recruited into the Moonies. She was locked in a dark closet for weeks and was raped and starved. Later she became an active member of the group as "Tania." She passed up chances to escape and even participated in a bank robbery, for which she was convicted and served a jail term.

Unfortunately, Hearst was the victim of an ignorant judge and jury. She was eventually granted a full pardon by President Clinton, in 2001.

The SLA may have succeeded in brainwashing Patty Hearst, but, on the whole, the coercive approach hasn't had an outstanding success rate. Once people are away from their controllers and back in familiar surroundings, the effects tend to dissipate. The SLA succeeded with Patty Hearst because they gave her a whole new identity. They convinced her that the FBI was out to shoot her on sight. She was convinced her safety lay in remaining with the group rather than seeking rescue.

Brainwashing is especially effective in producing compliance to demands, such as signing a false confession or denouncing one's government. People are coerced into specific acts for self-preservation; then, once they have acted, their beliefs change to rationalize what they have done. But these beliefs are usually not well internalized. If and when the prisoner escapes their field of influence (and fear), they are usually able to throw off those beliefs.

Mind control is much more subtle and sophisticated. The victim typically regards the controllers as friends or peers, so is much less on guard. They usually unwittingly participate by cooperating with their controllers, and by giving them private information that they do not realize will be used against them.

Mind control involves little or no overt physical abuse. Instead, *hypnotic processes* are combined with *group dynamics* to create a potent indoctrination effect. The individual is deceived and manipulated—but not directly threatened—into making the prescribed choices. On the whole, the victim responds positively to what is done to them.

It is unfortunate that the word *brainwashing* is used loosely. People inside most cults aren't physically tortured, so when critics accuse them of having been brainwashed, the accusation doesn't ring true. When I was in the Moonies, I knew I hadn't been brainwashed. I do remember, however, Moon giving us a speech in which he said that a popular magazine had accused him of brainwashing us. He declared, "Americans' minds are very dirty—full of selfish materialism and drugs—and they *need* a heavenly brainwashing!"[77] We all laughed.

A Note On Hypnotism

The term hypnotism is also misused. We use the term hypnotism in our normal speech—we sometimes say such things as, "She hypnotized him with her smile." Actually, hypnosis is little understood by most people. When the term is mentioned, the first image that may come to mind is of a bearded doctor dangling an old pocket watch by its chain in front of a droopy-eyed subject. While that image is certainly a stereotype, it does point to the central feature of hypnotism: the trance. People who are hypnotized enter a trance-like state that is fundamentally different from normal consciousness. The difference is this: whereas in normal consciousness the attention is focused outwards through the five senses, in a trance one's attention is usually focused *inwards*. One is hearing, seeing and feeling internally. Of course, there are various degrees of trance, ranging from the mild and normal trance of daydreaming to deeper states in which one is much less aware of the outside world and extremely susceptible to suggestions that may be put into one's mind.

Hypnotism relates to the unethical mind control practices of destructive cults in a variety of ways. In many cults which claim to be religious, what is often called "meditation" is no more than a process by which the cult members enter a trance, during which time they may receive suggestions which make them more receptive to following the cult's doctrine. Non-religious cults use other forms of group or individual induction. In addition, being in a trance is usually a pleasant, relaxing experience, so that people wish to re-enter the trance as often as possible. Most importantly, it has been clinically established by psychological researchers that people's critical faculties are diminished in the trance state. One is less able to evaluate information received in a trance than when in a normal state of consciousness.

The power of hypnosis to affect people can be considerable. People who are "high hypnotizables"—can be put into a trance very quickly and perform remarkable feats. During stage hypnosis shows subjects have been directed to dance like Elvis Presley (to the audience's laughter); lie down between two chairs and assume a wooden boardlike rigidity; believe they are naked (when they are fully clothed) or behave as though their hands were "glued" to their sides. If people can be made to perform these acts in just a few minutes of influence, getting hypnotic subjects to believe that they are part of a "chosen few" with many hours, days or weeks of programming is very achievable.

Destructive cults commonly induce trances in their members through lengthy indoctrination sessions. Repetition, boredom and forced attention are very conducive to the induction of a trance. Looking at a group in such a setting, it is easy to see when the trance has set in. The audience will exhibit slowed blink and swallow reflexes, and their facial expressions will relax into a blank, neutral state. With people in such a state, it is possible for unscrupulous leaders to implant irrational beliefs. I have seen many strong-willed people hypnotized and made to do things they would never normally do.

Basic Principles Of Social Psychology And Group Dynamics

The political experience of World War II, in which thousands of apparently normal people operated concentration camps in which millions of Jews, Romanies, Slavs, blacks, gays and communists were killed, provoked considerable interest among psychologists.[78] How was it that people who had led ordinary lives prior to Adolf Hitler's rise to power became involved in a deliberate attempt to exterminate whole groups of people?

Thousands of social psychological experiments have been conducted since World War II, yielding great insights into the various ways people are influenced, both as groups and as individuals. The result of these studies has been the consistent demonstration of the remarkable power of *behavior modification techniques, group conformity* and *obedience to authority*. These three factors are known in psychological terms as "influence processes" and demonstrate that situations often determine human behaviors, often more than the values and beliefs of the individual. One of the most remarkable discoveries of social psychology is that people are hardwired to unconsciously respond to social cues.

For example, a class of psychology students once conspired to use behavior modification techniques on their teacher. As the professor lectured, the students would smile and seem attentive when he moved toward the left of the room. When he moved to the right, the students acted bored and listless. Before long, the professor began to drift to the left, and after a few classes he spent each lecture leaning against the left wall.

But when the students let the professor in on the experiment, *he insisted that nothing of the sort had happened.* He saw nothing odd about leaning against the wall, and angrily insisted that it was merely his personal lecturing style—something he had chosen to do of his own free will. This psychology professor was completely unconscious of how he had been influenced.

Of course, under ordinary circumstances, the people around us are not all secretly conspiring to make us do anything. They simply act more or less as they have been culturally conditioned to act, which in turn conditions us. This is the way in which a culture perpetuates itself.

In a destructive cult, however, the behavior modification process is completely stage-managed around new recruits, who of course have no idea of what is going on.

If behavior modification techniques are powerful, so too are the influences of conformity and obedience to authority. A famous experiment in conformity by Dr. Solomon Asch demonstrated that most people will conform—and even doubt their own perceptions—if they are put in a social situation where the most confident people in the group all give the same wrong answers.[79] Another social psychologist, Stanley Milgram, tested people for obedience to authority and found that over 90 percent of his subjects would obey orders, even if they believed that doing so caused physical suffering to another person. Milgram wrote, "The essence of obedience consists in the fact that a person comes to view himself as the instrument for carrying out another person's wishes, and therefore no longer regards himself as responsible for his own actions."[80]

Dr. Philip Zimbardo conducted a world-famous prison experiment in the basement of the Psychology building at Stanford University in 1971. He demonstrated the "power of the situation," which he described in detail in his book *The Lucifer Effect*. Healthy, normal young men were randomly divided into two groups: one of prisoners and one of guards, who were to manage the prisoners. This was to be a two-week experiment, but it had to be called off after only six days, because some of the guards had become sadistic, and some of the prisoners had broken down mentally.

Good people started behaving badly when put in a bad situation and were unaware of the mind control forces at work. We are unconsciously wired to adapt and conform to promote our survival. When we are confused or not sure what to do, we look to others in our environment and especially to people we deem to be legitimate authority figures. Most people conform to fit in. The groundbreaking work of Philip Zimbardo and others has enormous implications. Zimbardo, who is Professor Emeritus at Stanford University and former President of the American Psychological Association, taught a course for 15 years called *The Psychology of Mind Control*.[81]

The BITE Model: The Four Components Of Mind Control[82]

Clearly, one cannot begin to understand mind control without realizing the power of behavior modification techniques, as well as the influences of conformity and obedience to authority. If we take these insights from social psychology as a foundation, we may be able to identify the basic components of mind control.

As I have come to see it, mind control can be largely understood by analysis of the three components described by psychologist Leon Festinger, in what has become known as the "cognitive dissonance theory."[83] These components are *control of behavior, control of thoughts* and *control of emotions*.

Each component has a powerful effect on the other two: change one, and the others will tend to follow. Succeed in changing all three, and the individual will be swept away. However, from my experience in researching destructive cults, I have added one more component that is vital: *control of information*. If you control the information someone receives, you restrict his ability to think for himself.

These four components of mind control serve as the basic reference points for understanding how mind control works.

Cognitive dissonance theory is not as forbidding as its name might sound. In 1950, Festinger summarized its basic principle this way: "If you change a person's behavior, his thoughts and feelings will change to minimize the dissonance."[84] What did Festinger mean by "dissonance?" In basic terms, he was referring to the conflict that occurs when a thought, a feeling or a behavior is altered in contradiction to the other two. A person can tolerate only a certain amount of discrepancy between his thoughts, feelings and actions, which after all make up the different components of his identity. Festinger's theory states—and a great deal of later research has confirmed—that if any one of the three components changes, the other two will shift to reduce the dissonance.

How does this kind of shift apply to the behavior of people in cults? Festinger looked for a place to examine his ideas in the real world. In 1956 he published a book, *When Prophecy Fails*, about a Wisconsin flying saucer cult, whose leader had predicted the end of the world. The cult leader claimed to be in mental contact with aliens from another planet. Followers sold their homes, gave away their money, and stood at the appointed date on a mountainside, waiting all night to be picked up by flying saucers before a flood destroyed the world the next morning.

When morning came with no saucers and no flood—just a spate of satirical news stories about the group—the followers might have been expected to become disillusioned and angry. And a few did—but they were fringe members who had not invested much time or energy. Most members, however, became more convinced than ever. Their leader proclaimed that the aliens had witnessed their faithful vigil and decided to spare the Earth. Members wound up feeling *more* committed to the leader, even after they took a dramatic public stance that resulted in public humiliation. Most Jehovah's Witnesses responded to the failure of the group's many prophecies of the end of the world with renewed faith.

Cognitive dissonance theory helps explain why this heightened commitment occurred. According to Festinger, people need to maintain order and meaning in their life. They need to think they are acting according to their self-image and their own values. If their behavior changes for any reason, their self-image and values change to match. The important thing to recognize about cult groups is that they deliberately create dissonance in people this way and exploit it to control them.

To make it easier to remember, I call it the **BITE** model of mind control: **B**ehavior, **I**nformation, **T**hought and **E**motional Control. Let's take a closer look at each one of these components of mind control.

Behavior Control

Behavior control is the regulation of an individual's physical reality. It includes the control of their environment—where they live, what clothes they wear, what food they eat, how much sleep they get, and what jobs, rituals and other actions they perform.

This need for behavior control is the reason most cults prescribe a very rigid schedule for their members. Each day a significant amount of time is devoted to cult rituals and indoctrination activities. Members are also typically assigned to accomplish specific goals and tasks, thus restricting their free time—and their behavior. In destructive cults there is always something to do.

In some of the more restrictive groups, members have to ask permission from leaders to do almost anything. In other groups, a person is made so financially dependent that their choices of behavior are narrowed automatically. A member must ask for bus fare, clothing money or permission to seek health care—things most of us take for granted. Often the person must ask permission to call a friend or relative not in the group. Every hour of the cult member's day has to be accounted for. In these ways the group can keep a tight rein on the member's behavior—and on their thoughts and feelings as well.

Behavior is often controlled by the requirement that everyone act as a group. In many cults, people eat together, work together, have group meetings and sometimes sleep together in the same dormitory. Individualism is fiercely discouraged. People may be assigned a constant "buddy" or be placed in a small unit of a half dozen members.

The chain of command in cults is usually authoritarian, flowing from the leader, through their lieutenants, to their sub-leaders, down to the rank and file. In such a well-regulated environment, all behaviors can be either rewarded or punished. If a person performs well, they will be given public praise from higher-ups, and sometimes gifts or a promotion. If the person performs poorly, they may be publicly singled out and criticized, or forced to do manual labor such as cleaning toilets or polishing other members' shoes. Other forms of punishment may include prescribed fasting, cold showers, staying up for an all-night vigil or doing remedial work. Those who actively participate in their own punishment will eventually come to believe they deserve it.

Each particular group has its own distinctive set of ritual behaviors that help bind it together. These typically include mannerisms of speech, specific posture and facial expressions, as well as the more traditional ways of representing group belief. In the Moonies, for instance, we followed many Asian customs, such as taking off our shoes when entering a Moonie center, kneeling and bowing when greeting older members. Doing these little things helped make us feel we were special and superior. Psychologists call this "social proof."

If a member is not behaving sufficiently enthusiastically, they may be confronted by a leader and accused of being selfish or impure, or of not trying hard enough. They will be urged to become like an older group member, even to the extent of mimicking that person's tone of voice.

Obedience to a leader's command is the most important lesson to learn. A cult's leaders cannot command someone's inner thoughts, but they know that if they command *behavior*, hearts and minds will follow.

Information Control

Information control is the second component of mind control. Information provides the tools with which we think and understand reality. Without accurate, up-to-date information, we can easily be manipulated and controlled. Deny a person the information they require to make sound judgments and they will become incapable of doing so.

Deception is the biggest tool of information control, because it robs people of the ability to make informed decisions. Outright lying, withholding information and distorting information all become essential strategies, especially when recruiting new members. By using deception, cults rob their victims of "informed consent" and in the case of religious cults, this lack of honest disclosure most certainly violates people's individual religious rights.

In many totalistic cults, people have minimal access to non-cult newspapers, magazines, TV, radio and online information. Certain information may be forbidden and labeled as unhealthy: apostate literature, entheta (negative information), satanic, bourgeoisie propaganda, and so on. Members are also kept so busy that they don't have free time to think and seek outside answers to questions. When they do read, it is primarily cult-generated propaganda or material that has been censored to keep members focused.

Information control also extends across all relationships. People are not allowed to talk to each other about anything critical of the leader, doctrine, or organization. Members must spy on each other and report improper activities or comments to leaders, often in the form of written reports (a technique pioneered by the Nazis, with the Hitler Youth). New converts are discouraged from sharing doubts with anyone other than a superior. Newbies are typically chaperoned, until they prove their devotion and loyalty. Most importantly, people are told to avoid contact with ex-members and critics. Those people who could provide the most outside—that is, *real*—information are to be completely shunned. Some groups even go so far as to screen members' letters and phone calls.

Information is usually compartmentalized, to keep members from knowing the big picture. In larger groups, people are told only as much as they "need to know" in order to perform their jobs. A member in one city therefore does not necessarily know about an important legal decision, media story, or internal dispute that is creating turmoil in the group somewhere else. Cult members naturally feel they know more about what's going on in their group than outsiders, but in counseling ex-members, I have found that they often know far less than almost anyone else. Moonies are often ignorant of their cult's involvement in arms manufacture, and Scientologists of the imprisonment of eleven leaders for the largest infiltration of government agencies ever undertaken.

Destructive organizations also control information by having many levels of "truth." Cult ideologies often have "outsider" doctrines and "insider" doctrines. The outsider material is relatively bland stuff for the general public or new converts. The inner doctrines are gradually unveiled, as the person is more deeply involved and only when the person is deemed "ready" by superiors.

For example, Moonies always said publicly that they were pro-American, pro-democracy and pro-family. The Moonies *were* pro-American, in that they wanted what they thought was best for America, which was to become a theocracy under Moon's rule. They believed democracy was instituted by God to allow the Unification Church the space to organize a theocratic dictatorship. They *were* pro-family in believing that every human being's true family was Moon, his wife and his spiritual children. Yet the inner doctrine was—and still is—that America is inferior to Korea and must become subservient to it; that democracy is a foolish system that "God is phasing out";[85] and that people must be cut off from their "physical" (as opposed to "spiritual") families if they are at all critical of the cult.

A member can sincerely believe that the outer doctrines are not lies, but just a different level of truth. By creating an environment where truth is multileveled, cult directors make it nearly impossible for a member to make definitive, objective assessments. If they have problems, they are told that they are not mature or advanced enough to know the whole truth yet. But they are assured that all will become clear shortly. If they work hard, they'll earn the right to understand the higher levels of truth.

But often there are many inner levels or layers of belief. Often an advanced member who thinks they know a cult's complete doctrine is still several layers away from what the higher ups know. Questioners who insist on knowing too much too fast, of course, are redirected toward an external goal until they forget their objections or they object too loudly and are kicked out and vilified.

Thought Control

Thought control, the third major component of mind control, includes indoctrinating members so thoroughly that they internalize the group doctrine, incorporate a new language system, and use thought-stopping techniques to keep their mind "centered." In order to be a good member, a person must learn to manipulate their own thought processes.

In totalistic cults, the ideology is internalized as "the truth," the only map of reality. The doctrine not only serves to filter incoming information, but also regulates how the information can be thought about. Usually, the doctrine is absolutist, dividing everything into black versus white, or us versus them. All that is good is embodied in the leader and the group. All that is bad is on the outside. The doctrine claims to answer all questions to all problems and situations. Members need not think for themselves because the doctrine does the thinking for them. The more totalistic groups claim that their doctrine is scientific, but that is never truly the case.

A destructive cult inevitably has its own "loaded language" of unique words and expressions. Since language provides the symbols we use for thinking, using only certain words serves to control thoughts. Cult language is totalistic and therefore condenses complex situations, labels them, and reduces them to cult clichés. This simplistic label then governs how members think in any situation.[86] In the Moonies, for example, whenever a member had difficulty relating to someone who was either above or below them in status, it was called a *Cain-Abel problem*. It didn't matter who was involved or what the problem was—it was simply a Cain-Abel problem. The term itself dictated how the problem had to be resolved. Cain needed to obey Abel and follow him, rather than kill him (as Cain killed Abel in the Old Testament). Case closed. To think otherwise would be to obey Satan's wish that evil Cain should prevail over righteous Abel. Clearly, a critical thought about a leader's misconduct cannot get past this roadblock in a devout member's mind.

The cult's clichés and loaded language also put up an invisible wall between believers and outsiders. The language helps to make members feel special, and separates them from the general public. It also serves to confuse newcomers, who want to understand what members are talking about. The newbies think they merely have to study harder in order to understand the truth, which they believe is precisely expressed in this new language. In reality, though, loaded language helps them learn how *not* to think or understand. They learn that "understanding" means accepting and believing.

Another key aspect of thought control involves training members to block out any information that is critical of the group. A member's normal defense mechanisms often become so twisted that they defend their own new cult identity against their old, former self. The first line of defense includes denial—"What you say isn't happening at all"; rationalization—"This is happening for a good reason"; justification—"This is happening because it ought to"; and wishful thinking—"I'd like it to be true so maybe it really is."

If information transmitted to a cult member is perceived as an attack on either the leader, the doctrine or the group, a defensive wall goes up. Members are trained to disbelieve any criticism. Critical words have been explained away in advance—for instance, as "the lies about us that Satan puts in people's minds" or "the lies that the World Conspiracy prints in the news media to discredit us, because they know we're onto them." Paradoxically, criticism of the group is used to confirm that the cult's view of the world is correct. Because of thought control, factual information that challenges the cult worldview does not register properly.

Perhaps the most widely used, and most effective, technique for controlling cult members' thoughts is *thought-stopping*.[87] Members are taught to use thought-stopping on themselves. They are told it will help them grow, stay "pure and true" or be more effective. Whenever cult members experience a "bad" thought, they use thought-stopping to halt the "negativity" and center themselves, thus shutting out anything that threatens or challenges the cult's version of reality.

Different groups use different thought-stopping techniques, which can include concentrated praying, chanting aloud or silently, meditating, speaking in tongues, singing or humming. These actions, at times useful and valuable, thus become perverted in destructive cults. They also become quite mechanical, because the person is programmed to activate them at the first sign of doubt, anxiety or uncertainty. In a matter of weeks, the technique becomes ingrained. It becomes so automatic, in fact, that the person is usually not even aware that they just had a "bad" thought. They are only aware that they are suddenly chanting or ritualizing.

Through the use of thought-stopping, members think they are growing, when in reality they are just turning themselves into thought-stopping addicts. After leaving a cult that employs extensive thought-stopping techniques, a person normally goes through a difficult withdrawal process before they can overcome this addiction.

Thought-stopping is the most direct way to short-circuit a person's ability to test reality. Indeed, if people are able to think *only* positive thoughts about their involvement with the group, they are most certainly stuck. Since the doctrine is perfect and the leader is perfect, any problem that crops up is assumed to be the fault of the individual member. They learn to always to blame themselves and simply work harder.

Thought control can effectively block out any feelings that do not correspond with the group doctrine. It can also serve to keep a cult member working as an obedient slave. In any event, when thought is controlled, feelings and behaviors are usually controlled as well.

Emotional Control

Emotional control, the fourth component of the BITE model, attempts to manipulate and narrow the range of a person's feelings. All or nothing. Either you feel wonderful as a "chosen" member of the elite, someone really special and loved and part of a wonderful movement; or you are broken, unspiritual, have bad karma, are guilty of *overts*, are sinful and need to repent, try harder and become a better, more devoted member. Guilt and fear figure mightily. However, most cult members can't see that guilt and fear are being used to control them. They are both essential tools to keep people under control.

Guilt comes in many forms. Historical guilt (for instance, the fact that the United States dropped the atomic bomb on Hiroshima), identity guilt (a thought such as "I'm not living up to my potential"), guilt over past actions ("I cheated on a test") and social guilt ("People are dying of starvation") can all be exploited by destructive cult leaders. Members are conditioned to always take the blame, so that they respond gratefully whenever a leader points out one of their "shortcomings."

Fear is used to bind the group members together in several ways. The first is the creation of an outside enemy, who is persecuting the group and its members. For example, the FBI will jail or kill you; Satan will carry you off to Hell; psychiatrists will give you electroshock therapy; armed members of rival sects will shoot or torture you; and, of course, ex-members and critics will try to persecute you. Second is the terror of discovery and punishment by cult members and leaders. Fear of what can happen to you if you don't do your job well can be very potent. Some groups claim that nuclear holocaust or other disasters will result if members are lax in their commitment.

In order to control someone through their emotions, feelings themselves often have to be redefined. For example, everyone wants happiness. However, if happiness is redefined as being closer to God, and God is unhappy (as He apparently is in many religious cults), then the way to be happy is to be unhappy. Happiness, therefore, consists of suffering so you can grow closer to God. This idea also appears in some non-cult theologies, but in a cult it is a tool for exploitation and control.

In some groups, happiness simply means following the leader's directions, recruiting a lot of new members, or bringing in a lot of money. Or, happiness is defined as the sense of community provided by the cult to those who enjoy high status within it.

Loyalty and devotion are the most highly respected emotions of all. Members are not allowed to feel or express negative emotions, except toward outsiders. They are taught never to feel for themselves or their own needs, but always to think of the group and never to complain. They are never to criticize a leader, but to criticize themselves instead.

Many groups exercise complete control over interpersonal relationships. Leaders can and do tell people to avoid certain members or spend time with others. Some even tell members whom they can marry, and control the entire relationship, including their sex lives. Some groups require members to deny or suppress sexual feelings, which become a source of bottled-up frustration that can be channeled into other outlets such as harder work. Other groups *require* sexuality, and a member who hangs back is made to feel selfish. Either way, the group is exercising emotional control.

People are often kept off balance, praised one minute and tongue-lashed the next. In some groups, one day you'll be doing public relations before TV cameras in a suit and tie; the next, you'll be in another state doing manual labor as punishment for some imagined sin. This misuse of reward and punishment fosters dependency and helplessness. Such double-bind behavior is a commonplace in cults.

Confession of past sins or wrong attitudes is also a powerful device for emotional control. Of course, once someone has publicly confessed, rarely is their old sin truly forgiven or forgotten. The minute they get out of line, it will be hauled out and used to manipulate them into obeying. Anyone who finds themselves in a cult confession session needs to remember this warning: Anything you say can *and will* be used against you. This device can even extend to blackmail, if you leave the cult. Even when it does not, former members are often scared to speak out, just in case their embarrassing secrets are made public.

The most powerful technique for emotional control is phobia indoctrination, which was described in Chapter 3. Members will have a panic reaction at the thought of leaving the group. They are told that if they leave they will be lost and defenseless in the face of dark horrors. They'll go insane, be killed, become drug addicts or commit suicide. Such tales are repeated often, both in lectures and in hushed tones through informal gossip. It becomes nearly impossible for indoctrinated cult members to feel they can have any happiness, security or fulfillment outside the group.

When cult leaders tell the public, "Members are free to leave any time they want; the door is open," they give the impression that members have free will and are simply choosing to stay. Actually, members may not have a real choice, because they have been indoctrinated to fear the outside world. If a person's emotions are successfully brought under the group's control, their thoughts and behavior will follow.

Each component of the BITE model: behavior control, information control, thought control, emotional control—has great influence on the human mind. Together, they form a totalistic web, one that can be used to manipulate even the most intelligent, creative, ambitious and strong-willed person. In fact, it is often the strongest-minded individuals who make the most involved and enthusiastic cult members.

I have attempted to cover only the broadest and most common practices within each component of mind control. No one group does everything described in this section. Other practices are used by certain cults but are not included here.

Some practices could fall into more than one of these categories. For example, some groups change people's names in order to hasten the formation of the new "cult" identity. This technique could fall under all four categories. There are many variations between groups. For example, some groups are overt in their phobia indoctrination; others are extremely subtle. What matters most is the overall impact on the individual. Are they truly in control of their life choices? The only way to tell is to give them the opportunity to reflect, to gain free access to all information and to know that they are free to leave the group if they choose.

Three Steps To Gaining Control Of The Mind

It is one thing to identify the four components of mind control but quite another to know how they are actually used to change the behavior of unsuspecting people. On the surface, the process of gaining control of someone else's mind seems quite simple. There are three steps: *unfreezing*, *changing* and *refreezing*.

This three-step model was derived in the late 1940s from the work of Kurt Lewin,[88] and was described in Edgar Schein's book *Coercive Persuasion*.[89] Schein, like Lifton, studied the brainwashing programs in Mao Tse Tung's China, in the late 1950s. His book, based on interviews with former American prisoners, is a valuable study of the process. Schein's three steps apply just as well to other forms of mind control as they do to brainwashing. As he described them, *unfreezing* consists of breaking a person down; *changing* constitutes the indoctrination process; and *refreezing* is the process of building up and reinforcing the new identity.

Destructive cults today have the added advantage of many decades of psychological research and techniques, making their mind control programs much more effective and dangerous than in the past. Hypnotic processes, for example, are much more significant parts of modern mind control. In addition, modern destructive cults also tend to be more flexible in their approach. They are willing and able to change their approach to fit a person's specific psychological make-up, use deception and highly sophisticated loaded language, or employ techniques like thought-stopping and phobia indoctrination.

Let's take a closer look at this three-stage model to see how the step-by-step program creates a well-disciplined cult member.

Unfreezing

To ready a person for radical change, their reality must first be shaken up. Their indoctrinators must confuse and disorient them. Their frames of reference for understanding themselves and their surroundings must be challenged and broken down. Upsetting their view of reality disarms their natural defenses against concepts that challenge that reality.

Unfreezing can be accomplished through a variety of approaches. Disorienting a person physiologically can be very effective. Sleep deprivation is one of the most common and powerful techniques for breaking a person down. In addition, new diets and eating schedules can also have a disorienting effect. Some groups use low-protein, high-sugar diets, or prolonged underfeeding, to undermine a person's physical integrity.

Unfreezing is most effectively accomplished in a totally controlled environment, like an isolated country estate, but it can also be accomplished in more familiar and easily accessible places, such as a hotel ballroom.

Hypnotic processes constitute another powerful tool for unfreezing and side-stepping a person's defense mechanisms. One particularly effective hypnotic technique involves the deliberate use of confusion to induce a trance state. Confusion usually results whenever contradictory information is communicated congruently. For example, if a hypnotist says in an authoritative tone of voice, "The more you try to understand what I am saying, the less you will never be able to understand it. Do you understand?" the result is a state of temporary confusion. If you read it over and over again, you may conclude that the statement is simply contradictory and nonsensical. However, if a person is kept in a controlled environment long enough, and is repeatedly fed such disorienting language and confusing information, they will usually suspend their critical judgment and adapt to what everyone else is doing. In such an environment, the tendency of most people is to doubt themselves and defer to the group.

Sensory overload, like sensory deprivation, can also effectively disrupt a person's balance and make them more open to suggestion. A person can easily be bombarded by emotionally laden material at a rate faster than they can digest it. The result is a feeling of being overwhelmed. The mind snaps into neutral and ceases to evaluate the material pouring in. The newcomer may think this is happening spontaneously within themselves, but the cult has intentionally structured it that way.

Other hypnotic techniques, such as double binds,[90] can also be used to help unfreeze a person's sense of reality. A double bind forces a person to do what the controller wants while giving an illusion of choice. For example, a cult leader may say, "For those people who are having doubts about what I am telling you, you should know that *I* am the one putting those doubts inside your mind, so that you will see the truth that I am the true teacher." Whether the person believes or doubts the leader, both bases are covered.

Another example of a double bind is, "If you admit there are things in your life that aren't working, then by not taking the seminar, you are giving those things power to control your life." The message is: *Just being here proves you are incompetent to judge whether or not to leave.*

Exercises such as guided meditations, personal confessions, prayer sessions, vigorous calisthenics and even group singing can also aid unfreezing. Typically, these activities start out quite innocuously, but gradually become more intense and directed. They are almost always conducted in a group. This enforces privacy deprivation and thwarts a person's need to be alone, think and reflect.

At this stage of unfreezing, as people are weakening, most cults bombard them with the idea that they are seriously flawed—incompetent, mentally ill or spiritually fallen. Any problems that are important to the person, such as doing poorly in school or at work, being overweight, or having trouble in a relationship, are blown out of proportion to prove how completely messed up the person is. Some groups can be quite vicious in their attacks on individuals at this stage, often humiliating them in front of the whole group.

Once a person is broken down, they are ready for the next phase.

Changing

Changing consists of imposing a new personal identity—a new set of behaviors, thoughts, and emotions—to fill the void left by the breakdown of the old one. Indoctrination in this new identity takes place both formally (for instance, through seminars and rituals) and informally (by spending time with members, reading, and listening to recordings and videos). Many of the same techniques used in the unfreezing phase are also carried into this phase.

Repetition, monotony, rhythm: these are the lulling, hypnotic cadences in which the formal indoctrination is generally delivered. Material is repeated over and over and over. If the lecturers are sophisticated, they vary their talks somewhat in an attempt to hold interest, but the message remains pretty much the same.

During the changing phase, all this repetition focuses on certain central themes. The recruits are told how bad the world is and that the unenlightened have no idea how to fix it. This is because ordinary people lack the new understanding that has been provided by the leader. The leader is the only hope of lasting happiness. Recruits are told, "Your old self is what's keeping you from fully experiencing the new truth. Your old concepts are what drag you down. Your rational mind is holding you back from fantastic progress. Surrender. Let go. Have faith." Scientologists are told that they must put their minds under the control of a counselor, to show that their minds can be controlled.

Behaviors are shaped subtly at first, then more forcefully. The material that will make up the new identity is doled out gradually, piece by piece, only as fast as the person is deemed ready to assimilate it. The rule of thumb is, "Tell the new member only what they are ready to accept."

When I was a lecturer in the Moonies, I remember discussing this policy with others involved in recruiting. I was taught this analogy: "You wouldn't feed a baby thick pieces of steak, would you? You have to feed a baby something it can digest, like formula. Well, these people (potential converts) are spiritual babies. Don't tell them more than they can handle, or they will die." If a recruit became angry because they were learning too much about the real workings of our organization, the person working on them would back off and let another member move in to spoon-feed them some pablum.

The formal indoctrination sessions can be very droning and rhythmic—a way to induce hypnotic states. It is fairly common for people to fall asleep during these programs. When I was a cult lecturer, I was taught to chastise people and made them feel guilty if they fell asleep, but in fact they were merely responding well to hypnosis. Even while lightly dozing, a person is still more or less hearing the material and being affected by it, with their normal intellectual defenses down.

Another potent technique for change is the induced "spiritual experience." This is often contrived in the most artificial manner. Private information about the recruit is collected by the person's closest buddy in the group and then secretly passed to the leadership. Later, at the right moment, this information can be pulled out suddenly to create an "experience." Perhaps weeks later, in another state, a leader suddenly confronts a recruit about their brother's suicide. Knowing that they didn't tell anyone in this new place about it, the recruit thinks the leader has read their thoughts or is being informed directly by the spirit world. The recruit is overcome and begs forgiveness for not being a better member.

Destructive religious cults are not the only ones to engineer "mystical" experiences. One martial artist and self-professed mentalist who formed his own cult secretly paid hoodlums to mug his students on the street, in order to heighten their fear of the outside world and become more dependent on him. Another cult leader, a psychotherapist, manipulated one of his clients by confronting her inability to stay on her diet. She believed that he had special powers. He didn't tell her that he had seen her earlier that day eating an ice cream sundae. She believed that he had special "powers."

A common technique among religious cults is to instruct people to ask God what He wants them to do. Members are exhorted to study and pray in order to know God's will for them. It is always implied that joining the group is God's will and leaving the group is betraying God. Of course, if a person tells the cult leader, "I prayed, and God told me to leave," this will not be accepted.

Perhaps the most powerful persuasion is exerted by other cult members. For the average person, talking with an indoctrinated cultist is quite an experience. You'll probably never meet anyone else who is so absolutely convinced that they know what is best for you. A dedicated cult member also does not take no for an answer, because they have been indoctrinated to believe that if you don't join, either you are evil or *they* are to blame. This creates a lot of pressure on them to succeed.

When someone is completely surrounded by such people, group psychology plays a major role in the changing process. People are deliberately organized into specific small groups, or cells. People who ask too many questions are quickly isolated from the main body of other members.

In the Moonies, we would set up teams at the beginning of a workshop to evaluate the recruits. We would divide them into sheep and goats, and assign them to groups accordingly. The sheep were the ones who were "spiritually prepared." Goats were stubborn individualists who were not expected to make good members. If they couldn't be broken, their "negativity" was safely confined to a goat team where sheep couldn't see it, and they could be asked to leave. (After I left the Moonies, I was amazed to learn that entirely different cults were doing the same thing. I thought "The Family" had invented the technique.)

But the changing process involves much more than obedience to a cult's authority figures. It also includes numerous "sharing" sessions with other ordinary members, where past evils are confessed, present success stories are told, and a sense of community is fostered. These group sessions are very effective in teaching conformity, because the group vigorously reinforces certain behaviors by effusive praise and acknowledgement, while punishing non-group ideas and behaviors with icy silence.

Human beings have an incredible capacity to adapt to new environments. Charismatic cult leaders know how to exploit this strength. By controlling a person's environment, using behavior modification to reward some behaviors and suppress others, and inducing hypnotic states, they may indeed reprogram a person's identity.

Once a person has been fully broken down through the process of changing, they are ready for the next step.

Refreezing

The recruit must now be built up again as the "new man" or "new woman." They are given a new purpose in life, and new activities that will solidify their new identity. Cult leaders must be reasonably sure the new cult identity will be strong when the person leaves the immediate cult environment. So the new values and beliefs must be fully internalized by the recruit.

Many of the techniques from the first two stages are carried over into the refreezing phase. The first and most important task of the new person is to denigrate their previous *sinful* self. The worst thing is for the person to act like their old self. The best is for them to act like their new cult self, which is often fully formed within a few months, or even days.

During this phase, an individual's memory becomes distorted, minimizing the good things in the past and maximizing their sins, failings, hurts and guilt. Special talents, interests, hobbies, friends, and family usually must be abandoned—preferably in dramatic public actions—if they compete with commitment to the cause. Confession becomes another way to purge the person's past and embed them in the cult.

During the refreezing phase, the primary method for passing on new information is modeling. New members are paired with older members, who are assigned to show them the ropes. The "spiritual child" is instructed to imitate the "spiritual parent" in all ways. This technique serves several purposes. It keeps the "older" member on their best behavior, while gratifying their ego. At the same time, it whets the new member's appetite to become a respected model, so they can train junior members of their own.

The group now forms the member's "true" family; any other is considered their outmoded "physical" family. Some cults insist on a very literal transfer of family loyalty. Jim Jones was one of many cult leaders who insisted that his followers call him "Dad."

In my own case, I ceased to be Steve Hassan, son of Milton and Estelle Hassan, and became Steve Hassan, son of Sun Myung Moon and Hak Ja Han, the "True Parents" of all creation. In every waking moment, I was reminded to be a small Sun Myung Moon, the greatest person in human history. As my cult identity was put into place, I wanted to think like him, feel like him and act like him. When faced with a problem, Scientologists are encouraged to ask, "What would Ron (Hubbard) do?"

To help refreeze the member's new identity, some cults give them a new name. Many also change the person's clothing style, haircut, and whatever else would remind them of their past. As mentioned, members often learn to speak a distinctive jargon or loaded language of the group.

Great pressure is usually exerted on the member to turn over money and other possessions. This serves multiple purposes. First, it enriches the cult. Second, donating one's life savings freezes the person in the new belief system, since it would be too painful to admit that this was a foolish mistake. Consistency is an important aspect of influence. Third, it makes financial survival in the outside world appear harder, thus discouraging the person from leaving.

Sleep deprivation, lack of privacy, and dietary changes are sometimes continued for several months or even longer. Often the new member is relocated away from familiar surroundings and sources of influence, into a new place where they have never been anything but their new self. This further fosters dependency on cult authority figures.

The new member is typically assigned to proselytizing duty as soon as possible. Research in social psychology has shown that nothing firms up one's beliefs faster than recruiting others to share them. Making new members do so quickly crystallizes their new cult identity.

Some groups finance themselves by difficult and humiliating fundraising methods, such as all-day and all-night solicitations. These experiences become a form of glorious martyrdom that helps freeze commitment to the group. Running around a supermarket parking lot selling overpriced flowers in the pouring rain is a powerful technique for making you really believe in what you are doing!

After a few weeks of proselytizing and fundraising in the outside world, the member is often sent back for reindoctrination. This entire cycle may be repeated dozens of times over several years.

After a novice spends enough time with older members, the day finally comes when they can be trusted to train other newcomers by themselves. Thus, the victim becomes victimizer, perpetuating the destructive system.

Dual Identity: The Key To Understanding Cult Members

Given freedom of choice, people will predictably always choose what they believe is best for them. However, the ethical criteria for determining what is best should be your own, not someone else's. In a mind control environment, freedom of choice is the first thing that is lost. The cult member no longer operates as an individual. They have a new artificial *cult identity* structure, which includes new beliefs and a new language. The cult leader's doctrine becomes the master map of reality.

Members of a mind control cult are at war with themselves. Therefore, when dealing with a cult member, it is extremely important to always keep in mind that they have *two* identities. This applies even to people born into destructive cults—they too have an authentic, private self and a cult self.

Identifying these dual identities is often confusing for relatives and friends of cult members. This is especially true in the early weeks or months of the person's cult involvement, when their new identity is most obvious. One moment the person is speaking cultic jargon with a hostile or elitist know-it-all attitude. Then, without warning, they seem to become their old self, with their old attitudes and mannerisms. Just as suddenly, they flip back to the cult identity. (This behavior is very obvious to anyone who works with cult members.)

For the sake of convenience, we can call these dual identities *John* or *Jane* (when the person is most themself) and *John-cultist* or *Jane-cultist* (when functioning as a cult clone). Ordinarily, only one of these two selves occupies the person's consciousness at a time. However, the personality on duty most of the time is the cult identity. Only intermittently does the old self reappear.

It is essential for family members to sensitize themselves to the differences between the two identity patterns, in terms of both content (what the person talks about) and communication patterns (the ways they speak and act). Each looks and sounds distinctively different.

When John or Jane-cultist is talking, speech is robotic, or like a tape recording of a cult lecture—what I call a "tape loop." They will speak with inappropriate intensity and volume. Their posture will typically be more rigid, facial muscles tighter. Their eyes will tend to strike family members as glassy, cold or glazed, and they will often seem to stare through people.

On the other hand, when the authentic John or Jane is talking, they will speak with a greater range of emotion. They will be more expressive and will share feelings more willingly. They will be more spontaneous, and may even show a sense of humor. Their posture and musculature will appear to be looser and warmer. Eye contact with them will be more natural.

Such a stark description of a divided personality may seem overly simplistic, but it is remarkably accurate. It's an eerie experience to be talking with someone and sense that, mid-sentence, a different identity has taken over their body. As you will see in later chapters, recognizing the change and acting appropriately is the key to unlocking the person's real self and freeing them from the cult's bondage.

As much as cult indoctrination attempts to destroy and suppress the old identity, and empower the new one, it almost never totally succeeds. Good experiences and positive memories rarely disappear entirely. The cult identity will try to bury former reference points and submerge the person's past. Yet, over time, the old self will eventually exert itself and seek ways to regain freedom. This process is speeded up by positive exposure to non-members and the accumulation of bad experiences the person has while in the group. The real identity deep down—the hardware (self) beneath the mind control virus—sees and records contradictions, questions, and disillusioning experiences.

It still amazes me, even though I had such an experience myself, that my clients are able to verbalize very specific painful incidents that occurred while they were members. People are able to recall horrible things, like being raped by the cult leader or being forced to lie, cheat or steal. Even though they knew at the time that they were doing something wrong or were being abused, they couldn't deal with the experience or act on it while their cult identity was in control. It was only when their real self was given permission and encouragement to speak that these things came back into consciousness. Indeed, an essential part of helping counsel a cult member involves bringing that person's own experiences into the light, so that they can process them consciously with their real self.

In my work, I have seen time and again that a person's real self—their mental and emotional hardware—holds the keys to undoing the mind control process. Indeed, this real self is responsible for creating the frequent psychosomatic illnesses that cult members experience. I have met people who have developed severe skin problems, which excused them from the normal grueling work schedule and gave them a chance to sleep. I have seen people develop asthma and severe allergic reactions in order to seek outside medical attention and help. Migraine headaches, backaches, chronic fatigue are just a few more very real and painful things that members develop which may help them to exit.

The real self exerts itself in other ways as well. It can exert pressure on the cult self to go home to the family for a visit, using as an excuse the need to collect clothes or funds, or to look for new recruits. The real self can also drop hints, when speaking to family members or friends, that the member wants to be rescued. I have had several families contact me after their children in cults told them specifically *not* to get a professional counselor to get them out. Before the cult members made that remark, the families hadn't even known that there was someone they could contact to help.

People's real selves have also been responsible for generating thematic dreams. I have met hundreds of former members who reported having nightmares over and over again while in cults. These dreams typically involved being lost, hurt, or trapped, of being choked or suffocated, or of being imprisoned in a concentration camp.

Some people have told me of receiving a dream or "revelation" that they were supposed to leave the group. At the time, their cult identities didn't want to leave, but their "spiritual" experiences were so powerful that they followed instructions and eventually were able to receive counseling.

I like to use the metaphor that there is hardwiring in our DNA that influences our bodies and minds to move away from harm. The real self resists conditioning and indoctrination and any attempt to suppress wellbeing.

I wish to add something here. My own spirituality has evolved over the decades. My family and I belong to an independent Jewish community in Boston that is non-dogmatic, egalitarian and social justice-oriented. We do traditional services as well as Jewish meditation services. Temple

Beth Zion allows for both analytic atheists and more mystically oriented people to feel at home and be part of a community. Faith can be a wonderful thing if it is balanced by critical thinking.

For me, I still have the belief that somehow there is a transcendent force, One God that is the unifying power of love and creativity. Whether people the world over like to call that being God, Manitou, Jesus, Hashem or Allah—or the sound of breathing (as we do)—that force resonates and works through people. And despite all that I know about psychology and influence, there are still experiences that have happened in my life that I can't just chalk up to coincidence or confirmation-bias, and which I prefer to believe as mysterious and mystical. One of these experiences has to do with how I came to be rescued from the cult.

After I had been out of the Moonies for over four years, I accidentally overheard my mother saying to a friend, "And don't tell Steven, but I was praying for a whole year that God should break his leg! I said, Dear God, don't hurt him too much—just enough so we can find him and rescue him." Amazed, I asked my mother why she hadn't told me this after so many years. She answered, "It's not nice to pray that someone should hurt himself. I didn't want you to be upset." I wasn't. In fact, I thought back to what the emergency technicians told me as they were prying me out of the wreckage: "It's a miracle you weren't killed."

So, in my own life of faith, I choose to believe that God did answer my mother's prayers. Of all my injuries and what could have happened in the crash, the main injury was indeed that my leg was broken. I believe that on some deep unconscious level, the real me was influenced by my mother's love to fall asleep and wake up at precisely the right moment. Of course, there is no way I can prove this. But I have heard of others being involved in accidents that led them eventually to freedom.

I might add that I have had other mystical experiences during my life, like when I met my now wife, Misia. On our very first date, I knew we were meant to be together and have a child together. And so it has come to fruition. We got married within a year and are raising our amazing son Matthew together.

Of course, there are so many prayers that so many good people utter to ease suffering, to prevent harm, that seem to go unanswered. I do not believe in an anthropomorphized deity who sits on a throne with a beard, with the Book of Life on his lap deciding what events takes place on earth. That said, I encourage my clients to pray and have hope and do everything in their power to help their loved ones and friends who are still involved with cult groups.

No matter how long a person has been involved with a destructive cult, there is still hope that they can be helped. I have talked with an 85-year-old grandmother who left a destructive cult after 15 years of membership. Tears came to her eyes as she described how wonderful it was to be free again. I cried, too, as she spoke. I knew exactly what she meant.

Chapter 5

Cult Psychology

Since my departure from the Moon cult, I have counseled or spoken with many thousands of former cult members. These people come from every sort of background and range in age from 12 to 85. Although some of them clearly had severe emotional problems before becoming involved, the great majority were stable, intelligent, idealistic people. Many had good educations and came from respectable families. Many were born or raised into totalistic groups, but still managed to leave. Many were able to form relationships and have successful careers. Many more struggled and suffered from a myriad of psychological and life issues related to their cult involvement.

The fact that many were intelligent, well-adjusted and from good homes hardly surprises me. When I was a leader in the Moonies, we selectively recruited "valuable" people—those who were strong, caring and motivated. Indeed, a cult will generally target the most educated, active and capable people it can find. People with emotional problems, on the other hand, always had trouble handling the rigorous schedule and enormous psychological pressures we imposed on them. It took lots of time, energy, and money to recruit and indoctrinate a member, so we tried not to waste our resources on someone who seemed liable to break down.

Like any other business, large cult organizations watch these cost/benefit ratios. Cults that endure for more than a decade need to have competent individuals managing the practical affairs that any organization with long-term objectives must do.

The big groups can afford to hire outsiders to perform executive and professional tasks, but a hired professional is never trusted as much as someone who is psychologically invested in the group. Moreover, cult members don't have to be paid for their services. Cults thus try to recruit talented professionals—to run their affairs, to put a respectable face on their organizations, and to ensure their success.

Outsiders who deal with the leadership of destructive cults never cease to be amazed that they aren't scatterbrained kooks. I hear comments such as, "I never knew there were so many brilliant people in these types of groups," or "That leader is really a very nice, kind, insightful person. How could he ever join a group like this?"

Occasionally I am asked whether there is some kind of typical problem family from which cult members tend to come. The answer is *no*. Anyone, regardless of family background, can be recruited into a cult. The major variable is not the person's family but the cult recruiter's skill and the recruit's life situation.

Participation in destructive cults does sometimes provide some people with an outlet for aspects of themselves that they did not find in their family life or social activities. For example, many people have a genuine impulse to work together with others as a team for a variety of social or religious causes. Relatively few communities, though, offer such organized activity to idealistic people. Cult life gives them just such an opportunity, along with the apparent benefits of "belonging" that comes from an intense group experience. I support anyone's search for more meaningful ways to develop relationships with other people—but, as I have learned, people who are engaged in that search are often more vulnerable than others to cult recruitment.

I have also noticed that many idealistic young people recruited into cults are struggling to assert their individuality, and some are going through a period of rebellion. For these young people, cult membership can be a way of substituting cult authority figures who become a surrogate family when they are away from home. I have occasionally come across more serious problems, such as alcoholism or drug addiction within the family, which made the person feel a strong desire to escape the dysfunctional family as soon as possible. However, there does not appear to be a consistent pattern in the type of family from which recruits come. The majority seem relatively normal.

So, what makes a person vulnerable to cults? How does a friendly, kind, insightful human being become a member of a destructive cult? If he or she is like most cult members, he or she is probably approached during a time of unusual stress, perhaps while undergoing a major life transition.

Intense stress is commonplace in the modern world. Many people experience great pressure at work or school, or tension from family problems, social relationships, health concerns, new jobs, new homes, money crises, or combinations of several of these stresses at once. Usually our defense mechanisms help us cope, but we all have vulnerable moments. Human beings all have these "life-cycle" kinds of events: graduation, moving, death of friends and family, break-up of relationship or marriage, loss of job, and so on.

Although we may succumb to mind control in weak moments, it is by no means permanent. Whenever recruits leave the group environment long enough and they begin discovering revealing books, articles or testimonies by former members, they almost always break away. The problem occurs when people rely on the group for all key information. Not knowing any better, they give the cult the benefit of the doubt. They may assume that any problem is merely the result of a member's idiosyncratic behavior, not the system itself. One particular cult member I counseled told me that whenever he had caught his Moonie recruiter in a lie, he disregarded it because he assumed that lying was just a personal problem she had. Such judgment errors are common among people who are innocent of the nature of cults.

This chapter, then, is designed to help you put yourself in the shoes of a cult member—to understand the psychology and something of what their life in a cult is like. It endeavors to identify some of the most basic themes of life in destructive cults, the common denominators they all share, in terms of what members do and say.

The Cult Experience

What is it like to be in a destructive cult that uses mind control? How does it feel? How does one think?

Since there are so many different types of mind control cults, it would be impossible to describe the beliefs and practices of each one, or even each type. The best way to learn about a specific group is to locate a former member, or a former member's written or video account. Ex-members are a great source of information.

Still, certain themes of cult membership are more or less universal. Here are the nine most common ones.

The Doctrine Is Reality

There is no room in a mind control environment for regarding the group's beliefs as mere theory, or as a way to interpret or seek reality. The doctrine *is* reality. Some groups go so far as to teach that the entire material world is illusion. Therefore, all thinking, desires and action—except, of course, those prescribed by the cult—do not really exist.

The most effective cult doctrines are those "which are unverifiable and unevaluable, in the words of Eric Hoffer."[91] They may be so convoluted that it would take years to untangle them. By then people have been directed away from studying the doctrine to more practical pursuits, such as fundraising and recruiting. Doctrine is to be accepted, not understood. Therefore, the doctrine must be vague and global, yet also symmetrical enough to appear consistent. Its power comes from its assertion that it is the one and only truth—and that it encompasses everything.

Since mind control depends on creating a new identity within the individual, cult doctrine always requires that a person distrust their authentic self. The doctrine becomes the "master program" for all their thoughts, feelings and actions. Since it is the "Truth," perfect and absolute, any flaw in it is viewed as a reflection of the believer's own imperfection. They are taught that they must follow the prescribed formula, even if they don't really understand it. At the same time, the cult member is told that they should work harder and have more faith, so they will come to *understand* the truth more clearly.

Reality is Black and White, Good Versus Evil

Even the most complex cult doctrines ultimately reduce reality into two basic poles: black versus white; good versus evil; spiritual world versus physical world; us versus them. There is never room for pluralism. The doctrine allows no outside group to be recognized as valid (or good, or godly, or real), because that would threaten the cult's monopoly on truth. There is also no room for interpretation or deviation. If the doctrine doesn't provide an answer directly, then the member must ask a leader. If the leader doesn't have an answer, they can always brush off the question as unimportant or irrelevant.

"Devils" vary from group to group. They can be political or economic institutions (communism, socialism, or capitalism); mental-health professionals (psychiatrists, psychologists, or deprogrammers); metaphysical entities such as Satan, spirits, or aliens; or just the cruel laws of nature. Devils are certain to take on the bodies of parents, friends, ex-members, reporters, and anyone else who is critical of the group. The "huge conspiracies" working to thwart the group are, of course, proof of its tremendous importance.

Some groups cultivate a psychic paranoia, telling members that spirit beings are constantly observing them, and even taking possession of them whenever they feel or think in non-cult ways.

Moon once ordered me, and busloads of other members, to see the movie *The Exorcist*, which showed horribly graphic scenes of demonic possession. Afterward, we were brought to Tarrytown to hear Moon rant about "how God had made *The Exorcist* movie and how it was a prophecy of what would happen to people who left the Unification Church." It was years after I had left the cult when I started studying phobias that I was able to trace back my own programming to that very night. After watching that movie and then hearing that speech, fear of Satanic possession took over my unconscious. I never had any conscious doubts about Moon or the group until my deprogramming.

Elitist Mentality

Members are made to feel part of an elite corps of humankind. This feeling of being special, of participating in the most important acts in human history, with a vanguard of committed believers, is strong emotional glue that keeps people sacrificing and working hard.

As a community, cult members feel they have been chosen—by God, history, fate or some other supernatural force—to lead humanity out of darkness into a new age of enlightenment. Cult members have a great sense not only of mission, but also of their special place in history. They believe they will be recognized for their greatness for generations to come. In the Moonies, we were told that monuments and historical markers would someday be erected to commemorate us, because of our sacrifices.

Ironically, members of cults look down on anyone involved in other cult groups. They are very quick to acknowledge that "Those people are in a cult" or "*They* are the ones who are brainwashed." They are unable to step out of their own situations and look at themselves objectively.

This feeling of elitism and destiny, however, carries a heavy burden of responsibility. Members are told that if they do not fully perform their duties, they are failing all of humanity.

The rank-and-file member is humble before superiors and potential recruits, but arrogant to outsiders. Almost all members are told when they are recruited that they, too, will become leaders one day. However, advancement will be achieved only through outstanding performance or political appointment. In the end, of course, the real power elite stays small. Most members do not become leaders, but stay among the rank and file.

Nevertheless, cult members consider themselves better, more knowledgeable, and more powerful than anyone else in the world. As a result, cult members often feel *more* responsible than they have ever felt in their lives. They walk around feeling as though the world sits on their shoulders. Cult members don't know what outsiders mean when they say, "You shouldn't try to escape reality and responsibility by joining a cult."

The Group Will Over Individual Will

In all destructive cults, the self must submit to group policy and the leader's commands. The "whole purpose" or group purpose must be the focus; the "self purpose" must be subordinated. In any group that qualifies as a destructive cult, thinking *of* oneself or *for* oneself is wrong. The group comes first. Absolute obedience to superiors is one of the most universal themes in cults. Individuality is bad. Conformity is good.

A cult member's entire sense of reality becomes externally referenced. They learn to ignore their own inner self and trust the external authority figure. They learn to look to others for direction and meaning. Rank-and-file cult members typically have trouble making decisions, probably because of the overemphasis on external authority. In their state of extreme dependency, they need someone to tell them what to think, feel and do.

Leaders of different cults have come up with strikingly similar tactics for fostering dependency. They transfer members frequently to new and strange locations, switch their work duties, promote them and then demote them on whims, all to keep them dependent and off balance. Another technique is to assign impossibly high goals, tell members that if they are "pure" they will succeed, and force them to confess their impurity when they inevitably fail.

Strict Obedience: Modeling the Leader

A new member is often indoctrinated and groomed to give up old thought and behaviors by being paired with an older cult member, who serves as a model for the new member to imitate. In Bible groups, this is sometimes referred to as *shepherding* or *discipling*. The newcomer is urged to *be* this other person. Mid-level leaders are themselves urged to act like their superiors. The cult leader at the top is, of course, the ultimate model.

One reason why a group of cultists may strike even a naive outsider as spooky or weird is that everyone has similar odd mannerisms, clothing styles and modes of speech. What the outsider is seeing is the personality of the leader passed down through several layers of modeling.[92]

Happiness Through Good Performance

One of the most attractive qualities of cult life is the sense of community it fosters. The love seems to be unconditional and unlimited at first, and new members are swept away by a honeymoon of praise and attention. But after a few months, as the person becomes more enmeshed, the flattery and attention are turned away, toward newer recruits. Most members continue to believe that the group has the "highest level" of love on earth. However, experientially, the cult member learns that in the group, love is not unconditional, but depends on good performance.

Behaviors are controlled through rewards and punishments. Competitions are used to inspire and shame members into being more productive. If things aren't going well—if there is poor recruitment, or unfavorable media coverage, or defections—it is always individual members' fault, and their ration of "happiness" will be withheld until the problem is corrected. In some groups, people are required to confess sins in order to be granted "happiness." If they can't think of any sins, they are encouraged to make some up. Many people come to believe that they really committed these made-up sins.

Real friendships are a liability in cults, and are covertly discouraged by leaders. A cult member's emotional allegiance should be vertical (up to the leader), not horizontal (toward peers). Friends are dangerous, in part because if one member leaves, they may take others with him. Of course, when anyone does leave the group, the "love" formerly directed to them turns into anger, hatred and ridicule.

Relationships are usually superficial within cults, because sharing deep personal feelings, especially negative ones, is highly discouraged. This feature of cult life prevails even though a member may feel they are closer to their comrades than they have ever been to anyone before. Indeed, when cult members go through hardship (fundraising in freezing cold or broiling heat) or persecution (being harassed by outsiders or arrested for violating the law), they often feel a depth of camaraderie and shared martyrdom that is exceptional. But because the only real allegiance is to the leader, a closer look shows that such ties are actually quite shallow, and sometimes just private fantasy.

Manipulation through Fear and Guilt

Cult members come to live within a narrow corridor of fear, guilt and shame. Problems are always their fault—the result of *their* weak faith, *their* lack of understanding, *their* "bad ancestors," evil spirits, and so forth. They perpetually feel guilty for not meeting standards. The leader, doctrine and group are always right. They are wrong. They also come to believe that evil is out to get them.

Phobias are the ultimate fear weapon of mind control. Shame and guilt are used daily through a variety of methods, including holding up some member for an outstanding accomplishment or by finding problems in the group and blaming members for causing them.

In every destructive cult I have encountered, fear is a major motivator. Each group has its devil lurking around the corner, waiting for members so it can tempt and seduce them, to kill them or drive them insane. The more vivid and tangible the devil, the more intense the cohesiveness it fosters.

Emotional Highs and Lows

Life in a cult can be like a roller-coaster. Members swing between the extreme happiness of experiencing the "truth" with an insider elite, and the crushing weight of guilt, fear and shame. Problems are always due to *their* inadequacies, not the group's issues. They perpetually feel guilty for failing to meet objectives or not conforming to standards. If they raise objections, members are likely to get the "silent treatment" or be transferred to another part of the group.

These extremes take a heavy toll on a person's ability to function. When members are in a high state, they can convert their zeal into great productivity and persuasiveness. But when they crash, they can become completely dysfunctional.

Most groups don't allow the "lows" to last very long. They typically send the member back through indoctrination programs to charge them up again. It is not uncommon for someone to receive a formal reindoctrination several times a year. The Scientology 'Rehabilitation Project Force' usually takes several years to complete and reduces members to abject slavery.

Some long-term members do burn out without actually quitting. These people can no longer take the burden or pressure of performance. They may be permanently reassigned to manual labor in out-of-the-way places, where they are expected to remain for the rest of their lives. Or, if they become a burden, they may be asked (or told) to leave. One man I counseled had been sent home to his family after ten years of cult membership, because he started to demand more sleep and better treatment. They kicked him out because, as they told him, they didn't want him to "infect" other members, who might start making demands as well.

Changes in Time Orientation

An interesting dynamic of cults is that they tend to change people's relationship to their past, present and future. Cult members tend to look back at their previous life with a distorted memory that colors everything dark. Even the most positive memories are skewed toward the bad.

The cult member's sense of the present is manipulated, too. They feel a great sense of urgency about the tasks at hand. I remember well the constant feeling that a time bomb was ticking beneath my feet, and that the world might become a heaven or a hell, depending on how well I performed in my current project. Many groups teach that the apocalypse is just around the comer. Some say they are preventing the apocalypse; others merely believe that they will survive it. When you are kept extremely busy on critical projects all the time—for days, weeks or months—everything becomes blurred.

To a cult member, the future is a time when they will be rewarded, once the great change has finally come. Or else it will be the time when they will be punished.

In most groups, the leader claims to control—or at least have unique knowledge of—the future. He knows how to paint visions of future heaven and hell that will move members in the direction he desires. If a group has a timetable for the apocalypse, it will likely be two to five years away—far enough not to be discredited any time soon, but near enough to carry emotional punch.[93] In many cults, these predictions have a way of fading into the background as the big date approaches.

In other groups, the timetable is believed right until it actually fails to come true. Often the leader just issues a new timetable that moves the big event up a few years. After he does this a few times, a few long-term members may become cynical. Of course, by then there is a whole set of new members who are unaware that the leader has been shifting the timetable. The Jehovah's Witnesses failed in many predictions for the end of the world, yet it remains one of the largest contemporary cults, numbering millions.

When I was in the Moonies, no one knew about Moon's failed prophecies that the old world would end and the Moon movement would take over, first in 1960 and then in 1967.[94] Moon predicted that World War III would occur in 1977. When that didn't happen, all eyes were on 1981. People recruited around 1977 have told me how clearly they remember the magical, whispered excitement of the word "1981" on their lecturers' lips.[95] When 1981 produced nothing more dramatic for the Unification Church than President Ronald Reagan's inauguration (which Sun Myung Moon himself attended), talk had already turned to dates farther ahead.

No Way Out

In a destructive cult, there is never a legitimate reason for leaving. Unlike healthy organizations, which recognize a person's inherent right to choose to move on, mind control groups make it very clear that there is *no* legitimate way to leave. Members are told that the only reasons that people leave are weakness, insanity, temptation, brainwashing (by deprogrammers), pride, sin, and so on.

Members are thoroughly indoctrinated with the belief that if they ever do leave, terrible consequences will befall them, their family and/or humanity. Although cult members will often say, "Show me a better way and I will quit," they are not allowed the time or given the mental tools to balance the evidence for themselves. They are locked in a psychological prison.

This belief—that there is no way to leave and still be fulfilled and be a good person—is at the heart of Lifton's eighth criterion, "Dispensing of Existence" (first described in *Thought Reform and the Psychology of Totalism,* and found in the essay in the appendix to this book). Essentially, Lifton outlined the totalistic notion that if you are in the group, you have a right to exist and if you leave, you do not. Violent cults may take this to an extreme, to justify the killing of former members and reinforce the notion that people have to stay. They must work, fight and follow orders or else they will die—not just symbolically, as in the Moonies, but in actuality.

People who do actually leave cults are extremely courageous—and they can have a very important role. They can provide inspiration to those who are under mind control, especially if the former members are happy, accomplished and open about their cult involvement. These heroic people, by speaking out about their experience, are a potent and dangerous force to cult leaders and mind controllers everywhere. When former members hide their cult involvement—whether through shame, doubt, guilt, fear or anger—they are missing a valuable opportunity: to free themselves and, by their example, to help free others.

Chapter 6

Courageous Survivor Stories

Many people involved with destructive cults may have some experiences that are too painful to remember. Even after counseling, ex-members may not wish to communicate their experiences to anyone but the closest people in their lives. Others realize that the world at large needs to understand their suffering while under mind control, and overcome their fear of speaking out, publicly.

While I certainly understand the reticence of those who wish to guard their privacy, I admire the courage of those who come forward and tell their stories. Such people can make us all stronger for being able to share their personal experiences. They give us an invaluable insight into the dynamics of recruitment, life in a destructive cult, and the stress of leaving. They are role models to others in the groups they escaped from, proving that there *is* life after the cult.

There are millions of former members all over the world. One of my deepest hopes is to de-stigmatize mind control involvement and to encourage them to speak out.

I wish I had the space here to tell the stories of the literally hundreds of courageous men and women I have come to know who have overcome their programming, escaped to freedom and worked to help others.[96]

I am delighted to share a few of these stories.

Jon Atack and Scientology

Jon Atack left Scientology in 1983 and became one of the few outspoken critics of the group at that time—at great personal risk. He authored the must-read book, *Let's Sell These People A Piece of Blue Sky*, which was published only after a fierce legal attack by Scientology. This book is the first objective history of any post-war cult. It became a bestseller, and is the foundation for all subsequent work on Scientology.

Jon and I met in the late 1980s and we have remained friends ever since. He is one of the most talented people I know, and has an encyclopedic mind. Aside from his decades of work helping people understand Scientology, he is an accomplished drummer, painter, poet and author of numerous books.

Jon encountered Scientology when he was 19, after the abrupt end of a romantic relationship. Desperately searching for help to resolve his distress, he read a book by Scientology's creator, Ron Hubbard, and was impressed by what appeared to be a rational therapeutic approach. There was no mention of the supernatural beliefs he would be expected to adopt once he had joined.

Jon asked both a doctor and a vicar about Scientology. Neither knew anything, even though a UK government inquiry had condemned the cult only three years earlier.[97] The Scientologists at the local "Mission" were young graduates, all dynamic and friendly. Jon eagerly took up the study of Scientology. After the first few inexpensive courses, the prices spiraled out of his reach, but, unlike many other recruits, he rejected the frequent offers to join the staff. It costs about half a million dollars to complete Scientology's "Bridge to Total Freedom."

At the hard-sell urging of Scientology registrars, Jon borrowed money and studied Scientology, full-time, for a year. In his nine-year involvement, he completed six counseling courses, becoming a Class II and Dianetic "auditor."

By the time he escaped, Jon was on "OT V," the 25th of the 27 available levels of the cult's systematic indoctrination. According to promotional literature, Jon should have achieved supernatural powers by this time, but, as all Scientologists find, the technology just induces euphoric states and heightened suggestibility. Despite many boasts, to date not one Scientologist has taken up James Randi's million-dollar challenge to perform a psychic feat.[98]

When one of Jon's close friends was expelled from the cult, without justification, Jon followed the cult's complaint procedure exactly. After six months, Jon received a letter, purportedly from Hubbard, saying only, "Your letter is on my desk." He refused to sever communication with his friend—called "disconnection" by the group—and spoke to other so-called "Suppressives." Jon found that 11 cult officials, including Hubbard's wife, had been jailed in the U.S. for burglary, breaking and entering, theft, kidnapping and false imprisonment. Horrified by this and other evidence, he resigned from the cult.

Jon was briefly at the center of a burgeoning independent Scientology movement in the UK, but soon realized that Hubbard's claims to have been a war hero, a nuclear physicist, and a student of Oriental gurus were bogus. He also realized that the cult's "technology" was designed to reduce followers to unthinking compliance.

After leaving, Jon was harassed under the cult's "fair game" doctrine, whereby critics can be "tricked, sued, lied to or destroyed."[99] A stream of false reports was made against him to authorities, including a charge of child abuse (a standard accusation against critics). He was "noisily investigated" by private detectives, who visited his family and friends all over the world, saying they had uncovered his dreadful "crimes." His private confessions were published. Leaflets were distributed to thousands of households. Jon was accused of being a drug dealer, a rapist, a heroin addict and an attempted murderer. Scientologists picketed his house and academic conferences where he spoke. Their placards accused him of being an "anti-religious hate campaigner," even though his work was supported by every mainline Christian church. Jon worked on hundreds of media pieces and earned former members over $14 million in settlements, although he received almost no compensation for his assistance. However, he was bankrupted by litigation fees from a raft of cases brought by numerous Scientology organizations and individuals.

After 12 years of daily harassment, Jon retired from the scene. The cult continued to litigate against him for four more years. He returned to the work in 2013, because he realized that most former Scientologists simply do not recover from the intense hypnotic procedures and humiliating treatment they received in the cult.

Jon blogs at Tony Ortega's Underground Bunker (tonyortega.org). His work has been endorsed by over 40 academics from around the globe. Recently, Jon has been working on the review board of the Open Minds Foundation (OMF), an organization which seeks to educate the public about undue influence and reduce its impact."

Rachel Thomas and Sex Trafficking

Rachel Thomas has a master's degree from UCLA and is cofounder of Sowers Education Group, an educational organization dedicated to prevent human trafficking. We were introduced to each other by Carissa Phelps in the summer of 2013. Carissa's organization, Runaway Girl, was conducting human trafficking trainings for the Joint Regional Intelligence Organization (JRIC.org) of Southern California. As an outgrowth of that experience, I asked Rachel to be part of a panel on trafficking as a commercial cult mind control phenomenon. The video of that program is on our website.[100]

Rachel was an all-American girl from an upper-middle-class home in southern California. While she was a junior at Emory University in Atlanta, Rachel was approached by a well-spoken modeling agent with business cards, a nice suit, and a charming smile. He told her that he wanted to invest in her modeling career by paying for her first photo shoot and set of comp cards (i.e., a model's resume). Rachel accepted.

At the photo shoot, everything was professional and seemingly legitimate. A few days later, Rachel received a phone call from the agent. "Hey, beautiful! Guess what? You're already booked for your first gig!" Excited and impressed by his fast work, Rachel showed up to the gig—a music video for a Grammy-award-winning artist.

At the end of the shoot, the agent informed Rachel that she had earned $350 for her work that day and asked her to complete a W-9. She filled out the form, including her permanent address (her parents' home address in California), her current address (the apartment she shared with her best friend near campus), her social security number, and other information.

In the next three weeks, her agent used his connections throughout the city to secure her another paid modeling gig and an audition for a major magazine. To finalize their working relationship, the agent asked Rachel to sign a contract in which she agreed to pay him a regular retainer fee. She signed the contract.

During her fifth week with the agent, Rachel first saw him slap another model on her face in an instantaneous, unpredictable fit of rage. A day later, she tried to cancel her contract. The agent not only refused, but forced her to have sex with a stranger, threatening to kill her parents if she didn't obey.

From that point forward, she was caught in a web of force, fraud and coercion, regularly experiencing physical and psychological abuse from her trafficker. He threatened to hurt her, her roommate, and her family if she ever told anyone or tried to call the police. Then, once the fear had taken root and she had abandoned any hope for escape, the agent began to mentally manipulate her, to reinforce her acceptance of her new identity as his slave. He gave her a new name and told her to wear a wig. He made her verbalize and repeat that she had chosen this situation by signing the contract. Knowing that her father was a deacon and that she was raised a Christian, he used Bible verses to justify her submission to his authority. He set up a system of rewards and punishments based on her obedience and feigned enjoyment of her servitude. He taught her a specific hand sign to use when she and his other victims were in public.

Almost a year into this situation, Rachel received a call from the Atlanta Police Department. They had been given her name and number by another of the trafficker's victims. Shortly afterward, this man was arrested, and later sentenced to 15 years in federal prison.

The effects of the experience stayed with Rachel long after the trial. She moved back home to California to be near her loving family, but she still endured years of self-blame and isolation, in part because she didn't have much understanding of sex trafficking and knew no other survivors.

It was not until she read an earlier edition of *Combating Cult Mind Control*, and found a helpful church, that she began to experience true healing.

Today Rachel travels the nation, raising awareness about domestic sex trafficking. She asked me to be part of a team including Carissa Phelps and D'Lita Miller, to develop a curriculum called *Ending The Game*. Together we created the first national sex trafficking intervention curriculum, which focuses on resisting and recovering from psychological manipulation and coercion.[101]

Masoud Banisadr and MeK, an Iranian Terrorist Group

I first met Masoud Banisadr at an International Cultic Studies Association (ICSA) meeting in Barcelona, Spain in 2011. We spent hours together. I was fascinated to hear the story of his cult involvement, as I had never met a former member of an Islamist terror cult before. At the time, I remember thinking that my experience of mind control was like that of a kindergartener next to his—a college graduate. I was only in two and half years. He was involved for twenty years. His indoctrination was so much more extreme than mine. I was gratified when he said that my book had helped him understand mind control.

Masoud wrote his story in the 2004 book, *Masoud: Memoirs of an Iranian Rebel*. Since then he has dedicated his life to intensive scholarly study of cults and terrorism, culminating in the publication of another book, *Destructive and Terrorists Cults: A New Kind of Slavery*, in 2014. In this book, Masoud paints a gripping portrayal of the dynamics of cults and their megalomaniac leaders.

Here is a short summary of his story.

Masoud Banisadr was born into a prominent, educated, and liberal-minded Iranian family. He was 25 years old, in the final year of his mathematics Ph.D. in the UK—happily married, and the father of a two-year-old daughter—when he attended a political meeting organized by the Iranian revolutionary organization, Mojahedin e Khalq, or MeK. It was during the Iranian revolution and he supported what he thought was the group's purely political cause. Iran had finally overthrown the dictatorship of the Shah. It didn't take long for Masoud and his family to be sucked into the mind control of the group. Soon he had transformed into an obedient cult member, sacrificing everything he had to the ambitions of the group's leader.

MeK was originally a political organization that mixed Islam with Marxism. MeK played a prominent part in the mass demonstrations and paramilitary activity that led to the 1979 overthrow of the Shah of Iran. To recruit new members, especially young students from schools and universities, MeK's slogans focused on democracy, freedom and human rights. After the revolution, as an aspect of recruitment, MeK supported Ayatollah Khomeini and the new establishment.

Over time, MeK changed from a small guerrilla organization into a mass political movement with the support of hundreds of thousands of young students. On June 20, 1981, Rajavi, the leader of the group, felt he could follow Lenin's Bolshevik takeover of government. He demanded his supporters to pour into the streets to overthrow the new revolutionary government and make him the new Iranian leader.

The attempt failed. It also cost many lives, especially among young students.

After this futile endeavor, MeK changed dramatically. It became a clandestine terrorist group, turning some of its young members into human bombs. A young member (perhaps the first female "suicide bomber") blew herself up inside a mosque. A month later, Rajavi, and many high-ranking members fled to France.

After Rajavi sided with Iraqi dictator Saddam Hussein, during the 1980s Iran-Iraq war, he lost almost all his support, both inside and outside of Iran. In 1985, in an attempt to hold on to its remaining members and supporters, MeK followed a more totalistic destructive path and initiated the process of *Ideological Revolution*. This process of mind manipulation escalated with the announcement of the marriage of Rajavi to Maryam, the former wife of his close aide and friend Abrishamchi.

In 1986, Masoud Banisadr was made the representative of MeK to United Nations' agencies and human rights organizations, and later its representative in the United States, meeting well-known politicians.

By 1990, all members of MeK were intensely brainwashed, and forced to divorce their spouses and accept celibacy for the rest of their lives. A year later, in order to destroy any remaining family ties within the group, members were forced to surrender their children, who were adopted by other supporters in Europe and America. Masoud divorced the "love of his life" and was unable to see his children. Finally, in 1994 all members were forced to go through the final stage of *Ideological Revolution* called "self divorce"—total loss of their individuality and personality, and to act only through blind obedience of their cult identity to leadership.

By 1996, after almost 20 years in MeK, Masoud began to wake up, as if from a very bad dream, and was able to find a way to get away. He experienced extreme, crippling back pain, which forced him to distance himself and receive care. There were other ex-members of the MeK and his family who still dearly loved and missed him.

By then, almost all members of the group were living in camps in Iraq, isolated from the rest of the world, collaborating with the government of Saddam Hussein against their own country, Iran. In the largest of these, Camp Ashraf, cult leaders Masoud and Maryam Rajavi had created their own imitation Iran, complete with a pseudo-parliament and a replica of the Tehran bazaar. Their members, by now transformed into devoted, unquestioning slaves, helped the two leaders to live out their failed fantasy of being the only true leadership of Iran.

In 2009, Camp Ashraf was seized by American forces, and MeK had to surrender all its arms and munitions.

In August of 2014, I was invited by Richard E. Kelly of AAWA (Advocates for Awareness of Watchtower Abuses) to teach a workshop in London. I invited many of my friends and contacts to come attend. A press conference was also organized about *terrorism as a mind control cult phenomenon* and many important statements were given by colleagues. The videotape of the press conference can be found on my website.[102]

While in London, I was fortunate to be able to spend time with Masoud, even meet his ex-wife, who has remarried, and his wonderful daughter and son. It was a heartfelt experience being a part of a healing that continues to unfold. Masoud is dedicated to sharing his life experience to help prevent people being recruited into extremist cults and to develop programs to help those afflicted to exit and be rehabilitated. He is a respected and dear friend. His website is http://www.banisadr.info/

Josh Baran and Shasta Abbey, A Zen Buddhist Cult

Josh Baran owns and operates a highly successful company, Baran Communications in New York City. He does strategic communications, crisis management, publicity and public affairs. Josh has been a friend and ally since the late 1970's. It was then that he founded *Sorting It Out,* a nonprofit dedicated to helping people who had been harmed by spiritual groups, gurus, and cults. He was my counterpart on the west coast—and my go-to person whenever I had a case involving an eastern religious cult. Over the years he has helped bring media attention to many important cult mind control stories. I am proud to call him my friend.

Josh became a spiritual seeker in his early teens. He was very attracted to Asian religion and meditation and, when he was in his 20s, living in the San Francisco Bay Area in the late 1960s, he would attend presentations by visiting meditation teachers and spiritual masters from around the world. He was a regular at Stephen Gaskin's Monday Night Class, and one of the first Americans to be given a secret Transcendental Meditation (TM) mantra.

Zen especially attracted Josh because it focused on meditation and on direct, personal mystical experience. According to Zen, nirvana is here and now; and all you had to do, according to Zen stories and teachings, was wake up and see for yourself.

Then, in San Francisco, Josh met an Englishwoman in her 40s named Jiyu Kennett, who had lived in Japan, Hong Kong and Malaysia for six years. There she had become a Soto Zen nun, gone through the basic training, and been certified as a teacher. She was the first European to receive the 'transmissions' of a Zen master and be given permission to teach. She was charming, very accessible, friendly and charismatic.

Kennett, along with two western disciples, had set up a small Zen center in a two-bedroom apartment in San Francisco. Josh started meditating with the group and enjoyed the practice very much.

Kennett wanted her serious disciples to become official Buddhists, shave their heads, and be ordained as monks. Josh became a monk when he was 20.

A year later, the group moved up to Mount Shasta, near the Oregon border, where it had purchased an old motel with many small cabins. With the approval of her master, Kennett wanted to westernize Zen and liked using Christian terminology, so she named the organization Shasta Abbey.

Shasta became a fairly isolated country Zen monastery. Josh became its guest master, then its chief cook, and eventually its president.

For the first few years, Josh found the meditation and discipline important and valuable. In retrospect, he said, it "really did help me clear away some of my own inner fog. It also helped me grow up, become more mature, and led to what I often call spiritual adulthood."

After a few years, Josh received "dharma transmission"—a formal endorsement to teach Zen—and was named one of Kennett's "dharma heirs." Josh noted, "I could set up my own Zen center if I wanted, but it was also obvious to me that I wasn't enlightened. Maybe I was a tiny bit enlightened. I was a little bit more than a beginner, but, frankly, at most, I was an advanced beginner. I wasn't any kind of master. I wasn't a guru."

After those initial years, Kennett changed. She was suffering from chronic illness, and her friendly manner disappeared. She became authoritarian and self-aggrandizing. As Shasta Abbey grew, so did her grandiosity.

Eventually, she demanded absolute loyalty from everyone. No one was permitted to question or challenge her. "I think she was frankly stressed out and didn't know what to do," Josh observed. "The way I saw it was that she came to the end of what she knew how to teach. She only had three or four years of experience in Japan and a very limited insight...In her mind, she had to be this fully enlightened Buddha."

Not surprisingly, the group changed as well. It became more institutional, hierarchical, and rigid.

Eventually, loyalty became the group's absolute value. Even the slightest questioning of Kennett would provoke an extreme reaction. Monks would be yelled at, punished or demoted. However, Kennett's rages were seen as skillful, ego-busting Zen teachings. The only acceptable response was to bow and accept the emotional attack.

Josh thought the Buddhist teachings were great, and he still liked some of what Kennett taught. But he was dogged by questions. *Why is this place so toxic? Why is Kennett abusive and cruel and cold? If she's so enlightened, why is she such a bully? Is this genuinely Zen, or is it a complex and confused mess of half-baked Zen, monotheism, occultism, and self-adoration—a very strange personality cult?*

Eventually, in 1976, Josh knew it was time to leave. At the time, he was president of the organization, the Order of Buddhist Contemplatives.

There weren't any prohibitions against leaving, but senior members who had left earlier were invariably vilified as failures and losers, too weak to follow the Soto Zen path.

But in Zen there is something called *angya,* a kind of pilgrimage or walkabout in which longtime practitioners go away for an extended period. Josh told Kennett that, after much personal meditation and reflection, he felt that it was time to do an extended *angya.*

She acquiesced, but she was obviously not happy—and from that day on, she tried to persuade Josh to cancel or delay his trip. But Josh held firm to his decision.

A week before his departure, Kennett invited Josh to tea. She said she wanted to give him a "going-away present."

At the meeting, she tried one last time to talk Josh out of leaving, but he stood his ground and explained that he would be departing on schedule. Kennett then gave Josh her promised gift—three small folded pieces of paper. Each one, she said, contained a dime.

On the first tiny package, Kennett had written the word *JAIL.* Kennett said, "Here is the first dime. (This was obviously when there were still public "pay" phones). After you leave the Abbey, when you get arrested, use this dime to call me from jail and I'll come and bail you out."

Then she gave Josh the second package, on which was written *LOO-*

NEY BIN. "After you leave Shasta," she said, "when you fall apart and end up in a mental institution, use this dime to call me, and I'll come to get you."

The third package said *BROKE*. Kennett said, "When you totally run out of money and have nothing, use this last dime to call me, and I'll come and rescue you."

Her underlying message was clear: *Leave me and you will go crazy. Without me, you have no personal power or integrity or sanity. Without me, you will fail. Without me, you will lose the Buddha's Way. Without me, you are doomed.*

Now Josh was more certain than ever that it was time to break free.

Josh left on schedule—and never returned. He did not end up broke, in jail or in the looney bin. He lives in Manhattan, where he runs Baran Communications, a successful strategic communications and public relations firm, working for non-profit organizations, documentary and feature films, and special campaigns. Josh predicts that meditation, especially "mindfulness" as it becomes more "mainstream," will foster a whole new wave of destructive cult leaders.

Yves Messer and the Lyndon LaRouche Political Cult[103]

Yves Messer is a very talented artist, designer, architect and portrait painter who currently lives in England.[104] He is courageous—one of those rare former members of the LaRouche organization who dares to openly and publicly expose the group. We found each other over the Internet in 2008 and were able to meet in person in London, in 2014.

Yves was recruited into this political cult in 1983, when he was 22, and remained a member until 1994, based mostly in France and Germany. He was attracted by the group's apparent liberal political platform. "LaRouchies," as they are called, claimed to stand for economic progress and to be anti-war, pro-third World, in favor of science and the arts, and investment in infrastructure and high technology. They position themselves in a centuries-old tradition of humanism—that's how they catch idealistic people's interest.

At the center lies Lyndon H. LaRouche Jr., a bizarre personality. He ran for the U.S. presidency eight consecutive times, but almost no one, apart from his members, voted for him. Most people do not take him seriously, and might pass him and his followers off as gadflies—you may have seen LaRouchies in airports with signs like "Nuke Jane Fonda" or near post offices or grocery stores with posters depicting President Obama with a Hitler mustache.

But there is a deeply sinister side to the man and his organization. LaRouche exhibits the personal traits of a narcissistic psychopath—lack of empathy, delusions of grandeur, entitlement, paranoia, and a willingness to engage in criminal behavior. At least two deaths, first of Jeremiah Duggan, in 2003, and the suicide of Kenneth Kronberg, in 2007, have been linked to the group.

In fact, LaRouche and his followers believe themselves to be "at war." Like many cult leaders, LaRouche paints the world in black and white: us versus them, good versus evil. He talks about a "cosmic war" between two secret elites—the evil and the good—the outcome of which will decide whether or not civilization survives. He claims the world is about to be plunged into an abyss, variously described as a "New Dark Ages," World War III, total economic collapse and a great pandemic. A self-professed economist, he has predicted a financial crash nearly every year for the past 40 years. LaRouchies believe that saving the world from Armageddon is their ultimate goal, their cause, their reason for living—and that physical force may be justified.

A pacifist Quaker in his youth, LaRouche turned to violence in his 50s, moving away from the far-left towards the far-right and even associating with neo-Nazis and the Ku Klux Klan.

Young and naïve, when he joined in mid-1983, Messer dedicated himself to the group and was promoted two years later as their so-called "Executive Intelligence Review" correspondent in Paris. He was sent to a "secret" training camp, which turned out to be LaRouche's mansion in Germany, where he learned to use guns, shooting live bullets at targets, against the backdrop of lush woods. The purpose of this weekend training was to ensure LaRouche's security during his European tour.

In October 1986, hundreds of law-enforcement agents raided LaRouche's headquarters in Leesburg, Virginia. Two years later, he was sentenced to 15 years in prison for scheming to defraud the Internal Revenue Service and defaulting on more than $30 million in loans from supporters. He was paroled after serving five years of his 15-year sentence. Like many followers, Yves initially believed that LaRouche had been the target of a "political vendetta."

In 1992, in the Alsace region of France, Yves helped set up a citizens' aid convoy to help refugees of the genocide in Bosnia-Herzegovina during the war in the former Yugoslavia. The Alsace-Sarajevo aid convoy, as it was called, set off on February 17, 1993 with more than 60 vehicles and 130 people. The mission was a success—it actually saved lives—but some leaders in the group chastised Yves, for failing to prominently attach the LaRouche name to the convoy. Messer was surprised but, by then, he'd already become suspicious of the group's motives, which seemed largely designed to cater to LaRouche's vanity.

It happened that Yves was in contact with someone outside of the cult who had started a hunger strike to protest the atrocities in the former Yugoslavia. Yves spent several days with him, discussing all kinds of things including what they called "mind manipulation," going so far as to design seminars—along with Yves's partner at the time—for a hypothetical "Research Institute on Mind Manipulations." One day, several LaRouche leaders arrived at his home to, in their words, "debrief" him but it was clear they were checking out his loyalty. Yves decided to quit the group. He left with his then-partner, in 1994, thinking it was just a disappointing political movement. It took them years to realize that the LaRouche organization was a cult, one that controlled its members by keeping them from feeling that they ever achieved anything real and significant. "What is essential is to preserve the LaRouche doctrine over reality," Yves said. "The doctrine is the real, superior, and the *only* reality."

Forbidding children to members was another key way to control members. The policy of enforced abortions left hundreds of couples without any children.[105] Yves and his then partner, who are now separated, adopted a little girl from China, and moved to Britain, where he eventually joined with Erica Duggan, whose son died in the group, to expose LaRouche and his organization. Members of the LaRouche Youth Movement left the cult en masse, in 2012, inspired in part by reading my book and reading Yves' website, http://laroucheplanet.info/ and his efforts. Yves is still involved, through his websites and other activities, in combating cults and mind control.

Hoyt Richards and Eternal Values[106]

Hoyt Richards was one of the world's first male supermodels and is a writer, actor, producer and filmmaker. He is also an outspoken former cult member willing to give interviews and even help people to leave destructive cults. We were introduced to each other by a woman who had been mind controlled by a gypsy "psychic" in the summer of 2011.

During the late 1980s and 1990s, Hoyt traveled the world, walked the runways of Paris, Milan, and New York; graced the covers and pages of high-fashion magazines; and appeared in hundreds of commercials. However, throughout his entire 15-year career, he was a member of Eternal Values, a destructive cult that began in midtown Manhattan.

Eternal Values was founded by Freddie Mierers, a native New Yorker, who grew up in a Jewish neighborhood in Brooklyn. In the seventies, Mierers, a former model and interior designer, reinvented himself as "Frederick Von Mierers," a new-age astrologer and guru who focused on attracting wealthy WASPs as members.[107]

When he was 16, Hoyt met Von Mierers on the beach on Nantucket, where Hoyt's family vacationed every summer. Hoyt developed a friendship with Von Mierers over the summers. While attending college at Princeton, where he studied economics and played football, he would occasionally visit Freddie in Manhattan.

Hoyt explains, "My early memories with Frederick in New York were going to Studio 54. Frederick could get me and his troupe of attractive followers whisked right through the large crowd out front of the club. It was a crazy scene. Celebrities and beautiful women were everywhere. I was only 18 and it all seemed like a fairy tale. At the end of the night, we'd gather a group of hip club goers and go back to Frederick's apartment for his version of 'high tea.' We'd have these long spiritual conversations until dawn. I found it all terribly exciting and harmless, or so I thought. I remember, at the time, even feeling like *I* was taking advantage of *him*."

During Hoyt's sophomore year, a chronic shoulder injury worsened and he found himself in a dilemma. Doctors told Hoyt that he would need major surgery to both shoulders if he wanted to continue to play football, with no guarantee that the surgeries would be successful. The alternative was to give up football. "For me, it felt like an identity crisis. I had played football all my life and my closest friends were my teammates. I really felt lost. This is when Frederick swooped in to 'my rescue' and suggested I give modeling and commercials a try," Hoyt said.

Hoyt agreed and met with early success. This led to more trips to New York City for auditions. When he graduated with a degree in economics, Hoyt moved in with Von Mierers' group. The group was largely made up of younger yuppie types—Ivy League lawyers and architects and a smattering of actors and models.

Von Mierers' main theme was apocalyptic—he predicted that by the turn of the century, a cataclysmic geological event, known as a pole shift, would occur and most of the planet's population would perish. Only certain pockets of humanity would survive in secret "safe places." Highly evolved souls, like Von Mierers and his followers, would be lifted off the planet by space aliens, trained, and brought back to Earth in the aftermath, to lead the building of a new-age utopian society.

Hoyt lived with the group for 15 years, during which time he broke from his family. He didn't see his parents for 12 years. After Von Mierers' AIDS-related death in 1990, the group relocated to the Blue Ridge Mountains of western North Carolina. This was one of Von Mierers' designated "safe places." Von Mierers had been the only person with supposed access to the space aliens, so the group became more survivalist in nature. They built a large compound outfitted with bunkers, and stockpiled weapons and a four-year supply of vacuum-packed food.

Hoyt escaped the group in the summer of 1999. "I wish I could tell you I woke up one morning and had the realization, 'Yikes! This is a dangerous cult and I need to get the hell out of here!'" he said. "Actually it took me three attempts to escape before I actually did. My self-esteem was so beaten down. I was constantly being told that I had let down the group and however hard I tried to improve, it was never enough. I had resigned myself to accepting the truth that I was a hopeless cause. I felt I was unfixable and unworthy."

Earlier that year, he had voiced doubts about Von Mierer's apocalyptic prediction. At the time, he was traveling 300 days a year around the world modeling. "I guess you could say I still had one foot somewhat in reality. However, I paid heavily for expressing my doubts. Even though I was the group's primary source of income and had given them many millions of dollars over the years, I was instructed to move to their North Carolina compound. I was told I couldn't model anymore—they shaved my head weekly so I couldn't work even if I wanted to. I was quarantined to the premises and given every type of slave labor they could think of 'to teach me humility.' I had to be the first one up and the last one to bed. I was forced to live in the garage with the dogs on a mat. I was literally and figuratively in the dog house," he said.

"Luckily, I can laugh about it now. But it was a horrible period in my life. I even contemplated suicide. But the crazy part was, as I much I hated being in that situation, I also felt like I deserved it. Even though leaving the group felt like such an act of cowardice, I felt like dead weight—that I was holding them back. I honestly felt that I was wasting *their* precious time and goodwill. My primary drive to leave the group was not because I thought they were bad or abusing me, but rather to relieve them of the burden of my uselessness."

Fortunately, Hoyt did escape. He experienced PTSD, as many would expect. After about 18 months away from the group, he finally had the clarity to consider a new idea. "I was so convinced when I left Eternal Values that I was evil and cursed—that I had failed Frederick and even mankind. I felt I was doomed to a life of tragedy for betraying the cause. But I finally got to the place where the thought occurred that maybe the way I felt was not just because of me and my endless failings, but perhaps the *group I had been involved with had something to do with it*," he said.

"For years, people had been saying I was in a cult but I would never believe that. I just couldn't accept that I would ever do that. I was convinced that things like that didn't happen to people like me. I would never join a cult."

Desperate to find answers, Hoyt went on to the Internet and discovered an earlier edition of *Combating Cult Mind Control*. "I bought Steve's book because it was the bestseller on the subject. But my true intent was to reassure myself that my group wasn't a cult. Of course, I was wrong. Steve's book was the first step for me in accepting the truth of what my experience had been. It also gave me the tools and inspiration to move toward the road of recovery."

Once Hoyt was well into his recovery, he went on the offensive and sued Eternal Values and won, thereby effectively ending the group's existence.

He remains active in raising cult awareness and, at times, has assisted me to rescue others from cults or mind control situations. He explains our work together: "We share a common goal of wanting to demystify the overwhelming preconception that cults happen to a particular kind of person or profile—naïve kookoos, weirdos, damaged people from broken families, etc. I don't fault anyone for that point of view. It was the same one I held, until I went through what I went through. I'm living proof that it is just not accurate. In being open and transparent about my experiences, I also hope to demonstrate to other cult victims that there is no need to hold any shame around the experience. We are all survivors and we should be proud and hold our heads high.

"I'm delighted to say I'm working on several film and TV projects to help build awareness of how cults operate and understanding of mind control. Coming forward and telling our stories is one of the greatest gifts we can give to others."

Gretchen Callahan and the Truth Station

Some destructive cults are tiny in comparison with organizations such as the Unification Church and Scientology. Yet, small groups can do just as much harm to individuals as big ones.

Certainly this was true of Gretchen Callahan's involvement in a small fundamentalist Bible cult in southern California called the Truth Station.[108] Its 30 members were led by a man who was convinced that he was in direct communication with God. The group lived in a house together and spent much of their time being indoctrinated. They believed that they were the only people on Earth living as true Christians. They also believed in the practice of faith healing. Yet Gretchen had a personal experience of a faith healing that failed—with fatal consequences.

The group would routinely have long meetings in a crowded living room. The leader would spend hours putting members on the hot seat, verbally humiliating them, while everyone else watched. No one was allowed to get up and go to the bathroom. They had to stay and be part of the process.

Members were led to believe that the sin in each of them had to be "brought into the light" and destroyed. No one knew whose turn on the hot seat would come next, and each person would sigh inwardly with relief when another member's name was called.

Questioning the leader's authority was called "giving place to satanic spirits." Being fully committed to the infallibility of the leader and his interpretation of the Bible was seen as the mark of a true believer. People would go to great lengths to demonstrate that they were, indeed, true believers.

David, a young man in the group, felt the subtle power of the group pressuring him to become more "spiritual." To prove his commitment to the group and be more accepted, he decided to stop taking insulin for his diabetes, believing that God would heal him. The members applauded his faith and his decision to throw away his insulin.

In a matter of days, David's health deteriorated. By the end of the week, the leader ordered around-the-clock prayer teams. Gretchen's team was on when David took his last breath; yet the group, spurred on by the leader's anxious exhortations, was convinced that David would be resurrected. They prayed for 15 hours over his body. David's father, at that time a group co-leader, beat on his dead son's chest, rebuking Satan and the angel of death, while David's mother had to be removed from the room because her grief and anguish were viewed as spiritual weakness. Gretchen held David's hand much of the day, as his body turned blue and became stiff.

Even after the police arrived and the coroner took away the body, the group members continued to believe that the young man would return. For three months following his death, a place was set for him at the table, and members (including young children) had visions, dreams, and prophecies concerning his resurrection.

A few days after David's death, Gretchen's parents called her from their home in Jamaica, because they had heard about the incident. Gretchen succeeded in convincing them that the young man was not actually dead. The leader had told her it would be a great miracle when he awakened, and nonbelievers would flock to the group.

Two years after David's death, Gretchen was kicked out of the group for her "spirit of rebellion." She just couldn't take anymore. She had given and given to the group, and it was never considered enough. "I guess you could say I was burned out," she told former members of other groups during a meeting of an ex-cultist support group. "Something inside me just turned off. Even though I was still frightened of doing the wrong thing or being 'out of the Spirit,' I just couldn't feel repentant any more for the 'sins' they had fabricated about me. I noticed that no one was happy and smiling anymore. Everyone was afraid to talk to one another because they might not be speaking 'in the Spirit.' Yet, even after I was thrown out, I still believed they were right and held the exclusive key to salvation. It wasn't until my parents had me deprogrammed that I started to understand that I'd been struggling with the mind control abuses, not with my relationship with God."

A few months after Gretchen left, the group began to use physical beatings, especially on women and small children, to eradicate "satanic spirits."

"It has taken me years to fully understand how deeply they controlled my emotions and thought processes," Gretchen said. "If I hadn't received good counseling, I probably would have kept trying to return to the group."

Gary Porter and Soka Gakkai/ Nichiren Shoshu

Gary met and fell in love with Ann, a woman involved with Soka Gakkai, formerly known as Nichiren Shoshu of America (NSA). The organization originated in Japan and claims Buddhist lineage, although members of some other Buddhist sects question its authenticity. Under both names, this cult has been active in the United States since the early 1970s. They own and operate Soka Univeristy in California. Members believe that if they chant the words *nam myoho renge kyo* repeatedly in front of a rice-paper scroll called a *gohonzon*, they will gain the power to get whatever they wish.

Ann had been involved for over two years when she began to chant *nam myoho renge kyo* for hours a day, in order to meet and marry a doctor. "People would chant for parking spaces, a new job, good grades in school, whatever," Gary told former members at a ex-member support group meeting.

Gary, who had grown up as a Methodist, was at a low point in his life when he met Ann. "I was burned out from four years of chiropractic college. My best friend was killed in a car accident. My siblings were pressuring me to go home and take care of my mother, who was ill. I was a sitting duck for anything that promised the keys to solving life's problems," he said.

At first, Gary thought the group was weird, but he agreed to try the chanting. It gave him an incredible high. He bought a devotional scroll, a *gohonzon*, and married Ann—after all, he did have a doctor of chiropractic degree—and remained in the group for over five years.

NSA used its celebrity members such as Tina Turner and Patrick Duffy for recruiting and for confirming members' commitment. Its other big selling point was "working for world peace." NSA made members believe that only their chanting would save humankind from destruction. But, other than march in NSA-sponsored rallies, which were shunned by most mainline peace groups, members did little to promote peace. The NSA marches did, however, dominate members' time and energies. "We used to have to go to group meetings three or four times a week, not to mention the hours we would spend each day chanting," Gary said. The voices of doubters were muffled and conformity was rewarded.

Eventually, Gary had several confrontations with his leaders in NSA and was threatened with expulsion. Deep down, that was exactly what he hoped for. He was tired of the pressure and manipulation, and his chiropractic work was suffering, because of all the time and energy he was putting into NSA.

Gary and Ann were eventually kicked out of the group. Ann spent the next year on a couch, thinking she was dying of terminal cancer. In fact, she was not ill at all, only acting according to her indoctrination. She, like other members, had been taught that if she ever left NSA and stopped chanting, terrible consequences would follow.[109] Once Gary and Ann started to study material on mind control and destructive cults, they realized that NSA was using the same techniques as groups such as the Peoples Temple and the Moonies. It took them several years to piece their lives back together.

Born Into The Group

When *Combatting Cult Mind Control* was published in November 1988, the overarching thrust of the book was directed toward people, like me, who were deceptively recruited into a destructive cult.

Soon after the book appeared, I began receiving calls and letters from people who had been born into groups. One of the most memorable was a letter and a follow up call from Randy Watters, a former elder at Watchtower's Bethel, who ran FreeMinds.org. He said, "I loved your book! But can I ask you, why didn't you mention the Jehovah's Witnesses?"

I remember being startled by his question, and immediately responded, "Why, are they a cult?" He laughed and said, "Are you kidding? I underlined the entire book!" I responded, "Really?" He told me, "Absolutely!" and I responded, "Teach me." He told me to come to California and he would get a group of former Witnesses together—many of whom were born into the group. I could teach them about mind control and cults. They would teach me about Jehovah's Witnesses. And so my education began.

It was extremely interesting for me to learn that my book was being read by hundreds of people who were raised in the Watchtower, a group I'd encountered many times in my life, and especially while a Moonie. They would try to recruit me and I would try to recruit them. Jehovah's Witnesses are a high-control group that absolutely denigrates former members and forbids contact of any kind, including reading anything they write. What was so interesting was that because I *hadn't* written about them in the first edition, I was not on their index of banned books.

The Moonies were very high profile and Jehovah's Witnesses (JWs) knew they were a weird cult. So reading a book by a guy who was an ex-member was a curiosity for them. They would read the book expecting to learn about the Moonies and other cults, and wind up realizing they were in a cult.

I remember talking with my colleagues in the counter-cult world about my realization that Jehovah's Witnesses were a mind control cult. I met total resistance. I was told things like, "They've been around too long" and "They're too large!" My reaction was, "Since when have those been criteria for evaluating a mind control cult? I thought mind control was the criterion!"

I started working not only with people recruited into the Watchtower Society but also people who were born and raised in the group, and I received hundreds of letters and phone calls. Most of the folks who had read my books wanted to know, "What if I don't have a pre-cult self to go back to? How do I get well?" I knew that I needed to begin addressing the issues for those who had been influenced from childhood by a totalistic group.

Through my investigations and experiences, I have come to believe that human beings are all born with an authentic self as well as a desire for love, fairness, truth and meaning. It is something that no group can program out of a person and therefore there is always hope for real healing.

A subsequent chapter focuses on recovery strategies and a future book will be written on this subject.[110] However, I do wish to make a special note about courage. People who choose to exit a group where they know they will likely be cut off—shunned, disconnected from by all of their family and friends—face incredible suffering, pain and hardship. The level of pain is unimaginable for the average person. If those trying to exit do not succumb to the pressures to return to the group, they can become resilient and strong. They often become staunch atheists or strong believers in the Bible, God or some Higher Power.

People kicked out of these groups are most at risk for serious emotional breakdown, addiction, suicide and other major public health issues. Research must be done to ascertain what I believe is a monumental drain on our health care system by destructive cult involvement. Mental health professionals, unless sensitized and trained, do not know how to even do a proper intake when it comes to involvement with undue influence. However, I am working on a forthcoming book and a training curriculum to help address this profound need.

Over the decades, people who were being born into large cults—the Moonies, Scientology, Hare Krishnas, Children of God,[111] TM—began coming of age and started to question their group's programming. With the creation of the Internet, online discussion groups and support communities sprang up. These have been very helpful for people raised in cults.

I am pleased to share the stories of a woman raised as a child in TM, two former Jehovah's Witnesses, and a former Mormon. I understand that these organizations are very high profile and that the public generally does not think of them as psychologically harmful. The Watchtower Society and the LDS Church have been around since the 19th century and have millions of members worldwide and enormous resources. I understand that I risk being put on enemies' lists, though I hope their leadership has more foresight than to do this. My hope is that the leadership will actually read this book and take steps to reform the policies of their organizations.

Gina Catena and Transcendental Meditation (TM)[112]

Gina Catena is a Certified Nurse-Midwife (CNM) and Nurse Practitioner (NP), writer and courageous former member and activist. After she understood the commonalities between covert methods of TM and other exploitative cults the International Cultic Studies Association first invited her to present her story at their annual meeting in 2006. In 2010, I met Gina when I became enthralled by her presentation about the Beatles' involvement with Maharishi Mahesh Yogi and Transcendental Meditation.[113] She writes and speaks on a volunteer basis to raise awareness of the risks of involvement with TM, so that the loss of those who suffered or died in the group is not in vain. "My conscience dictates that I reveal the insanities I lived, so that others might be spared recruitment to TM's underbelly," she says.

Gina Catena was raised in Transcendental Meditation (TM), an organization founded by Maharishi Mahesh Yogi and his followers. Her parents were drawn in during the 1960's. As a teenager, Gina's parents sent her to live with the TM Movement, in 1974, when they established their permanent university and community in Fairfield, Iowa. Gina and her brother were raised to believe that they were in a spiritually privileged class—"children of the age of enlightenment." They participated in private initiation ceremonies, called pujas, each receiving a secret mantra that supposedly could induce an altered state of consciousness, release stress, free creativity, and ultimately cure all ailments. Like many TM children, Gina raised herself—her parents were often away meditating or traveling to expensive advanced training courses.

Still, Gina loved the close-knit TM community and recalls the feeling she received as a kind of "social heroin." Members were deeply entwined by their shared lifestyle and their goal to "save the world" through meditation. As she grew older, Gina became increasingly troubled by certain behaviors, in particular the group's habit of blaming individuals for their own problems, such as poor health, financial woes and relationship issues. These problems were chalked up to "bad karma," but in fact, they were often caused by the group's practices.

"Meditating every day for hours and hours drove some members to psychosis," she told me. Treating health conditions with expensive questionable herbal concoctions produced by Maharishi Ayurvedic Health Products International, or with costly mystical prayer ceremonies called "*yagyas*," instead of seeking professional medical help threatened the health of members and in some cases may have caused their deaths.[114] Donating thousands and even millions of dollars for Maharishi's schemes to create a perfect world through advanced meditation programs pushed many toward financial ruin. Some actually committed suicide.

Meanwhile, 'Mahesh' and his inner circle resided in luxury—in Swiss palaces and mansions and later in a custom built private enclave in the Netherlands.[115]

Gina observed other problems. TM markets itself heavily, drawing on pseudoscientific research to tout the health benefits of their brand of meditation—calling it a cure for everything from PTSD, ADHD, sexual exploitation, stress and poverty. In fact, it is a method of self-induced trance which can, in some people, produce anxiety and other adverse reactions. Instructors make light of these reactions, calling them a form of "un-stressing," and urging more meditation to release stress even further. It is important to differentiate TM's meditation method from other forms of legitimate meditation. In TM, the practitioner is given a single word, their secret *mantra*—often derived from the name of a Hindu diety—which is repeated until a trance state is achieved.

Though TM's marketing and front groups have changed names over the years, recruitment occurs largely through the *David Lynch Foundation*[116] and the *Center for Wellness and Achievement in Education*[117]—recruitment remains the same step-by-step process. Someone signs up for a beginner TM course. They are then encouraged to attend regular support meetings, where they are warmly welcomed, and given "suggestions" about which advanced courses they might take. Many people stop with the introductory course but some choose to go on. Eventually, they may sign up for the TM-Sidhi program which promises to teach mystical powers, such as yogic flying, for a mere $5,000 or more. Decades ago, a friend sponsored Gina to learn yogic flying. "It involved energetic butt-bouncing on high-density foam," she said.

In 1976, Maharishi promised devotees that if they could get the square root of 1% of the world's population to practice the TM-Sidhi program at the same time daily, they would create a "Maharishi Effect" of global peace, prosperity, perfect weather and health for the world. Many true believing TMers continue to devote their lives to practicing the TM-Sidhi program[118] for four to eight hours daily, in the belief they will positively affect the world. Some become addicted to the state of self-induced trance. They are dubbed "space cadets" by other TMers. Many of those same devotees struggle with cognitive dissonance as they decline with age despite Maharishi's promises of immortality.

Despite her growing doubts, Gina stayed in the group, married twice—in each case to a TMer—and had three children. In 1980, Gina left for India to attend a one-month course in "Vedic Science." She returned to Fairfield, Iowa, but something had shifted. "I never again attended a course. I still lived in the town but I conducted my own life as if I were living elsewhere," she said.

Finally, in 1988 she convinced her husband to move the family to California. They were both 30 years old. Gina enrolled her kids in public school and began taking courses at the local community college "My husband initially could not function. He played video games for about 15 hours daily—truly just another way to dissociate," she said. "He began following Sai Baba (another problematic Indian guru). I didn't follow anyone. I was too busy working (in retail), taking college classes and raising three children." The pair eventually divorced. Gina would go on to earn three degrees and currently works as a certified nurse-midwife at a major medical center.

"I still didn't realize it was a cult until 2003, 15 years later. I was 45," she said. A coworker told her about the work of Margaret Singer. "I had the ah-ha moment—'Oh shit! I was raised in a cult! My whole family is in a cult! That's why our lives are so screwed up!' Only then did I begin searching online for cult information, reading everything I could to self-counsel. I found a therapist who knows about cult recovery."

As a medical professional, she has devoted herself to exposing the ways in which TM can adversely affect a person's health. She maintains close relationships with other former members and with families who have been adversely affected by TM. She blogs at tmfree.blogspot.com and ginacatena.com and speaks and writes on a volunteer basis to raise awareness of the risks of involvement with TM.

Lee Marsh and Jehovah's Witnesses[119]

Lee Marsh is a former Jehovah's Witness, a retired Canadian counselor and is the president of Advocates for Awareness of Watchtower Abuses (aawa.co), a nonprofit group that helps educate the public about the group's violations of basic human rights, especially toward women and children.

When Lee was eight years old, her mother abandoned the family, and Lee was forced to live with her father. Shortly after that, her father began sexually molesting her. The crime was reported to the police when she was 11, and her mother, whom Lee had not seen in three years, was awarded custody. Her mom was then living with relatives and studying with Jehovah's Witnesses.

When Lee was 12, her mom's common-law husband sexually molested Lee and her teenage aunt. When this was reported to an elder at the Jehovah's Witness Kingdom Hall, the elder advised the family to keep it secret. When it happened again, the elders decided that it should not be reported to the police. Lee's aunt was sent to live with other family members, while Lee was placed in a foster home for the next three years.

At age 16, Lee went back to live with her mother, who was then a baptized Witness. A year later, Lee was baptized and encouraged to marry a Witness, a man she hardly knew. They had two children, and she remembers the enormous pressure on her to be a good example to others in the congregation. Meanwhile, her husband—who appeared to be a fine and upstanding Witness—sexually and emotionally abused her.

However, she carried a secret. On the outside, their family life looked good. But inside she was depressed and suicidal. She had never received counseling for her childhood abuse, and the emotional and sexual abuse in the marriage only exacerbated many of the long-term effects of abuse that she only realized later on.

The Watchtower, the Jehovah's Witnesses' prominent magazine, counsels Witnesses to be wary of therapy and counseling, as they are supposedly ways for the Devil to destroy their faith. But after struggling for years with bad *Watchtower* advice, Lee received permission from the elders to get counseling. However, she was forbidden to tell her counselor that she was a Jehovah's Witness.

After two sessions, Lee realized what was happening in her life, that her husband was a repetition of the abuse she endured as a child. She realized she needed to get out of the marriage. She also knew that this would not be easy, as there were only two acceptable ways to make that happen among Witnesses—death or adultery.

After talking to the elders about the situation, she was granted a trial separation. But Witnesses believe that a wife's role is to provide sex to her husband. So despite the fact that they were separated and her husband was living elsewhere, he believed he had the right to come to her house for sex. Understandably, she could not deal with sex-on-demand, and the only approved way to stop him was to commit adultery, so that is what she did.

After she told her husband and the elders about this once-only incident, she was "disfellowshipped," and everyone in her congregation—even her mother—was obligated to shun her. Her husband convinced their kids to live with him, and soon Lee was homeless.

She filed for divorce and it was granted. She needed to support herself, but had few marketable skills, because of the Witness taboo against college.

Lee went on public assistance and made the brave decision to register for college. She did well in her first two courses and decided to study full-time. In that environment, she began to thrive, ask critical questions, and challenge assumptions—none of which is permitted in the Witness world.

Lee graduated with honors, formed a small nonprofit organization to help incest survivors, and provided counseling for over 600 people over seven years before she retired, due to ill health.

Counseling others had helped her turn past childhood abuse into something positive. But it was now time to investigate her Jehovah's Witness experience. Using the Internet, she found a wealth of information about the Witnesses and cults in general, and the methods used to unduly influence members. When she finally proved to herself that Jehovah's Witnesses were a cult, it pinpointed many cult-induced phobias and fears that had lingered with her for years. She has since come to learn about the detrimental effects of the Governing Body's policies on child-rearing. This includes corporal punishment of children. Most repulsive is their organizational failure to call police when children were being raped by pedophiles in the organization. A number of high profile lawsuits have recently been brought against the Watchtower and several perpetrators. We can only imagine how many more victims will be coming forward.

Lloyd Evans and Jehovah's Witnesses

When I first met him, Lloyd was blogging on the Internet under the name John Cedars, as he was buying time to develop an exit strategy from the Watch Tower Society. He has a huge online following and is responsible for helping thousands of people reassess their obedience to this aberrant Christian group.[120] Their Governing Body's policy against blood transfusions, established in 1945, is a non-Biblical and erroneous interpretation of passages of the Bible that has led to countless deaths and needless suffering.[121]

For all the victims of Watchtower ideology, Armageddon is a real event that could strike at any moment. It is a time when divine forces will be unleashed to kill pretty much everyone who isn't a Jehovah's Witness, and the idea that Armageddon is "just around the corner" has been instilled in Witnesses of all ages for decades. The level of phobia indoctrination of this group, bolstered by their numerous false prophecies over the decades, restricts members from higher education, sports, voting, Christmas and birthday celebrations, and promotes total dependency.

Lloyd Evans got his first taste of this when he was a child. As part of his family-worship evening, his parents orchestrated a fake phone call, reporting to Lloyd and his sister that the Great Tribulation (the prelude to Armageddon) had started. Lloyd ran upstairs to pack his vital belongings, because the family had to flee with other Witnesses to escape the authorities under Satan's control. Only when panic-stricken Lloyd came back downstairs could he tell from the smiles on his parents' faces that this had been some sort of macabre joke.

By the time Lloyd was 20, he had started to see glitches in this high-control pseudo-religious group. But this formative awakening was put on hold when Lloyd's mother died of cancer in 2001, when he was 21.

When Lloyd was 25, he fulfilled one of his mother's dying wishes, by attending a two-month course designed to train young Witness men to better serve the organization. Within three years of graduating, he was promoted to the position of elder in his local congregation.

A year later, in 2009, Lloyd withdrew as an elder and decided that he and his wife would move to Croatia, to be near her parents. For the first year Lloyd attended the local meetings and tried to settle into his new congregation. However, due to the language barrier, he could no longer understand what was being taught at the meetings and gradually unplugged from his indoctrination. And he started to ask himself, "What do I believe?" Doubts from his youth began to resurface.

It wasn't long before Lloyd realized he no longer believed Jehovah's Witnesses were God's organization.

The more Lloyd awakened from his indoctrination, the more curious he became. He visited websites set up by ex-Witnesses. Though he had been taught to intensely fear so-called "apostate" websites, he found many of them informative and not spiteful, as he had been led to believe. He also read the book *Crisis of Conscience*, by former Governing Body member Raymond Franz, which convinced him that Jehovah's Witnesses were being deceived by their leaders.

Curious to find out how others felt, he set up the website jwsurvey.org to survey current and former Witnesses for their opinions. After three years, he learned that almost all Witnesses who did objective research disagreed with the teachings of their leaders.

Lloyd and his wife have since formally disassociated themselves as Witnesses, which prompted many of their family members to shun them. Though they admit it is extremely painful, Lloyd and his wife take comfort in knowing their daughter will grow up without experiencing the heartache of being shunned by her parents for ideological reasons.

Tom Hopkins and The Church of Jesus Christ of Latter-day Saints (LDS)

Tom Hopkins is a father, a humanitarian, a composer, a music producer and a guitarist. He was a faithful member of the Church of Jesus Christ of Latter-day Saints—more commonly known as the Mormons—for most of his life. He grew up in a loving, active Mormon family, and at 16 became a priest. He served as the assistant to the bishop, and he proselytized, influencing and baptizing several people. Later, during his mission work in Thailand, he averaged at least one convert baptism per month.

After returning from Thailand, Tom converted and baptized a woman who he later married. Together, they raised four children.

Tom became a Gospel Doctrine teacher, a scoutmaster, a high priest and second counselor in the bishopric, a counselor in the Sunday school, and stake mission presidency. He was also a faithful home teacher who tithed and made regular offerings.

Despite all this, certain doctrines and aspects of his Mormon faith never felt right to Tom. Like other faithful members of the church, he accepted some things on faith, expecting that someday, perhaps after he died, it would all make sense. Though he studied literature that answered many anti-Mormon arguments, he didn't give his own concerns, questions, or negative feelings much energy or credibility.

Tom was taught to believe that the Mormon Church represented everything in life that was good and true—and the only way to eternal happiness. He was also taught that anything contrary to the teachings of the church was false, evil and of the Devil—and, of course, would lead to unhappiness.

Tom loved his parents, his family, and his Mormon friends. They were good people, and Tom wanted them to love him, accept him and be proud of him. To Tom, this meant not taking seriously his doubts about the church. He felt stuck—like he had to play the game, believe in extraordinary events and theology and dedicate his life to the church.

In his late twenties, one of Tom's guitar students, a lawyer and former missionary, told him some very disturbing facts about the Mormon Church. Some he'd heard before; some he hadn't. Some of what Tom was told made sense, rang true and disturbed him more than any other discussion about the church that he'd had previously.

That night, after he came home, Tom cried in secret, seriously wondering for the first time in his life if Church doctrine might not be true.

But he didn't want to look into any of the things he'd been told that day. Instead, he pushed them aside, and redoubled his efforts to increase his testimony and his faith. For the next 15 years, he lacked the courage to investigate what his student had told him.

Meanwhile, the more perfectly Tom practiced his Mormon faith, the more he lived in a world of guilt and shame, always seeking forgiveness. He became obsessed with trying to be worthy, in order to have "the spirit" with him.

The routine of daily prayer, scripture study, church activities, seminary and institute classes, regular temple attendance, weekly sacrament meetings, priesthood meetings, and Sunday school constantly indoctrinated Tom and reaffirmed his faith. When he took the sacrament, or went to the temple, he made covenants to be obedient to the strict commandments of God and Church standards. But he also knew that, even as he made those promises, he—like everyone else—would fall short of perfection, and would need to repent over and over again. This routine often led to shame, hopelessness, two-faced hypocritical behavior and a habit of breaking commitments. This can be the perfect recipe to create addiction.

Yet Tom was determined to be a man of integrity. With help, he eventually came to the point where he felt that he would rather lose everything, face public humiliation and die with his integrity intact, than to live without it. Integrity became more important to him than his need to believe in the Mormon Church.

Armed with this new courage to be completely honest, and to follow his own convictions no matter what the cost, he was finally willing to deeply investigate his questions and concerns about the Church.

The more he studied, deliberated and prayed, the more clear it became that the Mormon Church was not what he had believed it to be. He found that it was full of ulterior motives and deception. This confirmed his own experience: he had known people in the Church who were power hungry or greedy.

To this day, Tom doesn't feel that the Mormon Church or its leaders are intentionally malicious—but that they do harmful things, because they believe that the ends justify the means. The church's leaders and followers are indoctrinated to believe that the Mormon Church is *the* true religion, and they cannot stand the idea of their friends and family suffering, or going to hell, or attaining a lower degree of glory, because they are not active in the Church.

Tom's story is online at iamanexmormon.com and he wishes to add his voice to those of other courageous former members at exmormonfoundation.org. I was invited to speak to their annual conference in 2008 when I explained the BITE model. For me, meeting two hundred and fifty former LDS people was quite an intensive education. I had helped people exit the Fundamentalist Latter Day Saints (FLDS) cult of Warren Jeffs but, until the conference, I was not clear on just how much the mainstream organization was problematic. The talk I heard at that conference given by Ken Clark, a former LDS CES Institute Director for 27 years, entitled: *Lying for the Lord: Deception as a Management Tool of the LDS Church* was an eye-opener for me.[122]

The people who were willing to share their stories in this chapter represent just a fraction of the amazing human beings I have come to know since my own exit from the Moon cult. There are so many other people whose stories deserve worldwide attention.

The Fundamentalist Latter-Day Saints (FLDS) is the largest polygamous cult in the U.S. and is far more extreme and destructive than the modern day LDS organization.[123] There have been many excellent books and documentaries on this cult. Rebecca Musser, ex-wife of "prophet" Warren Jeffs, published her biography, in 2013, The Witness Wore Red: The 19th Wife Who Brought Polygamous Cult Leaders to Justice.[124] Carolyn Jessop, with assistance from Utah Attorney General http://en.wikipedia.org/wiki/Mark_Shurtleff, had gone into print ten years before. Carolyn became the first woman who left an FLDS community to be awarded full custody of all of her children. She wrote the best-seller, *Escape*, in 2008. Her cousin Flora Jessop, who is an incredible activist helping victims of FLDS, published *Church of Lies*, the following year.

Special acknowledgment goes to my friend Tory Christman, an ex-30 year Scientologist, OT VII, who has made hundreds of video blogs and has helped me many times to assist people involved with Scientology. Please visit her on her ToryMagoo44 Youtube page. Exscientologykids.com is a website maintained by Jenna Miscavige, the niece of top leader David Miscavige, along with several of her friends. She published the book *Beyond Belief: My Secret Life Inside Scientology and My Harrowing Escape*, in 2013.

Donna Collins, born into the Moonies, has been an amazing force to help her family and friends exit the cult. She was featured in a BBC documentary on the Moonies, *Emperor of the Universe*, which is online.[125] If you wish to understand the Moon cult better and what they believe, watch this documentary! For an active ex-member site on the Moonies, please visit http://howwelldoyouknowyourmoon.tumblr.com/, and take a look at the Moon page on freedomofmind.com, which lists all of the Moon-owned entities around the world. This list is maintained by Private Investigator, Larry Zilliox, who has been helping me with cases for decades. In future editions of this book, I will add many more stories of courageous former members. I would like to include: a multi-level marketing survivor, a former member of a Large Group Awareness Training, a former member of a Jewish cult and a survivor of FLDS.

There is another book I hope to do about sexuality, cults and mind control. Hal Lanse's *Erasing Reason: Inside Aesthetic Realism - A Cult That Tried to Turn Queer People Straight* is an important book that is a window into the power of mind control. Straight people being convinced to be gay. Gay people being indoctrinated to believe they are straight. Heaven's Gate members mind controlled to believe they are aliens and eight men happy to have their testicles surgically removed. Transgender pioneer ex-cult activists Kate Bornstein[126] and Denise Brennan[127] speaking out after so many years in Scientology, being told by the cult they were not who they knew themselves to be. Inspiring!

Please come to the Freedom of Mind Facebook page and share your stories. There are also many groups in the Freedom of Mind group database: some are online, but most are not due to lack of resources. So if you do not see a group listed, do not assume we do not know about it or that the group you are investigating is not controversial.

Hopefully, I will do a book dedicated to telling the remarkable stories of former members I have had the privilege of knowing over the decades.

Hearing people tell their stories is a deep experience that can help inoculate the public to the dangers of undue influence and destructive cults. It is my profound hope that more people will be willing to share their stories and the stories of friends and family members who have been involved with this global epidemic of mind control. If you have a story to tell, please share it!

Chapter 7

How to Protect Yourself and People You Care About

Nobody joins a cult. They just postpone the decision to leave.
—Source unknown

I am frequently asked to help people who are involved with a group I've not heard of before. Over the years I have had to develop a way to evaluate a group and assess its negative impact.

Some organizations, I have found, may appear to be unorthodox or even downright bizarre, but do not practice mind control, and are not damaging to their members.

I have gotten dozens of calls from parents who didn't like the person their child was marrying, and accused them of practicing mind control. In some cases the accusation turned out to be true; but in many instances, I have simply refused to intervene or become involved. People are entitled to make their own decisions, even bad ones, if they are legally considered adults. While I am always interested in working to enhance people's opportunities for choice, perspective and good communication, I do not take every case that is offered to me.

Many groups have certain potentially destructive aspects, but are not inherently destructive. These groups fall into a gray zone—the middle of the continuum presented in Chapter 3. For some individuals, membership may have a destructive effect, while the organization as a whole may not meet the significant criteria of a destructive cult.

How can we discern whether or not a group is a destructive cult? What are the crucial elements that separate benign organizations from dangerous ones? In this chapter I'll discuss the general characteristics of destructive cults in more detail, so you can protect yourself and people you care about from their influence. I'll also answer some of the more frequently asked questions about cults. In addition, I'll include a list of questions you can use to begin evaluating any group.

In examining and evaluating a group that I suspect of being a destructive cult, I operate primarily in the realm of psychology, not theology or ideology. My frames of reference are the influence processes of mind control, hypnosis and group psychology. I look at *what a group does rather than what it believes* (or purports to believe). I analyze how an organization and its members communicate (or fail to communicate), rather than whether its principles, political outlook or interpretation of the Bible is the *right* one. I see if the group wants to convert the cult member into *its* own belief system. My approach is to encourage the individual to sort things out for themselves by researching and considering an array of perspectives.

A person's right to believe, however, does not grant them an automatic license to act indiscriminately on those beliefs. If it did, white supremacy groups would deport or kill every non-white person in the country, and criminal satanic cults would openly murder people in their rituals.

If a group believes it is all right to lie to non-members, in order to advance its cause, and that lie undermines the principle of informed consent and infringes on people's constitutionally guaranteed rights, it violates their freedom. Frederick Clarkson emphasized this point by saying that "destructive religious cults are violating people's religious rights by using undue influence." Likewise, if a group hides behind First Amendment privileges, routinely violates its members' civil rights, and works to destroy democracy, then freedom is not being supported. There must be equal protection of liberties under the law. People have a right to be free from undue influence, both in groups and as individuals.

Some people may think, *Why should I worry about all this? My rights are violated by someone every day and there's nothing I can do about it.* While many factors in life are beyond our control, people *should* have some control when it comes to membership in a group. And the truth is that there is quite a lot you can do. By preventing others from violating your rights, you can keep them from harming you. I'll say much more about this later in this chapter, but let me offer an example.

Suppose you meet someone whom you suspect is a recruiter for a destructive cult. You might not have even given this person the time of day, but, for some reason, you feel attracted to them. They keep trying to persuade you to meet them at a certain place. You aren't really interested in the group, but are toying with the idea of coming to know this person better. In a situation like this, there's one cardinal rule to follow: *Don't give them your phone number, e-mail address or snail mail address until you know more*. Hold back, even if it's hard to do so, because you might be on the verge of having your privacy violated by a very organized group that will not give up easily.

Many people eventually succumb to the social pressure. With your address or phone number, group members can apply that pressure in a very direct way. Once you become a member of a destructive cult, you lose your right to privacy completely, and more serious damage can be done to you later.

Take their contact information instead! That way *you* are in control.

I became involved in exposing destructive cults, because of my own experience, not because I believe that our government should restrict new religious groups or legislate the beliefs of any specific group. But every group can and should be held accountable for its *actions*. And that includes *active* deception.

Organizations that practice mind control have very specific characteristics that undermine individual choice and liberty. These involve *leadership*, *doctrine* and *membership*. By examining these three areas in any organization, you will quickly be able to determine whether it is (or has the potential to become) a destructive cult.

Leadership

Even though destructive groups cloak the true nature of their organizations, a good starting point for information gathering and assessment is *leadership*. Who is the leader of the group in question? What is the leader's life history? What kind of education, training and occupation did they have before starting the group? One cult group's leader, Eugene Spriggs of Twelve Tribes, was a carnival barker—he pitched sideshows to visitors.[128] Another leader, Werner Erhard of est and The Forum, sold used cars and, later, encyclopedias.[129] Another, Carl Stevens of The Bible Speaks, was a bakery truck driver.[130] Perhaps the most famous cult leader of all, Ron Hubbard of Scientology, started as a writer of adventure stories and pulp fiction.[131] One well-known cult leader, Victor Paul Weirwille of The Way International, received his Ph.D. in theology from a mail-order degree mill.[132] Hubbard's 'doctorate' also came from a diploma mill. I'm not suggesting that someone with a degree from Yale Divinity School could never become a cult leader, or that former bakery truck drivers aren't to be trusted. But a leader's professional background can be useful in helping you see the full picture of any group. Cult leaders usually make exaggerated biographical claims.

Contrary to public perception, not all cult leaders start a group because they lust after money or political power. Even the Rev. Jim Jones, who ordered the People's Temple massacre in Jonestown, was once a highly respected, ordained church minister who had a long history of helping the poor. His original intentions were in fact quite admirable. However, along the way, he reportedly started to use amphetamines, presumably so he could work longer hours and care for more people. He met others involved in fake faith healings and began experimenting with these and other techniques to "fire up" his congregation. As his power grew, he became more and more deranged.

Interestingly, many of today's cult leaders were themselves once victims of a mind control cult.[133] Whenever a person is subjected to mind control processes and leaves a group without understanding undue influence, it is easy for them to take what they have learned and practice it on others. Cults have methods to induce euphoria, and these methods are passed on by defectors who create their own cults.

Clearly, not every former member starts his own cult, but certain personalities are disposed to do so. It seems obvious that most cult leaders are narcissists and might even be full-blown sociopaths or psychopaths. Although many cult leaders demand material opulence, what they require above all is attention and power. In fact, power can and does become an extreme addiction. Over time, cult leaders develop a need for more and more power. Three things make these people terribly dangerous: 1) their psychological instability, 2) that they actually believe their own propaganda and 3) that they surround themselves with loyal devotees who are unlikely to disagree with them, so promote their narcissism.[134] They are not merely cunning con artists who want to make money or sexually dominate their followers. Most genuinely believe they are God, or the Messiah, or have gained enlightenment. But, as Martin Gardner said, it is possible to be both a crank and charlatan. Most cult leaders believe in their own superiority, against all of the evidence, so they project certainty, which is a highly desirable commodity at times of personal uncertainty.

Even more useful is knowledge of a leader's criminal background (or lack thereof). Has the group leader ever been arrested? If so, what were the charges? Were there any convictions? For example: Sun Myung Moon was allegedly arrested at least twice in Korea, though there are conflicting reports as to the charges.[135] In 1985, he served 13 months in a United States federal prison for conspiracy to commit income tax fraud.[136] Joseph Smith was convicted of fraud before he founded the Mormons. Ron Hubbard had convictions for check fraud, leaving a baby unattended in a parked vehicle, and, later, trying to obtain addictive barbiturate drugs by pretending to be a medical doctor.

It's not hard to use any search engine to research someone's criminal background. Type in their name (inside quotation marks, as in "Steve Hassan") plus the word *arrest*. Do the same with the word *convicted*, then with the word *crime*—and perhaps with the words *scandal*, *fraud* or *court*. Search many pages deep and not just the first page of any search engine. If nothing turns up, you might want to consider hiring a private investigator first—especially if you are considering going to an isolated retreat or making a large donation.

Although a leader's background does not necessarily indicate that they are a huckster or a charlatan, where there is smoke there is often fire. *Many* leaders of destructive cults have questionable backgrounds.

By looking at the leader's background, you can draw some general conclusions about how much trust you can place in them. For example, if someone is teaching a course on how to have a successful marriage, the fact that they have been divorced several times is significant. If a leader has a background of drug use and bizarre behavior, like Ron Hubbard, then be cautious in listening to their claims of being able to solve all of humanity's problems. [137]Sun Myung Moon repeatedly said he was working toward world peace—keep in mind he owned an M-16 gun factory in Korea.[138] Another important aspect of leadership involves its organizational flow of power. Does the organization have a structure with a true balance of power? Many destructive groups have boards of directors, but typically they are puppets of the leader. The true structure is that of a pyramid with the cult leader as omnipotent head at the apex. Below the leader is a core of lieutenants who are totally subservient. Below them are subsidiary leaders. The operating structure allows for no checks and balances. The leader has absolute power. Lord Acton said it well when he wrote, "Power tends to corrupt, and absolute power corrupts absolutely."

If a leader has a questionable personal background, and their organization is totally centralized and under their control, beware. If, however, there are checks and balances built into the system, power seems to be genuinely distributed among many levels, and the leader is committed to meeting members' needs and goals, you are probably looking at a much healthier organization.

Not every destructive cult has a leader who is glorified to outsiders, or who enjoys great personal wealth. Since many contemporary cult leaders were themselves former cult members, they may be acting out of nothing more than delusion, mental illness and a drive for power. I have counseled people out of several groups whose leaders were not in it for the money, but were simply addicted to personal power. Many destructive Bible cults have leaders who are not conspicuous consumers, and who appear to hold God and the Bible above themselves as higher authorities; yet their *interpretations* of the Bible and God's will are used to manipulate and control people.

Doctrine

Since the Constitution protects people's right to believe whatever they wish to believe, close scrutiny of a group's particular doctrine is unwarranted and unnecessary. But beware of groups with any belief system that is simplistic and makes all or nothing categorizations—good/bad; black/white; us versus them. Beliefs that claim things as facts, but actually have no evidence-based research to support these claims.

Absolutely key are honesty and transparency. Any group's beliefs should be freely disclosed to any person who wants to join, before any pressure to join is exerted.

Does the group's doctrine claim publicly to be one thing when it is in fact quite otherwise? Are there separate insider and outsider doctrines?

For a group to have integrity, its members must truly believe what it stands for (and says it stands for). However, destructive groups change the "truth" to fit the needs of the situation because they believe that the *ends justify the means*. Helping to "save" someone is a rationalization used to justify deceit or manipulation. Legitimate organizations don't change their doctrine to deceive the public.

Membership

This is my main focus whenever I evaluate a group.

Membership has three components*: recruitment, group maintenance* and *freedom to leave*. The impact of group membership on the individual, their identity, their relationships, and their goals and interests is crucial.

The basic feature of most cult ***recruitment*** is deception. This includes outright lying, leaving out important information or distorting information.

Destructive groups operate under the assumption that non-members are too ignorant or unspiritual to recognize what is best for them. They are blind to the truth, known only to the cult. Recruiters, therefore, take it upon themselves to make decisions for the people they recruit.[139] When an individual's critical faculties are intact and fully functioning, information supplied by the destructive cult is typically meager. Only when the individual's critical functions are worn down and less functional will the cult supply the next phase of their information.

Most cult recruiters will deny that they are trying to recruit anyone at all. When asked what they are doing, they normally say that they just want to share something meaningful, and want people to make up their own minds about it. Recruiters for multi-level marketing groups and large group awareness trainings are typically told not to disclose exactly what will happen in the program. That if they do, they will "spoil" the person's experience. Or that the person has to *experience for themselves* to know what it is all about. What they also do not tell the prospective convert is that they may have a recruitment quota to fill; they may feel like they are not honoring their commitment if they don't get a certain number of newbies to attend a cult function.[140] The practice of deception by destructive cults often extends to the use of various front organizations. This misleads and confuses potential recruits, and hides the real agenda of the organization. Universal Peace Federation, CAUSA, C.A.R.P., Freedom Leadership Foundation, the International Cultural Foundation, and many others were all Moon organizations.[141] Dianetics, the World Institute of Scientology Enterprises (WISE), the Citizens' Commission on Human Rights (CCHR) and Narconon are fronts for Scientology.[142] The average citizen is not usually aware of these connections.

The recruiter wants to draw as much information as possible from the potential convert, to determine the most effective way to bring them into the group. An effective recruiter knows how to home in on potential weak spots (called 'finding the ruin' in Scientology). These may involve a boyfriend or girlfriend, parents, family members, job, or school; the death of a close friend or relative; a move to a new town, and any other significant transition or dislocation. An effective recruiter knows how to make the target comfortable, so more willing to disclose highly personal and confidential information.

Meanwhile, the recruiter reveals as little as possible about themselves and (especially) the group, unless it is absolutely necessary. Most of the information comes from the person being recruited. This unbalanced flow of information is always a signal that something is wrong.

By far the most common impression potential recruits have is that they are making a new friend. However, in the real world, friendships take time to develop. Over time, each person shares more and more personal information in a reciprocal manner, giving and taking in a balanced way. There is also no hidden agenda.

Once a potential convert is invited to a cult function, there is a great deal of pressure, both overt and subtle, to make a commitment as soon as possible.[143] Cult recruiters, like good con artists, move in for the kill quickly, once they have sized up a person. It is not in their best interest to encourage thoughtful reflection. In contrast, legitimate groups do not lie to potential converts or pressure them into making a quick commitment.

A destructive group will recruit new members through the use of mind control techniques. Control of the individual's experience is essential in order to break them down, indoctrinate them, and build them up again in the cult image. During cult recruitment, the person's identity framework makes a dramatic shift. During the indoctrination, sometimes the person doesn't contact family and friends for days or weeks. When they eventually do, a radical personality change is evident. The individual often changes his style of clothes and speech patterns and behaves in an uncharacteristically distant manner. Often, the person's sense of humor is blunted. Previous interests, hobbies and goals may be abandoned "because they are no longer important."

This personality change does seem to wear off a bit over time, *if* the individual doesn't continue to contact the group or participate in its activities. However, when the person maintains contact, the new identity can and does grow ever stronger.

To family and friends, the person seems not only more distant, but deceitful and evasive. Sometimes the person can be coaxed into revealing what he now believes. Frequently, though, the new member asks family members and friends to talk to older members or leaders, because "they can explain it better."

The most telltale sign of the work of a destructive cult is this radical personality change. A person may have been politically liberal before, but is now a staunch conservative. They may have loved rock music but now think it is from the Devil. They may have been very loving and close to their family, but now don't trust them at all. They may have been an atheist; now, suddenly, God means everything to them. Time after time, I have heard family members say, "She's a different person now. We don't know her anymore!"

People have been known to change their names, drop out of school or work, donate their bank accounts and property, and move hundreds or even thousands of miles away from home once they become involved. However, the absence of these requirements doesn't necessarily mean that the group is not a destructive cult. Increasing numbers of groups have deliberately avoided such practices for some time in order to allay suspicion.

Each situation and each group should be considered individually in terms of its impact on a person's life. Recruitment is done incrementally; in some cases, a person's behavior changes over months, although more typically it takes only days or weeks.

The ***maintenance of membership*** is achieved by cult activities deliberately designed to undermine the new member's relationships with family and friends. One way this is achieved is by having new members recruit everyone they know. As long as friends and family are "raw meat," as Scientology refers to them,[144] recruits have permission to spend time with them and try to recruit them. But as soon as family members and friends express their concerns and declare that they will never join the group, cult leaders urge the new member to stop wasting time on them. If a family member or friend is critical enough, the new member will be instructed to "disconnect" from them. Mind-control groups cannot tolerate opposition of any kind. Either people agree with them and are seen as potential converts, or they are the enemy.

Once a person becomes a member, their sleep patterns often change significantly. Sleep deprivation is a common strategy for keeping people in line and in the fold. Anyone who has ever experienced several sleepless nights, or had to stay up all night to work or study, knows the difficulty of functioning normally without adequate sleep. Many cult groups make sure that members have only three to five hours of sleep each night. It's not that they have a formal policy of sleep deprivation; they simply make sure that the new member is so overworked that they have little time to sleep. In many cults, leaders are routinely praised for sleeping very little, and rank and file members are belittled for sleeping too much. In time, members learn to sleep a minimum amount and work for the group as much as possible.

Dietary changes also frequently occur during cult recruitment. Some groups practice strict vegetarianism, but feed new members excessive amounts of sugar to give them a high. Some groups encourage long and frequent fasts, with little or no care given to the body before and after. Some groups even make members forage in garbage cans for their meals.[145] Usually, drastic weight shifts occur. Although most people lose weight during their cult membership, some become significantly overweight.

What people eat, their attitude toward food and how they eat all contribute to a person's sense of self. If a member is made to feel that they have to "die to themselves" and their human needs, they may agree to fast a good deal of the time and deny themselves any pleasure in eating. On the flip side, if a cult member is very unhappy from too much work, not enough sleep, and not having their emotional needs met, they may overeat. Contrary to public misconceptions, most mind control cults do not systematically deprive members of decent food. If they did so for long, the members' bodies would break down and they would not be able to work.

Destructive cults *are* characterized, however, by doing little to maintain their members' good health in other ways. As we have seen, psychosomatic illnesses abound in members, perhaps as a reflection of their unconscious need for help and attention. Medical treatment is minimal, and in some groups virtually absent; in still others it is labeled as sinful.

In destructive cults, large amounts of time are spent in group activities, with a minimum of time allowed for privacy or time with friends and family. Little time is available for reading anything other than cult material, or for learning anything other than cult practices. Of course, members go out of their way to convince outsiders that they are living a "normal" life. Yet, if you involve cult members in a long discussion of current events, art or history, it becomes evident that most are out of touch.

One of the most obvious signs of a person in a mind control group is a lack of independent decision-making abilities. Even though cult members may try to convince outsiders that they are autonomous, once you probe beyond the surface it becomes obvious that they cannot make important (or, sometimes, even minor) decisions without first asking permission from superiors. This dependency is typical on all levels of cult membership, except at the very top.

One mother of a cult member I knew was happy when she thought that her son had decided to come home for Christmas. She was crestfallen when her son said, "No, Mom, the yogi told me that my place was to be with you over the holidays." In fact, the only reason he was allowed to come home was that she had never criticized the group, and had often invited some of its members to dinner.

Family members are often told by cult members that they "will see" if they can come home for important family events such as marriages, funerals and birthdays. What this means is that they will ask their leaders for permission.

In mind control groups, members have to ask permission to do many things that most people take for granted. Imagine having to ask permission of a priest to visit a sick relative. However, a member of one of these groups who doesn't ask permission, but simply does what they feel is necessary, is typically seen as selfish, rebellious, and antagonistic to "positive growth." The more controlled a group is, the less likely a member is to be allowed to attend a wedding, funeral or any other outside activity.

Some cults maintain membership by controlling all social relationships, telling members who they can or can't date or marry. Some of the most extreme groups tell members when they can and can't have sex, and what positions are acceptable. Some take members' children away from them in order to allow the parents more time to work and allow more thorough indoctrination of the kids.

Life in a destructive cult can vary a great deal. Some members live together in an ashram, center or group house, while other members may have their own living arrangements. Some members may have menial jobs that demand little or no thinking (for instance, as janitors, workers, cooks and cleaners); others may be engaged in quite demanding work (recruiting, public relations, and operating cult businesses). The Children of God actively encouraged its female members to become prostitutes. These "Happy Hookers for Jesus" used sex to make money, manipulate officials and gain converts.[146] Some people have outside jobs from nine to five, which force them to compartmentalize their cultic thinking process. These people typically continue their jobs once they join, because of the money, the prestige, and the opportunities to recruit and influence. Such people are fortunate to have time away from the group and extensive contact with non-members, and the detrimental effects are minimized.

In the day-to-day lives of members of destructive cults, there is often a wide variation in the degree to which they experience the BITE model: behavior control, information control, thought control and emotional control. Those persons who are forbidden to think "negative thoughts" or have contact with critics or former members, even though they may have outside jobs and live separately, may still be under mind control, though perhaps not as highly controlled as someone who is a full-time, completely devoted member.

The final criterion for judging a group is the members' ***freedom to leave***. To put it simply, members of destructive cults are psychological prisoners. As I have explained, destructive cults plant phobias into members' minds so that they fear ever leaving the group. By doing this, they shut the door on free choice. People had the freedom to join, but people don't have the freedom to leave a destructive group. In fact, in the eyes of a destructive cult, there is no "legitimate" reason for a person to ever leave the group.

Legitimate groups treat people as adults, capable of determining what is in their best interest. Although every organization wants to retain its membership, legitimate groups never go to the extremes of control through fear and guilt that destructive cults do.

Some of the most destructive cults actually try to hunt down and silence former members—through violence, legal harassment, intimidation, or blackmail. Paul Morantz, a lawyer who litigated against the drug rehabilitation program (and mind control cult) Synanon, was bitten by a rattlesnake placed in his mailbox by cult members.[147] Stephen Bryant, a former devotee of the Hare Krishnas, was murdered—shot in the head by a group member, allegedly at the instruction of one of the organization's leaders.[148] Bent Corydon, a member of Scientology for 22 years, was subjected to extreme forms of legal harassment for writing *L. Ron Hub-*

bard—Messiah or Madman? a critical biography of the group's founder.[149] Many critics of Scientology have been litigated into bankruptcy. Jeannie Mills, a former member of the Peoples Temple and an outspoken critic of Jim Jones, was murdered by persons unknown, along with her husband and children, after the massacre at Jonestown.[150]

Needless to say, people should always retain the right to decide for themselves whether to remain in a group. That freedom of choice should not be taken away from a person who has decided to join any organization.

Questions People Ask About Cults

One question I frequently hear is whether all destructive cults are equally dangerous. The answer is no. Not every group is as destructive as the Peoples Temple, ISIS or Boko Haram. Nor is every group as deceptive as the Moon group or as demanding as Jehovah's Witnesses. Nevertheless, all mind control cults fall at the negative end of the influence continuum.

Another question I am occasionally asked is whether destructive cults can change over time in significant ways. The answer is yes. Groups that use mind control may start off with extremely good intentions, but end up manipulating their members and deceiving the public. That was certainly the case in the Peoples Temple, which was originally an inner-city ministry oriented toward helping the poor. The tragedy is that the people whom the cult tried to help eventually became the group's victims, and then made victims of others.

Some cults simply fade away or disband. The Democratic Worker's Party of California decided to disband after its members became extremely disillusioned with their leader.[151] The Center for Feeling Therapy disbanded when its leaders simply walked away one day, leaving hundreds of confused and disoriented members.[152] Another issue is whether a particular destructive group is uniformly dangerous at every one of its locations throughout the world. This may or may not be the case. Despite the fact that many groups try to present an image of being large, powerful, and monolithic, they are usually not totally uniform. There can be major differences, depending on the local leader's personality, strictness, and style.

During my days in the Moonies, the lifestyles on the east and west coasts differed significantly. In the east—primarily because Moon lived there and oversaw operations personally—militaristic discipline and control were extreme. Men and women were not permitted to hug, kiss or hold hands unless they were married *and* given permission. On the west coast, where things were much looser, people did all these things. However, recruiters on the west coast were more deceptive in their tactics.

Because many destructive cults offer meditation or other possibly therapeutic techniques that are claimed to have universally beneficial results, another legitimate question is whether cults affect some people more adversely than others? The answer is yes.

For example, a significant proportion of people simply do not respond well to passive relaxation techniques, and suffer from "relaxation induced anxiety." Such a person recruited into an organization like Transcendental Meditation (TM) might suffer headaches, insomnia, increased anxiety and so forth. Since TM members believe that their form of meditation is good for everybody, a person who complains of negative effects may be told that they are simply "unstressing" and should continue meditating. Unfortunately, ignoring such problems may lead to serious health problems, nervous breakdowns and even suicidal tendencies.[153] Former TMers have complained of tunnel vision and, after the "yogic flying" course, at least one practitioner suffered a fractured coccyx.

Large group awareness training programs such as est (changed in the 1980s to The Forum and later Landmark Education) and Lifespring have been strongly criticized for their lack of professional screening. As a result, several of these organizations have been the subject of lawsuits by damaged participants.[154]

Lastly, there is the consideration of a group's size. Is a cult's destructiveness related to its size?

Not at all. I have seen one-on-one mind control relationships that have been as destructive as some of the world's most powerful and toxic cults. In researching battered-person syndrome, I have found many similarities and parallels with members of mind control cults.[155]

Some dysfunctional relationships, marriages, and families are essentially mini-cults of a few people. I've learned that many domestic abuse victims were forced into a nearly totally dependent relationship, often kept away from family and friends who might be critical of the controlling partner's behavior. Some people were not allowed to have access to money, to learn how to drive a car, or to work outside the home. Whenever they tried to communicate their wants or needs, they were beaten.

They were made to feel that any problem in their marriage was entirely their fault, and that if they only worked harder to please their spouse, everything would be fine. These people's self-esteem became so low that they came to believe there was no future for them without their partner. Some people had spouses who planted phobias in their minds, so they could never leave the marriage; in some cases, they were also told that they would be hunted down and killed if they ever left. Some controllers threatened to kill themselves if their victim ever left.

Asking Questions: The Key To Protecting Yourself

Learning to be an educated consumer can help save you time, energy and money. In the case of destructive cults, being an educated consumer can help protect your mind and possibly save your life. Thorough online research is your best first option. However, if you are ever approached by someone who tries to pry information out of you or invites you to participate in a program, you can ask some very specific questions which will help you avoid over 90% of cult recruiters. Simply asking these assertively will help you deflect recruiters, who will quickly realize that you are not a promising use of their time.

These questions work best if you ask them in a very direct yet friendly manner, and demand very specific answers.

Although most cults use deception while recruiting, most cult members don't realize that they are lying to potential new members. By asking these direct questions one after another, you can usually discover that either 1) you are not being told a straight story, or 2) the person doesn't have the straight story to begin with.

For example, Jehovah's Witnesses recruit by asking people if they would like to study the Bible with them. But what they do not say is that they use the New World Translation, published by the Watchtower, which is not accepted by Biblical scholars outside the cult. Of course, they have been told it is a better translation than all other Bibles.

Because members have been trained to avoid thinking negatively about the group, you will often receive vague generalities or evasions. For example, "We're just trying to help people to overcome their problems," or "We're having a free dinner tonight to discuss some of the world's problems" or "We're just getting together to study the Word of God."

Evasive remarks, such as "I understand you're feeling skeptical. I was too, before I really came to *understand,*" or "Is that what you *really* want to know?" should also ring warning bells.

Another common technique used by recruiters is changing the subject. For example, when you ask a question about whether or not a cult leader has a criminal background, you may hear a long monologue about the persecution of the world's great religious leaders. You may be told that Socrates was accused of child molestation and Jesus being accused of associating with prostitutes. Don't get drawn into a debate about Socrates or Jesus. You want a direct answer about the leader of *this* person's group. If the recruiter doesn't give a clear, concise, direct answer, something is wrong.

And remember: you can always simply walk away.

Most of all, though, you will find that the best possible advantage over a cult recruiter is the ability to ask him direct, penetrating questions. The following are some that I have found to be highly effective:

- **How long have you (the recruiter) been involved with this group? Are you trying to recruit me into any type of organization?**

First, this will help you find out very quickly who you are dealing with. A person who has been involved in a destructive cult for less than a year is usually very inexperienced and possibly less likely to lie, and any lies they do tell are less likely to sound convincing.

Second, if the person has been involved for many years, you can expect them to know and to be able give you concrete, specific answers to all your follow-up questions. If they don't, you can say, "You've been a member for years and you don't know the answer to such simple questions?"

When asked point blank about recruitment, the person may say, "No, I'm not trying to recruit you into anything. I just like you and wanted to share this with you. What you decide to do with the information will be totally up to you." Fine. Just keep this answer in mind, because if the group is in fact a destructive cult, it will eventually become obvious that you *are* being recruited. That means the recruiter lied to you. If and when you realize this, be appropriately annoyed and walk away.

- **Can you tell me the names of all the other organizations that are affiliated with your group?**

You are trying to uncover the names of front groups as well as the principle group. A cult recruiter will usually be taken off guard by this question and ask what you mean. Ask again; it's a perfectly clear and straightforward question. If the recruiter tells you they don't know, ask them to find out for you. Ask for their phone number—do not give them yours, of course—and say that you will call them tomorrow for the answer.

If the person tells you there are no other organizations, at some later point you may discover that this was a lie. If and when you realize this, be assertively annoyed and leave. Remember, cults like to create front groups for popular causes. For example, both the Moonies and Scientologists have front groups to presumably combat trafficking.

- **Who is the top leader? Tell me about their background and qualifications. Do they have a criminal record?**

You may or may not get a straight answer to these questions. The recruiter might use the name of the local sub-leader instead of the person at the top. They also might not know anything about the leader's background or criminal record, because they may not know themselves. You might then ask the person, "How could you have become involved with a group without checking these things out first?"

Remember, a destructive cult will try to get your commitment first, *before* disclosing important information. A legitimate group will always give information first, and ask for commitment later, only when you feel ready.

- **What does your group believe? Does it believe that the ends justify the means? Is deception allowed in any circumstances?**

Most cult recruiters will not want to explain what they believe right there on the spot. They are trained to use your curiosity to bring you to hear a lecture, watch a video or attend a program. This will give them a better chance of influencing you, because you will be in their environment.

If the person is not willing to summarize the key points of the group's beliefs, right there and then, you can be sure they are hiding something.

If they say that they're afraid you will misunderstand, if they give you only a short description, ask for it anyway. *Any legitimate group will be able to summarize its central beliefs*. Destructive cults will not want to do so.

If you find out later that this description was a gross distortion filled with inaccuracies, you have every right to be annoyed and leave. The cult members will most assuredly try to convince you that they *had* to lie to you because you have been brainwashed by the media against them, and you would have never listened if they told the truth. Don't buy this "ends justify the means" rationalization. No legitimate organization needs to lie to people in order to help them.

- **What are members expected to do once they join? Do I have to quit school or work, or donate my money and property, or cut myself off from family members and friends who might oppose my membership? What did you do for a living before you joined the group, and what do you do for a living now?**

If you are being approached by a destructive cult, the person you meet may tell you that you will be expected to do little or nothing once you join. However, this question will make most cult members very uncomfortable and defensive. Watch the recruiter's non-verbal reaction carefully when you ask this question. Ask the person what they did when they first met the group and what they are doing now.

- **Is your group considered controversial by anyone? If other people are critical of it, what are their main objections?**

These are nicely open-ended questions that allow you to probe just how much the person knows or is willing to discuss. If you ask these questions politely and with a smile, the person may say, "Oh, some people think we're a cult and that we're all brainwashed. Isn't that silly? Do I look brainwashed?" To that question you might respond, "So how are people supposed to look if they are brainwashed?" When I ask that question, the person I'm speaking to usually becomes very uncomfortable and, if I continue to probe, finds some excuse to leave.

- **How do you feel about former members of your group? Have you ever sat down to speak with a former member to find out why they left the group? If not, why not? Does your group impose restrictions on communicating with former members?**

This is one of the most revealing sets of questions you can ask. Any legitimate organization would never discourage contact with former members, particularly family and friends. Likewise, any legitimate group would support a member's right to leave, even though they might not like it.

Destructive cults, on the other hand, do not accept any reason for a person's departure, no matter what it is. Likewise, cult groups make sure to instill fear in members, insuring that they stay away from critics and former members. Although you might hear some experienced cult recruiters say, "Sure, some of my best friends have left," when you probe further and ask them for specifics, you may find out they have been lying. I always pursue such a response with questions such as "What specific reasons did they give for leaving?" and "Do they say that they are happier now that they have left?" Again, the recruiter is usually at a loss for words.

- **What are the three things you like least about the group and its leader?**

I can't remember how many times I have seen reporters and television hosts ask cult members whether or not they were brainwashed. The cult member usually smiles and says, "Of course not, that's ridiculous." It is absurd, however, to expect an objective answer from someone under mind control. A much better challenge for such people would be, "Tell me three things that you don't like about the group or the leader." If you get an opportunity to catch a cult member off guard and ask that question, I suggest you watch their face very carefully. The pupils in their eyes will dilate, and they will act momentarily stunned. When they do answer, they will very likely say that there is nothing they can think of that they don't like. Cult members will generally give some variation on that reply, because they are simply not permitted to talk critically, particularly on television.

- **What else would you rather do in life than be a member of the group?**

The answer is likely to be, "Nothing."

- **Did you take the time to talk with former members, and read critical literature about the group, before you joined, in order to make up your own mind? Is this something you'd be willing to do now?**

It's possible that the person might call your bluff and answer "of course" to the second question. This is fine. If they are in a destructive cult, it's probably a lie—but if the person does follow through, they will be well on their way out of the group, and you will have done them a favor.

If you make it through all the above questions and feel reasonably comfortable that the person was being straight with you—and you're still genuinely interested in learning more about the group—I strongly suggest you do two more things before attending any program: 1) ask other members of the group the same questions, and see if you get consistent answers, and 2) research the group intensively online.

Remember, though, that search engines can be manipulated, and cults have been known to put up phony blogs and websites to give disinformation to potential recruits.

If everything seems to look okay, go to the program with a trusted friend who is both skeptical and assertive. This way you will have someone you trust to discuss what you see and hear.

If the group is a destructive cult, at the program, members will try to find some convenient way to separate you from your friend. "Divide and conquer" is the rule. This may seem quite spontaneous and benign, but it is neither. Typically, one cult member will start talking to your friend, while another will question you. At first you and your friend will be standing next to each other; within minutes you will be several feet away; by the end of the evening you will be at opposite ends of the room. Resist this. Stick together, and don't let anyone split you up. Demand to stay with your friend. If you are pressured to conform, or are confronted by group leaders, simply walk out.

If you find yourself in an indoctrination session, stand up and announce loudly that you don't like being manipulated and controlled. The louder you speak, the faster you will be escorted from the room. Several other people might also jump at the opportunity to leave with you.

Don't let your curiosity get the best of you. If you are highly confident and assertive, and are comfortable challenging people loudly, directly, firmly and to their faces, kudos to you! But if, like most people, you don't like conflict and confrontation, be wise. Many people have been recruited into cults because they were overconfident they could handle themselves in any situation. Curiosity and overconfidence have been the downfall of many people, including me. Placing yourself in a potentially dangerous situation just isn't worth the risk.

Chapter 8

Curing the Mind Control Virus

When most people begin to search for ways to release friends or relatives from cults, they know little or nothing about mind control, the characteristics of destructive cults, or how or where to begin.

Some may think the only available option is deprogramming. Yet they have no idea that deprogramming involves forcible abduction of the cult member, a process that is lengthy and coercive, along with a price tag of 10-50 thousand dollars." I *do not* recommend coercive deprogramming, and know of no reputable person who currently practices it.

Non-coercive ways to help now exist. I and others now use therapeutic techniques that are well established in the mental health profession, along with the latest, innovative approaches. Furthermore, today almost all the professionals who help cult members break free are themselves former members of mind control organizations. They are more likely to understand what cult members are thinking and feeling, and can share personal experiences and insight.

This chapter is a guide to interventions: how the process of curing the mind control virus works. I've included three cases of interventions I have conducted. The dialogues are reconstructed from memory, but the stories themselves are faithful reflections of real events. These case histories took place some years ago. Since then my approach has evolved significantly, into the Strategic Interactive Approach, which is what I use today. Nevertheless, many of the key concepts, dilemmas and techniques that appear in these stories continue to apply in the present day.

First, though, it's important to give you some essential background on deprogramming.

Because I myself was deprogrammed in 1976, I am very familiar with its drawbacks. Back then, very few options were available to concerned relatives and friends of cult members. Either people tried to keep in contact with the member and hoped they would leave on their own, or they hired a deprogrammer. Cult leaders saw deprogramming as a terrible threat. They were losing many long-term, devoted members and leaders because of it. And those people were talking to the media and revealing details of the cults' operations. Ex-members who had simply walked away tended to be paralyzed with guilt and fear, and usually kept their former cult involvement very quiet. But deprogrammees had access to a support network that understood what they had been through and gave them the strength and encouragement to speak out.

By the late 1970s, cult mind control had become intertwined in the public eye with forcible deprogramming. This was partly the result of public relations campaigns financed by some major cults to discredit critics and divert the debate from the cults themselves.[156] The propaganda labeled deprogramming as "the greatest threat to religious liberty of all time." Deprogrammers were falsely portrayed as beating and raping people to force them to recant their freely held religious beliefs. Influenced by this campaign, at least one movie portrayed deprogrammers as money-hungry thugs who were just as bad as cult leaders.

For the record, I know of *no* instance of deprogramming (and I've met hundreds of deprogrammees) that involved any beating, rape or physical abuse. Furthermore, no family I have ever worked with would allow anyone, including a deprogrammer, to harm a family member in any way. Nevertheless, deprogramming is often emotionally traumatic, as well as legally risky.

In a classic deprogramming scenario, a cult member would be located and physically snatched off a street corner, pushed into a waiting vehicle, and driven to a secret location, perhaps a motel room. There the security team would guard the person for several days, 24 hours a day, while the deprogrammer, former cult members, and family members presented information and argued with them. Windows might be nailed shut or barricaded, because members had been known to dive out of them to avoid the so-called "faith-breaking" process. The member would sometimes be accompanied to the bathroom in an effort to prevent suicide attempts. They might be held for many days, until they snapped out of the cult's mind control—or, as occurred in some cases, pretended to do so.

In the small number of deprogrammings I participated in during 1976 and 1977, the cult member was usually confronted while visiting home rather than grabbed off a sidewalk. Even so, when they were told they couldn't leave, they almost always reacted violently. In various deprogrammings, I was punched, kicked, and spat on; had hot coffee thrown in my face; and had tape recorders hurled at me. Indeed, if I hadn't had a cast on my leg during my own deprogramming from the Moonies, I would have done something similar. Cult members are indoctrinated to behave that way: to stay faithful to the group, no matter what.

At the beginning of a deprograming, the cult member often becomes even more convinced that his family is the very embodiment of evil. *After all*, the person thinks, *look at the extremes they have gone to. I've been kidnapped, and now I'm going to be beaten, raped or both*. In the aftermath of such situations, the cult member's trauma, anger, and resentment can take years to dissipate, even if the deprogramming is successful.

I knew one woman who was deprogrammed from a short-term membership in the Moonies. Then she rejoined the group for over a year and quit on her own. It was as if, she told me later, she had to prove she could do it by herself. Unfortunately, during her second stint in the group, the Moonies paraded her around and used her to denounce deprogramming, all over the United States.

It is terrifying to be held prisoner and fear that you are about to be tortured or sexually abused. Remember, these are the experiences that cult leaders tell members to expect in a deprogramming. As you can imagine, good counseling in such a situation is difficult at best. The member immediately clams up and chants, prays or meditates to shut out any external influence. This thought-stopping may continue for hours or days, before they see that they aren't going to be tortured; that the deprogrammers are caring, sensitive people; and that there really are legitimate questions about their group involvement that they should look at. Only then does the person start to respond.

After being part of a small number of interventions, I believed it was imperative to find another approach. Legal, voluntary access to the cult member was essential. Family and friends are the key. But they need to become knowledgeable about cults and mind control, and they need to be coached in how to communicate effectively with a cult member.

The Strategic Interactive Approach, the non-coercive approach I have developed, accomplishes with finesse what deprogramming does with force. However, family members and friends have to work together as a team to plan and implement a strategy for influencing the cult member. Although this approach—like any approach—will not work in every single case, it has proved to be the best option possible.

This non-coercive approach requires excellent information in order to succeed. The information gathering and dissemination begins with the first phone call or meeting.

Let's walk through one such story, from relatively early in my career.

The O'Brien Family and the International Church of Christ[157]

In December 1987, Matthew O'Brien called me and expressed his concern about his son George's involvement with a group known as the Boston Church of Christ. The church was also known as Multiplying Ministries and the International Churches of Christ. (It should not be confused with the mainline Church of Christ, or with the United Church of Christ, an inheritor of the New England Congregational tradition).[158] He had heard of me from Buddy Martin, an evangelist then with the Cape Cod Church of Christ (another mainline church), who strongly denounced the authoritarian shepherding/discipleship cult tactics used by the BCC.[159] O'Brien told me he had grown more and more worried about his son's involvement. George had lost a great deal of weight, was always exhausted, and had abandoned his plans to graduate from a small liberal arts college in upstate New York. He was also becoming progressively more incapable of making simple decisions. He had to get his "discipleship" partner's advice, before doing almost anything.

O'Brien asked me about my own background, and whether I thought this particular group was a destructive cult. I told him that I had successfully counseled many dozens of people out of this particular group. He was very happy to hear this.

The O'Briens wanted to know what makes a group a destructive cult, and asked several probing questions about my own values and ethics. I told them that encouraging a person to think for themselves was paramount, and that I was always careful not to impose my own belief system on a client. My role was to present information, to do individual and family counseling as needed, and to facilitate family communication.

We talked for about half an hour, and I agreed to mail them information on my approach, as well as a background questionnaire and photocopies of articles on Kip McKean's Boston Church of Christ. I also gave them phone numbers of some other families I had worked with. I told them to answer the questions on my form as completely as possible. The more information the family and friends could supply about themselves, I said, the better.

Gathering written information from a family is always a good place to start. It forces the family to think through a variety of issues about themselves, the cult member, the cult member's involvement in the organization, and how they have responded to it, so far. It also gives me a good starting point for person-to-person discussions.

It matters to me how much effort a family will make to do a thorough job. Some families mostly provide one-line answers; on the other hand, one family provided me with a 44-page, single-spaced response. (Six to eight pages of responses is typical.) I'm particularly concerned with the answers to these questions:

- In the family, what are relationships like between siblings, and between the cult member and the parents?
- What kind of a person was the cult member before joining the group?
- Did the member have many friends?
- Did the member use drugs or alcohol?
- Did the member have clear-cut life goals?
- Did the member suffer any trauma or unusual stress during their life; such as the death of a close friend or relative, or the divorce of their parents, or a difficult move to a new city?
- Did they have a well-formed religious, political or social value system?

The healthier a person's family relationships and fully formed sense of identity were before they were recruited by a cult, the easier my job usually is.

In George's case, I wanted to learn who he was before he joined BCC and how he had changed, aside from weight loss and listlessness. I wanted to know who in the family he was closest to. I wanted to know his state of mind just before joining. I also wanted to know about his education, interests and hobbies, work experience and religious background.

As in all my cases, I also wanted to know how long it took for him to be recruited. Did he go straight in after being approached one afternoon, or did it take months or years before he became fully involved? What did he *think* he was joining? Does it bear any similarity to the group he now belongs to? How long has he been a cult member? Where has he been living—with other members, alone, or with non-members? How does he spend his time? Has he ever expressed doubts or difficulties about his membership?

Also, as in all my cases, I wanted to know how his family members and friends have reacted. What have they said or done about his membership of the group? What books or articles have the family read? What professionals and other people have they contacted? I wanted to know who *was* and who *was not* willing to help rescue George. Interestingly, a close sibling who may initially be unwilling to help can often become the most important element in a successful case.

With the O'Brien family, I followed my usual procedures, which look like this:

After studying the completed questionnaire, I talk again with the family by phone. I ask more specific questions to round out the picture and assess what to do next. In most cases, I also ask the family to gather more information from other knowledgeable people—and, sometimes, to obtain additional counseling. It's very important during this preparation period that the family meets and talks with others who have had the same problem—especially others who have successfully rescued a family member. It's also good for the family to talk to former members of the particular cult, to gain insight into their loved one's mindset.

Next I set up a meeting with as many family members and friends as possible, often in the family home. Here I observe how the people relate to each other. I spend a lot of time at this meeting teaching about cults and mind control, and coaching people on the parts they will need to play. It is crucial that people understand exactly what the problem is and what they can (and can't) do to help. I discuss ways to connect with the cult member and persuade them to open up. We also may begin discussing rescue strategy.

One thing I stress is that *everyone* must pull together and look at the rescue as a team effort. This takes the load off any one person's shoulders. It also guarantees that the cult member will be influenced by as many supportive people as possible. I urge them to contact other family members and friends and persuade them to help; to study books, articles, and videos; and to make files/keep a record.

If I am contacted within the first few months of recruitment, the prognosis for a successful exit within a year is extremely good. But if the person has been in a cult for ten years or more when I am contacted, it might be quite some time before a rescue can even be attempted.

That said, long-term members are by no means beyond hope. They just require a lot of patience and continued effort. In fact, in many ways it is easier to counsel someone out of a long-term membership, because the person knows the harsh realities of life in the group—the lies, the manipulations, the broken promises of cult leaders. In contrast, a new member may still be walking on air, as part of the honeymoon stage.

The O'Briens told me that George had been involved for two and a half years. He was living in an apartment with other believers. He was still in contact with his mother and father, less so with his sister, Naomi. His parents were not strongly religious. They objected to George's rigid belief in the group's equally rigid interpretation of the Bible. For his part, George had come to regard his parents' attitudes as non-Christian. As in so many other families, his cult membership had dredged up some angry and resentful feelings on both sides. The family was deadlocked.

By the time George's parents called me, they had long since realized that an oppositional approach was going nowhere. George's father decided to try the opposite tack. He asked George if he could attend a Bible study, and even went to a couple of BCC's Sunday services. Of course, George and his discipleship partners interpreted his father's attendance as a sign that God was moving in his father's life. Strategically, however, it was an important step in repairing George's relationship with his family.

O'Brien had explained to George that he wanted to learn more about his son's church because he loved his son and wanted to rebuild their relationship. This was true, but O'Brien—and everyone in the family—was also trying to learn as much as they could about the group.

To his credit, George never doubted his parents' love for him—nor, deep down, his love for them. But he had been taught that people were either part of God—that is, members of BCC—or on the side of Satan. George had no idea that his family was in touch with me or with Buddy Martin.

After many meetings and phone calls, the family and I began to make plans. The issue of whether to be deceptive was, as always, both important and thorny. The O'Briens had to come to terms with a variety of options. Should they simply tell George what they had learned and ask him to meet with Buddy and me? Ethically, that was what they wanted to do. Yet they were dealing with a mind control cult. If they told him they wanted him to meet people who would be critical of the group, would he tell his superiors? Would they advise him to break off contact with his family?

I encouraged the family to speak with several former BCC members and ask them how a group member would likely respond to the straightforward approach. Without exception, the ex-members told the family that George would immediately consult his discipleship partner for advice. From that moment on, the group would be forewarned, and would do everything in its power to convince him to avoid any contact with his family, since it was obviously being controlled by Satan's power.

My preference is always to have someone ask the cult member if they would be willing to hear a little of the other side of the story, and see what reaction this elicits. However, such a request needs to come from a sibling or a friend, rather than from a parent, so that it seems much less threatening. If the cult member accepts the opportunity, a place and time for meeting with former cult members should be agreed upon, immediately. The person who asks for the meeting must also directly raise the issue that if other group members find out, they will try to convince the member to break their agreement. They need to ask, "Will you fulfill your promise regardless of group pressure?" If the cult member says yes, a verbal contract is established.

This type of open agreement works best with people who are not yet fully indoctrinated, are having questions or doubts, or still trust and are close to their families. But I felt that George was already indoctrinated thoroughly.

I asked if George had ever expressed any dissatisfaction or disillusionment with the group. No, the O'Briens told me—absolutely none. He was totally committed. He only trusted people within the group. He was programmed to think that all others were "dead"—that is, unspiritual.

I advised George's family that, while the decision was theirs, there was only a small chance that they would get access to him if they tried the open approach.

We decided to get George away from the group by inviting him to his grandmother's 86th birthday party, on Cape Cod. After the party on Sunday night, his parents would find an excuse to stay overnight. They would tell George that they would drive back to Boston in the morning. The next morning, the family would tell him at the breakfast table that they were very sorry they had not told him before, but that they had arranged to spend the next three days with a Church of Christ minister, a counselor, and a former BCC member.

I coached the family extensively on what to say and how best to say it. I wanted them to make sure he didn't immediately phone the group, and to do their best to talk him out of simply running away. They would need to reassure him that they were not trying to hurt him, or take him away from God. All they wanted was for him to have access to information about the Boston Church of Christ that he otherwise would never hear. They would ask him to pray, and tell him they trusted that his faith in the power of God was stronger than his fear of Satan.

Once they explained all this, they would ask George to agree to a three-day period of research, during which be would be free to come and go, take as many breaks as he wanted and decide what topics he wanted to concentrate on. During this time, he would agree to not be in touch with any members of BCC. Most importantly, if he wanted to let people in the group know that he wasn't coming to services, he would simply call, tell them he was away on important family business, and would be out of touch for a few days.

Monday morning found me in a Cape Cod coffee shop with Buddy Martin and Ellen, a former member I had counseled out of the Paris branch of BCC the previous summer. We sat around a table and waited for four hours. Meanwhile, the family was in their home, trying to persuade George to agree to their terms. They called me half a dozen times for support and advice. The family did everything I coached them to do. But George was adamant. He would agree to nothing beyond meeting the three of us for a few hours.

We decided to go ahead and do the best we could. Before we left the coffee shop, a bunch of locals told us that we had just set a record for sitting in one spot. I laughed and thought, *Boy, if they only knew what was going on!*

George was flushed, angry and hostile when we walked in and met him. We introduced ourselves, and he was most surprised to meet Buddy. Here was a Bible-toting fundamentalist minister from a Church of Christ. Naturally, he was also scared and confused. We tried our best to make him as comfortable as possible, and to allow him some sense of control.

George asked to speak alone with each of us: first me, then Ellen, then Buddy. We agreed.

Sitting alone with George, I tried to help him see that this situation was an opportunity for him—to learn, to grow, and to prove to his family that he wasn't under mind control and knew what he was doing.

George proved to be as indoctrinated as anyone from the Boston Church of Christ that I had ever worked with. He was extremely resistant to the idea that he might benefit from anything that was being discussed.

Buddy Martin's participation turned out to be the key. In his turn alone with George, he began to cite specific Bible verses, and asked George what he thought each meant. Since the BCC had programmed George to believe in a literal interpretation of the Bible, he could hardly object to examining it. Slowly, one passage at a time, Buddy began to show George that, although the group claimed to be following the Bible, in fact they were taking passages out of context, and deliberately ignoring other verses that affected their meaning. This was the opening by which George began to admit the possibility that the group might be less than perfect.

With that foothold established, George became willing to listen to Ellen and me. I gave him some background on the cult's leader, Kip McKean, including his own recruitment and indoctrination by Chuck Lucas into Crossroads, a cult in Gainesville, Florida, back in the 1970s.[160] It was there that McKean likely learned to use the mind control methods he now used. George had never heard of Crossroads. We showed him a letter written by McKean in March 1986 to Crossroads Church leaders, saying he "owed his very soul" to them.[161] George was shocked.

Then we produced a 1977 letter from the elders of the Memorial Church of Christ in Houston, Texas, where McKean had been a minister. The elders announced they were firing McKean because of his un-Biblical teachings.[162]

With that as a starting point, we could begin discussing with George the characteristics of destructive cults and mind control. In this case, without the letters from McKean and the Memorial Church elders as frames of reference, it would have been impossible to show George what had happened to him.

Then I discussed with George the specific behavioral components of mind control, making sure to explain Lifton's eight criteria of Chinese Communist thought reform. Next I described what it was like for me inside the Moonies. Back then, many people had a negative view of the Moonies (except Moonies themselves, of course), so telling my own story usually helped to minimize any thought-stopping and defensiveness. The parallels between groups become blatantly apparent, and the person I'm speaking with usually makes a lot of connections without prompting.

This information was very intense and troubling for George. He needed to regulate the flow of what he was hearing. Every couple of hours, he would stand up and announce that he needed to go for a walk and pray. This happened several times each day over the three days.

At night I stayed at a nearby bed and breakfast where I was able to rest and map out strategy. Each time George walked out the door, we were never quite sure whether he would return. It would be easy for him to stick his thumb out and hitchhike back to Boston, or phone the cult for a ride. But to try to stop him would have ensured his lack of trust in us thereafter.

But we were in this for the long haul. If he walked out now, the family would simply have to continue giving him information each time they saw or spoke with him. We had to trust that George wanted to do the right thing.

At one point, George complained about the deception his parents had used to get him to his grandmother's house. They apologized profusely. I asked him to put himself in their shoes and suggest any other course of action they could have taken that would have been effective. He could think of none. He knew that if he had received any advance warning, he would have gone straight to his superiors and they would have dissuaded him from making the trip.

George's parents reminded him that he had turned down a previous offer to meet former members and read critical information. He was astonished; he didn't even remember it. They reminded him that he had met his cousin Sally a month earlier. At the O'Briens' request, she had made just such an offer, and George had turned her down cold. His parents told him they felt they had no other choice.

During those three days, I was able to do a good deal of counseling with the family on ways to communicate more effectively with George—and with each other. I also helped them work on some of their own issues and concerns, which were quite separate from their son's cult involvement. In this way, George could see that the whole family was learning and growing together, and that his renewed family involvement could be a stepping stone to developing closer relationships with everyone.

After the three days were over, George was not willing to say that he would never return to BCC. He did say that he wanted more time to study and think about what he had learned. He also decided not to return to his apartment, but to stay with his parents. There he would read books and articles, watch videotapes of shows on cults, and continue to speak and meet other former members.

Within a month, George declared to his family that he would never return to the Boston Church of Christ. He had attended services and Bible studies at the Burlington Church of Christ, one of the 18,000 mainline Churches of Christ, where he met some 65 other refugees from the Boston group.

He now says he feels far happier than when he was in the cult, and has a much better understanding of the Bible. Since leaving, he has spent a good deal of time helping others understand the destructive aspects of BCC.

Although George's parents would probably prefer that he attend their Unitarian church with them, they respect his right to choose his own way. For years, after the intervention, his father attended a weekly Bible study group with his son in order to learn and get closer to him.

Wisely, the O'Briens were willing to intervene in George's life only to the point where he would be able to recognize and understand the mind control practices of destructive cults. They did not want to bring George under their own control, or simply try to make themselves feel better. Their commitment was to help their son think for himself.

The Beliefs Underlying My Approach

Since cults lure people into what amounts to a psychological trap, my job as a counselor is to show a cult member four things.

First, I demonstrate to them that they *are* in a trap—a situation where they are psychologically disabled and don't feel able to leave.

Second, I show them that they didn't originally choose to enter a trap.

Third, I point out that other people in other mind control groups are also trapped.

Fourth, I tell the person that it is possible to escape from the trap.

While these four points might seem obvious to people outside a cult, they are not immediately apparent to anyone under undue influence. It often takes someone who has been caught in such a trap to convey this message with the necessary strength and determination. This is why former cult members, especially former cult leaders, are usually the most effective people for assisting the exit process.

My approach rests on several core principles (or, if you like, beliefs) about people:

One is that *people need and want to grow.* Life is ever changing, and people inherently move in a direction that will support and encourage growth.

It is important that *people focus on the here and now.* What has been done in the past is over. The focus should not be on what they "did wrong" or "didn't do," but on what they can do *now.* The past is useful only insofar as it provides information that may be valuable in the present.

It is also my observation that *people will always choose what they think is best for them at any given time,* based on their experiences and the information they have.

It is equally clear to me that *each person is unique* and *each situation is different.* Each person has a special way of understanding and interacting with reality. Therefore, my approach is totally client-centered. I adjust myself to fit each specific client's needs, and my client is always the cult member. I don't expect them to adapt to my needs or expectations. In my approach, the counselor's job is to understand the person thoroughly—what they value, what they need, what they want, and how they think. I have to step inside their head—in a way, to temporarily become them—in order to understand and help them do what *they* want to do. My approach depends on having faith that, deep down, even the most committed cult member wants out.

Lastly, *it's essential to be family-centered.* When someone is recruited into a destructive cult, everyone they know and love is affected. In any successful effort to help them exit, family members and friends are vital. They can be trained to be as effective as possible whenever they communicate with the cult member, and they can use personal and emotional leverage to gain the member's cooperation.

This way of working demands a lot from the family. They must be willing to learn new ways of communicating, and to deal with existing troublesome issues. If there are any significant family problems, they are best addressed—and, ideally, resolved—before any rescue strategy is implemented.

When the focus is kept on the family, everyone changes. The cult member becomes aware that positive things are occurring beyond the cult's involvement. Family members learn how to build rapport and trust, and how to plant questions in the cult member's mind. When family members learn how to interact effectively, they do a great deal to help the victim of mind control break away from the group. During any rescue effort, this factor often becomes crucial.

A family's love is a much stronger force than the conditional love given by cult members and leaders. A healthy family's love supports one's right to grow into an autonomous adult and make one's own life decisions. In contrast, a cult's love attempts to keep a person a dependent adolescent—and that love may well be withdrawn if the person makes their own decisions or fails to follow the leader's orders.

When I counsel a cult member, I never try to take the group away from them—or to take them permanently away from the group. If I did, they would only feel threatened, and rightly so. Instead, I always look for ways for them to grow, by offering different perspectives and possibilities. I help people to see choices they didn't know existed, then encourage them to do what they think is best for themselves. Throughout this process, I also do whatever I can to let them feel in control.

As we have seen, mind control *never* succeeds in fully erasing a person's authentic self. It merely imposes a dominating cult identity that suppresses the real self. Cult indoctrination downloads a mind control virus—a virus that can be cured. Once the virus is gone, a person's mental and emotional hardware can be repaired, and the person's real self can come forward once again and integrate the cult experiences, hopefully in a healthy way.

As a Unification Church member, I thought that I had successfully "died to myself." I, Steve Moonie, thought that the old Steve Hassan was dead. Yet the core me woke up again during my deprogramming. I was able to eventually remember all the contradictions, conflicts, and broken promises that I had experienced while I was a member. That realization enabled me to leave. My authentic self had been there all along.

Successfully connecting with a person's authentic identity is what enables me to help someone walk away from a cult. If the core identity is happy and content with cult involvement—a very rare occurrence—there is little I can do. Such a person would not be under undue influence; they would have genuinely chosen to be right where they are.

But I almost never encounter such people. Families call me because they observe something terrible happening. And I have discovered that when someone in slavery is given a truly free choice, is able to overcome the learned helplessness, they do not choose to stay enslaved—not when they could be making decisions for their own life, having normal relationships with other people, and pursuing their own interests and dreams.

The Strategic Interactive Approach has some other distinctive features. First, I focus on the *process* of change. What this means is that *how* people come to change is more important than *what* or *why* they change.

Since I believe that people are naturally interested in growing and learning, my approach is also educational. I do a lot of teaching—about psychology, communication, mind control issues, and other destructive cults, as well as a great deal of material about the particular group's history, leadership and doctrinal contradictions.

Difficult Cases

When a cult member refuses to speak with people who can offer them the other side of the story, or simply walks out of an intervention and returns to the cult, all is not lost. Communication about key issues has at least been opened. Often, the cult member feels badly about how they treated their loved ones and agrees to talk at a future date. It might take weeks or months for the family to re-establish a relationship with the cult member—but an opening for communication usually appears at a later time.

When rescue efforts fail, often it is because the timing was poor or unlucky. Perhaps the cult member just came from an intensive re-indoctrination experience, married someone in the group or received a promotion. Naturally, the best time is when the person is in a down period, but of course such periods are impossible to predict.

After a failed rescue effort, the family has two choices:

1) Back off, telling the cult member that when they want to look at more information or talk to former group members, the family will be happy to help.

2) Attempt to intervene further with the help of other people who can approach the person in other contexts.

This second option is more complex and time-consuming. It means trying to help the cult member without their knowing that the family is trying to help them re-evaluate their group involvement. I need to find a pretext to meet the cult member and find enough time with them to do some good. This is never easy.

Someone observing the preparations for such an effort would be reminded of the old television program or movie franchise starring Scientologist Tom Cruise, *Mission: Impossible*. A team is assembled. The target's psychological profile is scrutinized for vulnerabilities, interests, and patterns of behavior. A strategy is devised to meet them and get them sufficiently involved for the mission to be carried out. Ironically, in some ways these preparations parallel what cult recruiters do to lure unsuspecting victims into their organizations. Most notably, these rescue efforts involve an initial deception—the very thing cults are famous for. However, I am not trying to make someone into my follower; once my job of presenting information, laying out alternatives, and counseling is accomplished, it is up to the individual to make decisions for themselves.

This type of approach may be necessary, if a cult member's relationship with their family or friends has been severely damaged. Such cases frequently involve long-term cult members whose families long ago passed their limits of frustration and pain, and said or did things that severed the relationship.

Margaret Rogers and The Children Of God/ The Family[163]

Margaret Rogers was a member of Moses David Berg's Children of God cult (later renamed The Family) for ten years.[164] During that time, her two sisters and brother received only half a dozen letters from her. Margaret, who then went by a name given to her in the cult, traveled all over the world with this unusual group. She was married to another member, and they had three children.

Her family generally did not even know how to contact Margaret, except for one time when they were able to visit her in the Philippines. During that visit, all the family members witnessed moments when Margaret briefly returned to her authentic self. Her face and demeanor relaxed, and she became the person they once knew. This happened most often when her brother and sisters talked about memories of childhood, or people and events back in their hometown.

Her family pleaded with her to take some time away from the group and talk with former members. At first, Margaret showed a distinct willingness to do this. She also badly needed food and rest, as well as a thorough medical examination. The family didn't mention it to Margaret, but they knew the group was making her do "flirty fishing"—using sex to recruit new members. In fact, Berg called his female followers "Happy Hookers for Jesus."[165] This was a major way the cult earned money as well as attracting male converts. Berg was a pedophile who also encouraged sex among members and even with very young children.

It was also clear to Margaret's family that her husband was a hard-core cult member who showed no such flashes of his former identity. It was equally clear that he always made all decisions for her. Margaret's family returned home, glad to have seen her and her children—and committed to trying to rescue her.

Her parents attended one of my communication workshops for family members and asked me to help. They told me they wished they had had the workshop's guidance before their trip to the Philippines, or even that they had taken me along. I told them to keep learning all they could about the group: its buzzwords, lifestyle and beliefs. To this end I put them in touch with several former members. I also encouraged them to continue practicing the communication techniques I taught them. Within a year, Margaret contacted them from Mexico and asked if they could come to visit again.

I sat down with the Rogers family and discussed the options. How could they get me to her, keep the husband away as long as possible, and evoke a minimum of suspicion—all at the same time? We concluded that the parents should not make the trip at all. They represented the clearest threat to Margaret's cult involvement. Instead, only her two sisters and brother would go, for a week. I would go, too, posing as her sister Lisa's boyfriend.

We manufactured a story that Margaret's father was under doctor's orders not to take such a trip—he had a problem with his heart. His wife was unable to get time off from work and felt obliged to stay close to home to help her husband, if necessary. Margaret's brother Bob called up his company's branch office in Mexico City and talked them into giving a job interview to Margaret's husband, who, the family knew, was looking for a way to earn some legitimate, steady money. Bob convinced the husband to accept the offer of a job interview. Bob would accompany him to Mexico City for a few days to give us time alone with Margaret.

The plan was to assess Margaret's state of mind and try to convince her to come back to the United States, with her children. We hoped that after the previous visit, she might be homesick. Also, if she didn't really love her husband, as we all suspected, we had a good chance of success.

Everything started out smoothly. When we arrived, Margaret and her husband showed little or no sign of anxiety. We all spent the first day together. None of us indicated that we were bothered by Margaret's lifestyle. We went out to eat lots of good food, went shopping, bought the whole family new clothes, and generally had a good time. Margaret and her husband did not try to sell the group to us in any way.

Bob left with Margaret's husband the next day, and we invited Margaret to our hotel, where we took a room for her and the kids. We volunteered to take the kids out, and recommended that she lie down and catch up on some sleep in the meantime.

When we returned five hours later, she was still asleep. She was obviously exhausted. When she got up, her face had a lot more color. We ordered room service. It was clear that she was not used to eating so well or to being served in such a nice hotel. She thoroughly enjoyed it.

After dinner we started up a conversation. It began with talk of pleasant childhood memories. Then her sisters started talking about how they missed her, and how they felt robbed of the sister they loved so much. Tears started to flow and people shared long hugs.

Then the discussion turned to the children and their future. Was this the way Margaret had always envisioned raising a family? Was Tom her vision of an ideal husband?

The time seemed ripe. "Hey, listen, Margaret," said one of her sisters. "How would you like to come back with us to Connecticut?"

"Oh my gosh, I'd love that!" Margaret answered excitedly. But then she sank back into the couch and said, "Oh, I can't do that."

"Why not?" Lisa asked.

"Because I just can't."

I stepped in. "Is it because you believe God wouldn't like it if you did?"

"Yes," she said. "Besides, Tom would never do it, unless he was told to by Elias." Elias was their elder. This was the first time Margaret had mentioned this aspect of the group to her sisters.

"What would *you* like to do?" I asked again.

"I don't know. I don't think I can," she said with a tone of disgust.

I asked her, "What would happen if God told you to go back to Connecticut?"

"He would never do that," she answered.

"But what if He did?" I pressed. "What if He told you in a loud clear voice that His will was to take the children and go to Connecticut for a few months? Would you be obedient?" My voice rose. "Where is your commitment: to God or to the group?"

She thought about it for a while. Then she answered, "If God told me to go to Connecticut, then I would go."

"Even if your husband or another member told you to stay?" I asked insistently. I was pushing it, but I wanted to see how far I could get.

"If God told me to go, I would go, even if others told me to stay," she declared.

Very good, I thought. Now for the next step. I asked her "How would you *know* if God wanted you to go, if you don't pray and ask Him what He wants you to do? Have you ever asked God a question like this one?"

"No, but I will tonight. But I don't think He wants me to go to Connecticut."

"Oh, so you're going to tell God what to answer," I said. "Why don't you reach down to the bottom of your soul and pray without any foregone conclusions about what God wants for you and your children?" My voice was intense. "Pray fervently and clearly, putting your total faith that what He wants will be what is right for you."

Margaret asked me if I really believed in God that strongly. I told her I did.

Then she asked me about my spiritual life. That gave me all the opening I needed to launch into my experience in the Moonies—how I came to believe that God was speaking through my leaders, and how I couldn't doubt, ask critical questions, or even leave the group. I explained phobia indoctrination. I explained how I was finally able to imagine a future for myself outside of the group only because I had met so many former Moonies who were still good, very spiritual people after they left.

Margaret listened attentively. I explained that I had come to distrust my own inner voice when I was in the Moonies. I was taught to believe that the voice was evil—when, in fact, I came to learn, it was a direct link to God. I described how I had been controlled by fear and guilt, and how in both the Moonies and the Children of God there was complete control over the information we received. Both groups' leaders saw themselves as God's chosen One on Earth; both had absolute authority; and both were extremely wealthy.

Then I asked her, "Do you believe that God gave people free will, just so He could take it away through deception and mind control? Think about it: do you believe in a God who wants His children to be robots or, at the very best, slaves? If God wanted that, He never would have given Adam and Eve free will. Isn't it a huge contradiction?"

Margaret's mouth hung open. Her eyes were wide as saucers. I gave her a hug and excused myself. I announced that I was going for a walk; that it would be good to take a break and reflect. She needed time to absorb what I had said. I was confident that her sisters would help her start working it through and deal with her feelings as they came up.

Later that night, I talked with her for a few more hours, mostly trying to empower her. "You've got a good mind," I told her. "You should use it." I told her I knew she had always been an ethical person. Did she really believe that the ends justify the means? Was it Christian to use sex to recruit people? She loved her family. Would she let her fears be stronger than her love?

I also appealed to her maternal instinct. I asked how she felt letting her children grow up in virtual poverty, with no formal education, and with little or no medical attention. I knew that she was aware of other members' children who had died because they weren't allowed to see a doctor.

Before she went to bed, I reminded her to pray, and pray hard. "Pray like you've never prayed before. Beseech God to show you the way. Ask Him what *He* wants you to do."

That night we let the children sleep in her sister's room, so she could have an undisturbed night's rest. The next morning Margaret told us of incredible dreams, filled with symbols of great struggle and turmoil. In one dream she was lost at night in a forest, not knowing how to get out. In another she was alone in a small boat, being bombarded by stormy ocean waves. The third dream was of wandering in a field of wildflowers in the middle of a warm, sunny, Spring day.

Over breakfast I asked her if she was aware of God's answer to her question. She flashed a smile, which then turned into a frown. She got up from the table and walked to the window. Then, after staring outside for a while, she turned and said, "In my heart I think I should go back to the States, but I don't think I can."

I felt as though a hundred-pound weight had just been lifted from my chest, but I tried to show little excitement. Her sisters started to cry. "What is stopping you?" I asked.

She sighed and thought for a long time. Then she said, "I'm afraid."

Her sisters and I went over, and the four of us stood there in one massive hug. "Don't worry, " I reassured her. "We'll help you in every way we can. Trust God."

We acted as if that settled the matter. Now was the time to get moving.

Within two hours, we were on our way to the airport. We phoned ahead to her parents and told them the good news. Margaret left a long letter to Tom saying that we were on our way to the States, that she wanted to be alone with the kids and her family for a few weeks, and that she would contact him and let him know when he could come visit, if he wanted to. She assured him that she had decided on this voluntarily—that she had been very unhappy for a long time, and felt that God wanted her to do it.

There were no problems at the airport, and we boarded without incident. In situations like this an unexpected, crazy thing might happen. But this time we were lucky. No cult members showed up at the gate to haul Margaret away. On the plane ride home, I told Margaret that I had a few friends who were former members of the Children of God. But I decided that I wasn't going to explain my role until a couple of weeks had passed, so she would have time to stabilize.

When Margaret walked into her parents' house for the first time in ten years, she saw balloons and a huge WELCOME HOME! sign hanging from the ceiling. The house was filled with relatives and friends. Tears streamed down her face. She had forgotten how wonderful life had been for her there.

She told me later that she felt like a prisoner of war who had just been released from ten years of captivity. So many people had grown up and changed. The neighborhood had changed a lot. And she was totally unaware of the national and world events of the last decade. She had plenty of catching up to do. Within a couple of days I arranged for her to sit down with some former Children of God members. I was lucky enough to locate someone she had known while in the group.

Margaret improved dramatically, day by day. She put on weight, started to make jokes, and had color and expression in her face once again. Her children adapted quickly and joyfully to their new life. Arrangements were made later to help her husband, with the support of his family.

No one can come out of a long-term experience like that without emotional problems, and she was no exception. Not all cases, though, are successful. Especially in the early years of my counseling work, I took on several cases in which I was not able to help the person to leave the cult. In retrospect, some cases had just too many factors going against success, but I tried anyway. Some cases involved the psychopathology of the individual in the group, or in family members themselves. Other cases involved families who neglected to tell me everything about their family history, while in others, there was intentional sabotage by one of the family members.

Alan Brown and the Foundation for Human Understanding[166]

Herbert and Julia Brown's son Alan had been involved in Roy Masters' group, the Foundation for Human Understanding, for over two years. Masters is a professional hypnotist who, in 1961, began one of the first national radio talk shows called *How Your Mind Can Keep You Well.* Masters is still doing radio and has even published a book.

One purpose of the show is to recruit new followers. Alan got involved by listening one night, and sent in his money to order Masters' audiotapes on "meditation." I've listened to these tapes myself, and they are not about meditation. They are actually a powerful hypnotic induction to Masters' voice, causing listeners to open up to Masters' control.

Later, as I studied Masters, I learned that he had moved into the "exorcism" business: discovering people in his audience who he claimed were possessed and then liberating them—for a fee. His place of work was normally a hotel ballroom packed with people.[167] Unlike most of my clients, the Browns had serious psychological problems. Unfortunately, I didn't realize that until I came to Michigan for a rescue attempt with their son, shortly before he went away for a one-month residential course, at Masters' ranch in Oregon.

I knew something was seriously wrong when I walked in the door. The family dog was virtually uncontrollable: jumping, barking and running all over the furniture. The Browns apologized to me, but it was evident that they were at their wits' end. They were constantly undermining each other's authority with the dog: one would tell him to go lie down, and then the other would encourage the dog to sit on his lap. As a dog owner and lover, it was clear to me that they lacked basic awareness. They knew nothing about dogs, or how to train them. They did not understand how the dysfunction in their own lives had negative consequences on their dog and on their child.

Later, when I met Alan, I observed an only child who was obviously spoiled and overprotected. He was also slowly being driven crazy because he was constantly receiving conflicting messages from his two parents—messages they were unaware they were sending. One minute his mother would praise him for mowing the lawn, and the next his father would criticize him for taking two weeks to actually do it. The father would tell Alan he should get a job; then his mother would tell him he should wait a few more weeks.

It was obvious to me that Alan was desperately trying to get away from his parents' influence. He wanted to be independent, but he didn't know how to begin to do so. He wanted to prove to his parents that he was capable, but his self-esteem was so low that he seemed to be always on the verge of depression. I wasn't surprised to learn Alan had difficulties socially and had no friends outside of the Masters group.

In this case, the authentic Alan was not happy or successful. He was miserable. From a counseling point of view, there was little from the past that could be used for him to reconnect with his authentic self.

Despite the disturbing traits of Masters' cult group,[168] as long as Alan's parents continued their dysfunctional style of relating and communicating with him, it seemed to me that staying in the group, at least for the time being, was the better choice for him. At least the group offered him an opportunity to socialize with other people, as well as the hope that he would get better by following his "sinless" savior, Roy Masters.

Clearly, understanding mind control and destructive cults was not enough for Alan. He needed an alternative environment, and the whole family needed a good deal of personal and family counseling. Unfortunately, although his parents loved him, they were unwilling to get the help they needed. They merely wanted me to get Alan out of the cult, and that was all.

On top of that, the Browns didn't want to invest the money required in a good rehabilitation program for Alan. He absolutely needed to have the experience of being somewhere healthy—not at home, and not in the cult. Sadly, he didn't get it.

My efforts were doomed from the start. Alan's parents did not understand cults and mind control thoroughly, nor were they willing to examine their own behavior and take the necessary steps to change. Meanwhile, Alan was getting too much from the cult—hope, attention, and connection with people—to even consider giving it up.

Unfortunately, people like Alan rarely succeed within a cult, even by its own standards. More often than not, they get pushed to their limit, burn out, and either walk out or are kicked out. I hoped that when that day came, Alan would remember some of the things he and I discussed.

I learned several valuable lessons from this case, back in 1980. First, I learned that screening, meeting with, educating and properly preparing the family is vital. If the family is not willing to invest the necessary time, energy and money, I should not take the case. Second, if the family isn't willing to address its own problems and make an effort to change and grow, it will undermine any rescue effort, as well as the cult member's potential exit and recovery.

Over the years, I have come to understand the critical variables for success. I will only accept a case if I am sure it will be a positive step for the cult member and their family, even if we cannot rescue the cult member overnight.

In addition, I've learned that three full days of counseling is necessary for success. The only people I have been unsuccessful with went back to their cults without giving their families three full days' time, or were married or had family still in the group.

These are just three examples from the many hundreds of people I have worked with since my exit from the Moonies. I've learned the incredible lengths to which people will go for a cause they believe is great and just. I have also learned that no one wants to sacrifice their time, energy and dreams for a cause that is harmful and untrue. Once the phobia against leaving is addressed, I can make contact with the person's true self and let them know what has been done to them. At this point, they almost always choose to be free, because people will choose what they believe is best for them.

It is also important for former cult members and their families not to view everything that happened inside a mind control cult as negative. Sometimes people learn important skills. Sometimes they meet good people, who eventually also leave the group, and a good post-cult relationship evolves. I always encourage people to *remember the good and take it with them* when they decide to leave.

Still, there is no question that belonging to a destructive cult changes you forever. You realize how many things you've taken for granted: family, friends, education, your ability to make decisions, your individuality and your personal belief system.

Leaving a cult also affords a unique opportunity to sit "naked" with yourself and analyze everything you ever knew or believed in. Such a process can be liberating, and also quite terrifying. It is a chance to start your life all over again.

Chapter 9

How to Help

If someone you care about becomes a member of a destructive cult, you will probably find yourself facing one of the toughest situations of your life. In helping this person return to their authentic self, it's easy to fall into mistakes that will make your job even harder. But if you respond to the challenge in a planned, emotionally balanced way, the chances are good that your efforts will ultimately be successful. The experience will also be very rewarding and joyful. That is what I have seen time and time again in the families I've worked with.

This chapter will give you some basic, practical ideas of what to do and not do when trying to help a cult member leave their group. It will also explain what to do for yourself and other members of your family while involved in this effort. Taking a few basic precautions can save you a lot of frustration.

The best place to start is with two contrasting examples—one leading to success, the other to failure. The two stories that follow are composites, based on real people I have counseled. To protect their privacy, all of the people's names have been changed.

The Johnson Family and the Twelve Tribes[169]

When Bill and Lorna Johnson first noticed that their daughter Nancy was acting strangely, they simply wrote it off as the growing pains of a 19-year-old girl away from home for the summer. Her older brother Neil had gone through his own share of episodes of strange behavior, when he was about the same age.

Nancy was then in Milwaukee, selling magazine subscriptions door to door to earn extra money for college. Bill and Lorna knew she was experiencing a slump in sales. Yet when she explained her difficulties with her job to them in a phone call, she surprised them by sounding emotionally cool, as though she didn't have a care in the world. Knowing Nancy was a go-getter, Bill and Lorna expected their daughter to sound frustrated and anxious. Something wasn't right, but they couldn't put a finger on it.

Several weeks later they received a telephone call from Leslie, one of Nancy's close friends. Leslie told Bill and Lorna that she had just received a disturbing letter from Nancy. Leslie had hesitated before calling them—she didn't want to betray Nancy's confidence. But the content of the letter was so unlike Nancy that she felt she had to risk alienating her friend.

The letter read, in part: "I have truly found my place in the world, Leslie. God has summoned me to be part of the Twelve Tribes, the only true Christians on Earth. I have thrown away my blue jeans, for I realize that they were part of my Satanic past...A woman's place is beneath a man...the Word of God says so, and I am learning to destroy this vain ego of mine that longs to be part of this wicked world...I'm now living with the most holiest [sic] and most wonderful people on the planet."

Nancy's favorite clothes had always been her jeans. She had always been easy to get along with, because she was so nonjudgmental. Also, she had been something of a feminist. Such subservient sentiments were highly uncharacteristic of her. All these things bothered Leslie.

Nancy's parents were even more disturbed because Nancy had apparently been hiding her involvement with the Tribes from them. Why hadn't Nancy even mentioned this group to them? She had always been open and honest with them before. Whenever they asked her what was new, she had answered, "Not much." From her letter, a great deal seemed to be new.

The Johnsons immediately phoned to ask their minister's advice. He came right over. He agreed that Nancy was indeed acting strangely, and suggested that maybe she had become involved in a religious cult. At the mention of the word "cult," the Johnsons began to panic. At this point, Bill came close to making a typical mistake. His first impulse was to call Nancy and confront her about the group, her letter to Leslie and her secrecy. Fortunately, he didn't.

Lorna started to sob uncontrollably. She felt she had failed as a parent. Something must have been lacking in Nancy's life that would allow her to join a cult. Lorna began to mentally review every significant incident in Nancy's life that might have made her so susceptible. She decided to ask her son Neil to drop whatever he was doing and come over.

When Neil walked into the living room an hour later, his father was pacing back and forth, his mother was still in tears, Leslie was sitting near her on the sofa with her hands clasped on her lap, and the minister was standing next to the TV, with a bewildered expression on his face. "What's going on here?" Neil asked as he sat down and put his arm around his mother.

Lorna said, "We think Nancy has gotten into some type of religious cult."

"Nancy? Never. No way! She would never fall for something like that." Then his parents told him everything they knew. He was astonished.

Fortunately, the minister was able to persuade the Johnsons to do nothing for the moment. He assured them that he would do his best to try to find more information about the Twelve Tribes, and find advice about the best approach to take.

Through the minister's research and connections, he found my name and telephone number and gave them to the family. They called me the following day. I had them fill out my questionnaire, and we had several more phone discussions.

As soon as we were able to get enough concrete information, the Johnsons asked their friends and relatives to come over the next Saturday, to be part of a two-day counseling and training program. I advised them to try to get as much help and support as they could find. I was able to arrange for a former Tribes member in another city to make a video describing as much as he could remember about the group, its leaders, its beliefs and its practices. With this as the foundation, we were able to make a plan.

Since Nancy and her fellow Twelve Tribes members were unaware that her family knew about her involvement, it was relatively easy to surprise her. The family agreed that we would all fly to Milwaukee the following week, where a former member would join us.

We staked out the cult house the morning after we arrived, and waited for Nancy to leave. We figured that it would be much easier to talk with her if she was off the group's property and away from other members.

Within a couple of hours, she and another woman got into a station wagon and drove off. We followed them to a supermarket, in a nearby shopping mall. After they went inside, I coached the Johnsons on what to say and do. The plan was to try to wait until Nancy was by herself, if possible. At that point, they were to walk right up to her and give her a big hug and immediately invite her to lunch. They would also tell her that they needed to discuss some very urgent family business—and nothing more. We counted on Nancy being totally surprised. Since she hadn't told her family about the group, it would be more difficult for her to resist their insistent invitation to go out to eat. They would be affectionate and friendly, but firm. Neil would make sure that the other woman would not interfere with their departure.

I watched from a short distance away. Nancy put up no resistance at all. She seemed really happy to see her family, yet very shocked and confused. When Nancy said, "Let me go tell Claire," Neil volunteered to do that, and walked toward the store.

"I think she's in the produce department," Nancy called out to him.

"Don't worry," Neil said as he looked back. His parents were already walking toward the car, arm in arm with Nancy.

Neil waited inside the store for a minute and then came running out. "She said fine," Neil told her as he got into the car.

I took a cab back to the hotel and waited in the second room we had taken next door, until the family was ready for me. Meanwhile, I reported what had happened to Alexis, the former Tribes member.

We didn't have to wait long. As instructed, the Johnsons waited until they were settled in their room before telling Nancy that they had flown out because they were concerned about the group she was involved with. At first Nancy denied any involvement. Then Mr. Johnson produced her letter to Leslie. As Bill told me later, her face turned beet red and she started to cry.

"Why did you lie to us?" Bill asked sternly. "That's not like you, honey," Mrs. Johnson added. More tears from Nancy.

"We're here because we love you and we're worried about you," Neil said, wiping his own tears away.

"Why don't you tell us all about it?" Bill asked. "Start from the beginning."

Nancy recounted what had happened. At first she seemed her normal self, but after a few minutes her personality changed. Her face took on a faraway expression, and she started quoting from the Bible and her leader.

Lorna asked Nancy if, deep down in her heart, she loved them and trusted them. She thought for a moment and said, "Yes."

"Will you stay with us for the next three days, and not talk to Claire or see anyone from the group during that time?" Lorna asked.

"Why?" Nancy wanted to know.

"Because there's important information we think you'll want to hear.

We've arranged for some people to come to share what they know with you. We want you to think for yourself about what we'll discuss, without any interference."

Nancy thought about it for what must have seemed like an eternity. She wanted to know who these people were and why it had to be for three days.

Bill said, "Honey, you can find out for yourself. They're waiting next door. All that we ask is that you trust us, and that you give them a chance to tell you facts the group might not want you to hear."

Nancy listened eagerly, once she saw that everyone was sincere and that we didn't have horns on our foreheads. She was immensely grateful for all the concern and love shown to her. She had had her doubts about the group but, like most new cult members, thought that she just wasn't spiritual enough to question or analyze what the older members told her.

Within two days, the Twelve Tribes' hold on her was broken, and she returned to her old life.

Why the Johnsons Succeeded

Even though their daughter had been recruited into a destructive cult, the Johnsons were very fortunate. First, since they talked with Nancy weekly, they were able to notice some of the changes in her voice and personality very early on. They instinctively knew that they should stay in close touch, because Nancy was young, halfway across the country, and experiencing great stress in her sales work. While the Johnsons could have made sure that Nancy knew about destructive cults before she left, they didn't realize that the problem could affect anyone, even a member of their family. Furthermore, once they understood the techniques and effects of mind control, they were able to move quickly toward constructive solutions. They did not allow their initial guilt, and their fear that they had failed as parents, to undermine them.

Leslie turned out to be a hero. She overcame her fear of angering Nancy and acted like a true friend, by contacting her parents. Because she had done so, the Johnsons were able to quickly identify and resolve the problem. As soon as Nancy was out of the group, she thanked Leslie profusely.

The Johnsons were also quite fortunate in getting good advice from their minister, who quickly came to their aid. Not only did he help them to put a finger on the problem, but also he was able to keep them from making any of the classic mistakes. Unlike most clergy, their minister had attended a workshop on cults, earlier that year. He knew that the family should not do anything rash or confrontational. He also knew that it was not wise for them to try to rationally discuss the cult issue with their daughter, without guidance from cult experts. He understood that Lorna and Bill needed to slow down and make a plan with those experienced and skilled enough to do it successfully.

The Marlowes and The Way International

Roger and Kitty Marlowe were not as fortunate as the Johnsons. Their son Henry was recruited into The Way, a Bible cult, while he was away at college. They noticed some very drastic changes in his personality and his disposition, but for the most part they thought those changes had been quite positive. Henry had stopped swearing, and he told them that he had given up smoking and drinking. When they came to visit him on parents' day, they were delighted to see his dormitory room so neat, and that his once-favorite magazine, *Playboy*, was noticeably absent.

Henry introduced his parents to several of his friends from the group. They thought it was odd that he had become so religious. He had never before expressed an interest in religion. On the whole, though, Kitty and Roger were impressed by many of the people in the fellowship. They seemed to be well-groomed, were obviously intelligent, came from apparently good homes, and were very friendly. The Marlowes didn't even think to investigate The Way. On the surface, it seemed fine.

They did become concerned when they saw their son's grades at the end of that semester. Henry's A minus average had plummeted to a C plus. When they confronted him about his grades, Henry was very defensive. He told them he was doing the best he could, but he felt he had gotten really bad teachers that term. Besides, he was thinking of changing his major. Marketing no longer interested him. He wanted to become a religious studies major.

Henry had always been a headstrong, independent kid. His parents reasoned that he knew what he was doing. Of course, they also wanted him to be able to support himself. Yet, if he was feeling a spiritual calling, who were they to question it? He was an adult, almost 20 years old.

Another semester came and went, and still the Marlowes didn't quite understand what was going on. Henry did manage to pull his grades up to a B average—which was still well below what he had achieved in the past.

That summer, Henry told his parents that he was planning to go to Kansas for a "once-a-year gathering of believers." However, once he was there, he phoned to say that he had felt "called by the Lord" to take a leave from college. He was going to make a one-year commitment to go wherever The Way sent him, take a part-time job to cover expenses, and evangelize at least 20 hours a week.

Roger was infuriated. "Why don't you finish your senior year and then evangelize?" he said with considerable irritation.

Henry got angry at his father's tone of voice. "Because, Dad, I feel like this is the right thing for me to do! Please, Dad, I want your support on this."

Henry's mother had been listening on another phone. She said, "Why don't you come home and we can discuss this?"

"Mom, trust me. I know what I'm doing."

Roger and Kitty could now hear mumbling on the line. It sounded as though someone was standing next to Henry, coaching him.

"Is there someone telling you what to say?" his father demanded.

"What?" Henry asked.

"Is there someone there telling you what to say to us?" his father repeated.

"Uh, er, no," Henry stammered.

"Son, have you been sucked into one of those religious cults?"

"We're a Bible research and teaching fellowship," Henry said in a defensive tone, repeating the words as though he were reading them from a brochure.

"I want you to come home right now, young man!" his father ordered. "If you don't, I'll never respect you again," he threatened.

"Now calm down, Roger. Henry, your father is very upset. Henry, you're not in a cult, are you?"

"No, Mom, of course not," Henry answered.

"You see, Roger, Henry's not in a cult," Kitty said, as if repeating these words would magically make them true.

Henry did not return home to discuss anything with his parents. Instead, he went to St. Louis to work for the group, recruiting other members for The Way. He asked his parents to put some of his belongings in boxes, and they shipped them off to him as he requested. They even sent him $500 in cash to help him get started.

Henry's father was disgusted. He went to the library, started making copies of articles that described The Way as a cult, and mailed them to Henry. He thought these articles would convince Henry to leave The Way and come home. The move backfired. Henry simply swallowed the cult's line that his parents were possessed by the Devil and were not to be trusted.

Kitty believed that her son was too intelligent to stay in such a group for very long. She convinced herself that he would soon see his mistake and walk out.

When months passed and he became more and more distant, she grew hysterical, loading herself and her husband with guilt.

Henry's teenage sister Amy and adolescent brother Bernie became caught up in the emotional upheaval left by Henry. Day after day, they had to endure their parents' obsession with Henry's cult involvement. Eventually they got angry at Henry for putting the family through this ordeal.

Time after time, Henry's parents took turns confronting their son with new pieces of information they had found about The Way. They told him that the founder and leader of the group was a plagiarist, who drank and swore excessively. This information did not deter Henry.

Throughout this time, the Marlowes remained silent with their friends and relatives about Henry's cult involvement. Roger was a state politician and concerned about his career. Kitty felt that people would think she was a bad parent for her son to be so disturbed as to join a cult. Whenever friends or relatives asked about him, they merely said that Henry was fine, had taken a leave of absence from college, and had decided to work for a while. They were very afraid of what everyone would think if they told them the truth.

With each passing year, Henry became more and more estranged from his family. They spoke very infrequently on the phone and wrote only sporadically. Eventually Henry felt there was no reason to stay in contact with his family anymore. As far as he was concerned, they were under Satan's power.

Lessons To Be Learned

Here are two different families, the Johnsons and the Marlowes, whose responses to a cult problem were very different. The Johnsons were able to find out very quickly that something was wrong and received good advice. The Marlowes were slow to pick up the signs, and when they did realize that their son was in a cult, they didn't seek out help. Roger Marlowe lost a potentially valuable strategic position by quickly and directly confronting his son and issuing what amounted to an ultimatum. Some people actually disown children who have fallen victim to destructive cults. Unfortunately, the mistakes the Marlowes made are common and happen in the majority of families. In the case of destructive cults, parents' impulsive reactions frequently do more harm than good.

There are several lessons to be learned here. First, any sudden, uncharacteristic change in a friend or a loved one should be investigated quickly and thoroughly. If the person is suddenly spending a good deal of time away, find out why. Ask a lot of questions—in a non-threatening, reassuring tone, of course. Avoid wishful thinking. Remember: when people join cults, they often become deceptive or evasive when questioned about changes in their lives.

If you are concerned, consult with as many of the person's friends and relatives as possible. Don't do what the Marlowes did, and try to keep the problem hidden. If you do, you will cut yourself off from very valuable emotional support, as well as possible practical help. When people delay talking with others or getting help, in the hope that the person under mind control will magically snap out of it themselves, the consequences can be disastrous.

If someone you care about appears to have become involved with a cult, make sure to contact their family—but ask that they *not* talk to the person about it yet. Doing so could jeopardize the relationship. However, if the situation is handled mindfully and tactfully, the family *and* the person you care about will ultimately be grateful for your concern.

Classic Ineffective Responses

Since most people do not understand mind control and the practices of destructive cults, it is easy for them to act ineffectively, or even counterproductively.

The most common problem is that family members typically feel an *excessive amount of guilt and shame*. People blame themselves because of their loved one's cult involvement. This can be one of the greatest hindrances to positive, effective action. People need to know that they are not at fault. Cults exist. Mind control exists. A mind control virus can infect anyone, just as anyone can become infected with the flu.

Another common problem is that *people neglect their own needs*. The best way to help someone else is to make sure that you first take care of your own needs. You need to get enough sleep, food and down time to stay sane and balanced. You can hurt yourself *and* your loved one if you don't take the time to rest, relax and do other things to cope.

A loved one's cult involvement also has to be placed in a manageable perspective. You can do only what is within your capacity to do. Life has to go on. The Marlowes inadvertently punished their other children because they devoted too much time and energy to Henry, all of which they exerted ineffectively.

Another mistake is that people often *emotionally overreact to the cult involvement*. This can be even more dangerous than doing nothing. A person can get driven further into a cult by hysterical tirades and inappropriate uses of words like "cult" and "brainwashing." Getting emotionally aggressive with a cult member almost always backfires.

One other common error is *trying to argue the person out of their cult involvement by using a condescending, confrontational approach*. This direct approach is doomed to failure. Rational argumentation is simply not effective with someone who has been indoctrinated through mind control. Add condescension or arrogance, and you are playing right into the cult recruiter's hands.

Similarly, it is important not to blame someone for being recruited into a cult. Instead, you need to regard what happened as an example of undue influence. The person you care about has contracted a mind control virus. Get angry with the cult. Get angry at *all* mind control cults. But *don't get angry with the person who has been victimized*. It isn't their fault. I have been told many times by people who have left cults that they felt psychologically raped. Don't do emotional harm a second time by telling them it's their own fault.

If you want to get even with any mind control group, fine—but first work to help the person you care about. Then do as much as you can to expose the group to the general public. Take it to court, if you have the time, energy and resources. Make sure that you have competent legal advice from an attorney with experience of the cult you are dealing with. You should also write to your political representatives, giving a brief outline of the cult. See if you can use the law to ensure justice.

Most of all, though, focus on helping the person you care about. To this end, information and strategy are your two most important tools. The overall objective should be this: ***Do everything within your power to create the necessary conditions to help the cult member* change *and* grow.** Keep this objective in mind at all times when deciding what to do or say.

Notice that your objective should *not* be rescuing the person from the group. People leave destructive cults as a natural consequence of changing and growing. If people are focused on positive growth, there will be less resistance, and everyone's efforts will be more effective.

That said, it is also essential to adopt the consistent attitude that the person *is* going to leave the cult. The only questions are whether they will do so sooner or later, and whether the transition will be easy and smooth, or difficult and painful. People can do only that which is within their control to do. People can help to create the positive conditions necessary to help a person trapped in a cult to grow so that they can break the shackles of mind control.

The best way for you to help the cult member leave their group is for you to be adequately prepared to undertake the job. Here are some ways to make sure that you're able to handle the stress you'll inevitably encounter. Good preparation is the key to success.

Preparing For A Successful Effort

Take Care of Your Own Emotional Needs

Don't expect instant results. Pace yourself and keep a balanced perspective.

Your efforts to help the person you care about shouldn't be at the expense of your (or anyone else's) health. This is particularly true if the cult member has been involved for many years, and efforts to help them are complex and protracted.

One of my clients, from Germany, flew to the United States against his doctor's advice to try to see his son in the Moonies. He had a heart attack and died. Imagine the guilt the son might have experienced when he found out. Trying to suppress that guilt might have actually prolonged his cult involvement.

Remember that you are in a kind of war with the cult. As part of the preparatory process, identify and address everyone's concerns and emotional needs. Good individual and family counseling can be enormously helpful.

Parents and other family members should try to keep the cult problem in a balanced perspective. Life for them and their family has to go on, particularly if the person has been a member for a long time.

Let me repeat: life has to go on.

Consolidate Your Resources

Following the example of the Johnsons, involve as many family members and friends in your rescue efforts as you feel comfortable with. But also help to educate them. Invite them to attend workshops on cults, undue influence or mind control. Contact knowledgeable clergy, mental health professionals, former cult members, families who have had a cult problem, and anyone else who might be able to offer assistance. When it comes to helping cult members exit their groups, people can be extremely helpful and generous.

If a family member is very close to the person in a cult, do everything within your power to involve that person. Countless times, a brother or sister who had a lot of clout with the cult member has turned out to be a key player. But also quite often, that person initially did not want to help with a rescue effort. Either they didn't understand mind control or they felt a misplaced loyalty to their sibling. If necessary, plan a mini-intervention with that person first. Then, with them on your side, it may well be much easier to help the cult member exit the group.

Lastly, don't just consolidate your resources: use them as wisely as possible. Coordination, teamwork and good communication all combine for success.

Get Organized and Make a Plan

Learn as much as you can. Study the enemy—the specific cult group—as well as similar cults. Learn how they think and how they operate. Become knowledgeable about mind control. The more clearly you understand it, the more easily you will be able to explain it to others—including, when the time comes, the cult member. Start with the Freedom of Mind website, freedomofmind.com, which offers a very wide range of free resources, plus links to other helpful websites.

Keep organized files. Make copies of important articles to share with everyone concerned. Make copies of every letter written to the cult member and every letter received from them. These may turn out to be quite important during or after any rescue effort. I have frequently shown cult members letters they had written in which they lied to their families, or made promises that they later broke.

Update everyone concerned regularly. Make sure everyone is on the same page regarding the cult member.

Consistent communication with the cult member is usually better than sporadic contact. Send a little card or note once a week, every week. This is far better than writing a 14-page letter one week and then missing the next month. Short notes, texts, emails and letters about home and shared positive experiences are also good. Ask the cult member to call, whatever the time and wherever they are, if they wish to talk and do not have their own phone.

Selecting the right counselor is a key step in organizing and making a plan. They can help you plan, strategize and avoid missteps. Most cult counselors are very caring and have often helped a tremendous number of people out of mind control groups.

Above all, be a smart consumer. After the Jonestown tragedy, a dozen or so con artists calling themselves deprogrammers appeared out of the woodwork, took advantage of numerous families, and stole their money. Some of these people were actually cult members themselves, attempting to give deprogramming a bad name. Be careful.

A person's claims to be a cult counselor don't make them one. Check credentials and references from multiple sources. Check with several families the person has worked with over the years. Plug their name into a search engine—and dig deep; don't just look at what pops up on the first page. Be careful, as cults and others with a negative agenda will often post deceptive material about counselors. And trust your instincts. You have to feel that the *cult member* will be able to trust and relate to the counselor as a person.

In my opinion, the best cult counselors are people who were once cult members themselves. They know what it feels like to be under mind control. Also, the best counselors have had a lot of experience.

Don't assume that any good psychotherapist will be helpful. Most mental health professionals know nothing about helping someone involved in a cult.

Professional cult counselors charge fees that range from $500–$2500 per day. Former cult members who assist them receive between $100 and $300. Usually all reasonable expenses, such as travel and accommodations, are extra. Although each case is unique, most rescue efforts are accomplished within three days. The cost usually lies somewhere between $5,000 and $30,000. After the initial effort, some follow-up is typically required. This might involve a program at a rehabilitation center, or it might be as simple and informal as introducing the ex-cult member to as many other former cult members as possible.

Once you've accomplished all the preliminary preparations, it is important to make one-month, three-month, six-month, and one-year plans. Although rescue efforts should be undertaken as soon as possible, they also should not be rushed. Most require weeks or months of advance planning. In some cases, plans are finalized, but cannot be put into operation until a good opportunity presents itself.

Keep in mind that arrangements to reserve a professional team are ideally made several months in advance.

How To Help A Cult Member Change And Grow

It may seem that helping a cult member to go through personal changes is a long and circuitous way to help them break free of their group. After all, isn't it most important to get them away physically from the people who practice mind control on them?

Actually, no. It is vital to recognize that the only way to get people permanently out of destructive cults is to help them get back in touch with their real selves. *This* is your long-term objective. Only then can they start growing toward new personal goals that mean something to them.

While keeping this long-term objective in mind, everyone concerned with helping a cult member should also focus attention on three short-term objectives:

The first is *building rapport and trust*. Without trust, nothing you do will be effective.

The second is *gathering information* about how the cult member thinks, feels, and views reality.

The third is *planting seeds of doubt about the cult and promoting a new perspective*.

Let's look more closely at each of these.

Build Rapport and Trust

When you first become aware that someone you care about is a cult member, act as though you don't know they are in a cult—unless, of course, they've told you. Don't tell them that you are studying counter-cult information or that you have made contact with experts. If you do, the result will likely be a breakdown of trust.

A *curious yet concerned posture* is the most effective stance anyone can take in relating to the cult member. It is relatively easy to elicit rapport and trust when you are genuinely curious, because all you are doing is asking questions in a non-judgmental way. Because you care about the person, you want to know everything that is important to them.

Show approval and respect for the person, their ideals, their talents, and their interests. However, be careful to show only conditional approval of their participation in the cult. Let them know that you are withholding final judgment on the group, until all the facts are in. In some cases, it might be appropriate to tell them you have a feeling in your stomach that something is not right about the group, but you are not sure. If the cult member tries to give credit to the group for positive aspects of their life, like no longer using pot or drinking excessively, tell them you think that is great—but remind them that you think *they* deserve the credit for the positive changes, not the group.

Evaluate your present relationship with the person. Do the two of you have a great deal of natural rapport and trust? If not, start thinking about ways you can build or rebuild the relationship. Remember, the more the person feels connected to people outside of the cult, the better off they will be. They will always be closer to some people than others, but everyone should be making a natural effort to get closer to the person. Coordinate the flow of communication to the cult member. It wouldn't seem natural if ten people suddenly e-mailed them on the same day. Avoid anything that looks too suspicious.

Also do not send the person money, particularly cash, because it will most likely be turned over to the group. It is far better to send clothes, pictures, books and other gifts with more personal and long-lasting meaning. Grandma's homemade cookies can go a long way towards reminding the person of their true self and establishing rapport than a card and a check.

Ask the member what you can do to better understand them or build your relationship with them. Ask them to be specific. Try your best to accommodate their needs, but act sensibly. If they ask you to read one of the group's books, tell them that you would be willing to do a swap; ask them to read a book that you recommend. If they tell you they want you to stop criticizing their group, ask them how you can communicate your questions and concerns without seeming critical.

People have done many creative things to help build trust and rapport. They have written poems and short stories, put together elaborate photo albums, and painted pictures. They have sent shoes, winter jackets, and tickets to performances that they know the person will love. I know of several cases where people invited a cult member to go with them on a trip overseas, during which they were able to provide counseling.

Collect Valuable Information

Once rapport with the cult member is built, it will be much easier to gather information from them about the cult, their life in it, and their feelings about it. The more information you collect, the more you will be able to know what is going on inside their mind. Communicate as regularly as possible. If you can see each other in person, do so, and try to do it one-on-one. Unless you are highly trained, it is very difficult to make much progress while talking to two or more cult members at a time.

Expect that, at some point, you will be invited to talk with older members or leaders. Don't accept this invitation—but also don't merely say no. Stall for as long as you can. Tell the person that you care about them and trust *them*. You're not interested in talking with strangers. You want *them* to explain everything to you. If they say that they don't know the answers to some of your questions, you can gently point out that you are concerned that if they don't know the answers, they may have made a commitment to the group before they were ready to do so. Suggest that they take a step back and spend a few weeks researching the group. If the group is legitimate, what do they have to lose?

Information can also help you understand just how fully indoctrinated the person is. When I was speaking with Bruce, I was able to ascertain his stage of involvement, so I guessed that to tell him about the Moon pledge service would be disillusioning for him. When you know what someone knows and doesn't know, it makes the counselor's job much easier—and increases the chances of success.

Develop Specific Skills to Promote a New Perspective

When you are able to establish good rapport and accumulate a good deal of information, the last step is actually developing the skills and strategies to undermine or side step the mind control used by the group. Too many people try to jump to this step before they have accomplished the first two. This is a big mistake. Only when you have laid the groundwork can you really be effective.

Remember that you want to connect with and empower the person's real self, not the cult self. Reminding them of earlier positive life experiences is the most effective way to do this. For example, you might call the cult member and say, "Hi, it's Steve. I've been meaning to call for a while. You know, I was down visiting the old school today, and I remembered when you and I used to go early, so we could play handball on the school wall. Do you remember the time when the gym teacher chased us across the field demanding the ball, because we accidentally cracked his window?"

Or, a father might call his son and say, "You know, son, I was flipping through the channels on TV the other day and saw a show on bass fishing. We haven't done that in years. I sure would love to go back up to the lake with you sometime this summer. It would be so good to spend some time with you, just you and me and the fish." Evoking these positive feelings and memories can be a powerful way to undermine cult programming.

However, be cautious about overusing this technique and thus arousing suspicion.

By staying in close contact with the cult member, and pooling information gathered by other family members and friends on the rescue team, you can create effective strategic messages. For example, a cult member tells an old friend that they really miss skiing, and that friend tells the other team members. The cult member's family might then plan a family ski trip, and invite both the cult member and the friend. The cult member may think it is coincidental, or perhaps even spiritually destined. Even if the cult doesn't allow them to go, the invitation will stir a strong desire within them.

Whenever you communicate with the cult member, always concentrate on just one or two points each time. It is better to make one point thoroughly than to try a shotgun approach.

Follow-up is critical. For example, suppose you hear one of the group's leaders say on television that members can go home to visit whenever they want. You might e-mail the cult member a message like this: *Hey, remember a few months ago when people told you that it would bad to ask permission to visit? I just saw Rev. Josiah on TV and he said anyone could go home to visit at any time. I'm so happy about this—and so glad he said it publicly. So when can you come visit?* If they don't respond to this point in their next phone call or letter, ask them about it again. Gently but firmly point out the contradiction: *Was Rev. Josiah being untruthful? Did you misunderstand? Help me understand, because I'm confused.* In a non-threatening tone, force the cult member to have to think about the contradiction.

Too many people make really good points but don't follow up with them. Perhaps they find it difficult to ask the follow-up question in a non-threatening tone—one that forces the cult member to have to think about the contradiction.

Above all, *don't send the cult member unsolicited articles* that are critical of their group, as Roger Marlowe did. This typically does more harm than good.

Remember to be yourself—stay in character. The person will be suspicious if you act differently from your usual self. In any case, why should you act differently? You are gathering information, but you are also maintaining your relationship with someone you care about.

Do your best, and don't worry about making mistakes. If you feel like you're walking on eggshells, or that you have to weigh your every word and action, you will incapacitate yourself. Mostly be yourself, keep your eyes and ears open, and pay attention to what you see and hear. If you do make some mistakes, keep learning from them, and over time you will be effective.

Since every situation is different, no one book can possibly cover everyone's particular needs. Under ideal circumstances, someone who recognizes that a friend or loved one is becoming a member of a destructive cult will immediately seek out professional assistance. The important point is this: *don't delay.*

If you know someone in a cult, start planning the process of helping them now.

What would you do if they called you tonight and told you they wanted to come for a long visit tomorrow? As surprising as it sounds, this happens quite often. Usually, it is a thinly disguised appeal for help. Ideally, you will be ready to move forward with rescue efforts as soon as you hang up the phone.

The best thing you can do is to start preparing for such a possibility now.

Chapter 10

Unlocking Mind Control

Wherever I go—to the supermarket, to the gym, on an airplane—I meet people who are involved with destructive cults. My heart goes out to them, because I was once in a similar trap. With all the cult members I meet, I try to remember that they are *enslaved*. They are also somebody's son or daughter, sister or brother. Whenever I meet people like these, I feel extremely grateful that I am free. I was one of the lucky ones who had the opportunity to be counseled out. Since people helped me, I try to share my good fortune.

In these fleeting personal encounters, I know that I will have only a few minutes, but I try to say or do something to help. Usually I never hear from the person again, but occasionally I find out that our brief meeting had some long-term impact.

Back in 1980, I started to deliberately go out of my way to conduct impromptu mini-interventions that are really mini-therapeutic interactions. I was eager to research and practice non-coercive approaches to helping free someone. I looked at every cult member I met as an opportunity to hone my skills.

These encounters taught me more effective ways of communicating with cult members—methods that serve as keys to unlocking cult mind control. This chapter offers a summary of those keys, with some examples of how I use them—and how you can use them as well.

Briefly, these are the three most basic keys to helping a cult member:

- Key #1: Build rapport and trust.
- Key #2: Use goal-oriented communication.
- Key #3: Develop models of identity.

This chapter offers two examples of rescue efforts I have conducted, as well as a mini-rescue that was conducted on me when I was still a cult member. These examples will help to demonstrate the importance of the first three keys, and how they can be effectively employed. In the remainder of this chapter, I'll discuss the other five keys, which enable a rescue effort to be carried through to a successful conclusion:

- Key #4: Access the pre-cult (authentic) identity.
- Key #5: Help the cult member to look at reality from many different perspectives.
- Key #6: Sidestep the thought-stopping process by giving information in an indirect way.
- Key #7: Help them visualize a happy future outside the cult.
- Key #8: Offer the cult member concrete definitions of mind control and specific characteristics of a destructive cult.

Key #1: Build Rapport And Trust

I have already emphasized the importance of building rapport; several techniques for building non-verbal rapport can help. The first is to simply mirror the body language of the person with whom I am speaking. I also use a non-threatening/friendly tone of voice and line of questioning and try to avoid judgmental statements. Like riding a bicycle or learning a foreign language, rapport building is a skill that anyone can learn and develop.

Key #2: Use Goal-Oriented Communication

Practiced mainly in the business world, goal-oriented communication represents the best way to influence people in a deliberate way. This is drastically different from the approach people typically use when interacting with family members or friends. When we are intimate with people we usually say whatever we think or feel, because we are being "ourselves." We don't have an agenda to influence others.

In the business world, most people have to think through their goals and determine how best to accomplish them. Business leaders understand that they often have to establish a step-by-step plan to make their dreams a reality.

In helping someone break free from a destructive cult, it can be just as helpful to clarify your goal and then determine how best to accomplish it.

Your overall goal, of course, is to help the person you care about to begin thinking for themselves (hopefully, to help them leave a cult.) To accomplish this, you need to use communication to find out just who it is you're trying to influence. This means getting to know and understand your loved one's new mind controlled personality. It also means learning more about the real person underneath, if possible. Next, you need to use communication to build trust and rapport. Finally, you need to use communication to help the cult member begin to question, investigate and think for themselves.

Key #3: Develop Models Of Identity

By gathering information, family members and friends can thoroughly research the cult member they hope to influence. In order to be most effective, three models, or mindsets, will need to be constructed.

The first model is *who the person was before they joined*—how they thought about themselves, the world, their relationships, their strengths and their weaknesses. This is the way they viewed all these aspects of their life. This information is best gathered from what they have written or have said to friends and relatives.

The second model is that of *a typical cult member of that group*. Any former member can provide a useful generic model of how members of the cult view reality. Former members can serve as coaches and teach you how to think like a cult member. Ideally, people can role-play what it feels like to be a cult member. Just as the actor rehearses their lines in character, what is important here is the characterization, even though the lines are impromptu. Different family members can take turns interacting with the "cult member" as well as "being" the cult member. The more they are able to role-play and practice, the better they will understand how the cult member thinks.

The third model is that of *the specific person in the cult, as they are now*. By contrasting this with the models of the generic cult member and the person's real self, you can get a good idea when the person is being cultish, and when they are being their real self. Remember, though, that in every cult member, there is a war between their cult identity and their real identity. At any time, you may actually see the person switch back and forth.

Many cult members try to fight off their cult identities whenever they can. For example, in one cult, members were vegetarians and did not use drugs or alcohol. Yet I met several members from that group who told me they used to sneak off the communal property and drive 35 miles so they could have a hamburger and a beer. If you have a good rapport with someone in a cult, you might discover and be able to make constructive use of this type of information.

When I am brought in to help with a rescue effort, I want to have as complete a sense of all three mindsets as possible before I meet with the cult member. Then, when I am with the person, I refine all three models by asking specific questions. Within three days, I am able to develop a sophisticated set of maps.

Like an actor, I am able to step into a role and imagine myself as the person I am counseling. I immerse myself in their reality. Throughout the counseling process, I switch back and forth among the mindsets. I test out the model of who the person is now—i.e., their cult personality—by anticipating how they will respond by having an imaginary conversation with them in my head. Then I ask the actual person the same question and note how accurately I was able to predict their response. As the interaction continues, I am able to refine this model more and more.

The faster I am able to create an accurate model of the person's cult personality, the faster I can "become" them. Once I become them, I can then figure out what needs to be said or done to help them regain control over their life.

Ultimately, it is the person's real identity that shows me how to unlock the doors. They tell me what keys are necessary to use, where to find them, and in what order to use them. This process of discovery can be demonstrated in the following interaction with a young member of a cult that stresses meditation, under the leadership of a man named Guru Maharaj Ji, aka Prem Rawat.

A Sample Rescue Effort: Gary and the Divine Light Mission[170]

A young man and I were both waiting for the bus. I noticed some brochures he was carrying.

"I'm curious," I said. "How long have you been involved with Divine Light Mission?"

"For about seven years," he answered. His eyes moved up slowly until they focused on mine.

"That's a long time," I said. "How old were you when you first got involved?" I tried to sound innocent, as though I were an old friend.

"I was 20."

"Hi. I'm Steve," I said, holding out my hand to shake his. "I'm sorry if I'm bothering you. What's your name?"

"My name is Gary," he said, somewhat bewildered. He looked as though he didn't know what to make of me.

"Gary, I'm just curious: what were you doing at that time in your life?"

"Why do you want to know?" he asked with a look of puzzlement.

"I love to talk to people who have made unorthodox choices in their life. I like trying to figure out why people do what they do," I shrugged my shoulders a bit.

"Oh. Well, back then I was working for a construction company, putting up buildings."

"Anything else?" I asked.

"Yeah, well, I liked to hang out with my friends. I was also into animals. I had two dogs, a cat, some tropical fish and a rabbit." A warm smile lit up his face as he recalled his friends and his pets.

"You certainly were into animals. Was any one your favorite?" I asked.

"Well, my dog Inferno was pretty special. He and I used to be best buddies."

"What made him so special?" I asked.

"He had an independent spirit. He loved adventure. He loved to go with me into the woods." It was obvious to me that he missed his dog a great deal. I shared that I grew up with dogs and love them too. This increased rapport.

"So, you love an independent spirit. Do you admire anyone who stands up and does what they feel is right no matter what others say?" I was trying my best to empower Gary by reminding him of the qualities he used to admire.

"That's right. Inferno did what he wanted to do. And I loved him for that, too." Gary's tone was somewhat defensive and self-righteous.

"So, Gary, tell me—what was it that made you decide that the Divine Light Mission was the group you wanted to spend your life in?"

"I never thought of it that way," he said, his face growing sullen.

"Well then, what was it that got you involved?" I asked in an upbeat voice.

"At the time, my girlfriend Carol started going to *satsang*—you know, group meetings—and I went along. We listened to the people all talk so glowingly about their experience of *Knowledge*, and how high it made them feel."

I continued to probe. "Did you decide to get initiated first, or did Carol?"

"She did. At first I thought the whole thing was a bit strange. But after she started meditating, I got curious and decided to do it, too."

"What year was this?" I asked.

"1973."

"And at the time, what did you think of Guru Maharaj Ji?"

"I thought he was this young dude from India who was going to usher in an age of world peace," he said, with a touch of sarcasm.

"Were you at that big meeting at the Houston Astrodome?" I asked.

"Yes," he answered.

"And what ever became of Carol?"

"I don't know," Gary said, his face darkening again. "We sort of broke up a few months after we got involved with the group."

"When was the last time you spoke to her?" I asked.

"About four years ago she wrote me that she had decided to go back to school and wasn't going to practice *Knowledge* anymore."

"Why did she say that she wasn't going to be part of the group anymore?"

"I don't remember," he said, staring at the pavement.

"So the person who got you involved left the group four years ago?" I repeated.

"Uh huh."

"And you have never really sat down with her to find out why she left, after belonging to the group for three years?"

"Why are you looking at me like that?" Gary said, looking up at me.

I smiled, looked down, then looked him right in the eye. "Well, I don't understand, Gary. If my ex-girlfriend left the group that she introduced me to, I would certainly want to sit down with her and find out everything I could from her. She must have had some really good reasons why she left after three years. And she obviously cared enough about you to contact you and let you know her decision."

I paused. Gary stood there, silent. I waited some more. Then I continued, "I suppose there's no way for you to get in touch with her anymore."

"Actually, her parents probably live at the same address. I'm sure I could find it."

My bus pulled up to the stop. "Might be a good idea. Well, I wish you good luck, Gary. It was really good talking to you. Thanks."

He waved to me as my bus pulled away.

The preceding conversation demonstrates just how much can be done to help someone in a mind control cult in only a few minutes. During that time I was able to quickly establish rapport, collect very valuable information about Gary, and use what I learned to help him take a very important step away from his cult group.

If I had used a threatening or condescending tone, I would never have gotten anywhere with Gary. However, because I used a curious, interested tone, Gary was happy to kill some time and chat with a friendly stranger.

Once I found out how long Gary had been involved, I was able to quickly determine that he wasn't enthusiastic about the cult. It was relatively easy for me to get Gary to reminisce about his pre-cult life. When he remembered what he had done before, he was able to reaccess his real identity and get in touch with how he thought, felt and acted before being indoctrinated. He not only remembered his favorite dog, but also talked about how he used to value an independent and adventurous spirit. This was a valuable resource—one he would need to help him walk away from a seven-year commitment to Guru Maharaj Ji.

Gary also remembered what he had first thought of the group before becoming involved. He stepped back in time and looked at the group with his pre-cult eyes, thinking that it was a bit weird. Back then he certainly never intended to join the group for life.

An important strategy for reality testing is to go back in time and ask, "If you had known then what you know now, would you have made the same decision?" For Gary, apparently the answer would have been no.

Then, as I was fishing for more information, Gary stunned me by telling me that Carol, who initially recruited him, had left the group. Since everyone under mind control has been made to be phobic about leaving the group, it didn't surprise me that Gary didn't know why she had left. Four years earlier, he was probably not able to consider talking with her. However, it was clear to me that Gary was still curious as to why Carol left the group. He was now at a point in his life where he was more open to this possibility. I gave him a nudge to go talk to Carol.

My Own Experience of a Mini-interaction

When I first got out of the Moonies, I searched my memory for times when I had questions or doubts about the organization. I remembered several times when I was momentarily thinking outside the Moonie framework. Even though these experiences weren't enough to get me to leave, they proved significant when I was being deprogrammed.

One experience involved a caring person I met by chance. During my first year as a cult member, I was fundraising on a steamy summer day in Manhattan. I approached a man who must have been in his sixties, and asked if he wanted to buy some flowers.

"What are you selling flowers for, young man?" he asked with a warm smile.

"For Christian youth programs," I answered, hoping I could sell him a dozen carnations.

"My, my, you look very hot," he said.

"Yes, sir. But this cause is very important, so I don't mind."

"How would you feel if I took you inside this coffee shop and bought you something cold to drink?" he asked.

I thought, *This guy is nice, but he has to buy some flowers; otherwise he won't have a connection to Father.* Then I remembered Jesus saying that anyone who gives water to a thirsty person is doing the will of God.

"Just for five minutes," he said with a twinkle in his eye. "It will refresh you, so you'll be able to sell even more flowers."

"Okay. Thank you very much."

We walked into the air-conditioned shop. It felt so good to be out of the sun.

When we sat down at a table, he said, "So, tell me a little about yourself."

"Well, I grew up in a Jewish family in Queens."

"Oh, so you're Jewish," he said with a warm smile. "Me, too,"

I thought that perhaps God had sent this person for me to "witness to" (a term we used for *recruit*). We had been instructed that while fundraising, we should never spend more than a couple of minutes with any one person. But since my main job was recruiting, and I had been sent out on Saturday to fundraise, maybe it was okay to spend a few extra minutes with him.

In the end, I must have spent at least half an hour with him. He got me to do most of the talking. During that time I became incredibly homesick—not only for my family and friends, but for playing basketball, writing poetry and reading books.

Before I left, he insisted that I call home and walked me to the phone. He put in the dime himself. I remember feeling that this man reminded me of my grandfather, someone I loved dearly. I didn't have the willpower to refuse. Besides, it would look bad for the group if I refused to talk to my parents.

I spoke with my mom for a few minutes. After that, I felt that I had to pry myself away from this man. My cult identity was strongly exerting itself. I started to feel guilty that I hadn't been out raising money and allowing people to "pay indemnity" and connect themselves to the Messiah.

But I was "spaced out" and couldn't sell for the rest of the day.

Eventually, a Moonie leader told me that I had created a "bad condition" by going inside for a cold drink; that Satan had tempted me; and that I had failed. He told me that, in my weakness, I had crucified Jesus on the cross one more time. That evening I prayed and repented and tried to quash any memory of what had happened. I never thought of that experience again, until after I was deprogrammed.

Now, let's take a look at another full-scale intervention, this time with a Krishna devotee.

Phil and the Hare Krishnas/ Iskcon[171]

Although most Americans don't realize it, the Hare Krishna sect, also known as ISKCON or the International Society for Krishna Consciousness, is still very much around even though its founder passed away in 1977.

Below is an account of my efforts with Phil, who had been a member of the Hare Krishna sect for over three years. Phil had become involved with the group about six months after his twin brother, Tom, was killed in an automobile accident while walking to a neighborhood store. The death hit his family hard, and sent Phil into a severe depression. He seriously contemplated suicide. He received medication and therapy, but nothing seemed to help him. Then one day, while walking downtown, he was approached by a Krishna. Not long afterward, he became a member.

I met Phil during one of his infrequent visits to his family, and was introduced as a family counselor who had been working with his parents and his two sisters for many months. I told Phil that I felt I needed to speak with him alone, before I could do any sessions with him and the whole family. I told him that in my view he was a very significant member of the family, and that his participation was badly needed.

After introducing myself to him, I suggested we go outside for a walk, so that we could get acquainted. He was dressed in full Krishna clothes, including sandals. I spent the first few minutes explaining my background as a counselor who specialized in communication strategies and family dynamics, and who was committed to helping people grow and enjoy better relationships with their loved ones. He told me that he now went by the name Gorivinda.

"So, Gorivinda—Phil (it is best to use the pre-cult name)—would you mind telling me about how you feel toward your family now?" I kept my hands in my pockets and my eyes directed toward the pavement.

"I don't know," he responded, shrugging his shoulders slightly.

"Well, are you happy with your present relationship with your mother? Your father? Your siblings?"

He answered, "Things have gotten a lot better since they stopped criticizing my religious commitment."

"How do you feel when you come home for a visit?" I asked, as gently as possible.

"To be honest, it's a bit strange," he said.

I was glad at his response. "What do you mean?" I probed for more information.

"Well, it's like coming to another world. It's so different from devotional life at the temple."

"Are there any good feelings you feel when you come home?"

"Yes," he said warmly. "I love my parents and my sisters and brother very much." Then he caught himself and added, "But they're living in the material world."

"I see," I said, a bit disheartened that he had caught himself and injected the cult perspective. "Would you mind telling me about your twin brother and what his death meant to you?" I was hoping to steer him back into his pre-cult identity.

"Why?" he asked suspiciously.

"Because, as a mental health professional, I believe that your whole family is still suffering from that tragedy," I commented, hoping he would accept my sincerity.

When I said that, Phil started to cry and choke up. I was struck by the power of his feelings. Then he stopped walking, put his hands together, and started rocking back and forth. He was chanting to shut himself down. Thought-stopping. After a few minutes he was recomposed.

"Tom and I were very close," he said, already beginning to lose control of himself again.

"Tell me about him when he was alive. What was he like? What did he like to do?"

Phil's face started to shine as be reminisced about his brother. "Tom was bright, energetic, had a great sense of humor. He was the more aggressive of the two of us. He helped motivate me to do things, all of the time."

"Tell me, Phil, what do you think he would be doing today if he hadn't had the car accident?" I was hoping to get Phil to think again about the kind of life Tom would have had

"That's a hard one," Phil answered.

"Do you think he would have joined the Krishnas?" I asked with a smile.

"No, never," Phil said definitively. "Tom was never into religion much at all, although he was very spiritual."

"So what do you think *he* would be doing?" I repeated.

"He always said that he wanted to go into the media—to work in television. He wanted to be an anchorman for the six o'clock news."

"So he liked news. Did he like investigative journalism?" I knew that if he said yes, I would have another angle to work with later.

"That was his favorite!" he said.

Bingo. I decided to explore another angle first, though. I asked, "Back then, what did you see yourself doing?"

"Back then? I wanted to become a musician," he said with enthusiasm.

"That's right," I said. "Your sister mentioned to me that you used to play electric guitar. You used to write songs, too."

"Yeah." I felt that Phil was making some of the important connections I was hoping he would make.

"So, did you want to have your own band and make records—the whole bit?" I wanted Phil to remember as much detail as he could.

"Sure. I loved music so much. I remember singing my songs with

Tom. He would help me with the lyrics sometimes, too," he said with considerable pride.

"So you could imagine being a successful musician, living a happy and spiritually fulfilled life?" I asked, nodding my head. I wanted him to create as powerful a mental image as he could.

"You bet!" Phil said, his eyes defocused. He was obviously enjoying what he was imagining.

"Can you imagine how good it feels to be up on stage, singing your songs, touching people with your creativity, making them happy?" I asked. I wanted Phil to get in touch with how good he would feel as a musician.

"Yes! It's a wonderful feeling," he said.

"Great. Just imagine enjoying your music, and perhaps see your friends there, too. They must admire and respect your talent a great deal. Perhaps you are even happily married, maybe have kids." I knew that I was taking a risk, but he seemed to enjoy adding the wife and kids to his fantasy. I waited a few minutes in silence until Phil returned from his pleasant imaginary voyage.

"Now I have another question." I paused for a deep breath. "What do you think Tom would say now if he saw you in the Hare Krishnas?"

I have to admit I was caught off guard, when Phil burst into intense sobbing, which continued for a full five minutes. By this time we were sitting together in a quiet park. Phil clutched his chest and rocked back and forth. The loud crying seemed to echo from deep within. I debated with myself whether or not to put my arm around Phil and console him; I decided not to interrupt. Eventually, he stopped and collected himself once more. I looked compassionately at Phil and decided to try the question again.

"Really, what would you tell Tom?" I asked.

Phil wiped his eyes and stated quite categorically. "I don't want to talk about it anymore, okay?"

I nodded and remained silent for a while. I decided to let him think about the question some more, hoping he would answer it within himself. I suggested we get up and walk some more. I wanted him to shift his frame of mind.

"There are a few more things I would like to discuss with you before we go back to the house." I started up again. "If you could put yourself in your parents' shoes, how would you feel to lose a son?"

"What?" he asked looking up at me.

"Imagine being your mother," I said. "She carried Tom and you, gave birth to both of you, nursed, diapered, washed both of you. Cared for you when you were sick. Played with you, taught you, watched you grow to adulthood. Can you feel what it must have been like for her to lose Tom?"

"Yes. It was horrible," he said. He was, indeed, talking as though he was his mother.

"And your father. Can you stop and think about what it was like for him?" I added.

Phil said. "Dad was always the closest to Tom. It hit him real hard."

"Yes," I said. "Now can you imagine what it felt like to watch your other son become suicidally depressed and then a few months later change his name, shave his head, and move in with a controversial group?"

"It would be horrible," he repeated. "I would feel angry. I would feel like I lost two sons."

"That's exactly how they told me they felt," I said. "Can you see that now? That is why they were so critical of the group when you got involved."

I paused and let him think for a few more moments before I went on. "I'm curious to know what was going on in your mind when you first met the member of the group. What was it that caught your attention and attracted you to learn more?" I asked.

Phil looked up at the sky for a moment, looked down at the ground, took a deep sigh, and said, "Well, when he asked me why I looked so depressed, I told him about Tom's death. I told him that I just couldn't understand why it would happen to such a wonderful person. It just didn't seem right. He began to explain the laws of *karma* to me and how this material world is just illusion anyway, and how I should be happy that Tom left his material consciousness, so that he could come back as a more highly evolved being in his next life."

"I see—so the devotee helped you understand what had happened to Tom in a way that took away your fear and confusion," I said.

"And guilt," he added.

"And guilt?" I probed.

"Yes, you see, I had asked Tom to go to the store that day to buy me another guitar string. He was on his way there when he was killed," Phil said.

"So you blamed yourself for his death because you figured that if you hadn't asked him to go to the store, he never would have been in the accident?" I asked.

"I guess so," Phil said, sadly.

It occurred to me that I had better try to offer Phil some other perspectives on the incident. I began by saying; "If Tom had been killed in a swimming accident, at the far end of the lake, would you have blamed yourself for not staying closer to him?"

He thought for a moment. "Maybe."

"Can you imagine any way Tom could have died that wouldn't have been your fault?" I asked.

He paused again before answering. "I guess not. But the fact remains that he was going to the store for me."

"Is it possible that he also had some other things to buy, or some other errands to run? Is it possible that he decided to take a different route to the store than he ordinarily took, and that was where the accident occurred?" I asked.

Phil seemed nonplussed.

"How would Tom feel, now, if it had been you who had gone to the store one day and were killed in a car accident?" I asked. "Would he get depressed, think about committing suicide, and then join the Hare Krishnas?"

Phil laughed.

I knew this was a bull's-eye. Within a few minutes it was Phil who started asking *me* questions.

"How do you feel about the Krishnas, Steve?" Phil asked.

I thought he was genuinely trying to test his "reality," not just trying to find fault with me and write me off.

"Boy. That's a tough one," I said, scratching my head.

He then said, "I want to know."

"My role as a professional, Phil, is to do counseling and not to make value judgments on what people do with their lives. I do have personal feelings though," I said.

"I want to know what you think personally," said Phil, quietly.

"Well, to be honest, I am very concerned. You see, fourteen years ago I myself joined a religious group that my family disapproved of. I too had been depressed before I met the members and wasn't completely sure what

I wanted to do with my life. Back then, I thought that they were trying to interfere with my rights as an adult to choose what I wanted to do."

"What group?" Phil asked, with curiosity.

I decided to give the formal name first. "The Holy Spirit Association for the Unification of World Christianity. It is also known as the Unification Church," I said. "Anyway, I was a devoted member of the group for more than two years. I slept three hours a night, and even did several seven-day fasts, drinking just water."

"That's a long fast," Phil said admiringly. I could tell that he was listening to every word I said.

"Yeah. I lost an average of fifteen pounds at the end of the week. Anyway, in my group we revered the leader as one of the greatest spiritual masters who has ever lived. In fact, we believed that he had met with Jesus, Buddha, Mohammed, Krishna and every other great spiritual leader."[172]

"You believed *that*?" He was amazed.

"Yes. We believed in a spirit world. In fact, we believed that whenever someone died, like Tom, it was to pay indemnity for some past sin in the person's lineage. In this way, another member of the family could join the group, serve the man we revered as the living Messiah, and then later intervene to save the person who had passed on to the spirit world. In this way, God could not only restore the whole world back to its original state of goodness, but restore all of the spiritual beings in the spirit world who were unable to advance without earthly 'vitality elements' provided by those on earth."

Phil's jaw hung open a bit. He asked, "You really believed that?"

"At the time, absolutely," I said. "You see, in the Church, members were not allowed to ask critical questions of anything the leader said or did. We were taught to believe that anything that challenged the leader or the group's beliefs was 'negative' and was caused by evil spirits. We were taught to do thought-stopping to shut down our minds. In my group we did this by praying intensely as well as chanting whenever we started to doubt, or whenever we felt homesick."[173] "What was the name of the group again?" he asked.

"The Unification Church," I said. "You probably know it as the Moonies."

"You were in the Moonies? No—I don't believe it!" Phil exclaimed.

"It's true. In fact, I was a devoted follower of Sun Myung Moon. I would have gladly died on command, if he had told me to," I replied.

"That's incredible!" Phil said.

"Not only that, but we were literally made to feel that if we ever left the group our lives would fall to pieces," I continued. "We were told that we would be betraying God, the Messiah, ten generations of our ancestors—the whole world, in fact—if we ever left. We were told that all of our relatives now in the spirit world would accuse us throughout eternity for betraying God.[174] It was quite a heavy trip. We were told to avoid all former members because they were controlled by evil. If someone we were close to left the group, we were made to feel that he or she was now a Benedict Arnold and was possessed by demonic spirits.[175] Can you put yourself in my shoes and imagine what I felt when I was in there?"

"Yes." Phil said. "Amazing. How did you get out?"

"Well, I was in an automobile accident in which I was almost killed," I said. "After two weeks in the hospital and an operation on my leg, I was able to get permission to go visit my sister. She had given birth to my nephew over a year earlier, but I had never seen him. I had never been able to get permission from my central figure. Anyway, my parents hired some former Moonies to come talk with me."

"Didn't you try to resist?" asked Phil.

"Of course. I had been taught in the group about deprogramming," I said. "I was told that they would torture me and try to break my faith in God. Of course I tried to get away, but, with a broken leg and no crutches, I couldn't get very far."

"So then, what made you decide to leave?" said Phil. I could see he really wanted to know.

I explained to him all the things I had learned during my intervention. I told him I had realized that former members still loved God and were genuinely good people. I described them as people who had decided to leave the group, because they no longer wanted to follow a demagogue who was interested in creating a world in which everyone was identical in thought, feeling and action. The ex-members told me of their belief that God gave them free will, so that they could choose to do the right thing, and not be forced by mind control to do what the leader thought was right. I told him that any group that told its members not to think, but rather to obey their leaders blindly, was dangerous. I told him that any organization that told members not to talk to former members or read critical information was exercising information control—an essential component of mind control.

I told him that during my counseling I began to remember specific questions I had buried, and specific contradictions that I had observed, but had never had time to ponder, while I was surrounded by members, because as a "good" member I had to use thought-stopping nearly all the time. Once encouraged to get in touch with who I really was and rethink my entire experience objectively, I was able to see that I had really been very unhappy in the group: I had given up my individuality, my creativity, my autonomy.

"I was also involved in bringing others in the group and forcing them to be the same way. I had a lot of guilt over things that I had done while a member, Phil."

We talked for a long time before we went back to the house. I told the family that maybe we should take a few hours out before we started family counseling. Not surprisingly, Phil wanted to be by himself for a while and do some thinking.

The family counseling that took place later built on the work I had done with Phil. By the time we stopped for the evening, the family had communicated their intense desire to Phil that he give himself a chance to really listen to the "whole story." Phil agreed to spend several days listening and talking to former members, and re-evaluating his involvement in the Hare Krishna group. Several people were brought in to assist him in this process. I was able to help the family resolve some of their pain and conflict, and Phil eventually made the decision to leave the cult.

I'm very happy to report that Phil is presently pursuing a career in music.

For Every Lock There Is a Key

In my intervention with Phil, I built rapport, used goal-oriented techniques of communication, and developed models of his identity. I also deliberately tried to get Phil to look at his situation from another perspective. I then intentionally applied the keys to the remaining locks of his mind control, and he responded positively. These keys can often reach into the deepest levels of a person, beneath any mind control virus, into the hardware of their real self. Phil's sudden collapse into cathartic sobbing and surrounding his pain and guilt of his twin's sudden death was his key. The changes these keys unlock can be profound.

Key #4: Put the Person in Touch With Their Real Identity

When a person begins to remember who they were before becoming a cult member, I am able to re-anchor them to a time when there was no cult identity and, consequently, no mind control. I enable the person to review what they thought and felt at each stage of the recruitment process. Almost always, the person had significant doubts or questions at the time, but these were long ago suppressed.

It is within this pre-cult personality that I can learn exactly what the person needs to see, hear or feel in order to walk away from the group. For some people, this can be seeing how their leader misinterprets the Bible. For others, it may be to learn about the cult leader's criminal background and dealings. For still others, it is to be shown specific contradictions within the group's doctrine. Contradictions in the leader's biography can also be pivotal. For instance, Scientology's creator, Ron Hubbard, claimed in *My Philosophy*, issued in 1965, that he had been lamed with 'physical injuries to hip and back' and 'blinded with injured optic nerves' at the end of WWII, but this is contradicted by a 1957 lecture, where he claimed to have won a fight against three petty officers, only two weeks before the war finished.[176]

The question, "*How will you know when it's time for you to leave the group?*" can help to reveal that individual's bottom-line criterion. Will they leave if God tells them to? Will they leave if they discover that they've been lied to? As soon as a member can tell me explicitly what they would need to know to leave the group, then I can try my best to find them the proof they require.

In Phil's case, before joining the Hare Krishnas he was a depressed, suicidal person wracked with guilt because he felt responsible for his brother's death. If I hadn't been able to help him face his feelings and reframe his brother's fatal accident, he never would have been able to leave the group. (One could speculate that, on some unconscious level, he was punishing himself for his "sin" by being involved in the group.) Until he could rethink the circumstances of his brother's death and verbalize what he felt, he would never be able to take a fresh step forward.

In this, and other cases like it, if the individual was not happy or healthy just before joining the group, it is imperative to find some positive reference point for the person to use as an identity anchor. If there are no strong positive experiences to use for this purpose, then one has to be either created or cultivated.

Imagination can be used to create positive experiences. For example, one might ask, "If you had had a warm, loving family, what would it feel like?" or "If your dad had been everything you wanted when you were growing up, what qualities would he have had, and what kinds of things would you want to do together?"

In order for Phil to even consider leaving the Krishnas, he needed to remember his previous, authentic self, and recall how good it felt to play guitar, write songs and have fun with his friends and family. He needed to remember Tom as a person full of life, not just as a victim. In Phil's inner life, he was able to resurrect Tom—his desire to be an investigative journalist, his dislike of organized religion, and his assertive stance toward life. Since twins are almost always extremely close, it was imperative that Phil reestablish his positive emotional link with Tom.

Key #5: Get the Cult Member to Look at Reality From Many Different Perspectives

During my interaction with Phil, I asked him to look at himself from a variety of viewpoints. When I asked Phil to switch perspectives, and think like Tom, a dramatic shift occurred. I asked him, "What would Tom do, if you were the one who had died? Would he have joined the Krishnas?" Phil had become so frozen by grief that he had never been able to find a perspective on it. When I asked him, "What would Tom say, if he knew you were in the Krishnas?" the answer came back, "He'd laugh at me and tell me to rejoin the real world."

Another important perspective I wanted Phil to have was that of his parents. He needed to connect with *their* grief and sense of loss. Phil had been so wrapped up in his own pain that he hadn't realized how deeply everyone else had been affected. Indeed, his parents had kept themselves together in order to help their children. As a result, they had never been able to go through all the stages of mourning properly.

Helping Phil remember and process the experience of being recruited into the cult was also important. When I asked him to verbalize what he thought and felt when he first met the devotee, Phil's long-suppressed guilt feelings about asking Tom to buy him the guitar string came to the surface, for the first time in years. Furthermore, by recalling his recruitment, Phil was able to remember some of the questions and doubts he had at the time. He also remembered that when he first started chanting, it made the pain go away. He remembered thinking at the time, *This is a whole lot better than feeling suicidal.*

In all rescue efforts, it is important to introduce different perspectives. Each time a cult member takes a different perspective, the cult's hold on them is weakened.

In addition to asking a person to remember who they were before joining the group, it can also be quite valuable to ask them to imagine the future. What will they be like in a year, two years, five years, or even ten years? What do they realistically see themselves doing then? Selling flowers on street corners? If not, how would they feel if they were unable to do anything but sell flowers on the street in ten years?

Another valuable perspective can also be that of the cult's leader. In one rescue effort, I asked a Moonie, "If you were the Messiah, would you live the way Sun Myung Moon is living—in a palatial mansion, with two $250,000 personal yachts, limousines and an array of high-end luxuries?" She answered, "Definitely not. I would give all my money to help the poor. I would live very simply." I was then able to ask her why she thought Moon lived as he did. She told me, "It troubles me. It has always troubled me!" Most cult leaders lead opulent lives, while their followers live relatively poorly.

When I told Phil what it felt like to be in the Moonies, I especially tried to convey what it felt like to be around Moon—the excitement, the honor, the awe. I could have asked him to imagine what it feels like to be a Moonie who believes that Moon is ten times greater than Jesus Christ, to feel the incredible honor of living on earth and meeting the Messiah in person. When Phil stepped into the shoes of a Moonie, his experience as a Krishna devotee was altered forever.

Each time the member is able to step out of his shoes and into the shoes of another—whether a member of a different group, or even his parents or his leader—he is weakening his psychological rigidity. Indeed, encouraging a cult member psychologically to take another perspective enables him to test his reality. In this process, the virus of mind control that they have been infected with, is exposed to healing light.

The way to undo blind faith is to introduce new perspectives.

Key #6: Sidestep the Thought-Stopping Process by Giving Information in an Indirect Way

Every person in a cult has been programmed to stop all negative thoughts about the cult's leader, its doctrine or the organization itself. This thought-stopping process is triggered whenever the person feels that someone is attacking the validity of the group. In this way, thought-stopping acts as a shield to be held up against any perceived enemy. They have also been indoctrinated to believe that their group is superior to all other groups and distinct from all other groups.

However, a cult member does not use thought-stopping when there is no perception of danger. Since the person believes that they are not in a cult, but that certain other groups *are* cults, it is relatively easy to have long, detailed conversations with them about cults without them ever feeling that you are attacking their leader or their group.

Therefore, the way to communicate with a cult member is indirectly. If the person is a member of The Way International, they will not feel threatened in the least if you tell them about the Moonies. If you're talking with a member of the Moonies, they will not feel threatened if you tell them about The Way. In this way it becomes possible to outline mind control processes and techniques in a soft, subtle manner. Meanwhile, you will provide the person's unconscious—their real self—with some essential frames of reference to begin to analyze what has happened to them.

Notice that in Phil's case I was careful not to attack the Krishnas. If I had done so, he probably would have become defensive and started chanting; if I had kept up my attack, he would have walked away. All the information I gave him was based on the Moonies and other groups. This indirect method of conveying information bypasses the thought-stopping mechanism.

Key #7: Help the Person Visualize a Happy Future Outside the Cult

Phobia indoctrination—fear of ever leaving the group—is usually accomplished on an unconscious level. The cult identity never thinks of leaving the group. Indeed, they are perpetually happy, enthusiastic and obedient to their superiors. It is the authentic self which has been enslaved.

I helped Phil begin to unlock the phobia indoctrination, by asking him to visualize a picture of the future that he would really enjoy—playing music, friends, a wife, kids, being close to his family. Then I asked him to step into the picture and enjoy the experience. By doing this, I was helping Phil open a door out of the Krishnas. This simple visualization technique began to dismantle his phobia indoctrination. It became a bridge to another possible life.

In other cases, I often ask cult members, "If you had never met this group, and you were doing exactly what you wanted to be doing, what would that be?" I usually have to repeat the question several times. "Really, just imagine, if you were doing exactly what you wanted to be doing, so that you were totally happy, spiritually and personally fulfilled, and you never knew the group even existed, what would you be doing?"

The answers vary. "I'd be a doctor and work in a clinic serving poor people." "I'd be a tennis pro." "I'd be sailing around the world."

Once the person verbalizes the fantasy, I try to persuade them to step inside their visualization of a new life, and become emotionally involved in it. I am then able to begin neutralizing their programmed negative fears about doing something outside the cult. Once this positive personal reference point is established, the cult-generated picture of a dark, disaster-filled life outside the group begins to change.

When a positive picture is in place, a bridge to other possibilities opens. People outside the group can be seen as warm and loving. Lots of interesting things can be learned outside the group. There are lots of pleasures to be experienced. Religious and spiritual fulfillment can be found.

Once the outside world is seen as potentially filled with positive experiences, the cult loses some control over the person's sense of reality. They are then in a better position to decide whether they want to stay where they are or do something more valuable and fulfilling.

Key #8: Offer the Cult Member Concrete Definitions of Mind Control and Specific Characteristics of a Destructive Cult

My intervention with Phil shows the importance of giving a cult member specific information about cults. Because I established good rapport with Phil, I was able to get a lot of personal information from him, so that I could better help him. In the process, Phil became curious about me and wanted to know my opinions.

At that point, I was able to convey specific information about cults and mind control through my own story of being in the Moonies. I was able to explain what happened during my deprogramming, and show how it enabled me to understand that I had been subjected to mind control and that, in fact, I was in a destructive cult.

In my own case, until my counselors taught me what the Chinese Communists of the 1950s were doing, I did not truly understand the process of "brainwashing." Until my counselors were able to show me how other destructive cults, like the Krishnas,[177] were structured in the same authoritarian manner as the Unification Church, I had believed that the Moonies were different from any other group.

I was also able to show Phil that, as strange as they sounded, some of the Moonies' beliefs did seem to make sense, if you believed in Moon and therefore the whole doctrine. I made sure to include the Moonies' view on accidental deaths, so he could see that there were alternative belief systems that offered other explanations. It was also important for him to see that there are other groups which are led by people claiming to be spiritually superior. When I eventually told him that there were over 3000 cult groups, and that if one of them was in fact led by the one legitimate great leader (which I seriously doubted), then the odds that he would have found the right one on the first pick were 3000 to one. Not very good odds.

I also showed him that I had been a dedicated cult member, and that I chose to leave the group for the "right" reasons. I wanted to challenge his indoctrination that people who leave do so because they are weak or undisciplined, or want to indulge in materialism. I wanted him to know that I left the Unification Church out of strength and integrity. I came to see objectively what I had been doing. I had devoted myself to a fantasy created in the Moonie indoctrination workshops. I thought I was following the Messiah—the person who would be able to end war, poverty, disease and corruption, and establish a Kingdom of Heaven on Earth. I didn't mind sacrificing myself for these noble causes. I thought that as a member, I was teaching people the ultimate standard of love and truth, and living an exemplary life.

Instead, I realized that I had learned to compromise my integrity in the name of God. I realized that the higher I rose in the organization, and the closer I got to Moon, the more obsessed I became. Power had become almost an addiction, and I began making choices based on what would protect and enhance my power, not on what was morally right.

I left when I realized that deception and mind control can never be part of any legitimate spiritual movement, and that through their use, the group had created a virtual Hell on Earth, a kingdom of slaves. Once I was able to realize that even though I *wanted to believe* that Moon was the Messiah and the Divine Principle was Truth, *my belief didn't make it true*. I saw that, even if I remained in the group for another 50 years, the fantasy I was sacrificing myself for would never come true.

By being given clear definitions of mind control, I was able to see clearly how I had been victimized and how I had learned to victimize others. I personally had to come to terms with my own values, beliefs and ideals. Once I did that, even though I had invested so much of myself in the group, become a leader, and developed close bonds with many members, I had to walk away. I could never go back to becoming a "true believer" again.

Chapter 11

Strategies for Recovery

People can leave a mind control group in any of three basic ways: they walk out; they are kicked out (often in a very burned-out condition, both psychologically and physically); or they are counseled out.

Although they are all fortunate to leave their cults, adjusting to life in the real world can be extremely difficult for them. If they don't get good information, support and counseling after they leave, the cult phobias they carry with them can turn some people into psychological "time bombs." Also, many cult members have lived for so long without any kind of normal work or social life that the process of readjustment to adult life is an uphill climb.

As a result, some people leave cults only to return again and again, because they miss family and friends who are still involved, but who were ordered to shun them. While such people are in the minority, they demonstrate the vulnerability of people who have left a mind control environment.

Walk Outs

Without a doubt the largest number of former members falls into the first category, the walk outs. These are the people who have managed to physically remove themselves from the cult, but have received no counseling about cult mind control. I occasionally meet them socially and find that some of them, even years after the cult involvement, are still dealing with the problems of mind control indoctrination.

For example, I once met a woman at a dinner party who had "walked out" of the Moonies. During our conversation, she remarked that even though she had been happily married for more than six years, she was deeply afraid of having children. She told me that she couldn't figure this out at all, because she had wanted to have children ever since she was a little girl. Now she was in her early thirties and felt she wanted children, but she still couldn't get over her fear.

As we talked, I learned that she had been recruited into the Moonies in 1969—more than 12 years earlier—and had stayed in the group for only three months.

"When they started making too many demands on me, I left," she told me. It was clear that she had brushed off her encounter as simply a close call.

"Did it ever occur to you that your fear of having children might be related to your experience in the Moonies?" I asked.

She looked puzzled. "What do you mean?"

"Do you remember ever being told anything about having children when you were in the Moonies?"

She rolled her head up slightly, as if her eyes were scanning the ceiling. After a few moments, her face became flushed and she shrieked.

"Yes! I do remember something!" To my surprise, she took hold of my shoulders and shook me back and forth. "I remember being told that if anyone ever betrayed the Messiah and left the movement, their children would be stillborn!"[178]

Her excitement at remembering the source of her fear of having children was tremendous, and I couldn't help but share it. It seemed as though we could hear the psychological chains that had been locking her mind fall to the floor.

At that point, I realized that I had to explain phobia indoctrination to her. I told her that even though she had been involved with the Moonies for only a few months, her recruiters and trainers had successfully implanted a phobia of giving birth to a dead child in her unconscious mind.

"Even though I don't believe in Moon anymore?" she asked.

"The mind is capable of learning new information and retaining it forever," I said. "This goes for harmful things as well as helpful things. You may have thought that you were finished with the Moonies when you walked out the door, but it has taken you 12 years to locate and eliminate that fear bomb they put inside your mind."

Of course, it is rare to have a conversation with a former cult member like this—a social situation at a friend's house which suddenly leads to a breakthrough about phobia indoctrination. Yet, a great number of people, just like this woman, are somehow coping with the damaging aftereffects of undue influence. Their problems are often made worse by the fact that many mental health professionals are not knowledgeable about mind control and do not know how to effectively help people suffering from its lingering consequences.

People may be able to escape the cult if they are exposed to too much of the inner doctrine before they are ready to swallow it. For example, when one woman I was recruiting found out that Moon was soon going to assign her a husband, it so infuriated her that she stormed out. A man I was recruiting discovered that we believed Moon was the Messiah before we had had enough time to prepare him for that conclusion.[179] He turned and walked out.

Other people leave when they become victims of internal politics or personality conflicts. For example, many people get fed up and exit because they can't relate to or readily follow their immediate superior. Long-term members often walk out when they feel that group policy is not being fairly and uniformly applied, or if there is a struggle for power.

Over the years I have met a large number of people who have walked out of their group because they just couldn't stand it anymore, yet they still believed in the leader. There are thousands of ex-Moonies who still believe that Moon is the Messiah, but just can't tolerate the way the cult is run. In their minds they are waiting for the day that the group reforms its policies, so they can return. They do not understand that the group is structured and run the way it is *because* of Moon. The same pattern applies to ex-Scientologists who leave the group but who still think Ron Hubbard was a genius and that the "technology" works. These people call themselves "independents" or members of the "Free Zone." If they still believe Hubbard was a great humanitarian and discovered how to be "free", they are still suffering from undue influence.

Over the decades, I've met thousands of people who were born into cults, but walked out. Even as children, some of them could never swallow the weird belief system, particularly if they went to public school and had positive relationships with grandparents, aunts, uncles, cousins, teachers, coaches, and other caring people.

Kick Outs

I've encountered hundreds of people who were "kicked out" of their mind control groups because they bucked authority and asked too many questions. Others were abused to such an extent that they were damaged and no longer productive for the cult. Still others developed serious physical or psychological problems that cost too much money to be treated. They became a liability to their group.

People who have been kicked out are almost always in worse shape than people who walk out or have been counseled out. They feel rejected by the group and its members. In the case of religious cults, they also feel rejected by God Himself. Many of them devoted their lives to their cults, turning over their money and property. They were told that the group was now their family, and believed that it would take care of them for the rest of their lives. Then, years later, they were told that they were not living up to the group's standards and would have to leave. These people, phobic toward the outside world, felt cast into utter darkness.

For many kick outs, suicide seems a realistic alternative to their suffering.[180] No one knows how many people have committed suicide because of mind control. I personally knew of a number of people who killed themselves because of their cult involvement. Research should be done, as this is a major public health issue.

Those who unsuccessfully attempt suicide are typically given a psychiatric evaluation. Many are incorrectly diagnosed as having schizophrenia, schizoaffective disorder, bipolar disorder or borderline personality disorder. Of course, some people do have these disorders, but my experience is that cults avoid recruiting people who cannot be controlled and rendered dependent and obedient, so most are suffering acute psychosis brought on by mind control.

Uninformed mental health professionals can hardly be blamed for this. How else could they diagnose a person who screams for Satan to come out of them? How could they know, unless they investigate, that the person had been doing silent, high-speed chanting for hours, and that it was causing them to be so spaced out that they appeared catatonic?

One man I worked with was kicked out of a cult after his father threatened the group's guru with lawsuits and other forms of exposure. The young man had been programmed for six years to believe that leaving the guru meant instant insanity. After he left, he (surprise!) went crazy. His parents took him to a psychiatric hospital, where the doctors diagnosed him with schizophrenia. The young man interpreted this diagnosis as proof that his leader was right: anyone who leaves the guru *does* go crazy.

In the hospital, he started to pound his head vigorously against the wall. He was put in a straightjacket and put under constant surveillance. But no one asked him why he was behaving in this way.

I learned that, during his years in the cult, on a visit to India, he had been shown the rock the guru had supposedly banged his head against until (as the young man explained to me), "he managed to reach gross consciousness." In his effort to replicate his guru's spiritual path, the young man nearly killed himself. To top it all off, this only convinced the doctors that he had schizoaffective disorder or was schizophrenic.

Only when I began to work with him did he begin to undo his cult conditioning, and how he reinforced that conditioning whenever he internally repeated cult jargon, followed cult practices or thought about his cult leader's teaching uncritically.

This unfortunate man also struggled with the years of negative "help" he had received from mental health professionals while in "treatment." Some of his doctors actually told him that his involvement with the group was one of the healthier things he had done in his life. One caseworker even encouraged him to read cult literature. Meanwhile, he was heavily medicated and was told daily that he was a schizophrenic.

One occult-group ex-member I worked with was convinced that her spiritual body was disintegrating and that she was dying. She suffered tremendous anxiety attacks, particularly in the middle of the night, and felt pains in her chest. She had been tested by doctors for every conceivable problem, and it was determined that the difficulty was all "in her mind." She had been programmed by the group to self-destruct if she ever left it. Once she was out, that was exactly what started to happen—until she began to learn about cults and mind control.

When people who have walked out or have been kicked out are not able to receive specialized counseling, their suffering is usually prolonged. Still, many manage, with the help of family and friends, to pick up the pieces and move forward with their lives. However, if these people never come to understand mind control and how it was used to recruit and indoctrinate them, in my opinion, they will never be able to live as full a life as they might. These people may have temporarily managed to put their cult experience on a shelf and forget about it. At some point, though, it could burst back into their lives.

Rick was one of these people. He walked out of the Children of God with his wife and three kids after six years. Five years later, a piece of cult literature turned up in his mailbox. All his cult indoctrination was triggered by this one letter from the leader. His mind started racing out of control. A voice in his head told him to go upstairs and choke his children.

Fortunately, Rick got help and was able to keep his children safe. Today, he is a successful computer consultant.

Efforts to sensitize and train mental health professionals are much needed. I was invited to do a program for psychiatrist Judith Herman, who is one of the leading trauma experts and the author of the seminal book *Trauma and Recovery*. A two-hour cults course was added to her Trauma curriculum and I was able to do this, in 2014. I was grateful that a woman I'd had the good fortune to work with was willing to share her 11-year experience with mental health practitioners. Her prior caregivers did not realize that her 13-year involvement with the Bible cult International Churches of Christ was at the root of her depression and suicidal impulses. Laura later did a Dr. Drew[181] podcast on the issue of the need for mental health professionals to learn how to correctly identify and help victims of mind control. A video of my presentation and a link to the Dr. Drew podcast can be found on the Freedom of Mind website, freedomofmind.com.

Counseled Outs

People who had had assistance are the smallest group of ex-members. Most people who are counseled out of cults are able to find the help and information they need. However, some are still carrying around cult-related psychological baggage. Just because a person has been out of a group for years, this does not mean that all of their issues are resolved. This is particularly true of those who were deprogrammed. Some deprogramees report ongoing PTSD symptoms from the deprogramming itself. While I am eternally grateful that my family deprogrammed me, I have needed to do much self healing and also have needed to turn to experts for support. Those who were exit-counseled or experienced some voluntary form of intervention do much better. However, it takes time and good support to recover fully. If the person's family and friends did not understand mind control and cult psychology it undermines a smooth recovery. Some people are encouraged way too fast to find a job or embark on a career. A supportive cult-aware therapist can be very helpful.

Much more is now known about undue influence and cults than ever before. Today there are also many more former cult members who have become professional cult counselors.

Unfortunately, however, those are not always the professionals to whom ex-members turn. Often they spend many frustrating years working with therapists who know little or nothing about mind control. It is unethical for a therapist who is not trained in addictions to be in charge of treating someone with an addiction. Similarly, an otherwise-talented therapist, who is largely clueless about undue influence, should not counsel ex-cult members.

Therapists need to understand that it is essential to first make an accurate diagnosis by doing a thorough interview. Then the client should be referred to a professional with the proper training and experience. After all, it is the therapist's obligation to get proper help for a client.

Psychological Problems Of Ex-Cult Members

Former cult members report a variety of psychological difficulties after they leave.

The most common is *depression*, particularly during the first few months after leaving. It is difficult to describe the pain of realizing that you have been lied to and mentally enslaved—that your dream was really a nightmare. Many people who leave after decades of involvement have to face the lost years of missed opportunities. Some have no spouse or partner, no children, no education, no relationships with relatives, and no friends.

Many ex-cult members describe their experience with a cult as if they had fallen deeply in love, and given every ounce of their love, trust and commitment to someone, only to find out that the person was a false lover and was just using them. The pain and the sense of betrayal is enormous.

Others describe the realization in more graphic terms: feeling as though they had been spiritually and psychologically raped. The sense of personal violation is indescribable. I myself came to realize that all of the love and devotion I felt towards Sun Myung Moon and Hak Ja Han as my "True Parents" was totally one-sided. I realized after I left that they didn't care about me personally at all. Instead, I was automatically labeled "Satanic" and a traitor, and shunned.[182] When people are depressed, they tend to only see the bad side of things. Their pain can be so great that it blots out any hope of a positive future. It is essential that former members acknowledge and work through their pain, and go through the necessary grieving period.

Two realizations seem to help ex-cult members most: first, that some positive things came out of their involvement, and, second, that they now are (or can be) much stronger because of their experiences. It can also help to encourage them to put their experience in a manageable and hopeful perspective. There are almost always examples of people whose experience was much worse than their own, and who were able to thrive after exiting.

Another common problem is an overwhelming tendency toward *continued dependence* (learned helplessness) on others for direction and authority. In groups where members lived communally, most life decisions were made by leaders. Members were encouraged to be selfless and obedient. This form of dependency creates low self-esteem and undermines the healthy desire and ability for personal development.

When I first left the Moonies, I didn't seem to have that difficulty. My deprogrammers had told my parents that they should expect that I would have trouble making decisions. My parents were quite confused when we went out to eat, because I easily knew what I wanted. They told me later that they thought, in some twisted way, that this meant that I hadn't been deprogrammed. What they hadn't taken into account was that I had not been a rank-and-file member. I had been a leader and was used to making certain kinds of decisions for myself, as well as for others. Day-to-day decisions were easy for me; bigger decisions, like which college to choose, were more difficult.

Like most skills, decision-making becomes easier with practice. In time, people learn how to resume control over their lives. This process can be speeded up by the gentle but firm insistence by family members and friends that ex-members make up their own mind about what they want to eat or do. By bolstering the ex-member's self-esteem and confidence, the dependency problem is usually overcome.

Floating: Dealing With The Cult Identity After Leaving

A more difficult problem is a phenomenon known as *floating*.[183] The former cult member suddenly starts to mentally float back in time to the days of their group involvement, and starts to think from within their former identity. The experience is triggered when the ex-group member sees, hears or feels some stimulus that was part of their conditioning process. This can briefly jolt them back into the cult mindset. Here is an example.

Margot, a 19-year-old college student, was recruited into Lifespring during a summer job in 1987. Lifespring is a Large Group Awareness Training. She completed the basic course and was one weekend away from completing the leadership training course. Margot's mother, an ordained Methodist minister, saw some personality changes in her daughter, and was concerned enough to borrow money to initiate a rescue effort. The effort was successful, and Margot soon broke from the group. (As part of an investigation of Lifespring, ABC's *20/20* interviewed psychiatrist and cult expert Dr. John Clark of Harvard Medical School. Although Lifespring insists otherwise, Dr. Clark stated that Lifespring does, in his opinion, practice mind control).[184]

For Margot, one of the biggest problems after the intervention was hearing music come on the radio, including Steve Winwood's "Higher Love," and having flashbacks of the training. Groups such as Lifespring like to use popular music as part of their indoctrination for that very reason. It creates a strong association in the individual's unconscious, which without proper counseling can take months, sometimes years, to overcome. Music is used by many cults for indoctrination, because it forms a strong anchor for emotional states via memory.

This stimulus-response mechanism that caused the flashback, or "floating," can be a significant problem for former members. This experience is triggered when a former member sees, hears or feels some external or internal stimulus, which was part of the conditioning process. This can briefly jolt them back into the cult mindset.

For the first year after I left the Moonies, every time I heard the word *moon*, I would think, *Father*, and remember sitting at Moon's feet. Another example occurred about a month after I left the group. As I was driving to a friend's house, I had the thought, *This would be an excellent fundraising area!* I had to tell myself that I was no longer in the Moonies. This thought was triggered because for the last five months of my membership, I spent fifteen to twenty hours a day driving around looking for places to drop off members to solicit money.

For people who were long involved in a group that required excessive meditation, chanting, "decreeing,"[185] speaking in tongues, or other mind-numbing practices, episodes of floating can occur for at least a year after they have left the cult. Many of my clients have told me that suddenly, in the middle of a normal conversation, they would find themselves doing the mind-numbing technique they had practiced for years. This can be especially dangerous when you're driving a car. One former member of a Bible cult told me, "It's very frustrating to realize over and over again that my mind is out of control. Particularly when I'm in a stressful situation, I'll suddenly discover I'm babbling nonsense words and syllables (speaking in tongues) inside my head, and I've become disoriented from whatever I was doing."

If not properly understood and responded to, floating can cause a former cult member who is depressed, lonely and confused to go back to the group.

For people fortunate enough to receive good cult counseling, floating is rarely a problem. However, for people who don't understand mind control, it can be a terrifying experience. Suddenly, you flip back into the cult mindset, and are hit with a tremendous rush of fear and guilt for betraying the group and its leader. You can become irrational and begin to think magically, interpreting personal and world events from the cult's perspective. For example, you didn't get that job "because God wants you to go back to the group," or the Korean Air Lines Flight 007 was shot down by the Russians "because you left the Moonies."

When you start to float, simply but firmly remind yourself that the experience has been triggered by some stimulus, and that it will pass. If you can, try to connect as soon as possible with someone who understands mind control, and talk it over rationally with them.

The most powerful and effective technique of all is to identify the trigger. It could be hearing a song, seeing someone who looks like a member of the group, or watching someone act or gesture in a way that cult members often do. Once you know what triggers you, *deliberately call forth that stimulus,* but make a new, positive mental association with it. Think of something non-cult related. Do this over and over again, until the association becomes a new, learned response.

In my case, when I heard the word *moon*, I would form a mental picture of a beautiful full moon. I would say to myself, *The earth only has one natural satellite, the moon*. For about a week, I often said to myself "moon," and conjured up this image, until it stuck. I referred to the leader of my former cult as Mr. Moon, not wishing to call him "Reverend," since that was a self-appointed title anyway, and visualized him behind bars in prison garb. Similarly, for ex-Scientologists, it is better to speak of "Ron Hubbard" rather than "L. Ron Hubbard" or "LRH", and not to call the cult "the Church". Such loaded language is a significant trigger.

One ex-member of est told me that even though she loves the beach, she avoided it because the sounds of ocean waves always reminded her of her indoctrination. Even though she had been out of the group for five years, that association was still inhibiting her ability to enjoy something she had always loved. I encouraged her to change the association. She could hear the sound of waves and deliberately program in a new and personally gratifying association. I told her to repeat the new association until it automatically overrode the cult programming. Within a few days she was able to visit the beach again. Ultimately, exposure techniques are the fastest methods to override the programming and make new, healthy associations.

Also keep in mind that floating is a natural byproduct of subjection to mind control. It is not your fault and not a defect on your part. Over time, its effects will naturally decrease, especially if you practice the techniques described above.

Overcoming Loaded Language

Substituting real language for the cult's "loaded language" can speed up a person's full recovery. By eradicating the cult jargon put inside my head, I was able to begin looking at the world again without wearing cult "glasses." The cult's *loaded language* had created little cubbyholes in my mind, and when I was a member, all reality was filtered through them. The faster an ex-member reclaims words and their real meaning, the faster recovery happens.

When I was in the Moonies, all relationships between people were described as either a "Cain-Abel" or a "Chapter 2" problem. The term "Cain-Abel," as explained earlier, was used to categorize everyone as either a superior or a subordinate. "Chapter 2 problems" were anything that had to do with sexuality, and any attraction members felt towards others. Therefore, all personal relationships fell into either of these two categories.

The most common mistake made by ex-members is to tell themselves that they should not think of the cult word. The mind doesn't know how *not* to think of something. Language is structured so that we have to think in positive associations. So, if you are an ex-member, make a new association, just as I described for the problem of "floating." If you are an ex-Moonie and have trouble getting along with a person, think of it as a personality conflict or a communication problem. For anyone who has been a Scientologist, it is absolutely essential to stop using the enormous cult vocabulary to stop thinking in the loaded terms invented by Hubbard and recorded in two dictionaries totaling a thousand pages. These folks are still thinking in the cult cubbyholes of the human experience. This becomes an issue with ex-Scientologists because unless they have made the intense effort necessary to eradicate the cult jargon installed in their minds, they inevitably use this jargon with each other and triggering happens all the time. Check the real meaning of words in a proper dictionary. Choose your friends and reclaim your native language! It will speed up your healing!

Loss Of Psychological Power

Another common problem for former cult members is the loss of concentration and memory. Before I became involved in the Moonies, I used to read a book at one sitting, averaging three books a week. But during the two and a half years I spent in the group, virtually all I read was Moonie propaganda.

When I first left the cult, I felt frustrated whenever I tried to read non-cult literature. At first, getting through a single paragraph was nearly impossible. I would continually space out, or have to stop to look up words that I once knew but now couldn't remember. I had to read and re-read material before I was able to force the creaky gears of my mind into operation. I also needed to buy a 400,000-word dictionary to relearn the meanings of words I had once known. I needed to look at old photographs, read old college papers, and be reminded of people I knew and things I had done prior to being in the group.

Fortunately, the mind is like a muscle. Although it tends to atrophy from disuse, with effort it can be built up again. It took me nearly a full year to get back to my pre-cult level of functioning. It took a lot of will and many hours of effort. But I did it. When I first was deprogrammed, I knew I wanted to go back to college but knew I needed time to strengthen my mind before I could function again. It took me a full year to regain my ability to concentrate and read normally.

Nightmares, Guilt, Grief, And Remorse

Nightmares are a good indicator that a former cult member needs to receive additional counseling in order to work through their cult experience. These unpleasant dreams come from the unconscious mind, which is still wrestling with the issues of cult involvement. Nightmares indicate unresolved conflicts within the mind.

Common nightmares for people who have lived with mind control include being trapped, feeling that people are coming after them, and being in the midst of a storm or a war. Ex-cult members also frequently report having upsetting dreams in which people inside in the group try to get them to leave, while friends and family outside the cult pressure them to rejoin.

Another key issue for some former members is *guilt about things they did in the group*. Some people were involved in illegal acts, such as fraud, theft, breaking and entering, harassment of critics, arson, sex trafficking, and the use and sale of drugs. I have met people who went AWOL from the armed services because a destructive cult group recruited them, and had great trouble when they tried to clear themselves later.

Fortunately, the vast majority of ex-cult members have not been involved in such things. However, even if they were not coerced to break the law, most have to cope with how they treated their family and friends during their cult membership. For example, some people had parents who became ill, but cult leaders prohibited them from visiting the hospital. In some cases, a parent died, and the cult member was not allowed to go to the funeral, even though it might have taken place only 20 miles away.

It can be extremely painful for a person to leave a destructive cult and have to deal with the havoc and emotional damage that their membership caused. This is especially true for people born into a cult. When they leave, typical cult policy is to excommunicate or shun them. This means they are rejected by their own families and friends, whom they might never see or speak with again. Alternatively, they might experience extreme pressure from their loved ones to "come back to God."

When I first left the Moonies, I felt an incredible sense of guilt about my role as a leader. I blamed myself for lying and manipulating hundreds of people. I felt I had allowed myself to be used as an American front man, a stooge for the Koreans and Japanese, who really held the reins of power in the group. For me, speaking out and helping others to leave was a form of making amends for what I had been manipulated to do.

Another issue involves feelings toward friends still in the group. When I left the Unification Church, at first I desperately wanted to rescue those people I had personally recruited. Unfortunately, the Moonie leadership cleverly shipped the people who were closest to me away from New York. They were told that I was away on a secret mission. The people I had recruited, my "spiritual children," didn't find out that I had left the group for more than three months. I believe they were told then only because I had started appearing on television to speak against the group.

About six months after I left, I went back to Queens College, where I had started a chapter of C.A.R.P., and gave a public lecture on cults and mind control for the psychology department. In the audience were my top three disciples, Brian, Willie, and Luis.[186] They sat and listened to me lecture for over an hour about mind control. I gave specific examples of how I had lied and tricked each one of them into membership. After the lecture was over, I walked over to them, and anxiously asked them what they thought. Willie smiled and said to me, "Steve, you shouldn't forget the heart of the Divine Principle or the heart of Father." I was crushed. They didn't appear to have heard a single thing I had said.

At that moment I remembered how, when I was a member, I had been instructed by Mr. Kamiyama to raise my spiritual children to be faithful, even if I left the group. I didn't realize at the time why he had me do that, because I never imagined leaving. Now I understood. To my great relief, many years later all three of them eventually walked out. I am so relieved and hope that one day they will forgive me and speak with me again.

Many people involved in faith-healing cults have to deal with the death of a child or other loved one who was prevented from receiving medical treatment. The remorse they feel when they leave such a group should not be turned on themselves in the form of blame or guilt. *They need to realize that they were victims, too, and did what they believed to be right at the time.*

Other ex-cult members have to deal with the anger and resentment of their children, who in some cases were beaten, neglected or sexually abused. Many were deprived of an education and a normal childhood. Some were deprived of their own parents; certain cults, such as the Hare Krishnas, systematically separated children from their parents and allowed them to visit only infrequently.[187] Yogi Bhajan's 3HO group sent some of its members' children to the organization's school in India. By separating children from their parents, the allegiance of both generations became solely to the group.[188] For years, Scientology "Sea Organization" parents were only allowed to see their children for an hour a day, if their production statistics were up. Children ran wild with almost no adult supervision. Leader David Miscavige has since prohibited Sea Org members from having children, and many women have been coerced into having abortions.

For others involved in less destructive cults, the emotional toll on children can ultimately yield positive results. I saw that in the life of my client Barbara. She explained how, for most of her life, she had thought she was crazy. Then she realized, from talking with a friend, that the group her parents had been involved with for the previous decade was actually a destructive cult. Barbara had spent a good deal of her childhood growing up on the group's commune. She and her brother Carl had been taught since early childhood that all negative emotions were harmful. Sadness, anger, jealousy, embarrassment, guilt and fear were all to be avoided and not "indulged in." Of course, all of these emotions are entirely normal, but Barbara and Carl had been taught otherwise. They were very relieved to know that their lifelong problems were not signs of mental illness, and that help was available for them.

Growing up, Barbara and Carl had tried to do what they were told, and dutifully attended cult indoctrination programs, but had never felt right about it. Nevertheless, they loved their parents and tried to do what would please them. Now that they were in college, as soon as they discovered that the group was a cult, they arranged for me and a former group member to counsel them, and then planned a rescue effort for their parents.

Their parents were bright, successful people in their fifties. He was a practicing attorney; she was an elementary school teacher. He had been recruited into the cult by an old friend from college. As a lawyer, he was quite skeptical at first, but was eventually drawn further and further into the group. He and his wife became mid-level leaders, and eventually ran the group's meetings in their city.

The rescue effort was a complete success, and the entire family is now closer than ever before. Both parents have helped others in the group to reevaluate their commitment. Several have left it.

Harassment And Threats

Another issue for some former cult members involves harassment, threats, break-ins, lawsuits, blackmail and even murder, particularly if an ex-member goes public. Since cults believe that anyone who leaves is an enemy, there is always some risk that harm will be done to a defector.

I have been threatened many, many times by cult members—usually by mail or phone, but also in person, particularly when I am picketing, demonstrating or otherwise exposing a particular group's activities. I have only once been physically assaulted, however, when a Moonie punched me in the face and incited me to punch him back. I looked him in the eye and asked him, "Is this what the Kingdom of Heaven is going to be like—silencing the opposition?" I took him to court and he pleaded no contest. The judge ordered him to pay for a new pair of glasses for me, and gave him a stern warning to stay away from me. Years later, he left the group and contacted me. He apologized for the incident, and told me he was only doing what he had been instructed to do: "Take care of Steve Hassan."

Even though violence toward former cult members is relatively rare, the fear factor has kept many people from going public and telling their stories. What they don't realize is that once their story is told, it would be stupid for a group to retaliate, because that would only incriminate them more. When I started Ex-Moon Inc. in 1979, it was partly because I realized there would be much more strength and safety in numbers. That strategy was successful.

Some of the larger, more aggressive groups, such as Scientology, believe in attacking critics rather than defending against accusations.[189] Scientology has initiated hundreds of lawsuits against former members and critics, including Paulette Cooper, author of *The Scandal of Scientology*,[190] and Gabe Cazares, former mayor of Clearwater, Florida. Typically, these suits are filed purely to harass and financially drain cults' opponents. To a certain extent, this strategy has been successful: most former members of Scientology, for example, are afraid to take any public action against the organization.[191] However, when the FBI raided Scientology headquarters, documents were obtained that proved the illegality of many of the organization's activities, and Hubbard's wife and ten other Scientologists were sent to jail. Guilty verdicts have also been handed down in Canada and France.

Problems With Intimate Relationships

Inside cults, members often have little chance to form a normal, satisfying intimate relationship with a partner. They may be forced into celibacy, paired with someone they would never have chosen on their own, or coerced into a life of sexual servitude. When they leave the group and begin to live in the real world, sooner or later they have to deal with the fact that, for years, their need for a satisfying relationship was never met.

Yet the experience of having been taken advantage of, often for years, makes it hard for people to take the emotional risk of forming close relationships with others. Some people have denied their own sexuality for so long that they may have difficulty expressing it. In other cases, ex-members got into sexual relationships with trainers or leaders who manipulated them, with little regard for their feelings.

That said, I have met a number of people who married in a cult, raised children, left the cult and managed to navigate their lives together. They are by far the exception. Most relationships break up after exiting the group. Sometimes one person stays in the group, which makes it very difficult when there are young children.

Trust in yourself and learning to trust someone else, much less a group, is a really big deal for ex-cult members. Feeling your real feelings and learning how to express them in healthy ways is so important. Learning to respect yourself and your partner as a separate and individual human being is essential. How to problem solve and share power is another essential issue. Some Christian cults put women under the control of men, and it can be difficult to unlearn such subservience.

In all of these cases, it's best to seek therapy with a mental health professional who understands undue influence.

Ways To Heal Yourself

The most effective emotional support and information will usually come from former cult members who are further along in the healing process. But the actual healing is the responsibility of the former cult member.

Finding and becoming part of a *healthy* group can be a big step forward. It took me a full year, after I left the Moonies, before I gingerly involved myself with a group of any kind—in this case, a peer counseling organization at college, in 1977.

In 1986, I served for a year as the national coordinator of a loosely knit group of ex-cult members who wanted to help themselves and others. It wasn't easy to coordinate a group of people who have all been burned by group involvement! But my experience taught me that such a thing is possible.

Support groups for former cult members can be especially beneficial. One woman who attended such a group in Boston contacted me, after she heard me on a local radio show. Deborah had been involved with a political cult for ten years. One day she told me she broke one of the group's rules. She had lunch alone with a non-member, and rather than face being "grilled" by the cult leader in front of the entire membership, she called up her parents and asked them for a plane ticket. She later decided that she was afraid to go home and wound up living on the streets of Boulder for several months, until she was able to slowly work her way back into society. When I met her, she was a successful businesswoman.

Even though she had been out of the cult for eight years, she had never talked about her experiences in it until she began meeting with other ex-members. "I feel like the whole thing is one big black box, and I'm afraid to open it up," she explained. But soon, with the help of the group, she did open it. She mustered the courage to share an issue she was dealing with. "I know that I am being hampered in my ability to trust my boyfriend and make a commitment to him. I think it is connected to what I went through," she shared.

We were all amazed at how successfully Deborah was able to compartmentalize her mind control experience, for such a long time. When she did start talking about it, huge chunks of time were still unaccounted for. The more she talked, the more we asked her questions and prodded her memory. Month by month, she got more and more in touch with what had happened to her. She had been subjected to an unusually intense degree of emotional and personal abuse while in the group.

"I'm really glad I was able to meet and talk with other former members," she explained. "It's nice to see other bright, talented people who went through something like what I went through. I just could never talk about the group to anyone without them thinking that I was crazy or sick."

Being part of a support group can show people how mind control operates in a variety of different organizations. It also enables those who are still grappling with issues of undue influence that it is possible to recover and become a happy, productive person. For most people who leave a destructive cult, the first step should be getting a handle on their group experience. Then, if there are other issues or problems that existed before their membership, they can begin to resolve them also.

Support groups can also be a mixed bag, if they aren't run by experienced professionals. With the best of intentions, people in support groups can wind up further traumatized if there aren't clear rules and boundaries of respect.

Be a good consumer! When looking for a support group, be careful. Some "support groups" are, in fact, fronts for cults themselves, which use them to lure back people who have recently left the group, as well as to recruit vulnerable people who recently left other mind control cults. When researching support groups online, look for a legitimate e-mail discussion group and/or Facebook page. I also suggest not revealing your real name or *any* personal information, until you are confident that the group is legitimate. If there is no support group in your area, see if there is an online support group that meets your needs.

It becomes apparent to former cult members in the first year after leaving that any pre-cult problems they may have had were never resolved while they were members of a destructive cult. This can be very disappointing to the ex-member, because the illusion of becoming healthier was one of the factors that reinforced continuing membership, sometimes for many years.

This realization is often more difficult for long-term members. Imagine going into a group at age 18 and coming out at 30. You've been deprived of a huge amount of life experience. Your twenties, typically reserved for self-exploration, experimentation, education, skill development, career and relationship building, have been lost. Chronologically, you are 30, but psychologically, you probably feel 18. Friends from high school have good jobs; many are married; some have children; some have houses. At 30, you may be inexperienced at dating, and have been out of touch with world affairs for more than a decade. At a party, you have little to talk about except your cult experience, which only exacerbates the feeling of being in a goldfish bowl. You have to catch up on *everything*. You may feel an acute sense of having to make up for lost time.

Some long-term former members liken the experience to that of POWs coming home after a war. In fact, post-traumatic stress disorder (PTSD) seems to apply perfectly to some cult member veterans. When they come home, they have to catch up on everything. In the 1970s one person I worked with had never heard of the Watergate scandal, didn't know who singer/songwriter James Taylor was, and wasn't aware that we had landed and walked on the surface of the moon.

Paradoxically, however, you need to slow down and *take* time. You need time to heal, grow and develop. You'll need to discover or create your own path, and be concerned about your own unique needs, rather than compare yourself with other people.

One sensitive father of an ex-cult member said, "If someone gets hit by a truck, naturally you expect that it will take them time to recover. You wouldn't expect them to get up out of bed, and go and get a job the next week, would you?" His daughter lived with him for her first year and a half away from the cult. He didn't pressure her to move out or seek employment during that time. He recognized that she was doing the very best she could.

Every person who has been in a cult is different and has different needs. Some people are able to adjust quickly to the outside world. Others, who have been more severely traumatized, need more time.

Perhaps most importantly, former cult members need to *learn how to trust themselves again*. They have to become their own best friend, as well as their own best therapist. They have to realize that they didn't choose to be lied to or abused. They are not at fault. Eventually, as they learn to once again trust themselves and their own inherent wisdom and instincts, they also learn that it's okay to begin trusting others. They realize that all groups are not evil. In fact, the good part of being involved with a healthy group—be it a religious, social or political—is that you *can* exercise control over your participation. You do not have to stay one minute longer than you want. Nor do you have to sit silently and blame yourself, if you don't understand what is being said or done. You can question, and you can question some more. Not only is this all right, it is your Constitutional right.

Other Challenges And Issues

Another important aspect of growth for any ex-cult member is learning to get in touch with emotions and channel them effectively.

When someone first leaves a mind control group, many of the emotions may remain suppressed. But as they adjust to the outside world, they may begin to feel shame and embarrassment, then anger and indignation. They move from *What is wrong with me?* to *How dare they do that to me!* This is normal and healthy.

At some point, they may begin a voracious research project to find out everything they can about their cult and answer every one of their questions. This, too, is a very positive therapeutic step. Often, the number one priority of someone who has just left a cult is to help rescue the friends who were left behind. For cult members, their major regret in leaving is usually losing contact with people they came to know and care for in the group. It becomes particularly difficult when a former member realizes that the friendships they thought were so good were conditional on continued membership. A former member can quickly see the strength of mind control bonds when their closest friend in the group refuses to meet them, unless he brings another member along.

Eventually, when all their questions are answered, and all their cult issues are addressed, they reach a saturation point. They declare to themselves, "They're not going to take the rest of my life!" and start making plans for the future.

Sometimes there are additional issues that need more extensive individual counseling. Sarah, a former ten-year member of the Church Universal and Triumphant, had been forcibly deprogrammed more than five years earlier, yet was still experiencing cult-related problems. I agreed to work with her for ten sessions. Her first homework assignment was to begin writing down her entire cult experience. *This is something I recommend for every ex-member.* It was certainly something Sarah needed to do in order to reclaim her true self.

I also suggested that, since she had been involved for such a long time, she should begin by making an outline. I told her to take ten folders and number them from 1973 to 1983; put 12 sheets of paper in each folder; and label the sheets January through December. With that as a starting point, I told her to begin writing down everything she could remember that was significant, whether positive or negative. I told her not to worry if there were huge gaps. Eventually they would all be filled in.

In order to help her remember, I told her to think of specific places she had lived or visited. I also told her to think about significant people. Lastly, I told her to recall specific activities or events that were meaningful to her.

Step by step, she was able to fill in her entire experience. She recorded how she came to be recruited. She listed her likes and dislikes about the group and its leaders. She was able to chart her ups and downs as a member. She was also able to see that, at many different points, she was very unhappy and disillusioned, but had no way out. At one point she had actually come home to her parents, complaining about her unhappiness, and they had taken her to a psychologist, who unfortunately did not recognize her problems as being cult related. After two months at home, Sarah had gone back to the group.

By writing down her entire experience, Sarah was able to process her experience and gain a greater perspective on it. She no longer had to carry around a lot of swirling, seemingly contradictory thoughts and feelings. It was now all on paper.

As part of her therapy, I explained to her that the person whose story filled those ten folders no longer existed. I suggested that she think about that person as a younger Sarah, someone who was doing the very best she could. Back at the time of her recruitment, she didn't know about cults or mind control. If she had, she surely would never have gotten involved.

Then I had her imagine herself as a time traveler. I instructed her to go back in time and teach the younger Sarah about mind control, so she could avoid the group's recruiters. I asked her to imagine how differently her life would have turned out if she had never become involved with the group. This enabled her to see that with more information, she would have had more choices and could have averted the danger. This became very important for her later in her therapy.

I asked her to re-experience, one at a time, traumatic cult experiences. This time, however, she could correct her responses. She told off one of the leaders in front of the members and angrily walked out of the cult. Even though she knew that we were just doing an exercise, it provided her the opportunity to channel her emotions constructively and reclaim her personal power and dignity.

By standing up for herself and telling the cult leader to "Shove it!" she could walk out of the group on her own and avoid the trauma of the forcible deprogramming. Sarah knows that in reality, her parents did need to rescue her. However, through this process she was able to regain personal control over the experience. This was extremely important in order to enable Sarah to move forward with her life.

Like everyone else in her position, she needed to take all the things she had learned, and all the people she had met and come to care for, and integrate them into a new sense of identity. Integrating the old into the new allows former members to be unusually strong. We are survivors. We have suffered hardship and abuse, and, through information and self-reflection, we are able to overcome adversity.

Like all former members I have counseled, Sarah suffered from lack of trust in herself and others, and fear of commitment to a job or a relationship. By helping her to reprocess her cult experience, I was able to show her that she now has resources that the younger Sarah didn't have, and that she is no longer the same person who was tricked and indoctrinated into a cult.

She is older, smarter and wiser now. She knows on a very deep personal level that she can identify and avoid any situation in which she is being manipulated or used. She can rely more completely on herself, and if she needs assistance, she will be able to find what she needs. Likewise, she needs to not fear making commitments. She knows now to ask questions and keep on asking questions, and to distrust any job or relationship that requires anything that violates her core self, including her ethics and values.

Like anyone who has been molested or abused, former members need to learn to rebuild their trust in themselves and others step by step. In their own good time, they can learn to take little risks and test the waters. They don't have to jump in any faster than is comfortable for them.

Recovery Facilities For Former Cult Members

There are regrettably only a small number of facilities to help ex-cult members heal, recover, rest, and grow. One such recovery center is Wellspring Retreat, founded by Paul and Barbara Martin, in Athens, Ohio. Paul, now deceased, was a licensed psychologist and former eight-year member of the Great Commission International, a Bible cult.[192] Another is Meadowhaven, founded by Rev. Robert and Judy Pardon, in Lakeville, Massachusetts. Both provide healing and support, through a staff of trained counselors and former cult members.

For some former cult members, the opportunity to go to a safe place for a few weeks or months, where they can get intensive support and counseling, is invaluable. The problem is that these facilities are very expensive to operate and most people coming out of cults have no financial resources. Something must be done to offer the services that people need to recover!

Chapter 12

Next Steps

I know but one freedom & that is the freedom of the mind
Antoine de Saint-Exupéry

The unethical use of mind control has reached the point where it is a major social problem, not only in the United States but across the globe. Human traffickers enslave hundreds of thousands of people in this country and millions worldwide. Organizations such as the Unification Church, Scientology, Jehovah's Witnesses and countless others are affecting the lives of millions of people all over the world. Destructive cults such as ISIS/Daesh[193] and other extreme terrorist groups have gained considerable political attention (if not power) by playing out their grisly activities on the world stage. Some groups, such as Al Qaeda, have managed to invade our shores by influencing domestic terrorists, like those who committed the Boston Marathon bombing. Freeman-On-The-Land, also known as Sovereign Citizens, is listed on the FBI's domestic terror watchlist.[194]

Groups are exerting their influence economically, through their "training" courses for business people in key positions in corporate America. Cults are also gaining ground among the waves of Asian and Hispanic immigrants to the United States, moving beyond their traditional recruitment of the white middle class, which has allowed them to broaden their financial base. People in other parts of the world, who are enamored of the "American dream," are falling prey to U.S. based Bible cults and multi-level marketing (MLM) groups.

Many cult groups have become so skilled at their public relations work that they have gained a high degree of social acceptance, even among prominent professionals. One ploy taken by wealthier groups is to lure respected professionals—scientists, lawyers, politicians, academicians, clergy—to speak at cult-sponsored conferences by offering them large honoraria, often at conferences held in exotic locations, with all expenses paid. These invited speakers may not know or even care about the cult involvement, but their mere presence at such conferences gives tacit approval to the cult. For instance, former British Prime Minister, Edward Heath, attended Moonie conferences. Sociologist Eileen Barker, who wrote *The Making of a Moonie: Choice or Brainwashing* and made her professional career saying my life work was mistaken, admits to attending 14 such conferences, but claims that this has not affected her objectivity!

My concern about cults is broad and urgent. Their activities, if unchecked, will continue to wreak untold psychological and, at times, even physical damage, on many thousands, if not millions, of people who do not understand what constitutes unethical mind control. Unless legislative action is taken to make destructive cults accountable to society for violating the rights of their members, these groups will continue to deceive the general public into believing that they are doing nothing out of the ordinary.

Speaking practically, I realize that many will be reluctant to add yet another issue to their list of serious concerns. Every day, when we read a newspaper or watch the TV news, we are confronted by the threat of nuclear war, global climate change, massive destruction of the earth's natural resources, starvation in Africa, widespread political corruption, deadly microbes like the Ebola virus and so many other concerns. Why add another? Because like Ebola, the mind control viruses of cults sicken and drain life from human beings. Unless they are contained, they will continue to spread, infecting ever more people.

Furthermore, like biological viruses, cults adapt to take advantage of human weaknesses. They exploit legal loopholes to escape prosecution. They manipulate and subvert Internet search engines to bury criticism that might alert people to their unethical behavior. They pour out scorn and disinformation about former members. They use social media to recruit new members.

Thousands of stories about cults have appeared in the media in the past few years, yet few address the issue of mind control directly. They tend to be presented as stories about strange or controversial "religions" rather than about people who have been deceptively recruited and controlled through mind control. Media attention usually dies down after the big stories—Charles Manson, the Jonestown massacre, Waco, Heaven's Gate, and the Tokyo subway sarin gassing by Aum Shinrikyo.[195] It may seem that there are fewer cults because there have been fewer big stories, and as I've mentioned, many people with whom I come into casual conversation on the subject of destructive cults express surprise when I tell them that such groups are still a major problem in American society.

Imagine, then, how they react when I tell them that this lack of awareness is the result of disinformation campaigns, not just by cults but by the very institutions that are supposed to protect our constitutional freedoms.

Cults And The United States Government

Public reaction to the Jonestown massacre on November 18, 1978, was shock and disbelief. The murder of a United States congressman showed that some cult leaders would stop at nothing to keep anyone, especially someone in a legitimate position of authority, from exposing them to public scrutiny.

I was deeply saddened by news of the assassination of congressman Leo Ryan. I knew that he was highly knowledgeable and concerned about destructive cults. He had been a leading member of the Congressional investigation of Korean-American Relations headed by congressman Donald Fraser. Released on October 31, 1978—just a few short weeks before the mass suicide at Jonestown—the Fraser Report, as it came to be known, recommended that an Executive branch inter-agency task force be set up to pursue illegal activities committed by the Moon organization.[196]

No action was taken on that recommendation. (Moon was convicted four years later of felony tax fraud, and served thirteen months in a minimum security prison in Danbury, Connecticut).

It seemed that something was being done about the cult problem, given all the activity on Capitol Hill, in the late 1970s. After Jonestown, Congress launched a formal inquiry. On May 15, 1979, a House Foreign Affairs Committee issued its report, describing in detail the brainwashing tactics of Jim Jones and the Peoples Temple. They concluded by recommending that the National Institute of Mental Health be given funds to further research on mind control and destructive cult groups.

Nothing was ever done to follow up on that recommendation, either.

However, Senator Bob Dole did put together a hearing on cults after Jonestown at which I was invited to speak. On the morning of the hearing, I was suddenly told that no former cult member would be permitted to speak. We were told that this was to avoid allowing current cult members equal time to speak. Yet in the hearing room—which was filled with ex-members holding up signs saying, "Elect Bob Dole President, Repeal the First Amendment"—we found that Neil Salonen, the spokesperson for the Moonies, had, nonetheless, been allowed to deliver a statement. I was beginning to realize the political clout of the cults. But I came to realize much more.

What the Jonestown "inquiry" showed me—and many others—was that in the face of an outrageous and evil act, the best our government could do was to hold a highly-censored hearing—a public show that neither got to the details of what happened nor took steps to see that such terrible events would never happen again.

The government had failed us but, as we were soon to learn, it had done far worse. It turns out the Central Intelligence Agency (CIA) had been conducting its own mind control research. It was experimenting with some of the very same techniques—and some far more ruthless—that had killed over 900 people at Jonestown. What's more, it had been carrying out these covert experiments on an often unwitting group of Americans since the late 1940s. The government was guilty of the very offense it claimed to be protecting us from.

Credit goes to author John Marks, who in 1975 read one sentence in a government report that led him to investigate the CIA's secret activities. In 1979, he published his famous *The Search for the Manchurian Candidate,* to widespread national attention. Inspired by Marks' initial discoveries, Alan W. Scheflin and Edward M. Opton Jr. undertook complementary research, which culminated, also in 1979, with the publication of *The Mind Manipulators*.

Both books laid out in detail the mind control research that was being performed by the Central Intelligence Agency from the late 1940s through the early 1960s, and that involved subcontractors at over 80 American institutions. Code-named MK-ULTRA, the CIA's mind control research program was a clandestine and illegal program of experiments on human subjects that was intended to identify methods that could be developed for use in interrogations and torture. MK-ULTRA left no stone unturned in the quest to find ways to manipulate people's mental states, alter their brain functions, and control their behavior.

The techniques used in MK-ULTRA's experiments ranged from the chemical—LSD and other psychotropic drugs (including the notorious

BZ, which never leaves the human system and was given to hundreds of unsuspecting GIs); to the physical—brain surgery, electroshock; to the psychological—sensory deprivation, isolation, hypnosis, sexual and verbal abuse, and more. Scheflin and Opton actually uncovered a 1953 speech by Allen Dulles, then CIA director, frankly admitting this to be true.[197] Dr. Ewan Cameron, who was president of the Canadian, American and World Psychiatric Association, supervised mind control research in a Canadian psychiatric hospital.

This meant that at the same time that the government was dropping the ball on the Jonestown investigation, it was covering up a program far beyond anything that Jim Jones could have ever imagined.

Other researchers attempted to follow up on this work but, by then, the CIA—in violation of many federal laws—had destroyed almost all of its relevant files. The MK-ULTRA records were virtually all destroyed except for a few boxes of financial records, making it impossible for investigators to find out what really happened. ABC aired an excellent documentary on the secret program called *Mission Mind Control*.

In 1975, a Congressional committee, led by Senator Frank Church, decided to investigate. The Church Committee set out to unearth the full scope of the research but, at its hearings, it became clear that it had not been able to go beyond the discoveries made by private researchers. The committee was derailed by the same two CIA strategies, leaving the public in the dark.

First, the CIA leaked information about its attempted assassinations of world leaders, which sent the Committee—and the media—running after that story. It then claimed that the MK-ULTRA was a "rogue elephant"—the brainchild of a few overzealous agents who worked on it, without the knowledge of their higher-ups. Members of the committee bought these explanations, thereby missing the fact, stated explicitly in Dulles's 1953 speech, that knowledge of—and responsibility for—the program went all the way to the very top of the CIA. Thousands of people were experimented on, which makes it impossible to believe that this was not a significant program. It is also true that at that time almost all social psychological research was actually funded by the U.S. government. Thankfully, Milgram and Zimbardo published their results.[198] I knew first-hand that techniques for mind control were real—I had lived in a mind control environment and practiced it on others. I had researched the subject of mind control, and had the great fortune to speak with top experts on the subject, such as Robert Jay Lifton and Margaret Singer. I knew that no self-respecting psychologist would deny that there was useful information in mind control research—information that *could* be used to affect people, for better or worse. But the revelations about the MK-ULTRA—and its cover up—forced me to confront another set of questions that demanded answers.

Why wasn't the federal government informing the American people about the dangers of mind control? Why was the issue continually shuffled into a discussion of religious liberty and the First Amendment? To this day, there has been no official government statement on the existence—let alone the dangers—of mind control.

European countries, including Germany, France and Belgium, have recently recognized the dangers posed by mind control cults and have created task forces to investigate them. There is apparently no such initiative on the part of the U.S. government—not by the FBI, CIA, Homeland Security, or any other intelligence-gathering agency—despite the threat that they have posed to our national safety. It's about time the Surgeon General, or some other high-ranking government official, made such a statement.

Perhaps there are other political explanations for why the government does not admit to any knowledge of mind control techniques. Whatever the reasons, there is now little doubt that, during those decades, the American people unwittingly spent millions of dollars on mind control research. That money would have been far better spent investigating the devastating effects of mind control in cult groups. Former members present a tremendous opportunity for researchers, but there is no political will for such an investigation.

I am not against research into mind control. To the contrary, as a mental health professional, I am heartily in favor of ethically conducted research, which increases our knowledge of ourselves and the workings of the mind.[199] Nor, for that matter, am I opposed to the classification of some information in the interest of maintaining national security. But if the government has indeed been conducting research into mind control, then it has a responsibility to inform the American public that mind control exists.

In the absence of recognition by the government that mind control exists and that unethical mind control is wrong, *the government's silence indirectly condones the practice of undue influence by unethical people and organizations on the rest of society.* One only need look around to see the effects of that silence: mind control groups are proliferating at an unprecedented pace. The principles of freedom and democracy demand that the reality of mind control be exposed to full public scrutiny.

Cults, Mind Control And The Mental Health Profession

The U.S. government issues licenses to professionals who are responsible for restoring ailing people's mental well-being. Mental health professionals do this by developing specific techniques and therapies to address the problem that a patient or client may have.

One population that cannot count on having its mental health needs met is that of cult victims and other victims of undue influence. This is particularly strange because for years, the *Diagnostic and Statistical Manual of Mental Disorders (DSM)*—which is published by the American Psychiatric Association (APA) and is relied upon by clinicians, researchers, drug companies, health insurance companies, the courts and policy makers—has contained a designation for victims of cult brainwashing and thought reform.

The most recent version, the *DSM—5,*[200] identifies this group of patients under a special category: Other Specified Dissociative Disorder 300.15 (F44.9). If you go to page 305, number 2, you will read: "**Identity disturbance due to prolonged and intense coercive persuasion**: Individuals who have been subjected to intense coercive persuasion (e.g., brainwashing, thought reform, indoctrination while captive, torture, long-term political imprisonment, recruitment by sects/cults or by terror organizations) may present with prolonged changes in, or conscious questioning of, their identity."

I wish I could say that most mental health professionals *have* read it. To the contrary, it must be one of the DSM-5's least known categories. Therapists and other practitioners are largely unaware that a diagnosis of mind control can even be made and are certainly unfamiliar with the specialized approaches that have been developed to address it. Meanwhile, a subset of their patients continue to suffer as a result of their cult involvement—that is, unless they turn to a relatively small handful of people who have recognized their needs and are willing to treat them.

There was a moment in time when this could have changed. In 2002,

Professor Philip Zimbardo, who conducted the now-famous Stanford prison study, was President of the American Psychological Association (APA). He saw quite clearly that the APA had not served the interests of this suffering population. He asked Alan W. Scheflin, then a professor at Santa Clara University School of Law, to chair a panel, *Cults of Hatred*, at the APA's annual convention.

In his opening remarks, Scheflin said that the mental health community has not addressed the needs of two different populations: those who accurately believe that their minds have been controlled in cultic and other situations; and those who mistakenly believe they are the victims of mind control and may be suffering from delusions or paranoia. The event brought together academicians like Scheflin and Zimbardo; therapists, like myself, who work in the area of mind control; and former members of groups such as the Peoples Temple. It was, for me and many others, a momentous occasion.

Zimbardo tried to seize that moment by writing about it in the President's column of the APA Monitor.[201] His words were so eloquent that I have decided to reproduce them:

> "A basic value of the profession of psychology is promoting human freedom of responsible action, based on awareness of available behavioral options, and supporting an individual's rights to exercise them. Whatever we mean by "mind control" stands in opposition to this positive value orientation.
>
> Mind control is the process by which individual or collective freedom of choice and action is compromised by agents or agencies that modify or distort perception, motivation, affect, cognition and/or behavioral outcomes. It is neither magical nor mystical, but a process that involves a set of basic social psychological principles.
>
> Conformity, compliance, persuasion, dissonance, reactance, guilt and fear arousal, modeling and identification are some of the staple social influence ingredients well studied in psychological experiments and field studies. In some combinations, they create a powerful crucible of extreme mental and behavioral manipulation when synthesized with several other real-world factors,

> such as charismatic, authoritarian leaders, dominant ideologies, social isolation, physical debilitation, induced phobias, and extreme threats or promised rewards that are typically deceptively orchestrated, over an extended time period in settings where they are applied intensively.
>
> A body of social science evidence shows that when systematically practiced by state-sanctioned police, military or destructive cults, mind control can induce false confessions, create converts who willingly torture or kill "invented enemies," engage indoctrinated members to work tirelessly, give up their money—and even their lives—for "the cause."

Zimbardo hoped that APA board members would wake up to the reality of mind control. That did not happen. Previous efforts by others had fared no better. In 1983, Dr. Margaret Singer headed a task force on Deceptive and Indirect Methods of Persuasion and Control at the request of the APA.[202] Despite her efforts, the problem was not deemed serious enough to be taken up by the APA. Internal politics appeared to be at work to keep this body of knowledge from public attention.

The promise contained in previous editions of the *DSM* and in the current section of the *DSM-5* goes unfilled and, indeed, unrecognized. The fact that neither the government nor organized psychotherapy has stepped up to help those adversely affected by mind control is dreadful. But I am hopeful that this will soon change, through the efforts of enlightened mental health professionals and, importantly, the growing number of former members who are taking action and telling their stories to therapists and anyone else who will listen.

Mind Control Research And Its Application

Despite the lack of attention by the government and mental health profession, many people have been hard at work studying mind control and how it affects people. They have written numerous books and hundreds of papers.

After publishing his 1961 classic, *Thought Reform and the Psychology of Totalism*, former Air Force Intelligence psychiatrist Robert Jay Lifton went on to write two more books on the theme of mind control. In 1986 he published *The Nazi Doctors*, in which he describes the psychological process of "doubling" that German doctors underwent to enable them to obediently perform acts of unimaginable cruelty in service to Hitler. Lifton then wrote a book in 1999 about the Japanese terrorist Aum Shinrikyo cult entitled, *Destroying the World to Save It*, in which he applied his model of mind control to explain how cult members were manipulated into killing innocent people in order to bring about an "apocalypse" that would supposedly erase all of the bad *karma* of the Japanese population.

Margaret Singer wrote two books with Janja Lalich[203]—*Cults in Our Midst* and *Crazy Therapies*. In *The Lucifer Effect*, Philip Zimbardo detailed his famous Stanford prison study and applied its lessons to understand the horrible acts committed by American soldiers at the Abu Ghraib prison. Louis Jolyon West and Paul Martin wrote a paper on pseudo-identity disorder that is now considered a classic. Social psychologist Robert Cialdini's best-selling book, *Influence*, details six laws by which people can be made to alter their behavior and beliefs. Anthony Pratkanis and Elliot Aronson's *Age of Propaganda* shows how PR and advertising manipulate the public.

Former cult members have written their stories—such as Deborah Layton (Peoples Temple), Nori Muster (Hare Krishnas), Alexandra Stein (The O), and Richard E. Kelly (Jehovah's Witnesses)—using their first-hand experiences to shed light on the process of mind control. Some, like me, have become mental health professionals, in an effort to apply our life experience to help others overcome the predatory behavior of cult leaders and other victimizers.

Research now strongly suggests that cult leaders, dictators, pimps and human traffickers have one or both of two serious personality disorders: narcissistic personality disorder (NPD) or antisocial personality disorder (more commonly known as psychopathic/sociopathic disorder). Canadian sociologist Stephen Kent presented a wonderful paper at a recent meeting of the International Cultic Studies Association (ICSA), titled "Narcissistic Grandiosity and the Life of Sun Myung Moon," in which he took extensive quotes from Moon and fit them into the nine criteria of NPD as set out in the American Psychiatric Association's Diagnostic manual, the *DSM–5*.[204] Former cult member and respected therapist, Daniel Shaw, wrote an important book, *Traumatic Narcissism: Relational Systems of Subjugation,* which is really worth reading.[205] Sam Vaknin, Ph.D. has written a book called *Malignant Self Love: Narcissism Revisited*, and he has posted several informative videos on his youtube channel, samvaknin. Psychologist Anna Salter wrote what I think is the best book on sex abusers (and not surprisingly most cult leaders), *Predators: Pedophiles, Rapists, and Other Sex Offenders*.[206] On the other side of the cult equation, Dr. Flavil Yeakley, a respected psychologist from Abilene Christian University, has undertaken considerable research into the psychological profiles of cult members.[207] Dr. Yeakley administered the Meyers-Briggs Type Indicator (MBTI), a personality profile research device, to over a thousand members of different religious groups, both mainline and cultic. He asked members to fill out the questionnaire three times. The first time, they were asked to answer the questions in their present frame of mind. The second time, they were asked to answer the questions from the state of mind prior to joining the group. Finally, Dr. Yeakley asked his test subjects to respond to the questions as they thought they would answer in five years' time.

He administered this test to members of the Boston Church of Christ, the Church of Scientology, the Hare Krishnas, Maranatha, the Children of God, the Moonies and The Way International. The results showed a high level of movement toward certain standard personality types as defined by the test. In other words, people in certain cults appeared to be all moving toward having the same kinds of personalities, distinct to their particular group, regardless of the original personalities they brought with them into the group.

In comparison, when this test was given to members of the Baptist, Catholic, Lutheran, Methodist, and Presbyterian churches, there were *no* significant changes in psychological profiles over time. In short, there was no indication of any pressure to conform to a certain type of personality. People's fundamental personalities—their authentic selves—remained intact.

I wrote to Yeakley that I thought these findings offered support for my idea that cults actually give new personalities to their members—Yeakley refers to it as "cloning"—as they suppress the members' original identities. As Dr. Yeakley explained in a letter to me:

"In the Boston Church of Christ and in three of the cults, the shifting was toward the ESFJ (extrovert, sensing, feeling, judging) personality type. Two of the cults were shifting toward ESTJ (extrovert, sensing, thinking, judging) and one toward ENTJ (extrovert, intuitive, thinking, judging). There is nothing wrong with any of these three types. The problem is with the pressure to conform to any type. It is the shifting which is negative, not the type toward which the shifting takes place."[208] Much more research needs to be done. Well-respected mental health professionals who are experts on mind control—Lifton, Singer, West, and Zimbardo, along with John Clark, Edgar Schein, Michael Langone, Carmen Almendros, Rod Dubrow-Marshall, Bill and Lorna Goldberg, Steve Eichel and others associated with the International Cultic Studies Association (ICSA)—have researched, written on, and advocated for more awareness about mind control.

There is an especially profound need for epidemiological studies to investigate the public-health effects of undue influence. Psychotic breakdowns, violent acts by former cult members, suicides, drug and alcohol abuse, depression, and anxiety disorders are public health issues that can all be caused by mind control, either deliberately or as side effects.

There are exciting possibilities in the developing technology of functional magnetic resonance imaging (fMRI) which might help us understand whether brain function changes as a result of undue influence. I suspect it does. Functional MRI's have already shown a distinct signature when someone is in a hypnotic state—the anterior cingulate cortex (ACC) lights up distinctively. They have also shown that dissociative identity disorder (DID) produces a distinctive brain signature when a person switches identities.[209] Every day, in real-life contexts, cults are essentially performing unethical social psychology experiments. One way to stop them is to expose the biological effects of their manipulations. I believe that incredible good can come from this kind of research.

More research also needs to be done on the potentially *beneficial* use of ethical mind control techniques (for instance, for weight loss, motivation, smoking cessation, and so on). The use of mind control technology is not inherently evil. Like any technology, it can be used to serve or to harm, to empower people or to enslave them.

Severe depression affects millions of Americans and robs them of their ability to enjoy life. It may be possible to teach these people some helpful mind control techniques (like psychiatrist David Burns teaches essential cognitive-behavioral strategies in his seminal book *Feeling Good*) to support or hasten their recovery.[210] One such simple technique involves repeatedly imagining a better future. Such a technique is effective and ethical, but only when someone freely makes the choice to use it and the *locus of control* is within oneself.

Mind control techniques can also be used to help people currently stuck in the criminal justice system. There is a great need for massive reform of our prison system. Inmates can be taught more effective ways to break their cycle of low self-esteem and law-breaking behavior. Their voluntary use of mind control techniques may help them change their thinking, behavior, and relationship to society.

It is my belief that *people who know how mind control operates have a distinct advantage*, providing they use their knowledge for ethical purposes—to bring about positive change in themselves and others; and to protect themselves and others from the unethical use of mind control by less ethical people.

A measured approach, one that is guided by morality and wisdom, must be taken when using any powerful tool for altering the human mind. I hope that these issues will be thoroughly debated and protections built in to prevent any abuses of this technology.

These considerations represent just the beginning of societal understanding of mind control. Much more must be done to educate mental health professionals and empower them to help people who are still suffering.

Protecting Children From Cult Abuse

Children occupy a unique and challenging place on the spectrum of issues involving undue influence. There is so much research showing the damaging effects of abuse—be it physical, sexual, emotional or verbal—on the developing brain. (The good news is that there is also research showing that the brain is remarkably resilient: it retains its plasticity well into and possibly throughout adulthood.)

Children who are raised in isolated, totalistic cults may be indoctrinated to hate those outside the group or to believe that Armageddon is just about to happen. They are told that if they stray from the group, terrible things will happen: their families will suffer, they will lose their connection to God and spend all eternity in Hell. Extremist groups train even child members how to kill. These are forms of mental and emotional abuse. Any country that allows such activities to take place should be held accountable. The International War Crimes Tribunal at Nuremberg went so far as to suggest that this kind of abuse of children constitutes a crime against humanity.

David Cooperson, a veteran child protection social worker, has written a vitally important book, *The Holocaust Lessons on Compassionate Parenting and Child Corporal Punishment,* which convincingly shows how hitting, spanking or paddling children has detrimental effects on a child's development. He has a website, stoplegalchildabuse.com, and is on a quest to make it illegal to physically harm children in the U.S.. Forty countries have brought such legislation, including the Scandinavian countries and the UK.

Any country that grants tax-exempt status to organizations that abuse children, not just physically, but mentally, emotionally or spiritually, should be held responsible for that abuse. Tax-exempt organizations like Jehovah's Witnesses, that have had policies in place for decades that systematically protect pedophiles from criminal prosecution, and which disfellowships victims and their families for speaking out, should lose their exemption. The leadership should be prosecuted for conspiracy to cover up illegal activities. The tragedy is that many children or young adults who run away from totalistic groups, like the Watchtower, end up homeless and in the control of pimps who exploit and control them for money and sex. They move from one mind control situation into another.

Child pornographers are being identified and prosecuted, but not enough is being done to protect children from being kidnapped or sold to human traffickers. As a start, men have an absolute obligation to find out the actual age of anyone they have sex with. If they look underage, they probably are underage. Call the police and rescue this minor. There could be laws requiring people to report suspected child trafficking.

Some states still have laws that allow people to apply for a religious exemption when it comes to medical treatment. Christian Science continues to lobby State governments to allow parents to keep their children from medical treatment. Jehovah's Witnesses prohibit members from having blood transfusions and expect members to refuse transfusions and other medical treatment for their sick or hospitalized children. They routinely apply for religious exemption on the basis of belief. These laws can and must be amended to protect the health and lives of children. Gretchen Callahan's failed faith-healing story in chapter 6 is heartbreaking, but there are countless children similarly and needlessly suffering. Not all of these children die or lose a limb or an organ due to medical neglect. But they are often in physical pain and may also suffer emotionally, especially if they are made to feel that their illness is their fault or are told that their disease is spiritual and that all they, or their parents, need to do is pray for God to intervene.

Perhaps most concerning of all is the situation with those groups, like the Twelve Tribes and Followers of Christ, which do not register their children at birth. Sick children, who are often denied medical treatment, may die and be buried on the cult property without the outside world even knowing they ever existed. Linda Martin, a former member of Followers of Christ, is trying to bring attention to the large number of children who have died, due to the group's faith healing practices. Janet Heimlich's Child Friendly Faith Project is an outgrowth of her important book, *Breaking Their Will: Shedding Light on Religious Child Maltreatment*. I gladly joined its board of advisors and the organization has held two very important conferences in Austin, Texas.[211] Another aspect of cult life—and even of noncult life—that is devastating to see occurs during and after separation or divorce, when children are indoctrinated against one parent by the other parent. Parental alienation is a very real phenomenon. It goes on all the time when a parent leaves a cult. The cult parent may truly believe that their former spouse is evil for "leaving God" (and for leaving the family.) Some of these groups actually instruct cult parents to make up lies to get the child to believe that the ex-member parent molested them, in an effort to influence a judge to stop contact. Developmental psychologist Amy Baker has written, along with Paul Fine, a number of excellent books addressing this huge problem, including *Surviving Parental Alienation* and *Co-Parenting with a Toxic Ex*. Baker has developed a curriculum for middle school guidance counselors to use with children whose parents are undergoing a divorce, to protect them from abuse. Understanding the BITE model has proven to be vital for children who have been programmed to hate their parent. It helps them understand what happened to them, so that they can take the first steps towards reconciling with that parent.

I would be remiss if I did not mention homeschooling. While it may work beautifully in the outside world, the fact is, many destructive cults insist on schooling their children in order to keep them from that world, which they often consider to be "Satan's world." While there are legitimate homeschooling curricula, it is imperative that there be checks and balances to protect children.

On the other hand, if a child comes to public school with black and blue marks, or displays a severe trauma reaction, teachers and counselors must investigate and do what they can to protect the child from abuse. Similarly, if a child appears isolated and wary or avoids interacting with children and adults outside their insular community, this can be very detrimental to their development. The onus is on the school to investigate.

Cults And The Law

Current laws do not even recognize that mind control exists, except when there is the use of physical force or the threat of such force.

There *are* laws concerning undue influence that protect children and vulnerable adults—the elderly, the dying, people with certain mental illnesses, people with disabilities—from being taken advantage of by what California law used to call "artful and designing persons." Aside from the elderly, it is very difficult, if not impossible, for courts to agree that a healthy, functional individual can be subjected to undue influence and undergo a radical personality change.

This is not a new phenomenon. Years ago, judges had a somewhat similar attitude towards women who were physically abused by domestic partners. Those judges said, "Just leave." It took many years and many experts to persuade them that the psychological dynamics were nowhere near that simple.

When victims of cult abuse appear in court seeking a remedy for the harms that have been done to them, the odds are usually against them.[212] Part of the problem is that courts generally prefer not to be involved with what they view to be interpersonal "squabbles," especially in the absence of some kind of physical abuse or coercion. Legal theories that might protect cult victims either do not exist or have not been applied to this kind of situation. When experts testify in court, the literature they draw upon concerns brainwashing and mind control. These terms are seen by some judges as fanciful or outlandish—something out of Hollywood—and certainly devoid of scientific grounding. The law requires that, for an expert to testify, it must first be demonstrated that he or she will be testifying about matters of science. Judges do not think about mind control or brainwashing as matters of science.

There are legal causes of action that could be utilized by cult victims, such as fraud or "intentional infliction of emotional distress." But the law on these two subjects has not been applied or developed in relation to cult situations. Courts and judges might be disinclined to extend these time-honored legal doctrines to this more controversial arena.

Meanwhile, the same principles of influence that are used to recruit people into cults are being used by pedophiles to groom children and to turn people into human trafficking victims. The definition used by the U.N. for labor and sex trafficking is use of fraud, force, and coercion. Law enforcement and other professionals who routinely deal with these victims are beginning to finally understand that this adds up to mind control.

Laws to protect victims of sex trafficking are beginning to change as well. Several states now have what are called Safe Harbor laws, which protect minors who are arrested for prostitution (it should be called "trafficking" but isn't, yet). Instead of being put into jail, these young people are protected by social workers who advocate for their safety, health and well-being. There is a growing understanding that young sex workers are not exercising their free will; they are under the mind control of pimps or sex traffickers (this is also true of many adult trafficking victims). Loyola law professor Kathleen Kim has written numerous articles, including "The Coercion of Trafficked Workers," which argues the need for law to be applied fairly and in support of victims' rights.[213] The same is true for all victims of mind control.

Part of the problem facing lawmakers and the courts is that cults have sought to hide behind the constitutional guarantee of religious freedom. In this country, people's right to believe whatever they want is absolute, as it should be. What is *not* absolute is a group's right to *act* in any way that it likes. For example, a sect may believe that it is a sacred act to handle poisonous snakes, but the law prohibits snake-handling rituals because too many people have died as a consequence. Lawyers for cults do their best to ignore this difference, and try to turn mind control issues into issues of belief, rather than issues of behavior. Attorney Marci Hamilton's excellent book, *God vs. the Gavel: The Perils of Extreme Religious Liberty* brings to light the way in which groups with influence over lawmakers enjoy special treatment under the law.

Another way to frame this issue involves freedom *of* versus freedom *from*. The Constitution guarantees Americans the right to worship, think and speak as they please. But to what degree should we be protected *from* other people's attempts to make us worship, think and speak as they want us to? Legislators and courts are still struggling with this.

Cult recruitment and conversion are particularly difficult to analyze. Does a group really have the right to deceive potential converts who would stay away if they knew the truth? Likewise, does a group have the right to manipulate a person's thoughts, feelings and environment in order to create a conversion experience? If so, where should the line be drawn between legal and illegal manipulation? I will say more about this shortly.

So far, it has been difficult to determine scientifically whether a person is under mind control. Any evaluation has had to be subjective. Mind control experts have been seeking a legal vehicle that will allow them to satisfy the law's requirement that they will be testifying from scientific data.

They now have one. Alan W. Scheflin, who is Professor Emeritus at Santa Clara University School of Law, in an important paper, argues that *all* human beings have the right to protection from undue influence, a concept the law has recognized for at least five centuries. With this legal precedent in place, the remaining issue is qualifying experts to testify on the basis of science.

In his paper, "Supporting Human Rights by Testifying Human Wrongs," which appeared in the *International Journal of Cultic Studies*,[214] Scheflin describes what he calls the Social Influence Model, or SIM, for determining whether undue influence has occurred. This model provides a structure for the presentation of scientific data. It involves an analysis of six elements: the influence itself; the influencer's motives; the influencer's methods; the circumstances under which the influence occurred; the influencee's receptivity or vulnerability (regardless of their designation as a minor, a vulnerable adult, or a non-vulnerable adult); and the consequences for both parties. For each of these elements, there is abundant social science data that an expert may use to give the judge and jury a clear picture of why the communications that occurred should be labeled *undue* influence.

Currently, the law tends to protect cults more than it protects their victims. In part, this is because of the enormous wealth of some mind control groups, which allows them to hire the best attorneys and to file harassment lawsuits (unwinnable, but very troublesome to the person or organization being sued). In addition, there is the first amendment issue. Sadly, some of the leaders of the American Civil Liberties Union (ACLU) have historically sided with cults, invoking the First Amendment and ignoring mind control research.

Still, brave former members of many different cults have initiated civil lawsuits against their groups. The results have been mixed. But when the Moonies sued the London *Daily Mail* newspaper for libel over two articles it published in 1978, they lost. In the longest libel suit in the history of England, the court found that the Moonies did "brainwash their members and did try to cut people off from their families." Because British law requires that whichever party loses the suit is responsible for the expenses of both sides, the Moonies were required to pay some $2 million in expenses.[215]

There has been a trend of cases over the last few decades holding that cult critics who describe a group as a "cult" and accuse it of using "mind control" or "brainwashing" are protected under the First Amendment from liability for defamation.[216] Therefore, former members should feel encouraged to speak out about their experiences. There are a small handful of lawyers in the United States that have offered to assist cult victims in these types of suits at low rates or pro bono. Attorney Paul Grosswald (who himself is an ex-Scientologist) is such a pioneering individual. He has truly stepped up to the plate regarding a recent libel suit brought by "God the Mother" of the World Mission Society Church of God (WMSCOG) against former member Michele Colon for writing on the examiningthewmscog.com website that the group was a cult and broke up her marriage.

There is little doubt, as well, that if the American economy gets shaky, cult-owned businesses will flourish. Many cult-owned businesses are able to undercut competition because they have free labor. They can also avoid paying taxes because their bookkeeping systems show payment of full salaries, yet those paychecks are in reality turned over to the tax-exempt organization. It therefore appears the business is making a marginal profit in comparison with the monies it is actually taking in.

In other cases, new employees will be expected to attend all company—sponsored "workshops" and "seminars." Even now, business executives are flocking to programs that can teach them how to better influence and control people. Cults have actually taken over the running of some companies in this way.

Despite the progress, there is still much more work that needs to be done. The threat of lawsuits by cults chills many people and makes them refrain from expressing themselves. It has also caused the media—which is entrusted with reporting difficult truths—to hang back or shy away altogether. Heather Kavan of Massey University in New Zealand wrote an important paper, "Falun Gong in the Media: What Can We Believe?" [217] I have personally seen how fear of cult lawsuits can affect the media. In early 1988, the editor of a popular magazine saw me on television and asked me to write a review of the then-new book *L. Ron Hubbard—Messiah or Madman?* by Bent Corydon, a former 22-year Scientologist. As it happened, I had just finished the book the week before, and happily agreed. However, the review was never published. The publisher later told me she was afraid of being sued by the Church of Scientology. She regretted not being able to print it, but said that it just didn't make good business sense for them to do so. Prior to its publication, eleven publishers told Jon Atack that they would like to publish his book, *A Piece of Blue Sky*, but that they were afraid of litigation from the Scientology cult.

With the creation of the Internet and the coming forward of many top former leaders of cults, information is much more available than ever before. There have been many books, websites, documentaries and stories published. It is difficult for cults to do information control when there is an open Internet.

Destructive Cults And Business:

The Case Of Multi-Level Marketing Groups

On October 24, 2013, an *ad hoc* committee of about forty consumer advocates, bloggers, attorneys, economists, and others—including Douglas Brooks, Robert L. Fitzpatrick, and Bruce Craig—filed a formal petition with the Federal Trade Commission (FTC) requesting that it investigate the multi-level marketing (MLM) industry, and that it formulate regulations to protect consumers from unfair and deceptive business opportunities. On March 12, 2014, the FTC announced that it was investigating the supplement company Herbalife. Over the years, other MLM companies, such as Amway, have been sued by the FTC, the Securities and Exchange Commission, and state Attorneys General. Any company that tells people that they can become millionaires by buying and selling their products and by recruiting others to do the same may be found to be a pyramid scheme by government regulators, and should be viewed with suspicion by anyone who is being recruited by them.

According to the consumer group Pyramid Scheme Alert (pyramidschemealert.org), the MLM industry may now be facing its greatest challenge. Fitzpatrick, Brooks and Craig have released a white paper which dissects the entire MLM industry.[218] In the white paper, Brooks and Craig—two of the foremost legal experts in the area of pyramid schemes—carefully researched and evaluated the federal court cases that define and outlaw pyramid selling schemes. (These are found in Section 5 of the Federal Trade Commission Act.) They applied these cases to the widespread practices of MLMs today to see if they are legal. Their white paper is the most in-depth and current evaluation of MLM legality ever produced. The analysis has become especially important now that the FTC has launched an investigation into the legality of Herbalife.

As a crucial part of the white paper, Fitzpatrick conducted a statistical analysis of MLM economic performance and of the MLM business model to determine its financial value to consumers and society, which is included in the white paper. The white paper is a must-read for attorneys, regulators, journalists, financial analysts and any interested consumers who want to determine how the FTC investigation could affect not just Herbalife but all MLMs, their shareholders and their distributors.

While they take an important first step, Brooks, Craig and Fitzpatrick ignore a critical aspect of the MLM phenomenon. What they don't report is how some MLM recruiters deceptively recruit and keep people dependent and obedient by following the BITE model. New recruits are pressured to attend rallies and conferences where they are influenced to buy materials, such as books and CDs; to keep a positive, unquestioning mental attitude; and most importantly not to give in to family and concerned friends who raise questions. They are told to never talk negatively about the company and, if they have questions, to ask only their recruiter, known as their "upline."

The cost of involvement, unless the person is in the top one percent of earners, is very high, in part because their earnings are so low. Bank accounts are drained, marriages are strained and broken. Relationships with family and friends can end up in tatters. People often wind up leaving the group, ashamed, embarrassed, depressed and sometimes even suicidal.

These groups should not be in business. It is up to our government to make sure the public is protected.

Until that time, *caveat emptor*: let the buyer beware.

Cults And Religious Freedom

The major defense that cults use whenever any criticism is directed against them is that it is an attack on their right to freedom of religious belief. This right is one of the most fundamental principles recognized by law and it has been memorialized in every major international covenant concerning human rights. When pilgrims were fleeing persecution in Europe and elsewhere, they sought refuge in the U.S. to practice their beliefs without government suppression. The Founding Fathers were wise to put freedom of religious belief in the very First Amendment of the Constitution. It is that important.

The strong legal protection afforded to freedom of religion refers to religious *beliefs*. It does not necessarily protect *behaviors*. For example, human sacrifice to the gods may be part of a person's belief system, as it was in earlier times, but if carried out in modern-day Boston or anywhere in the U.S., it is homicide. Courts have routinely banned snake-handling rituals, because of the many deaths that have resulted from that practice. It has famously been said, by judges and others, "Your right to swing your arms ends just where the other man's nose begins."[219] The U.S. Constitution emphasizes the individual's right to freedom of speech but it, too, has limits. The law does not allow me to take a bullhorn at 3 o'clock in the morning and wake my neighbors with religious or any other kind of speech. In fact, the law may regulate the content of speech under what is called the "clear and present danger" doctrine. Speech that is designed or likely to cause a riot or serious harm to other people is not given protection. Religion does not enjoy immunity from these legal limitations.

Frederick Clarkson, in his 1997 book, *Eternal Hostility: The Struggle*

Between Theocracy and Democracy, showed how the men who shaped our nation's approach to religious freedom were well aware that even religion's rights had their limitations. As we hear cries of religious persecution by groups that specialize in violating the rights of others, it is worth considering how the framers of the Constitution thought about these things.

Clarkson notes that James Madison, writing about religious freedom in one of the most influential essays of his time, denounced the "invasion" of an individual's "conscience" by other "Sects." Madison's conclusion was simple. The role of government should be "protecting every citizen in the enjoyment of his Religion with the same equal hand which protects his person and his property; by neither invading the equal rights of any Sect, nor suffering any Sect to invade those of another." Clarkson notes that Madison was not the only founding father to hold such a view. He quotes Thomas Jefferson as writing that a church is a "voluntary society" of which a person "should be as free to go out as he was to come in."

In recent years, there has been an interesting twist in the discussion about religious freedom. While there is general acceptance of the concept of freedom *of* religion, there is mounting concern for the adoption of freedom *from* religion. In much the same way that my freedom to move my fist stops at your nose, there is also a belief that your freedom to worship stops at my head, or more specifically, my mind. The Constitution guarantees Americans the right to worship, think and speak as they please. But to what extent should we be protected *from* other people's attempts to make us worship, think and speak as they want us to?

It seemed to Clarkson, as it seemed to Madison—and it seems to me—that if there are laws that protect people from being conned out of their property, there should be laws that protect people from being conned out of their beliefs, thoughts and opinions. The point is not to diminish or disparage a particular religion, but instead to show equal respect for the rights of others to believe or not believe as they choose. The protection of religion should not require the sacrifice of individual liberties and social values.

With regard to cults, the point may be more directly stated as follows: it is not your beliefs that require regulation—it is your practices. It is not *what* you bring people to believe. It is *how* you bring them to believe it.

Clarkson declares that "inducing people to secluded locations and willfully impairing critical faculties of recruits and members for purposes of indoctrination and continuation of membership is a far cry from Jeffersonian—or any other definition of voluntary association."

According to Clarkson, "Respect for religious freedom means respect for the integrity of the conscience of the individual." He continues: "Groups that use deception and coercive forms of persuasion to induce people to abandon their own conscience and adopt the beliefs of another, certainly violate the religious freedom of individuals, even if governments and cult apologists turn a blind eye to such abuses and the slow corrosion of this area of constitutional rights."

It takes significant knowledge as well as maturity on all of our parts to navigate our religiously plural society. The protections we each enjoy under the Constitution are also enjoyed by people with whom we disagree. Unless we are able to embrace this concept in ways that inform our thinking on every aspect of counter-cult work, we risk undermining our own cause.

We can take a hint from none other than George Washington, who famously wrote to the Touro synagogue in Newport, Rhode Island in 1790 about the meaning of religious freedom and citizenship. "For happily," he wrote, "the Government of the United States gives to bigotry no sanction, to persecution no assistance, requires only that they who live under its protection should demean themselves as good citizens, in giving it on all occasions their effectual support."[220] *To bigotry no sanction and to persecution no assistance*. That is a good principle to guide us in our work.

Nothing would grieve me more than to learn that this book has caused anyone to become religiously intolerant. I remember how I felt being spat upon, kicked, punched and verbally abused because I was a Moonie. Such treatment, always uncalled for, only served to reinforce my feelings that I was being persecuted for my faith in God. And it also had the opposite effect to what people desired. By reinforcing cult leaders' claims about persecution, it made me dig my heels in deeper into my cult identity. It made me less willing to have dialogue with people who wanted to insult me and consequently with those who wanted to help.

I was able to reconnect with my Jewish faith after I left the cult, but it was *my* freedom of choice to do so. Not everyone makes the same kind of decision. For some, the cult experience ruined their ability to have faith in any kind of organized religion.

My point is, discrimination toward *anyone* for their beliefs—or their lack of belief—is illegal.

In principle, I am against banning cults. That will only force them underground.[221] Much as I abhor their practices, I also believe they have the right to exist, so I would not support legislation prohibiting them. On the other hand, I would love to see the government supporting an inoculation program against destructive mind control and cults in which citizens young and old were provided with an understanding that kept them free from undue influence.

The Future

Much can be done to stop the spread of cults and undue influence. Here is a brief checklist of practical steps that people can take:

Everyone

- Learn more about cults, mind control and undue influence. Many wonderful documentaries have just been done—including HBO's *Going Clear* (on Scientology), *Truth Be Told* [222] (on Jehovah's Witnesses), and *Prophets Prey* (on Warren Jeffs' Fundamentalist Latter Day Saints [FLDS] cult). Watch them! Visit websites such as openmindsfoundation.org (Open Minds Foundation), icsahome.com (International Cultic Studies Association) and Families Against Cult Teachings (familiesagainstcultteachings.org). Please visit my website, freedomofmind.com. Read widely. You may appreciate my other books *Releasing the Bonds* and especially the more recent *Freedom of Mind: Helping Loved Ones Leave Controlling People, Cults and Beliefs*.
- Stay up-to-date with our social media. Follow us on Twitter(@CultExpert) and Facebook (facebook.com/FOMinc).
- Read the United Nations Universal Declaration of Human Rights and share it widely.[223] Share these resources with others. Discuss one of them in your book or movie group. Tweet about them. Put up relevant articles on your blog. Write reviews on Amazon.com and Goodreads.com
- Protect yourself—research any potential organization carefully before agreeing to attend its events. When in doubt about an organization, ask the questions provided in Chapter

7. Don't give out personal information of any kind to *anyone* until they have demonstrated that they are trustworthy. Do not put personal information up on the Internet. If someone enters your life with "psychic" powers, you should assume they found your personal information online.

- Lobby your politicians—local, state and federal. Set up appointments to tell them your concerns. Ask them to stand up for human rights.
- If you suspect that someone you know is under the sway of a group or individual and may be a victim of undue influence, don't turn a blind eye. Act quickly. Express your concerns to the person's friends and family.
- If you know a former cult member whose involvement kept them from gaining a formal education or employment, please go out of your way to help find them a job or re-enter the educational system. Do whatever you can to help them integrate into society.
- If you are a former member, help de-stigmatize the whole area of cult involvement. Tell people your story. Help them understand that those of us who were in a cult do not have something "wrong" with us. Help the public see that we were unduly influenced.
- If you are in a position to help the efforts to assist current members to reevaluate their life and exit to freedom, please do! If it is prudent not to do so publicly, there is much you can do behind the scenes to help people who are actively setting up websites, social media campaigns, contacting authorities, hiring attorneys and private investigators to find out vital background information.

Government: Federal and State

- Ask the Surgeon General—or some other high-ranking and credible government official—to state definitively that undue influence exists and that destructive cult mind control is bad for public health.
- Educate law enforcement and intelligence agencies, so that they can more effectively combat human trafficking and terrorism.[224]

- Pass lobbying laws and impose stiff penalties for those who subvert the Constitution and abrogate human rights.
- Consider carefully any "religious" organization that applies for tax-exempt status. Take action against those who currently have such status, such as Scientology.[225] Tax-abiding citizens should not be forced to subsidize such organizations!
- Set up a special agency where people can report infractions and/or blow the whistle on questionable groups. Hire experienced investigators to investigate and collect evidence. Questionable groups should be asked to reform their policies and pay damages, or they will lose their IRS exemption. Groups that are found guilty should be stripped of their tax-exempt status and made to sell property and other assets to compensate victims.

Media

- Please accept the responsibility to support investigative journalism aimed at protecting the public good!
- Do not hide the truth from the public because of the threat of lawsuits that might hurt the "bottom line." Perhaps there should be some federal agency set up to fund attorneys who defend investigative journalists who have been sued or threatened. The government might consider funding an independent media resource designed for the public good.
- Fire reporters and editors who are on the payroll—or the ideological hook—of known totalistic cults, especially those which systematically engage in criminal behavior or have stated agendas of taking over the world and violating non-members' civil and human rights.
- Your archives are filled with documentaries and shows that have exposed destructive cult groups. Open them to the public! Many of these shows—like 60 Minutes, Dateline, Nightline, 20/20 and shows like Donahue and others—should be online for the public good, either free or at a reasonable fee.
- Words matter and so do names. Using the term "ISIS" is not just misleading—it is an affront to Muslims. The destructive group is not a "State" nor does it represent the overwhelming majority of Muslims, most of whom do not wish to revert to 7th century shariah law. Switch to the term that many Mus-

lims use: Daesh. As a start, use *ISIS/Daesh* or *Daesh/ISIS*. As people become familiar with Daesh, drop ISIS altogether. Be precise when labeling an Islamist group. Do not call the tiny Wahhabi sect, to which Al Qaeda and Daesh/ISIS members belong, "Sunnis." This is like calling the Branch Davidians at Waco "Christians." Most Muslims want nothing to do with terrorism. It is no part of their faith.

- Write more stories about undue influence, mind control, former members, whistleblowers, and anybody else who stands up to injustice. Hold them up as courageous heroes.
- There is an idea afloat to collect one dollar from every citizen of the United States to fund a truly independent investigative journalism entity whose job will be to truly look out for the public good and who is not beholden to politicians or advertisers or special interest groups. Where facts that are indisputable could be published online for all to see. Such an institution is vital to keep our democracy functioning, as the existing system is declining rapidly. There is a recent report that advertisers are now influencing some editorial boards to do stories that will include "product placement" within their report. Very upsetting and confusing.

Educators

- If you're sufficiently knowledgeable about mind control and undue influence, offer a program, unit, class or curriculum. If not, bring in a qualified speaker.
- Create an atmosphere in your classroom that encourages questioning, open discussion and respect for a wide range of beliefs and opinions.
- Teach students how to think critically and analytically. Rather than teaching to the test, teach young people how to think for themselves. Teach them to look out for others—to be responsible citizens.

Attorneys

- Study and use Alan W. Scheflin's SIM model of Undue Influence.

- Please consider representing former members without fee or on a no win/no fee contingency basis.
- Educate judges.
- Make presentations at American Bar Association meetings.
- Contact Steven Hassan and Freedom of Mind for legal strategy, research, and expert witness work.

Mental Health Professionals

- Attend a class or workshop in the basics of mind control and cult dynamics. Find training or supervision from a qualified expert.
- When beginning to work with new clients, ask questions to help determine if they have been victims of undue influence. If you do not have the appropriate training, refer them to professionals who do or get trained yourself.

Spiritual Leaders

- Talk about undue influence and cults with your congregants and your networks.
- Bring in speakers on the subject of cults, mind control and undue influence.
- Practice, encourage, demonstrate and speak about spiritual discernment.
- If you suspect a congregant is a victim of mind control, act quickly. Speak with their family members and friends. Speak with a cult expert.
- Insist that schools and seminaries offer courses on how to counsel victims of undue influence. Clergy are often first responders in crisis situations, and many are not well prepared to respond effectively.
- Practice tolerance and organize programs that bring together people of different faiths as well as humanists. Less isolation and more ecumenism.
- Sign and participate in Karen Armstrong's CharterforCompassion.org

Philanthropists

Cults have the money. We don't! If people made contributions of money, it could be used to:

- Fund those established scholars and practitioners who do not have the resources to research and write about cults, mind control and undue influence.
- Establish a major think tank where this research can be gathered and analyzed and where resources to help victims and their families can be centralized.
- Develop educational programs exploring the vulnerability and strength of the human mind.
- Support Philip Zimbardo's Heroic Imagination Project (heroicimagination.org)! It is one of the most inspiring teaching tools I know. With new modules on cults, trafficking and terrorism that I hope to help create, it will be one of the best methods for inoculating people against mind control and undue influence all around the world.
- Develop facilities that help victims of human trafficking and other cult mind control situations to understand and recover from undue influence.
- Support the Child Friendly Faith Project (CFFP) (childfriendlyfaith.org) and Against Violent Extremism (AVE) (againstviolentextremism.org)—two non-profits I am involved with.
- I hope to find some angel (or some foundation) who will help me with the resources needed to train, along with others I respect in the field, like Jon Atack and Joe Szimhart, the next generation of people who can help people to understand how to step out of "self-sealing systems" to freedom of mind.
- Tell other philanthropists about this cause. The need is huge but so is the reward.
- Crowdsource! Choose projects that interest you and get others to help you support them.

Final Thoughts

Writing this book is the fulfillment of my long-standing desire to contribute a practical, informative guide to the problems of mind control, undue influence and destructive cults.

It has been a long, often difficult, road but also an incredibly rich and rewarding one. I can't imagine having followed any other path. Despite the many difficulties, I am grateful to have been allowed to do this work, and, given the choice, I would not follow any other career path. I have had a very rewarding life.

Through my writing and my counseling work, I have had the privilege of helping people to free themselves from mind control situations of every kind imaginable, as well as some that are unimaginable. My hope is that this book enables many, many others to understand more clearly how undue influence operates within destructive cult groups and other situations that may be occurring in their own or their loved ones' lives.

It was important, I think, to tell the whole story, and to include my methods for helping people leave cults and other mind control situations, even though I have worried that it might make these destructive groups more sophisticated in their programming. By demystifying my work—and theirs—I hope that countless numbers of people will be motivated and able to start working to help themselves and those they love.

I also hope that this book will help to create a powerful public consumer awareness movement about mind control and destructive cults. I hope that the government will finally acknowledge the problem and take steps to protect the public. In the meantime, I hope readers of this book will join OMF, ICSA and other counter-cult groups and subscribe to their news-letters and journals. Furthermore, I encourage those people who have been through a cult mind control experience to get involved and make a stand. We need your help! Sharing your knowledge and experience—telling your story—can be incredibly powerful. It is freeing and empowering to tell it. And it can be freeing and empowering to hear it. You can save lives.

As destructive cults and mind control come to be better understood, the social stigma attached to former cult membership will begin to dissolve. Former members will come to realize that we were not to blame for our involvement. People will see that we have a lot to give back to society given the chance. Many of my former clients and friends have gone on with their lives and become happy, productive citizens. They are doctors, lawyers, dentists, chiropractors, psychologists, architects, artists, teachers, parents and social activists. Support groups can help a lot, but it takes active participation. Whether you are in need, or have something to give, or both, I urge you to take a positive step. You can make an enormous difference.

In the words of Edmund Burke: "The only thing necessary for the triumph of evil is for good men to do nothing."

Or as Margaret Mead put it: "Never doubt that a small group of thoughtful, committed citizens can change the world; indeed it's the only thing that ever has."

Appendix

Lifton's Eight Criteria of Mind Control

The following excerpt from Robert Jay Lifton's *The Future of Immortality and Other Essays for a Nuclear Age* (New York, Basic Books, 1987) is a concise explanation of Lifton's eight criteria for defining mind control. These are:

1. Milieu control

2. Mystical manipulation (or planned spontaneity)

3. The demand for purity

4. The cult of confession

5. Sacred science

6. Loading of the language

7. Doctrine over person

8. Dispensing of existence

The essay from which this selection is taken is entitled "Cults: Religious Totalism and Civil Liberties." In it, Lifton frames his comments in relation to what he calls *ideological totalism*. This was the environment in which Chinese thought reform was practiced, as Lifton came to know of it from the Korean War and afterward.

Ideological Totalism

The phenomenology I used when writing about ideological totalism in the past still seems useful to me, even though I wrote that book in 1960. The first characteristic is "milieu control," which is essentially the control of communication within an environment. If the control is extremely intense, it becomes an internalized control—an attempt to manage an individual's inner communication. This can never be fully achieved, but it can go rather far. It is what sometimes has been called a "God's-eye view"—a conviction that reality is the group's exclusive possession. Clearly this kind of process creates conflicts in respect to individual autonomy: if sought or realized in such an environment, autonomy becomes a threat to milieu control. Milieu control within cults tends to be maintained and expressed in several ways: group process, isolation from other people, psychological pressure, geographical distance or unavailability of transportation, and sometimes physical pressure. There is often a sequence of events, such as seminars, lectures, and group encounters, which becomes increasingly intense and increasingly isolated, making it extremely difficult—both physically and psychologically—for one to leave.

These cults differ from patterns of totalism in other societies. For instance, the centers that were used for reform in China were more or less in keeping with the ethos of the society as it was evolving at the time; and therefore when one was leaving them or moving in and out of them, one would still find reinforcement from without. Cults, in contrast, tend to become islands of totalism within a larger society that is on the whole antagonistic to these islands. This situation can create a dynamic of its own; and insofar as milieu control is to be maintained, the requirements are magnified by that structural situation. Cult leaders must often deepen their control and manage the environment more systematically, and sometimes with greater intensity, in order to maintain that island of totalism within the antagonistic outer world.

The imposition of intense milieu control is closely connected to the process of change. (This partly explains why there can be a sudden lifting of the cult identity when a young person who has been in a cult for some time is abruptly exposed to outside, alternative influences.) One can almost observe the process in some young people who undergo a dramatic change in their prior identity, whatever it was, to an intense embrace of a cult's belief system and group structure. I consider this a form of doubling: a second self is formed that lives side by side with the prior self, somewhat autonomously from it. Obviously there must be some connecting element to integrate oneself with the other—otherwise, the overall person could not function; but the autonomy of each is impressive. When the milieu control is lifted by removing, by whatever means, the recruit from the totalistic environment, something of the earlier self reasserts itself. This leave-taking may occur voluntarily or through force (or simply, as in one court case, by the cult member moving across to the other side of the table, away from other members). The two selves can exist simultaneously and confusedly for a considerable time, and it may be that the transition periods are the most intense and psychologically painful, as well as the most potentially harmful.

A second general characteristic of totalistic environments is what I call "mystical manipulation" or "planned spontaneity." It is a systematic process that is planned and managed from above (by the leadership) but appears to have arisen spontaneously within the environment. The process need not feel like manipulation, which raises important philosophical questions. Some aspects—such as fasting, chanting, and limited sleep—have a certain tradition and have been practiced by religious groups over the centuries. There is a cult pattern now in which a particular "chosen" human being is seen as a savior or a source of salvation. Mystical manipulation can take on a special quality in these cults because the leaders become mediators for God. The God-centered principles can be put forcibly and claimed exclusively, so that the cult and its beliefs become the only true path to salvation. This can give intensity to the mystical manipulation and justify those involved with promulgating it and, in many cases, those who are its recipients from below.

Insofar as there is a specific individual, a leader, who becomes the center of the mystical manipulation (or the person in whose name it is done), there is a twofold process at work. The leader can sometimes be more real than an abstract god and therefore attractive to cult members. On the other hand, that person can also be a source of disillusionment. If one believes, as has been charged, that Sun Myung Moon (founder of the Unification Church, whose members are consequently referred to frequently as "Moonies") has associations with the Korean Central Intelligence Agency and this information is made available to people in the Unification Church, their relationship to the church can be threatened by disillusionment toward a leader. It is never quite that simple a pattern of cause and effect—but I am suggesting that this style of leadership has both advantages and disadvantages in terms of cult loyalty.

While mystical manipulation leads (in cult members) to what I have called the psychology of the pawn, it can also include a legitimation of deception (of outsiders)—the "heavenly deception" of the Unification Church, although there are analogous patterns in other cult environments. If one has not seen the light, and it is not in the realm of the cult, one is in the realm of evil and therefore can be justifiably deceived for the higher purpose. For instance, when members of certain cults have collected funds, it has sometimes been considered right for them to deny their affiliation when asked. Young people have been at centers of a particular cult for some time without being told that these were indeed run by it. The totalistic ideology can and often does justify such deception.

The next two characteristics of totalism, the "demand for purity" and the "cult of confession," are familiar. The demand for purity can create a Manichean quality in cults, as in some other religious and political groups. Such a demand calls for radical separation of pure and impure, of good and evil, within an environment and within oneself. Absolute purification is a continuing process. It is often institutionalized; and, as a source of stimulation of guilt and shame, it ties in with the confession process. Ideological movements, at whatever level of intensity, take hold of an individual's guilt and shame mechanisms to achieve intense influence over the changes he or she undergoes. This is done within a confession process that has its own structure. Sessions in which one confesses to one's sins are accompanied by patterns of criticism and self-criticism, generally transpiring within small groups and with an active and dynamic thrust toward personal change.

One could say more about the ambiguity and complexity of this process, and Camus has observed that "authors of confessions write especially to avoid confession, to tell nothing of what they know." Camus may have exaggerated, but he is correct in suggesting that confessions contain varying mixtures of revelation and concealment. A young person confessing to various sins of precultic or pre-institutional existence can both believe in those sins and be covering over other ideas and feelings that he or she is either unaware of or reluctant to discuss. In some cases, these sins include a continuing identification with one's prior existence, if such identification has not been successfully dishonored by the confession process. Repetitious confession, then, is often an expression of extreme arrogance in the name of apparent humility. Again Camus: "I practice the profession of penitence, to be able to end up as a judge," and "the more I accuse myself, the more I have a right to judge you." That is a central theme in any continual confessional process, particularly where it is required in an enclosed group process.

The next three patterns I describe in regard to ideological totalism are "the sacred science," the "loading of the language," and the principle of "doctrine over person." The phrases are almost self-explanatory. I would emphasize especially sacred science, for in our age something must be scientific as well as spiritual to have a substantial effect on people. Sacred science can offer considerable security to young people because it greatly simplifies the world. The Unification Church is a good example, but not the only one, of a contemporary need to combine a sacred set of dogmatic principles with a claim to a science embodying the truth about human behavior and human psychology. In the case of the Unification Church, this claim to a comprehensive human science is furthered by inviting prominent scholars (who are paid unusually high honoraria) to large symposia that stress unification of thought; participants express their views freely, but nonetheless contribute to the desired aura of intellectual legitimacy.

The term "loading the language" refers to a literalization of language—and to words or images becoming God. A greatly simplified language may seem cliché-ridden, but can have enormous appeal and psychological power in its very simplification. Because every issue in one's life—and these are often very complicated young lives—can be reduced to a single set of principles that have an inner coherence, one can claim the experience of truth and feel it. Answers are available. Lionel Trilling has called this the "language of nonthought" because there is a cliché and a simple slogan to which the most complex and otherwise difficult questions can be reduced.

The pattern of doctrine over person occurs when there is a conflict between what one feels oneself experiencing and what the doctrine or dogma says one should experience. The internalized message in totalistic environments is that one must find the truth of the dogma and subject one's experiences to that truth. Often the experience of contradiction, or the admission of that experience, can be immediately associated with guilt; or else (in order to hold one to that doctrine) condemned by others in a way that leads quickly to that guilty association. One is made to feel that doubts are reflections of one's own evil. Yet doubts can arise; and when conflicts become intense, people can leave. This is the most frequent difficulty of many of the cults: membership may represent more of a problem than money.

Finally, the eighth, and perhaps the most general and significant of these characteristics, is what I call the "dispensing of existence." This principle is usually metaphorical. But if one has an absolute or totalistic vision of truth, then those who have not seen the light—have not embraced that truth, are in some way in the shadows—are bound up with evil, tainted, and do not have the right to exist. There is a "being versus nothingness" dichotomy at work here. Impediments to legitimate being must be pushed away or destroyed. One placed in the second category of not having the right to exist can experience psychologically a tremendous fear of inner extinction or collapse. However, when one is accepted, there can be great satisfaction of feeling oneself a part of the elite. Under more malignant conditions, the dispensing of existence, the absence of the right to exist, can be literalized; people can be put to death because of their alleged doctrinal shortcomings, as has happened in all too many places, including the Soviet Union and Nazi Germany. In the Peoples Temple mass suicide/murder in Guyana, a single cult leader could preside over the literal dispensing of existence—or more precisely, nonexistence—by means of a suicidal mystique he himself had made a part of the group's ideology. (Subsequent reports based on the results of autopsies reveal that there were probably as many murders as suicides.) The totalistic impulse to draw a sharp line between those who have a right to live and those who do not—though occurring in varying degrees—can become a deadly approach to resolving fundamental human problems. And all such approaches involving totalism or fundamentalism are doubly dangerous in a nuclear age.

I should say that, despite these problems, none of these processes is airtight. One of my purposes in writing about them is to counter the tendency in the culture to deny that such things exist; another purpose is to demystify them, to see them as comprehensible in terms of our understanding of human behavior.

Dr. Lifton wrote *Witness to an Extreme Century: A Memoir* (Free Press, 2011). I was fortunate to sit him down for two videotaped interviews which are on the freedomofmind.com website.

Acknowledgments

To Misia Landau—anthropologist, science writer, artist, photographer, and my loving wife, who is strong enough to deal with all the stresses of life with an activist—thank you for all your incredible support on many levels. You have helped me write, strategize, and cope. You have been my number one. Special thanks for putting your own writing projects and art classes aside to help me ready this book for publication by editing and advising every step of the way. Thank you in ways far more than words could ever communicate.

To our son Matthew, who is the joy of our lives: what a gift you have been. Thank you for being you.

With heartfelt gratitude, I thank my parents, Milton and Estelle Hassan, for all their love and support. Whenever I needed them, they were there for me. They risked everything to rescue me from the Moonies, and I will be forever grateful that they did.

I wish to thank my sisters, Thea and Stephanie, as well as my brothers-inlaw, Doug and Ken, for all they have done throughout the years. Thea and Doug helped save me more than once. They also did much to take care of my folks in their waning years.

To their sons, Michael and Scott, and their families: thank you.

My aunt and uncle, Phyllis and Mort Slotnick, and their children Debbie and Mark, whom I grew up with, have always provided strong support.

To Misia's sisters, Lauren Broch and Ricki Grossman; their husbands, Danny and Dennis; and my niece Sarah and my nephews Ben, Noah, and David: thanks for being my extended family.

I wish to thank Gary Rosenberg, Michael Strom, Nestor Garcia, and Gladys Gonzalez for their willingness to spend five very difficult days in 1976 counseling me back to reality. Without their help, I might have spent many more years in the Moonies. I have recently rediscovered Nestor on LinkedIn; he is now a psychiatrist in Florida. Gladys also lives in Florida and is a social worker. Gary, unfortunately, passed away. Mike, where are you?

Special acknowledgments go to my first wife of seven years, Aureet Bar-Yam, who lived through the creation and the original publication of this book. She died in a tragic accident, trying to rescue our Golden Retriever from an icy pond in 1991. I will always remember her for her love, talent, intelligence, and willingness to help others. Her parents, Drs. Zvi and Miriam Bar-Yam, and their children Sageet and Yaneer and their families, have continued to be sources of much love, inspiration, and help, in ways too numerous to recount.

A special thanks to Eric Rayman and his wife, Sue Horton. As an attorney, Eric gets all the credit for helping me reacquire the rights to this book so it could have a second life. He has also helped over many years with legal support and advice in getting my work to the broader public. Susan, thanks for being a friend.

I would also like to thank a few other friends: Marc and Elyse Hirschorn, Monica Weiss and Dan Hanson, Elissa Weitzman, Shepherd Doeleman, Karen Magarian, Gary Birns, Russell Backer and Susan Mayer, Michael Stone, Ron Cooper, Steve Morse, Chris Kilham, Hoyt Richards, Taryn Southern, Josh Baran, Masoud Banisadr, and others too numerous to mention here. They know who they are.

Some individuals have been my teachers and, at times, my inspiration. I would like to thank Robert Jay Lifton, M.D., Alan W. Scheflin, Daniel Brown, Ph.D., Bill and Lorna Goldberg and Stephen Lankton.

Thank you, Christopher Sonn, for your teaching, healing, and guidance on web issues—and for your friendship.

I wish to also thank Jorge Carballo, Cathy Colman, Karen Kaplan, and Rebecca Johnston for all of their support. You helped me transform my pain into creativity, flexibility, and creative energy.

Special thanks to Dr. Philip Zimbardo, my hero, who taught a course at Stanford University called The Psychology of Mind Control for 15 years. The class uses two chapters of the original *CCMC* as part of its required reading. Zimbardo has been my mentor and one of my biggest supporters. His Heroic Imagination Project deserves to become a standard curriculum used around the world.

Thanks so much to my personal board of advisors: Hank Greenberg, Richard E. Kelly, who put in many hours helping me with this book, Jay Livingston, Ellen Krause Grossman who have helped be my business coach.

Jon Atack has been a friend and a source of enormous assistance. He helped me a great deal with this book. Thank you forensic psychologist teacher of mine for decades, Daniel Brown. Thank you Alan Scheflin for your friendship and advice over the years and for ideas to make the final chapter stronger. Thank you Fred Clarkson for all your assistance and clarity with the religious freedom issue and the Moonies. Cell Whitman gets über kudos for sending me Moonie material.

My work at Freedom of Mind Resource Center has led me to many sources of help over the years. My private investigator, Larry Zilliox, has helped me with many cases and maintains the Moon front-group list. My friend and associate in Los Angeles, Rachel Bernstein. I also wish to thank Greta Ioug, my assistant who worked tirelessly to help me bring the 2015 book project to fruition. Thanks to Jane and Kimmy for helping me so much with FOM. Thanks to the folks at Artists for Humanity for helping me design my logo and book cover. Further thanks to my wife Misia, who oversaw the design development. Thank you Artists for Humanity for helping make the book trailer.

Thanks to Mike White and Ghost River Images for helping to put the book together and publishing help.

Special thanks to Sue Hall for PR assistance, and to Terri VandeVegte, Elise Hirschorn and Jefferson Hawkins who helped me proofread the galleys of this book.

Thanks to James Elliott, P.I., who read the original *Combatting Cult Mind Control* book years ago and asked me to fly to California to help with the issue of human trafficking. He also introduced me to Carissa Phelps, who brought me out to assist with two trainings done by Runaway Girl for over 600 law enforcement personnel. At those trainings in the summer of 2013, I became acquainted with Rachel Thomas, D'lita Miller, and many other wonderful sex trafficking survivor/mentors. That meeting evolved into my first workshop for Lisa Goldblatt Grace and the wonderful people at My Life, My Choice, which now uses my work to help human trafficking survivors. Thanks, too, to ICSA, the International Cultic Studies Association, for which I put together a panel on the theme of trafficking as a commercial cult phenomenon. At the ICSA meeting in Washington, D.C., Christina Meyer, Rachel Thomas, Christine Marie Katas, and I met Christina Arnold, a Children of God survivor and the founder of Prevent Human Trafficking. Rachel Thomas, Carissa Phelps, D'lita Miller and I created Ending the Game, a state of the art curriculum for helping trafficking survivors understand mind control and strategies for reclaiming their power.

Thanks to Janet Heimlich and the Child Friendly Faith Project. I am proud to be on CFFP's board of advisors. The organization works to ensure that children have medical treatment, are protected from pedophiles, and are not corporally punished. This work is crucially important. Deep thanks to all of CFFP's wonderful board members.

A special shout-out to Zainab Al Suwaij, president of the American Islamic Congress, for her pioneering work in supporting women's and children's rights, and in promoting peaceful, collaborative Islam.

Masoud Banisadr gets special praise for his intelligence, humility and courage to educate the world about terrorist groups as mind control cults.

Many other people have helped me substantially along the way, providing me with information, insight, and editorial comments. So I would also like to thank James and Marcia Rudin, Bob, Barbara and their son Paul Grosswald, Dave Spector, Pascal Zivi, Arnold Markowitz, Bernhard Trenkle, Michael Langone, Rod and Linda Dubrow-Marshall, Joe Szimhart, Sue Hall, Marc and Cora Latham, Bo Juel Jensen, Lee Marsh, Mickey Hudson, Lee Elder, Paul Grundy, and John Hoyle and all the people at AAWA, Advocates for Awareness of Watchtower Abuse. Special thanks to Randy Watters of Free Minds, who was the first former elder of the Watchtower who contacted me, educated me, and supported me through the decades.

To friends, supporters, and heroes who are no longer alive—Herb Rosedale, Bob Minton, Denise Brennan, Milton H. Erickson, M.D., Margaret Singer, Ph.D., Louis Jolyon West, M.D., Dr. John Clark, and Carol Turnbull—thank you for all your support and contributions.

Thank you Reb Moshe Waldoks and Rav Claudia Kreiman, and the amazing spiritual community of Temple Beth Zion in Brookline, Massachusetts. You have been my grounding for so many life events, including my bout with Hodgkin's lymphoma in 2006, and the illnesses and passing of both Misia's and my parents.

Some people mentioned here—friends, colleagues, and former clients—were willing to share their stories of cult involvement, thereby enriching this book. I am most grateful for their assistance and encouragement.

In the many years I have been involved in the field of cult awareness, I have met some of the best, most talented, and most caring people in the world. Thank you all.

About the Author

Steven A. Hassan, M.Ed., LMHC, NCC is one of the foremost authorities on cults and mind control. He has been involved in educating the public about mind control, controlling groups and destructive cults since 1976. He holds a master's degree in counseling psychology from Cambridge College, is a Licensed Mental Health Counselor (LMHC) in the Commonwealth of Massachusetts, and a Nationally Certified Counselor (NCC). Steve has written three books that have received extensive praise from former cult members, families of former members, clergy, cult experts, and psychologists. *Combating Cult Mind Control: The #1 Best Selling Guide to Protection, Rescue, and Recovery from Destructive Cults* (1988, 1990, 2015), *Releasing the Bonds: Empowering People to Think for Themselves* (2000), and in July 2012, he published the paperback and ebook, *Freedom of Mind: Helping Loved Ones Leave Controlling People, Cults & Beliefs*, (Second Edition 2013).

Hassan's insightful perspective and expert commentary have made him a definitive source for hundreds of national, international and local media outlets including: USA Today, The Wall Street Journal, New York Times, Washington Post, Los Angeles Times, Newsweek, People Magazine, CNN, 60 Minutes, Dateline, NightLine, The Today Show, and Good Morning America. He has also appeared on the Oprah Winfrey Show, Dr. Phil, Larry King Live, Dr. Drew and countless others.

Mr. Hassan pioneered a new approach to helping victims of mind control called the Strategic Interactive Approach (SIA). Unlike the stressful and media-sensationalized approach known as deprogramming, this non-coercive approach is an effective and legal alternative to help cult members. It teaches family and friends how to strategically influence the individual involved in the group.

Since 1976, Mr. Hassan has helped thousands of people who were victimized by cult-related mind control. He has led many workshops and seminars for mental health professionals, educators, and law enforcement officers, as well as for families of cult members.

Mr. Hassan was deceptively recruited into Sun Myung Moon's Unification Church at the age of 19, while a student at Queens College. He spent the next 27 months recruiting and indoctrinating new members, fundraising, and doing political campaigning. He personally met with Sun Myung Moon on many occasions in leadership sessions. Mr. Hassan ultimately rose to the rank of Assistant Director of the Unification Church at National Headquarters.

Following a serious automobile accident, he was deprogrammed by several former Moonies, at his parents' request. Once he realized the insidious nature of the organization, he authorized police officials to take possession of his personal belongings, which included a massive set of private speeches documenting Moon's secret plan to take over the world.

During the 1977-78 Congressional Subcommittee Investigation into South Korean CIA activities in the United States, he consulted as an expert witness and turned over to the committee these private speeches.

In 1979, following the Jonestown tragedy, Mr. Hassan founded Ex-Moon Inc., a non-profit educational organization composed of over 400 former members of the Moon group. Although now defunct, it was one of the first and largest ex-member organizations in the world.

In 1999, Mr. Hassan founded the Freedom of Mind Resource Center, Inc. (freedomofmind.com), a consulting, counseling, and publishing organization dedicated to upholding human rights, promoting consumer awareness, and exposing abuses of undue influence, mind control, and destructive cults.

He has co-developed a groundbreaking curriculum, Ending The Game, to help victims of sex trafficking to understand psychological coercion used by pimps and traffickers. He does trainings for mental health professionals and law enforcement groups including the Joint Regional Intelligence Organization (JRIC.org). He has blogged for The Huffington Post and is often quoted in newspaper and magazine articles. He has addressed hundreds of religious, professional, and educational groups throughout the world.

Mr. Hassan is a member of The Program in Psychiatry and the Law at Harvard, a forensic think tank. He has established a non-profit Freedom from Undue Influence, a division of Dare Association, where he is researching undue influence under the supervision of Dr. Michael Commons. He is a doctoral student at Fielding Graduate University and is seeking to do quantitative research on the BITE model of mind control as a potential forensic instrument.

In his commitment to fight against destructive cults, Mr. Hassan devotes a major portion of his time and energy to actively consulting with individuals and organizations.

Please see his websites at freedomofmind.com and freedomfromundueinfluence.org or on Facebook for updated information.

Endnotes

Chapter 1

1. Report of the Subcommittee on International Relations, U.S. House of Representatives, Oct 31, 1978 (also known as Fraser Report), 338-348.

2. Fraser Report, 316.

3. Steve Kemperman, *Lord of the Second Advent* (Ventura, California: Regal Books, 1982), 13.

4. Gary Scharff, "Autobiography of a Former Moonie," *Cultic Studies Journal* (Vol. 2, No. 2, 1986), 252.

5. Frederick Clarkson, *Eternal Hostility: The Struggle for Theocracy and Democracy*, Common Courage Press, 1997. 65-66.

6. Moon's original name is Yung Myung Moon, which means "Thy Shining Dragon." Cited in "Honor Thy Father Moon," *Psychology Today* (Jan 1976).

7. "Jury Finds Rev. Moon Guilty of Conspiracy To Evade Income Tax," *The Wall Street Journal* (May 19, 1982). Lyda Phillips (UPI), "Rev. Moon free after year in prison for tax evasion," *The Boston Globe* (July 5, 1985).

8. Frank Greve, in "Seeking Influence, Rev. Moon Spends Big on New Right," *Philadelphia Inquirer* (Dec 20, 1987), states the numbers to be even lower.

9. Sun Myung Moon, "On Witnessing," *Master Speaks*, (January 3, 1972). James and Marcia Rudin, *Prison or Paradise*, (Fortress Press, 1980), 25. Robert Boettcher, *Gifts of Deceit–Sun Myung Moon, Tongsun Park and the Korean Scandal* (Holt, Rinehart and Winston, 1980), 175-176.
   Gary Scharff, "Autobiography of a Former Moonie," *Cultic Studies Journal* (Vol. 2, No. 2, 1986), 252.

10. Michael Warder, "Bribemasters," *Chronicles,* June 1988. Gary Scharff, "Autobiography of a Former Moonie," *Cultic Studies Journal* (Vol. 2, No. 2, 1986). Douglas Lenz, "Twenty-two Months as a Moonie," Lutheran Church of America Partners, February 1982. Barbara Dole, "Former Member's Story," *The Advisor,* Feb/March 1981. Michael Lisman, statement about his membership, 1981.

11. Sun Myung Moon, "Completion of Our Responsibility," *Master Speaks* (October 28, 1974, 8.

12. Sun Myung Moon, "Relationship Between Men and Women," *Master Speaks,* (May 20, 1973).

13. Sun Myung Moon, "Moon Tells How He Regulates Sex," *San Jose Mercury,* (May 27, 1982).

14. Fraser Report, 338-348. Fred Clarkson, "The New Righteous Plan a Third Party," *The Washington Herald,* (February 8, 1988).

15. Laura Knickerbocker, "Mind Control: How The Cults Work," *Harper's Bazaar,* (May 1980).

16. Fraser Report, 311-390.

17. Fraser Report, 354.

18. Fred Clarkson, "Moon's Law: God is Phasing Out Democracy," *Covert Action Information Bulletin,* (Spring 1987).

19. Ibid., 36.

20. See Frederick Clarkson, *Eternal Hostility: The Struggle Between Theocracy and Democracy*, Common Courage Press, 1997; Jon Lee Anderson and Scott Anderson, *Inside the League: The Shocking Expose of how Terrorists, Nazis, and Latin American Death Squads Have Infiltrated the World Anti-Communist League*, Dodd Mead, 1986; David E. Kaplan, Alec Dubro, *Yakuza: Japan's Criminal Underworld,* (University of California Press, 1986).

21. Douglas Lenz, "Twenty-two Months as a Moonie," (Lutheran Church of America Partners, February 1982), 13-15. Josh Freed, *Moonwebs,* (Dorset Publishing, Inc., 1980), 191.

22. Fraser Report, 326, 366.

23. (UPI) "Ousted Editor Says Church Controls *Washington Times*," *The Boston Globe*, (July 18, 1984).

24. Fred Clarkson, "Behind the Times: Who Pulls the Strings at Washington's #2 Daily," *Extra*!, (Aug/Sept 1987).

25. James Ridgeway, "Bush Sr. To Celebrate Rev. Sun Myung Moon—Again: Ex-president's keynote speech at Washington Times bash this month is latest link between Bush and Unification Church founder," Mother Jones magazine, (April 29, 2007). http://www.motherjones.com/politics/2007/04/bush-sr-celebrate-rev-sun-myung-moon-again

26. Sun Myung Moon, "The Significance of the Training Session," *Master Speaks* (May 17, 1973).

27. Frank Greve, *The Philadelphia Inquirer, Knight-Ridder News Service* (December 20, 1987).
"Moon/Mormon Conference for Legislators," *City Paper* (Washington DC July 25-31, 1986).

28. Andrew Ferguson, "Can Buy Me Love: The Mooning of Conservative Washington," *The American Spectator*, (September 1987).

29. Frank Greve, *The Philadelphia Inquirer*, (syndicated by *Knight-Ridder News Service*, December 20, 1987).

30. James Ridgeway, "Bush Sr. To Celebrate Rev. Sun Myung Moon—Again: Ex-president's keynote speech at *Washington Times* bash this month is latest link between Bush and Unification Church founder," *Mother Jones* magazine, April 29, 2007. http://www.motherjones.com/politics/2007/04/bush-sr-celebrate-rev-sun-myung-moon-again

Chapter 2

31. Douglas Lenz, "Twenty-two Months As a Moonie," Lutheran Church of America Partners (Feb 1982), 13-15. Josh Freed, *Moonwebs* (Toronto: Dorset Publishing, Inc., 1980), 191.

32. "Jacob's Curse and Our Life in Faith," (May 27,1973), 3. Robert Boettcher, *Gifts of Deceit–Sun Myung Moon, Tongsun Park and the Korean Scandal* (New York: Holt, Rinehart and Winston, 1980), 343-344.

33. Kamiyama was co-convicted with Moon for conspiracy to defraud the U.S. government of tax revenues. U.S. vs. Sun Myung Moon and Takeru Kamiyama: Kamiyama accused of aiding/abetting filing of false returns, obstruction of justice, and perjury.

34. Michael Warder, "Bribemasters," *Chronicles* (June 1988). Fraser Report, 313.

35. "The Seven Day Fast," *Master Speaks* (Oct 20, 1974), 19.

36. "Children's Day," *Master Speaks* (Aug 4, 1974), 12.

37. Moon and Hak Ja Han, his third wife, were regarded by members to be the perfect Adam and Eve. Moon's theology says that the original Eve was tempted into sexual intercourse by Satan before she had grown to perfection, and then she seduced Adam. Therefore, all mankind were the offspring of tainted blood. The kingdom of heaven will be established when God sends a perfect man again in order to establish the "pure" lineage. Jesus was killed before he had a chance to marry and have perfect children. Therefore, Moon (being 'perfect' himself) can spiritually "adopt" members into his "true family" and assign them marriage partners in order to redo their spiritual lineage. Moon married more than 2,000 such couples in Madison Square Garden in 1984.

38. Vernon Scott, "Controversy Shrouds Obscure Movie, 'Inchon,' " *Santa Barbara News- Press* (Oct 10, 1982). "Times Kill Review," *Washington Post* (Sept 18, 1982), C1. "Stars Tricked into Making Cult Movie," *Globe* (June 8, 1982).

39. Fred Clarkson. "The Messiah Who Bilked IRS," *The Sacramento Bee* (Sept 15, 1985). Herbert Rosedale, "Moon's Conviction Justified by the Record," The Cult Observer (Nov 1984).

40. Douglas Lenz, "Twenty-two Months as a Moonie," Lutheran Church of America Partners (Feb 1982).,12. Steve Kemperman, *Lord of the Second Advent* (Ventura, California: Regal Books, 1982), 14.

41. Christopher Edwards, Crazy for God (Englewood Cliffs, New Jersey: Prentice-Hall, Inc., 1979), 144-145.

42. Douglas Lenz, "Twenty-two Months As a Moonie," Lutheran Church of America Partners (Feb 1982), 12. Jerry Carroll and Bernard Bauer, "Suicide Training in the Moon Cult," *New West* (Jan 29, 1979), 62.

43. "God's Plan for America," Sun Myung Moon (Dec 18, 1975).

44. Marcia R. Rudin, "The Cult Phenomenon: Fad or Fact?" *New York University Review of Law and Social Change* (Vol. IX, No. I), 31.

45. Fraser Report, 311-392.

46. To learn more about Aureet's life and her important contributions, please see http://bar-yam.org/aureet/ Aureet Bar-Yam Hassan's (index all) Theory of Interpersonal Development, which deserves much wider attention, please see http://bar-yam.org/aureet/Psychologist/Theory/index.html

Chapter 3

47. Kidnappedforchrist.com is the web site of a powerful documentary made about such a boot camp in the Dominican Republic.

48. Glenn Collins, "The Psychology of the Cult Experience," *The New York Times* (March 15, 1982).

49. Fraser Report, 326, 351-53, 368. "The Outline of Rev. Moon's Hand in Central America: The Unification Church, the World Anti-Communist League, CAUSA and John Singlaub," (Ford Greene, 1987), 13-17.
"Moonie Interests Said to Choose Montevideo as Centre," *Latin America Regional Reports* (Oct 14, 1983).
Tim Cain, "Moonie Recruiting Groups Have Ties to Contras in Central America," *Sandpaper* (Oct 16, 1987).
Jean Francois Boyer and Alejandro Alem, "Moon in Latin America: Building Bases of a World Organization," *Manchester Guardian Weekly* (March 3, 1985).

50. Fraser Report, 345.
"The Way International," Anti-Defamation League Report (Spring 1982).
"Government Probe of The Way Disclosed Political Activism, 'Pattern' of Harassment of Witnesses," *CAN News* (July-July 1987), from "Religious Group's Political Activities Subject of Probe," *Bangor Daily News* (Nov 21, 1986).

51. Louis Trager, "Evidence Points Toward North Tie to Rev. Moon," *San Francisco Examiner* (July 20, 1987).

52. "Moonie Interests on the Rise: The Empire Consolidates" *Latin America Regional Reports* (April 1984).

53. "Significance of the Training Session," *Master Speaks* (May 17, 1973).

54. John Marks, *The Search for the Manchurian Candidate* (New York: Times Books, 1979), 72, 133, 182-192.

55. Patricia C. Hearst with Alvin Moscow, *Patty Hearst: Her Own Story* (New York: Avon Books, 1982).

56. Ted Patrick with Tom Dulack, *Let Our Children Go* (New York: E. P. Dutton and Company, Inc., 1976).

57. Allan Maraynes, producer, "Scientology," *60 Minutes* (Volume XII, Number 51), aired Aug 31, 1980.
Eugene H. Methvin, "Scientology: Anatomy of a Frightening Cult," *Reader's Digest* (May 1980), and "Scientology: The Sickness Spreads," *Reader's Digest* (Sept 1981).
Bent Corydon and L. Ron Hubbard, Jr., *L. Ron Hubbard: Messiah or Madman?*
(Secaucus, New Jersey: Lyle Stuart, 1987).
Russell Miller, *Bare Faced Messiah: The True Story of L. Ron Hubbard* (Great Britain: Penguin Books Ltd., 1987).

58. Patricia Ward Biedernan, "$1.5 Million Award to Former C.U.T. Member," *Los Angeles Times* (April 3, 1986).
Karen Kenney, "Church Universal and Triumphant: Of Church business, Public and Private," *The Valley News* (Feb 1, 1980).
"Fear of Church Grips Montana Town," *Daily News* (Feb 4, 1982).

Mark Reiter, "One Man's Story: Why Would a Man in His 50s Join a Cult? Listen to Gregory Mull's Tale," *50 Plus* (Oct 1981).
Kerry Webster, "Her Will Be Done: Elizabeth Claire Prophet and the Church Universal and Triumphant," *Herald Examiner* (Jan 27, 1985) (six-part series).
Jim Robbins, "A Question of Good Neighbors," *Boston Globe Magazine* (Aug 9, 1987).

59. Wendy B. Ford, "Way Seduction 'Invisible,'" *The Journal Herald* (Jan 13, 1981).
Jan Pogue, "The Mysterious Ways of the Way: Victor Paul Wierwille has quietly built a huge religious following. He believes that if people would just listen to what God told him 40 years ago, he could 'remake the world.' Some who know him well are afraid he's right." *Today, The Philadelphia Inquirer* (Aug 1, 1981).
Anne Cocroft Cole, "Janney Lost Career Dreams as Follower of 'The Way,'" *Loudoun Times-Mirror* (Dec 10, 1981), and "Janney's Life in the Way: Sacrifice and Obedience," (Dec 17, 1981), and "Now Out of 'The Way' Janney Warns Others," (Dec 24, 1981).

60. Win McCormack, "Bhagwan's Bottom Line: Rajneesh's Far-flung Empire is More Material than Spiritual," *Oregon Magazine Collector's Edition/The Rajneesh Files* (1981-86), 91.

61. "The LaRouche Network–A Political Cult," *ADL/Civil Rights Report* (Spring 1982, Vol. 27, No. 2).
Howard Blum and Paul Montgomery, "U.S. Labor Party: Cult Surrounded by Controversy," *The New York Times* (Oct 7, 1979), and "One Man Leads U.S. Labor Party on its Erratic Path," (Oct 8, 1979).
John Mintz, "Lyndon LaRouche: From Marxist Left to Well-Connected Right," *The Washington Post National Weekly Edition* (Feb 25, 1985).

62. "MOVE Leader Wanted 'Absolute Control,' *The Boston Globe* (May 15, 1985 and May 16, 1985).
"New Life for 'Move' Child in Wake of Philadelphia Disaster," *The Cult Observer* (Jan/Feb 1986), from the *Wall Street Journal* (Nov 1, 1985).

63. Chip Berlet, "White, Right, and Looking for a Fight: Has Chicago Been Targeted by a New Alliance of White Supremacists?" *Reader* (June 27, 1986, Vol. 15, No. 39). "Idaho Bombings Part of Race War

Planned by Neo-Nazi Splinter Group," *CAN News* (Oct 1986), from *Couer d'Alene Press*, Idaho.
Press Oct 8, 1986, and the *Spokane Spokesman-Review* Oct 9, 1986.
"Racist Groups Meet," *The New York Times* (July 14, 1986).
"Two Neo-Nazis Convicted in Slaying," *The Cult Observer* (Jan/Feb 1988) from "Two Convicted in Radio Host's Death," *The Fort Wayne News-Sentinel* (Nov 18, 1987).

64. Peter Siegel, Nancy Strohl, Laura Ingram, David Roche, and Jean Taylor, "Leninism as Cult: The Democratic Workers Party," *Socialist Review*. 58-85.

65. Marcia R. Rudin, "The Cult Phenomenon: Fad or Fact?" *New York University Review of Law and Social Change* (Vol. IX, No. 1), 18-19.

66. Scientology, Transcendental Meditation and the Moonies all have fortunes in excess of a billion dollars.

67. For instance, Hill and Knowlton were employed by Scientology to improve its image. The cult later employed Jack Trout of Reiss and Trout.

68. For more information on treatment of phobias, contact the Anxiety Disorders Association of America, 600 Executive Blvd., Suite 200, Rockville, MD 20852-3801, (301) 231-9350.

69. James and Marcia Rudin, *Prison or Paradise* (Philadelphia: Fortress Press, 1980), 103.
Lorraine Ahearn, "Mind Control Called the Way of The Way," *The Capital* (Annapolis, April 2, 1986), 12.

70. Diane Salvatore, "The New Victims of Cults," *Ladies Home Journal* (Aug 1987)
Andree Brooks, "Cults and the Aged: A New Family Issue," *The New York Times* (April 26, 1986).

71. Webpage of the largest Christian Apologetic Site on Followers of Christ.
http://www.apologeticsindex.org/2459-followers-of-christ-church

72. "Public Hearing on the Treatment of Children by Cults," The Assembly of the State of New York (Aug 9-10, 1979).
Shirley Landa, "Hidden Terror: Child Abuse in 'Religious Sects and Cults,'" *Justice for Children* (Fall 1985, Vol. I, No. 5).

73. Routledge 2013.

Chapter 4

74. Robert Jay Lifton, *Thought Reform and the Psychology of Totalism* (New York: W.W. Norton & Company, 1961).

75. I, Louis Jolyon West, Jon Atack and others believe that the personality is formed of a continuum of many identities, so the authentic *personality* is overtaken by the cult *identity. These "parts" are also referred to by therapists who do "ego-state" therapy.*

76. "Jury Indicts 9 Linked to Synanon," *The Cult Observer* (Oct 1985), from *The New York Times* (Oct 2, 1985).
"Point Reyes Light Wins $100,000 settlement from Synanon," *The Cult Observer* (March/April 1987).
Steve Allen, *Beloved Son* (Indianapolis, New York: The Bobbs-Merrill Company, Inc., 1982), 187-194.
Myrna Oliver, "Two Synanon Members Get Year in Jail," *Los Angeles Times* (November 22, 1980).

77. Moon made this speech to an audience of several hundred people during the summer of 1975 in upstate New York.

78. See Adorno, Frenkel-Brunswik, Levinson, Sanford, *The Authoritarian Personality* (New York: Harper & Brothers, 1950).

79. Solomon Asch, "Effects of Group Pressure Upon the Modification and Distortion of Judgment," in *Groups, Leadership, and Men*, ed. M.H. Guetzkow, (Pittsburgh: Carnegie, 1951).
Solomon Asch, "Studies of Independence and Conformity: A Minority of One Against a Unanimous Majority," *Psychological Monographs*, 70 (1956).

80. Stanley Milgram, Obedience to Authority (New York: Harper & Row, 1974), xii.

81. He used this chapter and the preceding one of this book in the course materials. I conducted a videotaped interview with Dr. Zimbardo on mind control which is on the freedomofmind.com site.

82. The original edition of *Combatting Cult Mind Control* used the four components, but it was Rev. Buddy Martin who suggested that I change the order and use the acronym BITE instead. Many thanks!

83. Leon Festinger, Henry W. Riecken, and Stanley Schachter, *When Prophecy Falls* (Harper & Row, 1964).

84. Ibid.

85. Fred Clarkson, "Moon's Law: 'God is Phasing Out Democracy,'" *Covert Action Information Bulletin No. 27* (Spring 1987), 38.

86. The appendix to George Orwell's *Nineteen Eighty-Four* gives an excellent description of the use of language to restrict thought.

87. Michael Mahoney and Carl Thoreson, *Self-Control: Power to the Person.* (Monterey, California: Brooks/Cole, 1974).

88. Kurt Lewin, "Frontiers in Group Dynamics: Concept, Method, and Reality in Social Science," *Human Relations*, 1947.

89. Edgar H. Schein, *Coercive Persuasion*, 1961 (The Massachusetts Institute of Technology, W.W. Norton, 1971).

90. One of the best books I've read on linguistic double binds is Milton Erickson's *Hypnotic Realities* (New York: Irvington Publishers, 1976).

Chapter 5

91. Eric Hoffer, *The True Believer* (New York: Harper & Row, 1951), 77.

92. Yeakley, Flavil. *The Discipling Dilemma,* (1988), Gospel Advocate Co, Nashville TN.

93. For instance, Ron Hubbard: "A handful of us are working our guts out to beat Deadline Earth. On us alone depends whether your kid will ever see sixteen or your people will ever make it at all. A few of us see the world has got a chance if we don't dawdle along the way.

Our chance is a thin chance at best. We are working as hard as we can in Scientology. And, the only slim chance this planet has rests on a few slim shoulders, overworked, underpaid and fought —the Scientologist. Later on, if we make it, what will be your answer to this question? Did you help? ... The world has an optimistic five years left, a pessimistic two. After that, Bang or just a whimper. On us alone depends whether your kids will ever see sixteen or your people will ever make it at all. Our chance is a thin chance at best. We are working as hard as we can in Scientology." *Auditor Magazine*, (1967), 9.

94. Michael Warder, "Bribemasters," *Chronicles* (June 1988), 31.

95. "Central Figure," *Master Speaks* (Feb 13. 1974), 6.
"Untitled," *Master Speaks* (Jan 3. 1972).
"Parents' Day," *Master Speaks* (March 24. 1974).

Chapter 6

96. One amazing thing is that with the Internet and some dedication to searching for them, their information and their efforts can be found. The Wayback Machine is a valued resource of past Internet sites, especially of former members who were eventually silenced by cult harassment.

97. *Enquiry into the Practice and Effects of Scientology*, Sir John G. Foster, KBE, QC, MP; Her Majesty's Stationery Office, by order of the House of Commons, 21 December 1971.

98. http://web.randi.org/the-million-dollar-challenge.html

99. Hubbard Communications Office Policy Letter, 18 October 1967, issue IV, *Penalties for Lower Conditions.*

100. Video of Trafficking Panel (2014) at ICSA is at https://freedomofmind.com//HumanTrafficking/HumanTrafficking.php

101. Why *Ending the Game*? Pimps call what they do—enslaving people to sell sex—"The Game." So we chose our course name to let people know they can only win by leaving the game. The web site for the program is endingthegame.com.

102. The Video of the Press Conference In London about Cults and Terrorism is on https://freedomofmind.com//Info/terrorism.php

103. See Dennis King's book *Lyndon LaRouche and the New American Fascism* (1989) for LaRouche's connections to neo-Nazis and the KKK.
Regarding "physical force may be justified" I can safely refer to his 1973-74 "Operation Mop-Up" use of violence against CPUSA: http://www.publiceye.org/larouche/Mop-Up.html
On Kenneth Kronberg's suicide: http://www.kennethkronberg.com/kk/
On Jeremiah Duggan's death: http://justiceforjeremiah.yolasite.com/
On the Youth movement massive departure in 2012, here is their (long) document http://laroucheplanet.info/pmwiki/pmwiki.php?n=Library.LYMwhyweleft "Why we left"
BITE model applied to LaRouche http://laroucheplanet.info/pmwiki/pmwiki.php?n=Cult.Bite
Yves's role in the aid convoy to Sarajevo : http://artwithconscience.blogspot.co.uk/2014/02/my-story-of-1992-93-alsace-sarajevo-aid.html

104. http://messer-art-design.com/

105. Scientology is also notorious for enforcing abortions on live-in members.

106. A thorough article was published about the cult. See *East Side Alien* by Marie Brenner, *Vanity Fair*, (March 1990, Volume 53, Number 3).

107. White Anglo-Saxon Protestants. WASP is sometimes considered to be a detrimental term but it was one Hoyt used to describe the cult's recruitment focus.

108. Doug Johnson, "Former Truth Station Member Tells of Secret Practices," *Victor Valley Daily Press* (March 5, 1981), A1.
"TV Producer Charges Kin Abused by Religious Cult," *Oxnard Press Courier* (March 5, 1981), 2.

109. Michael Kelly, "A Couple Still Hearing the Chant," *Cult Awareness Network News* (Jan-Feb 1985), 3.

110. *Take Back Your Life*, (Bay Tree Publishing1994, 2006) by Lalich and Tobias is a very helpful text on recovery.

111. Miriam Williams, *Heaven's Harlots: My Fifteen Years in a Sex Cult*, Eagle Books, 1998 and *Something Somebody Stole* by Ray Connolly (2011) and ex-member resource page is at http://www.xfamily.org/index.php/Main_Page

112. Cult or Benign Cure-all? Life in Transcendental Meditation's Hidden Society - http://www.commonwealthclub.org/events/2014-10-20/cult-or-benign-cure-all-life-transcendental-meditation%E2%80%99s-hidden-society
http://www.papermag.com/2015/03/fairfield_iowa_maharishi_transcendental_meditation.php

113. 2010 ICSA Conference handbook is online at https://drive.google.com/file/d/0B4dmoPK1tYNjanFOQkZ6azg5UjA/edit?usp=sharing

114. Yagyas http://www.maharishiyagya.org/ Maharishi Ayurvedic Products (MAPI) latest site(2015): http://www.mapi.com Scientific basis under "Our Story" section: Maharishi was unyielding when it came to the authenticity of these ancient formulations and their purity. In the early days of Maharishi Ayurveda, Maharishi, surrounded by the greatest Ayurvedic experts in India, rejected formulas due to minor deviations from the ancient original texts or due to lack of purity in the formula. This is the foundation of vpk® by Maharishi Ayurveda: Authentic, Pure, Effective and Safe. - See more at: http://www.mapi.com/our-story/our-story.html#sthash.iCxtzXMk.dpuf
Wikipedia references show lack of science on MAPI products. Wikipedia has a senior editor assigned to TM-related pages to keep the pro-cult trolls in check:
http://en.wikipedia.org/wiki/Maharishi_Vedic_Approach_to_Health

115. Source of Swiss palaces and private enclave in The Netherlands — my life. But here are the links:
http://www.meru.ch/index.php?page=kurse-in-seelisberg
http://www.ayurveda-seelisberg.ch/index.php?page=home&hl=fr_FR
http://www.globalcountry.org/wp/full-width/links/
http://en.wikipedia.org/wiki/Maharishi_Peace_Palace
http://www.peacepalaces.com/home.htm

116. David Lynch Foundation: http://www.davidlynchfoundation.org

117. Center for Wellness and Achievement in Education: http://cwae.org/

118. links TM-Sidhi program :
https://www.mum.edu/about-mum/consciousness-based-education/tm-sidhi-program/
https://www.mum.edu/core-skill-departments/development-of-consciousness/learning-the-tm-sidhi-program/
http://www.amazingabilities.com/amaze9a.html
Expose links TM-Sidhi Program :
http://minet.org/www.trancenet.net/secrets/sutras/
http://www.suggestibility.org/sidhi.shtml

119. MACLEANS January 5th, 2015 *Against Their Will: Inside Canada's Forced Marriages* by Rachel Browne http://www.macleans.ca/news/canada/against-their-will/
(Courtois, *Healing the Incest Wound.* 1988)

120. Walter Martin's book, *The Kingdom of the Cults*, Bethany House (1965), has a chapter on Jehovah's Witnesses and the Watch Tower Society and critiques them theologically. It was important for me to understand that the Bible JWs use deviates substantially from those commonly endorsed by scholars. For example, the New Testament in their Bible has "Jehovah" inserted where the Greek text would have said "Lord." As Bible scholar Bart Ehrman notes: "The divine name 'Jehovah' doesn't belong in either Testament, old or new, in the opinion of most critical scholars, outside the ranks of the Jehovah's Witnesses. That's because Jehovah was not the divine name." http://ehrmanblog.org/

121. The Hebrew Bible does direct people to observe the dietary law of *Kashrut* and drain the blood of animals they cook and eat. See http://www.myjewishlearning.com/practices/Ritual/Kashrut_Dietary_Laws.shtml
However, I have asked numerous Christian and Jewish scholars about the Watch Tower policy. Not one thinks there is a shred of legitimacy to the Governing Body's policies on blood transfusion. In fact, the Jewish religion is always in favor of saving life! Please see http://ajwrb.org/ for detailed information about the changing policies on blood by the JW Governing Body over the years.

http://ajwrb.org/children/my-child-is-dead is a heartbreaking story. For a summary of the blood issue, explaining the Watch Tower history of the doctrine, and why it is not based on sound Scriptural reasoning, please visit http://www.jwfacts.com/Watch Tower/blood-transfusions.php.

122. The talk I heard at that conference given by Ken Clark: https://www.youtube.com/watch?v=gKt7ozdKeBk&list=PLA92A1F6CFEA252A2. Richard Packham's 2013 talk, "Truth Will Prevail: All About Proof, Evidence, Fallacies and Lies" is worth your time https://www.youtube.com/watch?v=SXl1FjwSMBQ

123. https://en.wikipedia.org/wiki/Fundamentalist_Church_of_Jesus_Christ_of_Latter-Day_Saints

124. (Grand Central Publishing, 2014). The Witness Wore Red: The 19th Wife Who Brought Polygamas Cult Leaders to Justice.

125. BBC's *Emperor of the Universe* is online at http://www.democraticunderground.com/discuss/duboard.php?az=view_all&address=364x2967341

126. Kate Bornstein, *A Queer and Pleasant Danger: The true story of a nice Jewish boy who joins the Church of Scientology, and leaves twelve years later to become the lovely lady she is today*, (Beacon Press, 2012).

127. Larry Brennan, *The Miscavige Legal Statements: A Study in Perjury, Lies and Misdirection.* Self-published. Posted on WhyWeProtest.net Activism Board. Please watch my video interview with Denise when she came out and her final interview before passing away: https://freedomofmind.com//Media/video.php?id=53.

Chapter 7

128. Andrea Estes, "Cult Attracts Trouble in Travels: The Ex-Carnival Barker Turned Church Apostate," *The Boston Herald* (June 23, 1984).
Mark Starr, "The Kingdom at Island Pond," *Newsweek* (Nov 29, 1982).
Joan Guberman, "Another Jonestown: The Kingdom at Island Pond," *The Advisor* (Feb/March 1983).

129. Mark Brewer, "We're Gonna Tear You Down and Put You Back Together," *Psychology Today* (Aug 1975), 82.
Richard Behar and Ralph Kina, Jr., "The Winds of Werner: The IRS, The Order of Malta and a Swiss Banker Have a Problem: A One—time Used Car Salesman from Philadelphia," *Forbes* (Nov 18, 1985).

130. Dianne Dumanoski, "The Gospel According to Stevens: Evangelist Carl Stevens Started Out as a Bakery Driver. Now he's a shepherd in the Berkshires, with a flock of born-again Christians—and newly acquired fields," *Boston Phoenix* (May 24, 1977).

131. Robert Lindsey, "L. Ron Hubbard Dies of Stroke; Founder of Church of Scientology," *The New York Times* (Jan. 29, 1986).

132. Phil Garber, "The Way: Religious Sect a Center of Controversy," *Daily Record* (March 30, 1986).
Wendy B. Ford, "Way Seduction 'Invisible,'" *The Journal Herald* (Jan 13, 1981).

133. Erhard, Da Free John, Paul Twitchell and Harvey Jackins were all Scientologists, as was the leader of the UFO cult studied by Leon Festinger. Over 200 cults have been started by ex-members of Scientology, according to Jon Atack's research.

134. See Ira Chaleff, *The Courageous Follower,* to understand how followers can better limit a leader's narcissism.

135. Robert Boettcher, *Gifts of Deceit–Sun Myung Moon, Tongsun Park and the Korean Scandal* (New York: Holt, Rinehart and Winston, 1980), 35.
Moonwebs, 50.

136. Lyda Phillips (UPI), "Rev. Moon Free After Year in Prison for Tax Evasion," *The Boston Globe* (July 5 , 1985).

137. Bent Corydon and L. Ron Hubbard, Jr., L. Ron Hubbard: Messiah or Mad-Man? (Secaucus, New Jersey: Lyle Stuart, 1987).
Russell Miller, Bare Faced Messiah: The True Story of L. Ron Hubbard (Great Britain: Penguin Books, 1987).
Richard Behar, "The Prophet and Profits of Scientology," *Forbes 400* (Oct 27, 1986), 314-315.

"Penthouse Interview: L. Ron Hubbard, Jr." *Penthouse* (June 1983), 111, 174-175.

138. Fraser Report, 387.

139. Hubbard instructed his recruiters, 'You tell him that he is going to sign up right now and he is going to take it right now ... One does not describe something, one commands something. You will find that a lot of people are in a more or less hypnotic daze ... and they respond to direct commands in literature and ads. Hard Sell means insistence that people buy.' (HCO PL 26 September 1979, Issue III).

140. All Scientologists are considered 'field staff members' and 'professional FSMs' are given specific recruitment targets.

141. Ibid., 313, 316, 333-334.

142. Eugene H. Methvin, "Scientology: The Sickness Spreads," *Readers Digest* (Sept 1981), 5.
"Penthouse Interview: L. Ron Hubbard, Jr." *Penthouse* (June 1983), 113.

143. "This technique is labeled 'buy now' in Scientology."

144. Raw meat: 'One who has never had Scientology processing.' Hubbard, HCOB, *Starting of Preclears (*16 January 1968).

145. Rachel Martin, *Escape: The True Story of a Young Woman Caught In the Clutches of a Religious Cult* (Denver, Colorado: Accent Books, 1979)

146. Deborah Berg Davis, *The Children of God: The Inside Story* (Grand Rapids, Missouri: The Zondervan Publishing House, 1984).
Herbert J. Wallerstein, Final Report on the Activities of the Children of God to Honorable Louis J. Lefkowitz, Attorney General of the State of New York. Charity Frauds Bureau (Sept 30, 1974).
Una McManus, *Not for a Million Dollars* (Impact Books, 1980).

147. Steve Allen, *Beloved Son: A Story of the Jesus Cults* (New York: Bobbs-Merrill Company, Inc., 1982), 192-193.

148. Lindsey Gruson, "Two Hare Krishna Aides Accused of Child Molesting," *The New York Times* (Feb 18, 1987).
"Murders, Drug and Abuse Charges Shake Krishnas," *Akron Beacon Journal* (June 22, 1986).
Eric Harrison, "Crimes Among the Krishnas: The world wouldn't listen to Stephen Bryant's charges against his religion's leaders, until he was murdered," *The Philadelphia Inquirer Magazine* (April 15, 1987).
John Hubner and Lindsay Gruson, "Dial Om for Murder: The Hare Krishna church, once brimming with youthful idealism, has became a haven for drug traffickers, suspected child molesters—and killers," *The Rolling Stone* (April 9, 1987), 53.
"Krishna Killer Ordered Extradited," *CAN News* (Sept-Oct 1987) from "Dreschner Ordered Extradited," *The Intelligencer* (Aug 14, 1987).
"Hare Krishna Leader Reported to be Linked to Murder of His Critic," *The New York Times* (June 17, 1987), 9.

149. "Scientology's 'Campaign of Harassment," *The Cult Observer* (Nov/Dec 1987) from "Scientologists In Dirty Campaign to Stop Book," *The Sunday Times* (London, Oct 18, 1987).
"Scientologists Try to Block Hubbard Biography," *The Cult Observer* (July/Aug 1987), from "New Hassle over Scientology Book," *The New York Post* (Aug 4, 1987) and "Lawsuits Surround Book on L. Ron Hubbard," *Publishers Weekly* (Aug 1987).

150. Robert Lindsey, "Two Defectors from People's Temple Slain in California," *The New York Times* (Feb 28, 1980), A 16.

151. Peter Siegel, Nancy Strohl, Laura Ingram, David Roche and Jean Taylor, "Leninism as Cult: The Democratic Workers Party," *Socialist Review*, 58-85.

152. "Center for Feeling Therapy Founder Fights to Keep License," The Cult Observer (Jan/Feb 1987) from the *Los Angeles Times* (Sept 21, 1986).
"Center for Feeling Therapy Psychologists Lose Licenses," *The Cult Observer* (Nov/Dec 1987) from "Psychologists In Feeling Therapy Lose Licenses," *The Los Angeles Times* (Sept 29, 1987).

153. Darrell Sifford, "Psychiatrist Probes the Effects of Transcendental Meditation," *Philadelphia Inquirer* (June 19, 1988).

The Various Implications Arising from the Practice of Transcendental Meditation (Bensheim, Germany: Institute for Youth and Society), 80.

154. Marc Fisher, "I Cried Enough to Fill a Glass," *The Washington Post Magazine* (Oct 25 ,1987), 20.
Alfrieda Slee, Administratrix to the Estate of Jack Andrew Slee, vs. Werner Erhard, et al. Civil Action #N-84-497- JAC, United States District Court for the District of Connecticut.
Evangeline Bojorquez vs. Werner Erhard, et al, Civil Action #449177, Superior Court of the State of California in and for the County of Santa Clara.
Nancy Urgell vs. Werner Erhard and Werner Erhard Associates, Civil Action
#H-85-1025 PCD, United States District Court, District of Connecticut.

155. Teresa Ramirez Boulette and Susan M. Anderson, "Mind Control and the Battering of Women," *Community Mental Health Journal* (Summer 1985, Vol. 21, No. 2).

Chapter 8

156. Alan MacRobert, "Uncovering the Cult Conspiracy," *Mother Jones* (Feb/March 1979, Vol. 4, No. 2), 8.

157. The names of the cult member and his family have been changed to protect their identities.

158. For a complete listing of all of the groups affiliated with the Boston Church of Christ, see the appendix of *The Discipling Dilemma* by Flavil Yeakley (Nashville, Tennessee: Gospel Advocates, 1988).

159. Buddy Martin has put together information packets on the Multiplying Ministries. Videotapes of his lectures are available through the Memorial Church of Christ in Houston, Texas.

160. Daniel Terris, "Come, All Ye Faithful," *Boston Globe Magazine* (June 6, 1986).
Linda Hervieux, "The Boston Church of Christ: Critics Call It a Cult, but Members Maintain Their Church's Legitimacy," *Muse*

Magazine, Boston University (Feb 18, 1988).
Gregory L. Sharp, "Mind Control and 'Crossroadism,'" *Gospel Anchor* (March 1987), 23.
Jeanne Pugh, "Fundamentalist Church Gathers Campus Converts... and Critics," *St. Petersburg Times* (July 21, 1979), 1.

161. Letter published in the Crossroads bulletin (March 16, 1987).

162. Letter from Memorial Church of Christ elders, (March 1977), firing McKean.

163. The names of the cult member and her family have been changed to protect their identities.

164. See Deborah Berg Davis, *The Children of God: The Inside Story* (Grand Rapids, Michigan: The Zondervan Publishing House, 1984).

165. Kathy Mehler, "Published Preachings: Even Prostitution Can Attract Converts to Cults," *The Daily Illini* (April 16, 1981).

166. The names of the cult member and his family have been changed to protect their identities.

167. Larry Woods, "The Masters Movement, Puns I and II," Turner Broadcasting Systems, CNN (Jan 13, 1986).

168. Ray Richmond, "Masters–A Healer in Bluejeans?" *Los Angeles Times* (Dec 1, 1985), 90.
Paul Taublieb, "Masters' Touch," *US Magazine* (April 23, 1984), 39-41.
Lauren Kessler, "Roy Masters: 'I Can Do No Wrong'", *Northwest Magazine* (Sept 4,1983).

Chapter 9

169. Also known as Messianic Communities. One of their popular businesses is the Yellow Deli restaurants. Former members complain of child labor trafficking, corporal punishment and lack of adequate medical treatment, especially during childbirth. See web site by former members at http://www.twelvetribes-ex.com/ and http://www.twelvetribes-ex.org/whyileft.html
and

http://www.independent.co.uk/news/uk/home-news/twelve-tribes-community-nspcc-demands-police-inquiry-into-christian-sect-that-canes-children-8847622.html

Chapter 10

170. Elan Vital, Inc. is a newer name than Divine Light Mission. See Michael Finch's *Without the Guru: How I took my life back after thirty years*, (Babbling Brook Press 2009). http://www.MikeFinch.com
http://www.ex-premie.org/pages/hinduismtoday83.htm
http://www.apologeticsindex.org/r23.html
http://arthurchappell.me.uk/cults-divine.light.mission.htm

171. Steven J. Gelberg's, *India In A Mind's Eye: Travels and Ruminations of an Ambivalent Pilgrim*, (Spiraleye Press, 2012) and http://surrealist.org/betrayalofthespirit/gelberg.html
Ex-Krishna Nori Muster's Betrayal Files http://surrealist.org/betrayalofthespirit/betrayalfiles.html And her book, *Betrayal of the Spirit: My Life behind the headlines of the Hare Krishna Movement.* Urbana: U of Illinois, 1997. Print.

172. Indemnity and Unification," *Master Speaks* (Feb 14, 1974), 11-12. Christopher Edwards, *Crazy for God* (Englewood Cliffs, New Jersey: Prentice Hall, Inc., 1979), 173-174.

173. Douglas Lenz, "Twenty-two Months as a Moonie," Lutheran Church of America Partners (Feb 1982). 14.

174. Steve Kemperman, *Lord of the Second Advent* (Ventura, California: Regal Books, 1982), 87.

175. Ibid.

176. Hubbard, PAB No. 124, (15 November 1957), *Communication and Isness.*

177. John Hubner and Lindsay Gruson, "Dial Om for Murder," *The Rolling Stone* (April 9, 1987), 53.

Chapter 11

178. Cf. "Relationship Between Men and Women," *Master Speaks* (May 20, 1973), 2.
Although this is a dramatic example of the things members are told by the Moonies, I have heard many similar tales from ex-members.

179. Gary Scharff, "Autobiography of a Former Moonie," *Cultic Studies Journal* (1986). Vol. 2, No. 2, 254.

180. See Marcia R. Rudin, "The Cult Phenomenon: Fad or Fact?" *New York University Review of Law and Social Change* (1979-80). Vol. IX, No. 1, 31-32.

181. Dr. Drew's podcast with Steve Hassan and former 15 year ICC member is at: https://freedomofmind.com//Media/videos.php

182. See Steve Kemperman, *Lord of the Second Advent* (Ventura, California: Regal Books, 1981), 87.

183. Floating has also been linked to "Post Traumatic Stress Disorder," from which many Vietnam veterans suffer.

184.Geraldo Rivera, "Lifespring Part 2," ABC's "20/20" (Nov 6, 1980).

185. Decreeing is used by only one group that I am familiar with: Elizabeth Claire Prophet's Church Universal and Triumphant. It is a high-speed recitation of the group's "prayers." It is done so fast that anyone listening will not understand what a member is saying. In my opinion, it is a highly effective technique for trance induction and thought-stopping.

186. During my time in the Moonies, I had personally recruited fourteen people and influenced hundreds of people to join.

187. Francine Jeane Daner, *The American Children of Krishna: A Study of the Hare Krishna Movement* (New York: Holt, Rinehart, and Winston, 1976).
Hillary Johnson, "Children of Harsh Bliss: In a West Virginia Commune, An Extraordinary Look at Life and Love Among the Krishnas," *Life Magazine* (April 1980).
Eric Harrison, "Crimes Among the Krishnas: The world wouldn't listen to Stephen Bryant's charges against his religion's leaders, until he

was murdered," *The Philadelphia Inquirer Magazine* (April 5, 1987).

188. See 3HO/Sikh Dharma Publication, *Beads of Truth*, Preuss Road, Los Angeles, California.

189. Richard Behar, "The Prophet and Profits of Scientology." *Forbes Magazine* (October 27th, 1986).

190. Tony Ortega wrote a wonderful book entitled, *The Unbreakable Miss Lovely* (Silvertail Books, 2015) about Paulette Cooper and Scientology's harassment of this pioneering writer. I became friends with Paulette in 1976 when I first exited the Moonies and was declared an SP. I have a 2013 video interview with her on my web site, freedomofmind.com.

191. Flo Conway and Jim Siegelman, *Snapping* (New York: Dell Publishing Co., 1978), 249.
"Penthouse Interview: L. Ron Hubbard, Jr." *Penthouse* (June 1983), 112.

192. Jim Healey, Sharry Ricchiardi, and D. Vance Hawthorne, "ISU Bible Study Group: Wonderful or a Cult?" *Desmoines Sunday Register* (March 9, 1980), 1B.
Michelle M. Bell, "I think I was Brainwashed: Religious Group Criticized as Cult-like is now al KSU," *Daily Kent Stater* (Dec 3, 1982), 1.

Chapter 12

193. Words matter in 'ISIS' war, so use 'Daesh". http://www.bostonglobe.com/opinion/2014/10/09/words-matter-isis-war-use-daesh/V85GYEuasEEJgrUun0dMUP/story.html

194. http://www.fbi.gov/?came_from=http%3a//www.fbi.gov/stats-services/publications/law-enforcement-bulletin/september-2011/sovereign-citizens and Stephen A. Kent 2003 paper for the European Federation of Centres of Research and Information on Sectarianism FECRIS.org "FREEMEN, SOVEREIGN CITIZENS, AND THE THREAT TO PUBLIC ORDER IN BRITISH HERITAGE COUNTRIES" online at http://griess.st1.at/gsk/fecris/copenhagen/Kent_EN.pdf

195. CBS *60 Minutes* flew me to Tokyo right after the sarin gas terrorist attack to be their "in the field" expert for the segment they aired. Dr. Robert Jay Lifton's *Destroying the World to Save It* applies his 8 criteria in this book and is an excellent account of the Aum Shinrikyo mind control cult.

196. Fraser Report: https://freedomofmind.com//Info/docs/fraserport.pdf

197. US Navy Intelligence launched the first mind control program, Operation Bluebird, in the 1940s. There were various other programs, including MK Naomi. Curiously, the first mention of these sinister experiments was made by cult founder, Ron Hubbard, in his 1951 book *Science of Survival*, where he spoke of "pain-drug-hypnosis." It is not impossible that Scientology itself was part of such a program. It would certainly explain the reluctance of the U.S. government to curtail its activities.

198. See Professor Christopher Simpson, *Science of Coercion, Communication Research & Psychological Warfare 1945-1960*, (1994), OUP, NY: 'Military, intelligence, and propaganda agencies such as the Department of Defense and Central Intelligence Agency helped to bankroll substantially all of the post-World War II generation's research into techniques of persuasion, opinion measurement, interrogation, political and military mobilization, propagation of ideology, and related questions. The persuasion studies, in particular, provided much of the scientific underpinning for modern advertising and motivational techniques. This government-financed communication research went well beyond what would have been possible with private sector money alone and often exploited military recruits, who comprised a unique pool of test subjects.' pp.3-4.

199. Studying destructive cult behavior and its effects on human beings is a window into what should be impermissible scientific research experimentation.

200. http://dsm.psychiatryonline.org/doi/book/10.1176/appi.books.9780890425596

201. *Mind Control: Psychological Reality or Mindless Rhetoric?* By Dr. Philip G. Zimbardo (November 2002, Vol. 33, No. 10).

202. http://en.wikipedia.org/wiki/APA_Task_Force_on_Deceptive_and_Indirect_Methods_of_Persuasion_and_Control

203. Janja Lalich is professor of sociology at California State University, Chico and has authored many important books, including *Bounded Choice: True Believers and Charismatic Cults* (University of California Press, 2004).

204. Stephen Kent, *Narcissistic Grandiosity and the Life of Sun Myung Moon*, (July 5, 2014, International Cultic Studies Association, Silver Spring, Maryland).

205. Routledge Press, 2014.

206. Basic Books, 2003. Sam Vaknin, Ph.D., *Malignant Self Love: Narcissism Revisited.*

207. Flavil R. Yeakley, *The Discipling Dilemma* (Nashville: Gospel Advocate Press, 1982).

208. *The Discipling Dilemma* is now available online at http://www.somis.org/tdd-01.html

209. Guochuan Tsai, Donald Condie, Ming-Ting Wue, and I-Wen Change. "Functional Magnetic Resonance Imaging of Personality Switches in a Woman with Dissociative Identity Disorders." *Harvard Review of Psychiatry* 7 (1999): 119-22.

210. Dr. Burns' web site is http://feelinggood.com/ He has an excellent and statistically valid set of measurement tools for evaluating people's progress and for teaching people how to develop control over their thoughts, emotions and behavior. This is a totally ethical mind control approach emphasizing that people's locus of control should be within themselves, not with some external authority figure.

211. There are videos of the CFFP annual conference in 2013 for free and the 2014 is available for purchase. I moderated an amazing panel of survivors of child abuse in 2013 and the video of that program is at http://childfriendlyfaith.org/conference-2013/videos-from-cffp-conference-2013/. Bethany Brittain, a board member, spoke about being a victim of extreme corporal punishment by her Christian parents who were followers of Roy Lessing's guidelines. Joel Engleman was a victim of a pedophile in the Satmar Hasidic

group in New York. He is involved with an organization, Footsteps, which helps people leave the orthodox Jewish groups. Liz Heywood lost her leg as a member of Christian Science. Rev. Jaime Romo was a victim of a priest pedophile in the Catholic Church.

212. Alan W. Scheflin, "Supporting Human Rights by Testifying Against Human Wrongs," 6 *International Journal of Cultic Studies 69-82* (2015).

213. Loyola Law School Legal Studies Paper No. 2010-53 96 Iowa L.R. 409 (2011).

214. Alan W. Scheflin, *Supporting Human Rights by Testifying Against Human Wrongs, International Journal of Cultic Studies 69-82* (2015).

215. William Borders, "Moon's Church Loses a Libel Suit in London over Recruiting Tactics," *The New York Times* (April 1, 1981). George Greig and Ted Oliver, "Daily Mail Wins Historic Libel Action: The Damning Verdict on the Moonies," *Daily Mail* (April 1, 1981), London. Otto Friedrich, "Om… The New Age, Starring Shirley Maclaine, Faith Healers, Channelers, Space Travelers and Crystals Galore," *Time* (Dec 7, 1987).

216. See, e.g., NXIVM Corp. v. Sutton, 2007 U.S. Dist. LEXIS 46471 (D.N.J. June 27, 2007) (the word "cult" is not actionable, nor is an article which compares the scholarly work of Robert Jay Lifton on cults and their common, shared characteristics with the materials distributed by NXIVM to its enrollees, because such statements constitute protected opinions); Nicosia v. De Rooy, 72 F. Supp. 2d 1093 (N.D. Cal. 1999) (statements accusing someone of being a manipulative "Svengali," with "Napoleonic aspirations," who carried on an "exploitative business relationship" are not actionable because they are protected opinion); Church of Scientology v. Siegelman, 475 F. Supp. 950 (S.D.N.Y. 1979) (statements in Snapping, a book about cults, are not actionable where they are "replete with opinions and conclusions about the methods and practices used by the Church of Scientology and the effect such methods and practices have . . . ."); Beaverton Grace Bible Church v. Smith, No. C1121174CV (Or. Cir. Ct. July 23, 2012) (blog posts saying that a pastor is a "cult leader" who "destroy[s] relationships" are not actionable because they constitute protected opinions); Harvest House Publishers v. Local Church, 190

S.W.3d 204 (Tex. App. 2006) (being labeled a "cult" is not actionable because the truth or falsity of the statement depends upon one's religious beliefs); Sands v. Living Word Fellowship, 34 P.3d 955 (Alaska 2001) (statements that a group is a "cult" and that a person is a "cult recruiter" are not actionable because they are pronouncements of religious belief and opinion). But see Landmark Education Corporation v. Conde Nast Publication, No. 114814/93, 1994 WL 836356 (N.Y. Sup. Ct. July 7, 1993) (an allegation that a group is a "cult" can be actionable when presented as hard news by a reporter in a publication known for journalism). See World Mission Society, Church of God A NJ Nonprofit Corporation. v. Colón, No. BER-L-5274-12 (N.J. Sup. Ct. Feb. 9, 2015) (statements alleging that World Mission is a "cult" that uses "mind control" and "destroys families" are protected opinions and are not actionable).

217. Heather Kavan is a lecturer in the Department of Communication, Journalism and Marketing at Massey University. Her paper, "Falun Gong in the Media: What can we believe?" ANZCA08 Conference, Power and Place, Wellington, July 2008 online at https://www.massey.ac.nz/massey/fms/Colleges/College of Business/Communication and Journalism/ANZCA 2008/Refereed Papers/Kavan_ANZCA08.pdf

218. Available at http://pyramidschemealert.org/wordpress/wp-content/uploads/2014/03/The-Pyramid-Scheme-Industry-FINAL.pdf

219. http://quoteinvestigator.com/2011/10/15/liberty-fist-nose/

220. Touro Synagogue National Historical Site, "George Washington and His Letter to the Jews of Newport," http://www.tourosynagogue.org/history-learning/gw-letter

221. When Scientology was banned in two Australian states in the 1960s, it merely changed its name to The Church of the New Faith

222. The Documentary about the Jehovah's Witnesses can be found at: http://buy.hereliesthetruth.com/

223. The U.N. Universal Declaration of Human Rights is online at: http://www.un.org/en/documents/udhr/

224. ISIS Is a Cult That Uses Terrorism: A Fresh New Strategy http://www.huffingtonpost.com/steven-hassan/isis-is-a-cult-that-uses-_b_6023890.html

225. It's Time to End the Church of Scientology's Tax-Exempt Status by Steven Hassan http://www.huffingtonpost.com/steven-hassan/its-time-to-end-the-churc_b_555843.html

Bibliography

Allen, Charles. *God's Terrorists: The Wahhabi Cult and the Hidden Roots of Modern Jihad*. Cambridge, MA: Da Capo, 2007. Print.

Atack, Jon. *Let's Sell These People a Piece of Blue Sky*. Worthing, England: Richard Woods, 2013. Print.

Atack, Jon. *SCIENTOLOGY - The Cult of Greed*. Worthing, England: Richard Woods, 2014. Print.

Baker, Amy J. L., and Fine, Paul R. *Co-parenting with a Toxic Ex: What to Do When Your Ex-spouse Tries to Turn the Kids Against You*. Oakland, CA: New Harbinger Publications, 2014. Print.

Baker, Amy J. L., and Fine, Paul R. *Surviving Parental Alienation: A Journey of Hope and Healing*. Rowman and Littlefield, 2014. Print.

Banisadr, Masoud. *Destructive and Terrorist Cults: A New Kind of Slavery: Leaders, Followers, and Mind Manipulation*. Research Institute on destructive Cults. CreateSpace Independent Platform, 2014. Print.

Banisadr, Masoud. *Masoud: Memoirs of an Iranian Rebel*. London: Saqi, 2004. Print.

Blass, Thomas. *The Man Who Shocked the World: The Life and Legacy of Stanley Milgram*. New York: Basic, 2004. Print.

Brown, Daniel P., Alan W. Scheflin, and D. Corydon. Hammond. *Memory, Trauma Treatment, and the Law*. New York: W.W. Norton, 1998. Print.

Buonomano, Dean. *Brain Bugs: How the Brain's Flaws Shape Our Lives*. New York: W.W. Norton, 2011. Print.

Cialdini, Robert B. *Influence: The Psychology of Persuasion*. New York: Morrow, 1994. Print.

Clarkson, Frederick. *Eternal Hostility: The Struggle between Theocracy and Democracy*. Monroe, ME.: Common Courage, 1997. Print.

Collier, Peter, and Horowitz, David. *Second Thoughts: Former Radicals Look Back at the Sixties*. Lanham, MD: Madison, 1989. Print.

Cooperson, David A. *The Holocaust Lessons on Compassionate Parenting and Child Corporal Punishment*. N.p.: CreateSpace Independent Platform, 2014. Print.

Doidge, Norman. *The Brain That Changes Itself: Stories of Personal Triumph from the Frontiers of Brain Science*. New York: Viking, 2007. Print.

Falk, Geoffrey D. *Stripping the Gurus: Sex, Violence, Abuse and Enlightenment*. Toronto, Ont.: Million Monkeys, 2009. Print.

Farley, Melissa. *Prostitution and Trafficking in Nevada: Making the Connections*. San Francisco, CA: Prostitution Research & Education, 2007. Print.

Feldman, Deborah. *Unorthodox: The Scandalous Rejection of My Hasidic Roots*. New York: Simon & Schuster, 2012. Print.

Finch, Michael. *Without the Guru: How I Took My Life Back after Thirty Years*. United States: Babbling Brook, 2009. Print.

Fontes, Lisa Aronson. *Child Abuse and Culture: Working with Diverse Families*. New York: Guilford, 2008. Print.

Hamilton, Marci A. *God Vs: The Perils of Extreme Religious Liberty*. Cambridge: Cambridge UP, 2014. Print.

Hawkins, Jefferson. *Counterfeit Dreams: One Man's Journey into and out of the World of Scientology*. Porland, OR.: Hawkeye, 2010. Print.

Heilman, Samuel C., and Friedman, Menachem. *The Rebbe: The Life and Afterlife of Menachem Mendel Schneerson*. Princeton, NJ: Princeton UP, 2010. Print.

Hill, Miscavige, Jenna and Pulitzer, Lisa. *Beyond Belief: My Secret Life Inside Scientology and My Harrowing Escape*. NY: HarperCollins, 2013. Print.

Jones, Celeste, Jones, Kristina, and Buhring, Juliana, *Not without My Sister*. London: HarperElement, 2008. Print.

Kelly, Richard E. *Growing up in Mama's Club: A Childhood Perspective of Jehovah's Witnesses*. Tucson, AZ: Parker Ridge Publications, 2008. Print.

Kelly, Richard E. *The Ghosts from Mama's Club*. Tucson, AZ.: Richard Kelly, 2012. Print.

Koch, Molly Brown. *27 Secrets to Raising Amazing Children*. Baltimore, MD: Sidran Institute, 2007. Print.

Kramer, Joel, and Alstad, Diana. *The Guru Papers: Masks of Authoritarian Power*. Berkeley, CA: North Atlantic /Frog, 1993. Print.

Lalich, Janja, and Tobias, Madeleine. *Take Back Your Life: Recovering from Cults and Abusive Relationships*. Berkeley, CA: Bay Tree Pub., 2006. Print.

Lehrer, Jonah. *How We Decide*. Boston: Mariner, 2010. Print.

Lloyd, Rachel. *Girls like Us: Fighting for a World Where Girls Are Not for Sale: A Memoir*. New York: HarperPerennial, 2012. Print.

Muster, Nori J. *Betrayal of the Spirit: My Life behind the Headlines of the Hare Krishna Movement*. Urbana: U of Illinois, 1997. Print.

O'Reilly, Patrick, and Rosen, Phyllis. *Undue Influence: Cons, Scams and Mind Control*. Point Richmond, CA: Bay Tree, 2013. Print.

Payson, Eleanor D. *The Wizard of Oz and Other Narcissists: Coping with the One-way Relationship in Work, Love, and Family*. Royal Oak, MI: Julian Day Publications, 2002. Print.

Phelps, Carissa, and Larkin, Warren. *Runaway Girl: Escaping Life on the Streets, One Helping Hand at a Time*. New York: Viking, 2012. Print.

Pratkanis, Anthony R. *The Science of Social Influence: Advances and Future Progress*. New York: Psychology, 2007. Print.

Schwartz, Harvey L. *Dialogues with Forgotten Voices: Relational Perspectives on Child Abuse Trauma and Treatment of Dissociative Disorders*. New York: Basic, 2000. Print.

Shaw, Daniel. *Traumatic Narcissism: Relational Systems of Subjugation*. S.l.: Routledge, 2013. Print.

Shermer, Michael. *The Believing Brain: From Ghosts and Gods to Politics and Conspiracies—How We Construct Beliefs and Reinforce Them as Truths*. New York: Times, 2011. Print.

Stein, Alexandra. *Inside Out: A Memoir of Entering and Breaking out of a Minneapolis Political Cult*. St. Cloud, MN: North Star of St. Cloud, 2002. Print.

Tavris, Carol, and Aronson, Elliot. *Mistakes Were Made (But Not by Me): Why We Justify Foolish Beliefs, Bad Decisions, and Hurtful Acts*. Orlando, FL: Harcourt, 2008. Print.

Taylor, Kathleen E. *Brainwashing the Science of Thought Control*. Oxford: Oxford UP, 2004. Print.

Wright, Lawrence. *Going Clear: Scientology, Hollywood, and the Prison of Belief*. New York: Alfred A. Knopf, 2013. Print.

Yapko, Michael D. *Trancework: An Introduction to the Practice of Clinical Hypnosis*. New York: Brunner-Routledge, 2003. Print.

Young, Jeffrey E., and Klosko, Janet S.. *Reinventing Your Life: The Breakthrough Program to End Negative Behavior ... and Feel Great Again*. New York: Plume, 1994. Print.

Zimbardo, Philip G., Pilkonis, Paul, Anthony and Marnell, Margaret Esther. *Shyness: What It Is, What to Do about It*. Reading, MA: Addison-Wesley Pub., 1990. Print.

Zimbardo, Philip G. *The Lucifer Effect: Understanding How Good People Turn Evil*. New York: Random House, 2007. Print.

Zimbardo, Philip G., and Boyd, John. *The Time Paradox: The New Psychology of Time That Will Change Your Life*. New York: Free, 2009. Print.

A more extensive bibliography can be found on our website: https://freedomofmind.com/Bibliography/

Index

A

B

C

E

F

G

K

L

N

O

P

Q

R

S

T

U

Z